Sporting Jowetts

The Javelin of John Batten, D.C. Hodgson and Robbie Mackenzie-Low in the 1952 Monte Carlo Rally. (JCC)

Sporting Jowetts

NOEL STOKOE

First published 2009
Reprinted 2022

The History Press
97 St George's Place,
Cheltenham, Gloucestershire, GL50 3QB
www.thehistorypress.co.uk

© Noel Stokoe, 2009

The right of Noel Stokoe to be identified as the Author
of this work has been asserted in accordance with the
Copyrights, Designs and Patents Act 1988.

All rights reserved. No part of this book may be reprinted
or reproduced or utilised in any form or by any electronic,
mechanical or other means, now known or hereafter invented,
including photocopying and recording, or in any information
storage or retrieval system, without the permission in writing
from the Publishers.

British Library Cataloguing in Publication Data.
A catalogue record for this book is available from the British Library.

ISBN 978 0 7524 4775 9

Typesetting and origination by The History Press
Printed by TJ Books Limited, Padstow, Cornwall

Contents

	Acknowledgements	7
	Introduction	9
one	Pre-War Jowett Activities	11
two	Post-War Rallies and Races	67
	What the Papers Had to Say	221
	Bibliography	249

The author in his 1952 Jowett Jupiter.

Acknowledgements

As with all my previous books, I would like to dedicate this one to my wife, Jane, who is always a great support to me in all things Jowett. I would also like to dedicate it to my children, Jonathan, Jessica and Ben, and to our lovely grandchildren, Luke, Daisy, Jack and Oliver. All four have been enrolled by us as 'Jowett Juniors' of the Jowett Car Club, so hopefully they will continue the Jowett tradition in future years.

Thanks also to: Phill Green, Eden Lindsay, Geoff McAuley, Edmund Nankivell, Göran Norlander, Ian Priestley.

The Authors and Publishers have made every possible effort to trace copyright holders; we apologise for any erroneous use of copyrighted material and would welcome contact from the original copyright holder.

Noel Stokoe
December 2008

Other titles by the same author

(Images of Motoring) *Jowett 1901–1954*
My Car was a Jowett
Jowett: Advertising the Marque

All available on The History Press website.

Introduction

Over the last twenty-five years or so, as librarian of the Jowett Car Club, I have collected a great mass of information regarding Jowetts in competition, mainly onwards from the 1949 Monte Carlo Rally when a Javelin was entered in a competitive rally for the first time. This involvement lasted through to the mid-1950s beyond the closure of the factory in 1954, but very little beyond then, as by that time the Javelin and Jupiter were becoming less competitive. There is also a small sprinkling of pre-war trials and record making/breaking attempts, but these are limited, as the ethos in those days was squarely on cheap, robust and reliable transport for the working man, with little thought of rallying, etc.

The contents of this book are in two formats, the first being personal accounts by drivers, several of whom were motoring journalists who covered the events they took part in. These have been collected from articles in the motoring press, Jowett Car Club publications going back to the 1960s and books published by some of the drivers themselves. There are also a large number from people who, after being in correspondence with me, have agreed to put their memories down on paper, which I am most grateful for. The second source of information has come from period newspaper and magazine articles; many local papers would cover local entrants for the Monte Carlo Rally etc. These were not 'known' rally drivers in many cases, but local enthusiasts deciding to 'have a go'. The beauty of this period was that in the early years after the war private individuals could enter these prestigious events and stand a chance of doing reasonably well. Big business and corporate backers had not moved into the sport at that time, but sadly, this situation did not last for long. By the late 1950s the private entrant no longer stood any realistic chance against the 'big boys' and their sponsors.

I have particularly enjoyed the personal accounts, as they help to give you a real picture as to what these events were like, particularly the Monte Carlo and Alpine rallies, as many of the mountain passes used were not even proper made-up roads at that time. I am sure that most of these accounts are basically factually correct, though many do tend to say, 'We could have won if such and such a thing had not happened', but I find them great fun in any case. Also two accounts of the same event are very entertaining; a typical example of this was the twelve-hour Class G record set at Brooklands by J.J. Hall and Horace Grimley in 1928. In Horace's account, which I am sure is a fair and balanced report, he says that he did all the maintenance on the attempt (this included replacing three blown head gaskets) and almost three-quarters of the driving. In J.J. Hall's account Horace hardly gets a mention, but it is still enjoyable reading nonetheless!

The next debate I had with myself was how to publish these accounts. I wondered about a list in date order to include personal accounts and press clippings. I felt that this would be difficult, as several personal accounts listed more than one event, in some cases over a five-year period. So what I have decided to do is to split the book into three sections, the first two being personal accounts, firstly pre-war and secondly post-war, where I have listed all of the individual writers' articles together, rather than split them up. The third section is a collection of newspaper and magazine reports, which I have decided to list in date order. It seems a logical way of doing things to me, so I do hope you agree with my way of thinking.

I would stress that this is not a text book as there are, I am pleased to say, plenty of them around now. It is a light-hearted selection of Jowett drivers' reminiscences, as written. On occasions I have added my own notes where things are clearly incorrect, but I have tried to keep these to a minimum so I do not spoil the flow of the accounts. I hope you have as much pleasure reading them as I did locating them and compiling them.

one

Pre-War Jowett Activities

From the early 1920s Jowett's had built up a reputation of rugged reliability, so this attribute was brought to the attention of would-be buyers at every opportunity. It was also important to show a car could perform overseas as well as in the home market; two examples of this advertising in 1925 came in the form of *Where there's a way the Jowett will go* and *East from Siwa*. I have included the texts from these, as both are personal accounts, probably written by Major McMullen, whom I refer to in more detail at the end of the second article. Clearly, many home-buyers would have read these sales booklets, which must have encouraged some to enter their cars in Trials in this country. Jowetts excelled in these, as speed was not the main factor, the 'go anywhere' characteristics being much more important.

From Alexandria across the Libyan desert to Siwa, and back via Gara or the little Oasis, 840 miles in all

The Jowett was the only British car in the convoy, and helped all the American cars of treble its power up hills, across bogs and deep sand. No other car made the journey entirely under its own power.

This full story of the journey should be read by every British motorist. It proves the undoubted superiority of a British car over high-powered American cars, which hitherto have been looked on as indispensable for such journeys. By the way, the Jowett averaged 47mpg, and no water was added until 390 miles.

This little account of a British light car on a desert journey of great difficulty is only one of many similar experiences of Jowett owners, and the pity is that you are too busy to read them all.

We publish it with some pride, because the success indicated proves still more conclusively the capacity of our cars to go anywhere where wheels can grip. Further, it proves Jowett car wheels will grip where other cars will not.

Just one moment, please, before we proceed to the narrative. Why can a Jowett go in places where all other standard cars fail? Here's the reason. Where ordinary cars cannot go there is usually no hard surfaced road. Lack of road means mud, sand or dirt. On this surface every ounce of weight counts. Consider, then, the average car used on virgin country. Weight about a ton, say 5cwts per wheel, plus load carried, say 6 cwts., making 6½cwts per wheel.

Now take the Jowett, weight 10 cwts or 2½cwts per wheel, plus 6cwts load, making 6cwts load per wheel. There's a 50 per cent greater load per wheel on the average car, hence it sinks deeper if the 'road' should be called by any other name.

The Jowett two-seater is half a cwt per wheel less even than the above. Simple, isn't it?

And now for the narrative...

At dawn on 20 March 1925, three American and one British car left Alexandria to visit the oasis at Siwa following the caravan 'roads'.

Mersa Matruh (189 miles) was reached at 5.30 p.m., the British Jowett only requiring 4 gallons of petrol to fill up. No oil or water was added, though the car was heavily laden with 32 gallons of benzene, 2 gallons of oil, and 2 gallons of water, together with kit and camp equipment for the driver and passenger. Some load for a 7hp car! The other cars all needed water and oil, and they did not do 47 miles to a gallon of petrol.

Matruh was left at 6.20 a.m. on the 21st, to Siwa, 390 miles from Alexandria. Three distinct zones were encountered: first the rocky hill country, then a wilderness of desert vegetation, and finally 50 or 60 miles of barren desert.

The Jowett had consumed only 10 gallons of benzene up to this point, and no water had been added to the radiator; 39mpg over such country is surely marvellous, is it not?

The 22nd was spent exploring Siwa and the neighbourhood, a visit being paid to 'The Hill of the Dead' and the famed 'Spring of Khorshed' and the 'Virgin's Well' – an old Roman well in which it is customary for each young Senussi maid to bathe on the day of her marriage. Siwa itself is fashioned from mud and marble, built in terraced formation on the side of the hill, house standing upon house. The more valuable material was probably looted from some unknown temple. The Temple of Jupiter Ammon, the once outstanding centre of Roman domination in North Africa, was next visited. British soldiers did much to preserve for future generations what remains of this famous pile.

Dawn on the 23rd saw a start for the little oasis of 'Gara'. Since there was no real track, and camel tracks are soon obliterated, a Bedouin guide was taken for this stage. Also, the precipitous drop to Gara must be known ... Gara or El Qara is otherwise known as Un Es Seghir. Here every available receptacle was filled with water to the brim, before the long trek to the coast across the waterless, and for the most part trackless, journey through the Ghoreb Pass. Even the Bedouins get lost; the way they took us was over terribly rocky outcrops, which played havoc with our springs.

After many tyre troubles with the American cars the Pass was reached at sunset. This serpentines upwards from ledge to ledge of rock, with precipitous rocky slopes between each ledge. We had been told that all the cars would have to be pushed up in turn. This was the case with all except the little Jowett, which went up without a falter, pushing its cheeky nose up on to ledge after ledge, taking things steadily until the top was reached.

Some 10 miles further on the Jowett was ahead of the convoy looking for a good camping site, which was found in a valley after descending a steep slope of soft sand. As the other cars did not appear, the Jowett returned up this slope unassisted to look for its companions, and lead the way down again to the camping site.

The conditions of the slope can be realised when I tell you that one of the other cars stuck in the sand going down and had to be helped out. A start was made for the coast at dawn on the 24th, and the difficulties increased instead of the reverse, as had been anticipated.

A tremendous and unusual rainstorm swept the coastal belt on the Sunday. The whole country was flooded and swampy, and the conditions of the earth track indescribable. The Jowett forged through all the swamps and floods unaided, but all the other cars were bogged down in turn and were hauled out by the Jowett.

At sunset, near Sidi Abd El Rahman, the car following the Jowett through a swamp became hopelessly bogged down in water and mud well over its back axle, and was not extricated till 4 a.m., after much jading, packing, and eventually being hauled out by the Jowett and another car as well. Here the Jowett had its first and only tyre trouble (a small leak at the tube joint) but the spare was speedily fitted, causing no delay to the convoy, whereas the other cars' frequent tyre trouble did necessitate a hold-up on several occasions.

During the final run into Alexandria on the 25th the American cars were bogged again two or three times, and again suffered much from tyre and carburettor trouble. The Jowett ran through to Alexandria without a falter, and was the only car in the expedition that was at no time bogged or pushed or towed. In the words of the other members of the party, the Jowett was 'simply marvellous'. It is a standard 1924 two-seater, and has already done 9,000 miles.

Yours faithfully,
Seven Horse Power

Clearly, the Jowett advertising department was delighted to have had this glowing endorsement, and finished off this little advertising booklet with the following:

A British 7hp car thus proved itself superior to American cars of more than treble the power. It probably cost a third to run, but what is more important, it ran everywhere, and was never pushed or towed. With an average petrol consumption of 47 miles to the gallon, and only one minor tyre trouble, its reliability was 'simply marvellous', and its economy in cooling water amazed everybody. Can any car be expected to run more than 390 miles across a desert without adding water to the radiator, or oil to the engine, yet the Jowett was not 'dry' by any means when filled at Gara, but was replenished before starting across 200 miles of waterless desert.

Such a car would serve you well, it costs less to run than any other, and a little more to buy than the cheapest. It's built to last a lifetime, and does. Tell your friends about this triumph of British light car over its American rivals. We shall be more than pleased to post a copy or copies of this leaflet to your friends in any part of the world, on receipt of the necessary names and addresses.

East from Siwa

To most of us desert travel conjures up visions of Arab steeds, bright of eye, with flowing mane and prancing step – Sheiks in gorgeous array who greet us with a courtly yet skilful flexion of a lithe body as they swoop by enveloped in a cloud of sand. Or maybe hold us to ransom and take off the prettiest maiden to some far desert encampment.

Gee! But the desert is full of romance and sand.

The word sand, when we know it, brings us back to earth, or at least to thoughts of lumbering, halting camels, patient beasts of burden but God-made for this purpose. In short we never dream of motorcars in such surroundings.

This narrative of an epic journey made by two standard, unaltered Jowett cars proves their undoubted ability to overcome any obstacle likely to be met with…

Well within the chartered Western boundary of Egypt, in that part of the Libyan Desert lying between the fertile oasis of Siwa and the Wadi Natrun, are large tracts of desert quite unknown by modern explorers and cartographers. The age-old caravan routes, meandering from oasis to oasis, traverse this wilderness, but modern topographical information is extremely scanty.

From Mersa Matruh or Sollum southwards to Siwa is fairly well known, but eastwards from the oasis is in the main 'terra incognita'. This explains the interest attached to the crossing by four Cairo and Alexandria men some three weeks ago.

On 21 October 1925 Mr T.M. Moore, secretary of the Cairo Motorcycle Club, set out with Mr A.G. MacDonald in a Jowett car with the object of making Siwa and then dashing south to Baharia across a span hitherto untraversed by mechanical transport. Such desert runs are indulged in by Mr Moore as a pleasant relaxation from business, and his acquaintance with the desert goes back to the later period of the war, and after, when he was with the light car patrols. The car, a standard two-seater Jowett, unconverted or improved for this task by extra fittings of any kind carried, besides the two passengers, 40 gallons of benzene (a quantity calculated to allow for a fair margin of safety over the needful amount for a 1,000-mile journey), a spare wheel and two extra tyres, a petrol can of fresh water, and food.

Leaving Cairo at 9 a.m., the car headed for Wadi Natrun, past Giza and the pyramids, and on to El Burg, which was reached at dusk, the men passing the night at the Frontiers Administration rest-house. Next morning they were joined by Major D.J. McMullen (who did the Alexandria to Siwa trip, the subject of a previous Jowett Booklet), and Mr R. Rahm in another Jowett, coming from Alexandria, and the two cars made Mersa Matruh (310 miles from Cairo) at 7 p.m. that evening, the night again being passed in a rest-house. The 200-mile stretch to Siwa was crossed uneventfully in very good time, the oasis being reached at 5.30, with an hour's halt at midday. This part of the way was in much the same line as the Masharab (camel track) el Istabl, which it crossed at intervals.

After reporting to the Mamur, the travellers had a refreshing dip in the 'Ain Tamoussa', a pool of Roman construction among the many springs in the oasis, and the night again spent under the wing of the Frontiers Administration, this time in tents. The following day was passed in the town and in resuming acquaintance with the local sheiks met in former years.

When the destination of the visitors, Baharia, was made known to the Mamur, that worthy was much perturbed and tried to get in touch with the acting governor of the province for the necessary permission. The acting governor, however, was at Alexandria and much of that day was wasted trying to communicate with him. The next day was also mainly spent in attempting to get through to Alexandria by telephone, and before the wire broke down a message was received from the office of the governor forbidding the continuation of the planned route, presumably because the abilities of the car to tackle sand dunes were not known.

While awaiting the verdict, the Mamur and the elder sheik were taken on joyrides along the sand dunes beyond Siwa – a region considered as a hopeless prospect for motor cars to attempt. The run opened the eyes of the Mamur to the ease with which the Jowett could negotiate the loose sand, but, while convinced that the cars could make Baharia without any trouble, he could not permit the trip – even though the visitors offered written assurances that all risks would be on their own shoulders and accepting all responsibility for their own safety.

Determined not to return to Cairo by any of the known ways, search was made for a path offering excitement; the map showed a virgin, unspotted expanse of white paper between the oases of Gara and Moghara, and a decision was made to attempt a direct crossing of that region. Siwa and Aghurmi were left behind on the morning of the 27th and Gara was reached at midday after a moderately good patch of 78 miles, via the Mashrab el Khalda. A short stop was made to look over the car and examine the water cans, then a turn northwards was made and persued for 9 miles. Here a compass bearing due east was followed and the most interesting part of the journey, over the barren arid wilderness forming part of the great depression in which the oases lie, commenced. The terrain was found to provide extremely difficult going over a surface of pure salt; during the rains this part probably is saturated with water, while evaporation and following expansion and contraction had driven the tortured earth into the exaggerated semblance of ploughed land, over which hardly 4mph could be made by the cars, working carefully on low gear. This section, the narrowest of the salt band, was 5 miles in width. Another compass bearing, direct for Moghara, was obtained and the cars speeded over absolutely featureless sand; the total absence of any mark that could be picked up made the maintenance of direction exceedingly difficult, the party having to rely for direction on the shadows cast by the cars. Here it was noted that a second car could follow, practically without any control of the wheel, in the ruts made by the first car. This indicates the depth to which the cars sank in the soft sand. Occasionally the bee-line followed, crossed, or touched an old and deserted caravan track, the Mashrab el Nahashas. The surface quality of the sand was very varied, the greater part being soft and loose; in regions where the winds had swept the grains into waves, in others into high dunes with knife-like edges, where negotiation required the nicest judgement of speed. Too low a speed allowed the wheels to sink, and too great drove the car over the crest with a rush that often ended in a pancake landing if the edge, as often occurred, was undercut. All ideas of distance and perspective were lost. Nothing beyond sand to the horizon was viewed, except occasionally when the remains of petrified trees were passed, apparently perfect in form even to the minor branches. Later, gazelle were also spotted, and the tracks of the addax were identified, but only two birds were seen – one being the ubiquitous wagtail. Moghara was hit in the full centre, the direction of the last few miles being aided by the sight of the escarpment that runs northwards from the oasis, and the run was ended.

A little search discovered the wells. A most interesting touch of nature was seen in the tameness and friendliness of the wagtails, perched on our hands and shoulders, and once even attempting to nibble the sprouting beard of one of the members of the party. The night was spent in the open.

The next day's run, to Wadi Natrun, gave an opportunity of speeding up and there the party divided, Major McMullen's car going on to Alexandria. At Wadi Natrun Mr Moore met a Desert Survey Inspector, who was starting a seven months' survey of the region just traversed by the Jowetts. The Survey man, hearing of the featureless state of the desert region, decided to bestow his attention to the escarpment district.

This is probably the first occasion in the history of motoring that an extended journey has been made over uncharted country by the sole aid of a compass bearing. If this be true, it is fitting that the honour falls to the Jowett, for its record of journeyings over desert and other road-less places is unapproached by that of any other car of orthodox design.

It would be unfitting on our part to close this narrative without offering our very hearty congratulations to Major McMullen, Mr T.M. Moore, Mr A.C. McDonald and Mr R. Rabon on their extraordinary performance in thus blazing a trail by light car across hitherto untraversed desert country.

The journey was accomplished by absolutely standard cars in every respect, and the knowledge of their success will not fail to impress upon us, as manufacturers, the vital necessity of using only the very finest of materials in our vehicles, for we cannot know which of our cars will be required to undergo a similar searching test, on the success of which the very lives of the participants inevitably depend.

It is our great honour to build a car on which such reliance is placed, and we certainly shall not fail in our side of the bargain.

We would like to assure the motoring public that this journey was undertaken without any arrangements for spare parts or service of any description en route. It is usual to organise depots where any likely mishap can be rectified and considerable expense is thereby entailed. The Jowett cars appear to be used for such adventures purely as a matter of course.

How easily, then, will such a car perform your less exacting requirements. May we tell you more? Our catalogue tells you everything, and is remarkably well illustrated with real photogravures. It's free!

Statistics of the run
Total mileage – Cairo to Cairo, 930.
Major McMullen did Alexandria also, mileage unknown.
Petrol consumption – lowest 21mpg; highest 36mpg.
Oil sumps needed a mere cupful to replenish to the original level.
Water was only added to replenish that lost by bumping over rough hard places, and the cars would, apparently, average thousands of miles per gallon of water – a unique feature of great importance in desert travel.

Major Johnstone taking part in the Scottish 6 Days Trial, which took part between 5-10 June 1922. His later sports model of 1926 still exists and is now owned by William Jowett's grandson, Mike Koch-Osborne. (JCC)

Speed 21-36mph according to condition of sand.
Mr Moore informs us that the cars proved amazingly fast and only rarely dropped below the 20mph average. Tool boxes untouched throughout the run except to open a petrol tin, which you will remember is sold in quite different containers overseas. You break open the tin (no screwed stopper) which is discarded when empty.

There can be no doubt that these two adventures, which were turned into sales booklets, will have increased the sales of Jowetts dramatically. They will also have helped with promoting the basic no-nonsense ruggedness and economy of the cars, a virtue relied heavily upon right up to the outbreak of the Second World War. They must surely have helped the Jowett brothers decide to pick up the gauntlet thrown down the following year by Frank Gray regarding the crossing of Africa in cars, as both of these journeys were over a quarter of the mileage involved in an African crossing. Major McMullen in fact took part in both journeys in the same car, so it did give a good indication that the cars were capable of such an arduous trip. The 'Wait and See' trip was a great success, and as they say, the rest is history. Probably due to this publicity, Jowetts were very popular in Egypt in the mid-1920s; in fact there was even a branch of the Jowett Car Club based in Cairo!

Major Donald Jay McMullen appears to have been a very interesting person: he was born in 1891 and joined the Royal Engineers in 1911 and served with them during the First World War. He was seconded to the Egyptian Government from 1920–29 to work on railway administration. From 1930–34 he was a Railway Training Centre Instructor for the Royal Engineers. He was the Assistant Director of Transportation for Egypt, Palestine and Trans-Jordan from 1936–37. He was Director of Transportation for the British Expeditionary Force from 1939–40, and Director of Transportation with the War Office from 1940–45. He later became Deputy Chief of Transport Division with the Control Commission Germany from 1945 up to his retirement in 1948. At the time of his two Jowett journeys in 1925 he was thirty-four years old and already a major, at the end of his career he was a major-general and later became Sir Donald Jay McMullen.

Wait and See ... 1926

In 1926 the ex-MP for Oxford, Frank Gray, threw down the gauntlet to the British car manufacturers to provide him with two cars that could cross Africa unaided. Needless to say, Jowett took up the challenge, where the car's 'go anywhere' characteristics were tested to the full.

I have previously seen several accounts of this epic trip, the first was in a Jowett publicity booklet entitled *Across Africa in 60 Days*, the second was in a book by Frank Gray published in 1928 entitled *My Two African Journeys*, the second journey being the Wait and See crossing. I have chosen to quote from the Jowett publicity booklet to start with as it features the cars throughout. Frank Gray's account from *My Two African Journeys* would be rather too long for use in this book as it also covers other aspects of the trip in greater detail. After detailing the Jowett publicity booklet, I will detail some more interesting references to the trip from other sources. – NS

Across Africa by Car in 60 Days
*It was a romance to cross Africa – The Jowett made it
a commercial proposition – Frank Gray*

The full story of such a journey can never be told, but here is an attempt to put on record at least a resume of much that Mr Frank Gray has disclosed. Based on his diary as published exclusively in *The Daily Sketch*, it contains much additional information imparted by Mr Gray in conversation with the present writer, who has been intimately concerned with the expedition from the moment the Jowett Company accepted the gauntlet thrown down by Mr Gray.

It will be remembered that he accused British manufacturers of producing the wrong kind of car for use overseas. The writer (on behalf of the Jowett Company) promptly took up the challenge in the most rigorous way possible, and Mr Gray purchased two absolutely standard 7hp Jowett cars for his intended Expedition, although he was offered two other British products free during the negotiations. The true facts of the case are that Mr Gray never had the slightest doubt but that, if any other car in the world could do such a journey, that car would be a British car, and his challenge was his way of spurring British manufacturers to take a lively and immediate interest in his proposal.

Jowett Cars Limited were, as usual, the first to accept his challenge, as was the case when the Royal East African Automobile Association invited British manufacturers to submit a car for test to destruction (if possible) in order to prove the superiority of British products. That is another story, however, now more than three years old, but it is well known the car performed prodigies and incidentally influenced Mr Gray's choice in the present instance.

Before proceeding with the actual narrative, let us examine the requirements of the expedition:

1) The journey had never previously been attempted in any form of mechanical transport, and it is doubtful if it has ever been accomplished by any living person, white or black, afoot or on camels – in other words it was a positively pioneering trip.

2) Greater distances would have to be accomplished without assistance than had been the case in any previous expedition by automobile, and this presupposed not only ultra-reliability but capacity for hauling heavy loads of fuel, water and food.

3) It was intended that the journey should be done in the shortest time possible; no advance arrangements were to be made for petrol, oil, spares or mechanical assistance in any shape or form, and everything that could not be purchased from the natives was to be carried on the cars.

4) The country to be traversed was almost devoid of roads in the accepted 'overseas' interpretation of the name, a large proportion of the route was absolute desert, water was scarce throughout and for one stage petrol, oil, water, food, kit and spares for 1,600 miles had to be housed on the cars or (as finally decided) hauled by the trailer attached to the cars.

Yet Mr Gray's choice fell on the diminutive-engined Jowett. In four days from receipt of his order, we had built two cars each with a Safari body built into the rear of the normal long two-seater passenger arrangement. In other words we ensured touring comfort for the driver and native boy whilst providing a very capacious flat body behind.

Mr Gray never saw the cars until he reached Lagos, where they were shipped from Liverpool; Mr John Sawyer driving one from Bradford in the company of a Jowett tester, who drove the other. Not much experience, you will say, before starting out on a trans-continental trip of the nature that will be indicated as you read the following pages.

But why did Mr Gray's choice fall on the Jowett, the smallest-engined real car in the world? We have ventured to put forward what we consider these reasons to have been, at the end of this narrative, and without more ado, we commend you to the story. Here follows the story of the most wonderful journey ever accomplished on a mechanically propelled vehicle.

Unlike my fellow adventurer, Mr John Sawyer, I had no opportunity of visiting the Jowett works before starting, and had never seen the cars until I landed at Lagos. But I met Mr William Jowett and the Company's General Manager, Mr Mitchell, at Liverpool where the party spent an interesting and informative evening prior to the departure of the SS *Elmina*. Mr Mitchell has been telling gags against me regarding my ability as a driver (or Sawyer's opinion of it), so I retaliate as you shall see in my narrative. He has already forgiven me.

I cannot but express my amazement at the enthusiasm shown by the band of Jowett drivers in Liverpool, who, on hearing I was about to embark at the port, decided to come and see me off on the *Elmina*. I would like to tell them that their enthusiasm greatly assisted in the quelling of those uneasy feelings one cannot prevent prior to an undertaking of this description. Whenever I find myself saying 'Will seven horsepower do it – is my choice right?' I found the answer at once – it was the answer of those Liverpool motorists.

Chapter 1

We landed in Lagos on 13 March 1926, and found the cars, which had been shipped by an earlier boat, almost ready for us. But this is Saturday, followed by Sunday when all West Africa rests.

Monday, and 1001 things to be done: those things of detail that shorten our lives – licences for the cars, licences to drive, and so forth. We decide to take two black boys and I secure the services of Bismark as mechanic and Peter as cook and steward-boy.

On this our first day in Africa, we have a great stroke of luck. I go to the Secretariat to enquire the most likely route by which we might drive our cars to Juby for no other car has ever even done this, the first stage of our journey. Preparations are already being advanced for an attempt to make the journey by the Governor and Lady Thompson. Their intended route is Lagos, Jebba, Bida, Zungera and Zaria, crossing the Niger at the long and famous Jebba railway bridge. What a stroke of luck.

I lunched with the Governor and Mr Ormsby-Gore and suite, and the Governor and Lady Thompson take it in quite good part that we anticipate their novel journey by ten days, and the whole party cordially wish us good luck.

It was not till we got back to England that I learnt that, although the Governor and his party were much more completely and expensively equipped than my party (with three powerful cars), they failed to reach even Kano. I must not laugh at the expense of others, but the Jowett is such a cheeky little car.

It is going to be a race, first of necessity (because we *must* race to escape the rains of Southern Nigeria) and second, because we want to see how quickly the journey can be accomplished, bearing in mind the slow progress of similar trans-continental expeditions.

Tuesday 16 March finds us ready to embark on the great adventure. We stand waiting for the dawn and – amid the hearty plaudits of our friends – we were off with the first glimmer of daylight. Abeokuta, of separate government and revolution fame, was reached, lunch is provided by kindly friends, and on we go to our first night's halt at Ibadan. One hundred and eighteen miles is not bad for our first day out. Nothing great, you in England say, but these are tropical roads and this is a tropical sun – we are more 'seasick' than tired.

Our next day (Wednesday 17 March) we intended to attempt the complete run to Jebba *via* Ilorin, and thus pass from Southern to Northern Nigeria. It was a desperate journey of 180 miles, and though we found much to rouse our attention, we had great difficulty in not falling asleep at the wheel. We struggled on in the intense heat, when 'See' slips off the sandy road down into a ditch. No help from natives here, and the four of us had to struggle and pant in the darkness and at last get the car back onto the road without damage. We were two weary white men who drove into Jebba that night, but we had accomplished the almost impossible – 180 frizzling miles in one day. We did not do so much again in a day.

In the morning light we overhaul the cars, wait for a train to cross over the bridge and then under the guidance of the railway foreman we essay the attempt to get the cars up the high embankment. We start (I at least a little white in the face), a rush over the hastily prepared track, a quick turn at right angles, and I am astride one set of rails and safe. Over the seven-span first part of the Jebba Bridge, a rush down the embankment, across the island on a cattle track, up and down the embankment again, and we are on and over the second or South Jebba Bridge and on the mainland again.

So much for the Niger. The Kaduna River we tackle differently. We lashed two native canoes together with a plank platform, and so carefully crossed with one car at a time. This was not the first, and by no means the last occasion on which we thanked our stars for the 'handlability' and lightness of the Jowett.

Once across the river we have a run of 12 miles over a good surface to the romantic walled city of Bida. Through the city we drive, passing under the further gateway and to the British District Offices, where we are right royally received, fed and accommodated. One hundred and ten miles on our third day in the tropics over alleged roads.

On the morrow we make for Zungeru, where we meet the railway again after travelling east by south one day and north by east the next, the railway meanwhile heading about nor'-east. We buy stores from the train and refill our 5-gallon condensed water tank – the only safe water to drink here.

Mr Newton, the Resident, and Mr Ross (his District Officer) entertained us to lunch, after which we pushed on across the Kaduna River again, this time over the railway bridge. How the heat radiated from the front of our cars and added to our discomfort as we bumped and jolted across the bridge. Bad enough going but much better than the Jebba Bridge.

Across the Kaduna we visit and pay our respects to that great personality, Dr Cameron Blair, the one and only white man who has decided to retire and die in this fever-laden country. After covering 108 miles in the day we reach the rest-house at Nshiba. The chief brings gifts of fowls and eggs, and sends his women to bring us water and firing – the women do all the work out here, man being in truth the lord. I give a more than suitable sum of money and thus preserve the courtly exchange of gifts (not payment) between chief and traveller.

Off at dawn on 20 March (we have almost forgotten the day of the week – it doesn't matter here) and after 45 miles of varying 'road' and bush, when horror of horrors – I smell burning rubber – the wires on the dashboard are fusing!

For three hours we pant and sweat in the heat of the day, trying to find the mischief and put it right. We fail, and couple up direct to the accumulator till we can perhaps get help in Zaria.

We reach Birnin Gwari, a lone bush station, and find two Assistant District Officers. 'Hallo!' says one, 'Where on earth have you come from and where are you going?' I reply, 'We are making from Lagos to the Red Sea.' 'My God,' says he, 'come in and have some lunch.' We did. Lunch over, a mascot presented to us, and we make for and reach a rest-house where the road branches to Zaria and Kaduna.

We decide at our evening meal that Jack Sawyer shall go straight on to Zaria on the morrow with the wounded 'Wait', while I cut due east for Kaduna to keep an appointment with the Lieutenant-Governor, who gave me much information and advised his officers by telegraph of my coming and instructed them to help.

After lunch I set off for Zaria (whence Jack had preceded me on the injured 'Wait' by the other route), Mr Palmer (the Lieutenant-Governor) leading me for the first 4 miles. I reached Zaria in the pitch dark after a very difficult and anxious drive, to find Sawyer more than pleased to see me. Thus we brought to Zaria the first two cars ever to reach that spot on wheels from Lagos.

Chapter 2

I followed the shorter but very exciting direct route from Zaria to Kano; Jack waiting behind while 'Wait' was put right. Thus 'See' saw Kano first and 'Wait' had to 'Wait and See'. Terrible puns, but how these little things rise to your mind when struggling over obstacles, across sandy river beds and bush! Once I said, 'Damn Wait, she is living up to her name.' Kano is a grand old walled city of 13 miles – with thirteen gates – wherein dwells civilisation, not of the West, but of the East, exactly as it was known 2,000 years ago, with a courtliness which we have never tried to emulate, or having tried, failed ignominiously.

There is excitement at Kano on my arrival, driving 'See', the natives being slow to believe that it had been driven from Lagos. They said, 'Him no fit come Lagos.'

On the arrival of 'Wait', trailers were attached to both cars to enable sufficient petrol and stores to be carried between Maidugari and El Obeid, since no supplies of any description will be available for the distance of at least 1,600 miles between these places. We had to abandon clothing and even our camp beds at this stage, and thereafter sleep in the open as best we could.

So on the morning of the 25th we started on the second main portion of our journey. Our progress is slow on account of our great weight and in the almost blinding heat driving becomes mechanical. We struggle on, our 'cold tea' is quite warm when we halt for lunch, but we stick it and accomplish 107 miles to a rest-house at Jemaari, where we arrive in the gloom of evening. At dawn we are ready to start again, when we were told the King of the district was to call on us, but having learned the necessity of getting as far as possible ere the sun is up, we moved off – much to the terror of the King's officials.

Perhaps an idea of our daily itinerary will be of interest here:

4am usually found us with the cars pointing in the direction we intended to travel, waiting for the dawn, after breakfast of tinned salmon and tea. We drove until 9.30 a.m., when we partook of second breakfast of tinned cheese and lime juice. Twenty minutes then off again till 1.30 lunch, twenty minutes and another spell until 6.30 p.m. when quite dark. Our own rations consisted of tinned salmon, tinned meats and cheese, lime juice and tinned fruits, the latter being best. For our evening meal, the boys would go off to find natives whenever practicable, from whom they bought chickens, eggs, and anything else procurable in addition to water and firewood. We had some wonderful dinners, but it is best not to ask what they consisted of and not to enquire too closely how prepared, or even obtained.

Such then, were our days, or hours, and after 500 miles Sawyer, having become hardened to the strenuous existence, soliloquised under the big brilliant African moon, somewhat as follows. 'This is a joy-ride, Gray, and I can't understand why English people with money don't attempt such journeys more often.' I smiled. After another 500 miles, at the end of a perfectly appalling day, after sweating bucketfuls, our lips badly swollen, and generally 'fed up', I said: 'Now you know why they do not come over in battalions, don't you.' No answer but a groan.

But to our story. After leaving Jemaari on 26 March, we first crossed the Bunga 'river', a wide stretch of sand, deep and soft, which it is very difficult to believe ever was a fast-flowing river, and more difficult to believe that it will be again. Misfortune then overtakes us within 5 miles of our day's halt at Gheljevina. My boy Joseph, sitting behind me, yells as the car lurches forward. The trailer has parted company with the car and deposited most of its load of petrol in the bush. The tow-bar had broken. We redistributed the load between the two cars and one trailer, and dragged the other trailer into the next camp, and so on to Maidugari, 280 miles from Jemaari as the crow flies.

At Maidugari we receive a royal welcome, and run a great risk of being undone with hospitality. We had to take great care of ourselves, and feasting must be avoided at all costs with the worst part of the journey still ahead of us. Colonials are always so jolly and kind. Here we obtained a new tow-bar (made by a native, notwithstanding it happened during the great 'fast') and made preparations for the third stage of our journey – across French Equatorial Africa.

Chapter 3

From Maidugari to El Obeid is at least 1,500 miles, without a chance of picking up petrol or supplies *en route*, and a good reserve supply of water is necessary. We dump all but essentials. We have now only the clothes we stand up in. In the name of the goddess petrol we here sacrifice everything, except food and water. 188 gallons of petrol alone is no small load, yet we dare take no risks. Calculating on 20mpg we considered we had a reserve sufficient for any emergency. Our experience to date was such that we could have done with much less, and as it proved we were able to assist others. But would you have risked carrying less than the cars would haul?

And what a load for two small 7hp cars. Each carried a dead load of 12cwts in addition to its own weight. Truly our choice of vehicle was right.

Away then on 27 March, for the great trek across the heart of Africa. We cover the first 50 miles with our big load and reach the Arabic fort of Dikwa, where we are fed and entertained by the cheery District Officer – Wilmar – a white man alone on this outpost of the Empire – the last Englishman we shall see for many a day.

It was good, that rest at Dikwa. It prepared us for the terrible day ahead. What a journey from Dikwa to Fort Lamy. Miles and miles of dreary tracks of heat-exuding sand, giving birth to unhealthy brown scrub and bush. They talk of the road to Lamy. In truth there is no road; there is a treacherous dry-weather track; there are rough bridges of sand-covered logs, and the first of these nearly proves our undoing. It trembles and shakes under us; then a wheel of the leading car fixes itself deep in the bridge. Then, four of us in this deserted lonely country sweat, fume and pant under the scalding rays of the sun, and heat reflected from the sand.

Here it was that Sawyer, wide of eye, parched of throat, and mad beyond description with anything connected with Africa, remembering Mr Mitchell's keen desire that we should take pictures of such incidents, said, 'So this is where Mitchell expects us to photograph. I should smile.' But we took them, nevertheless, for who could refuse to supply all the evidence possible concerning the wonderful efforts of these heroic little cars?

At Fort Kousserie, we are greeted by two French officers and seek a rest-house to await the morrow to cross the river, which, after 100 dreary miles of sand, looks like sparkling sapphires. Of the 100 miles covered on this day's flight at a speed of only 7mph, at least 80 have been done in second gear, ten in top, and ten in bottom – truly a test for the sturdiness of the gears. The cars are not exhausted, but the drivers are.

Well will this day (Wednesday 31 March) be remembered by us. Leaving Kousserie, we set out to get on a raft to cross the Chari River, just beyond which lay Fort Lamy. After half a mile we reached an impossible confusion of sand dunes, dry sand, stream beds and scrub.

Twelve o'clock and we are back in Fort Kousserie, dishevelled and weary. After rest and refreshment, another start was made; we gain the bank of the river at last and slide bodily down the big sand bank. We manhandle one car and trailer aboard the raft, and have an hour's journey down stream before we find a place to get off again for Fort Lamy. With the aid of fifty natives we get up the bank from the raft, and one car is safe. The other is down river on a raft, and it is now quite dark so we mount a guard over it till dawn. A whole day covering 2 miles. Four miles from Fort Lamy we lose the trail, so back to Lamy for a fresh start, swearing at our luck.

The day is full of adventure. After a short distance, there is a bump at the back of my car. Joseph has gone overboard amid an array of tinned meats, milk and fish. He and the 'chop' box have gone over the top – unparted, as becomes a faithful cook. By every rule of the game, that boy should have been seriously injured, if not killed. I go to him in fear and trembling. He rubs his head, blinks, and starts to collect the 'chop'.

I should digress to explain that I had exchanged Peter for Joseph at Kano, Joseph being selected on the grounds that he spoke English, French, Arabic, and Hausa, could cook and valet. A great claim for a native, and was substantially true. Joseph turned out to be a first-class rogue, a great personality, and always great in the hour of trial and adversity. He claimed to have many qualities, but never claimed the greatest one he had – loyalty in adversity.

Thus for a day and a half – on to Mongo – we fight loose, dry sand. Sand is everywhere; in our eyes, our ears and our mouths. To think that once in our lives we used to long for sand to play in! At last stands up a blue hazy dome. We are coming to a mountain range, the Ouera. We drive now over caked mud, with yawning cracks which must be skilfully traversed, as they are deep enough to bury the wheels. We are reminded of an unbelievably wet season in this land, but the going is better.

Up in the hills, we find a pagan village. The chief, with all his retinue, comes out to meet us. They are very friendly, and we exchange all sorts of favours. These natives fought vigorously for a discarded tobacco tin, and even threw away the contents of a tin of cheese, but retained and prized the shiny tin.

Chapter 4

Sunday 4 April was a bad day.

After only 2 miles, bang goes the car I am driving into a concealed hole, and bang goes the universal joint.

We take the injured forging back to Mongo and find a native to undertake repairs. He drives a pointed piece of metal into the ground for an anvil. This, with a hammer and a large pair of tongs or pliers, appear to be his total outfit, and I protest against any attempt to straighten the forging whilst cold. He laughs and produces an object made of baked clay, two cylinders, centring into a third, and a smaller one with a nose: attached to each of the larger cylinders is a goat skin. With exceeding skill, a boy manipulates these two skins, a small quantity of charcoal is put into a hole in the ground, and lo, we have a furnace, complete with bellows. In an hour, this native craftsman had completed the straightening of the fitting, and we return to refit.

We covered 44 miles following our mishap, fighting our way across the sand, bush, broken bridges and baked, cracked mud. That forging hauled our load to the end of the journey without further trouble, a good article cleverly repaired by a native craftsman, in the middle of Africa. In consequence of the crash in the hole, I was unable to change gear, and drove all the way from Mongo to El Fasher in second gear, except where it was necessary to use bottom, when Jack Sawyer tapped the gear home with a piece of iron. Says Jack, 'It would please Mr Mitchell I should think, to see us smack the gear with a bit of iron every time we stop.'

And now further misfortune overtakes us. At our evening camp, 50 miles east of Mongo, Joseph upsets a saucepan of boiling water over both legs of our mechanic Bismark, and is thrown out of action.

We were told there may be a doctor at Um Dam, 95 miles away, and we decide to drive there without resting him, for all we could do was dress his legs with lubricating oil. After another hard day's driving we reach Um Dam, only to find there is no doctor! I call in a priest doctor to Bismark, and thus we bow to circumstances. He proclaimed him fit to travel (by car) on the morrow. We have another 120 miles to go before there is any chance of a real doctor.

In four more days we reach Adre, the last French post before British Soudan. We pass through Abechir, where we obtain proper medical treatment for Bismark. The doctor dresses him, and pronounces him fit to walk and work. He refuses to do either and we threaten to abandon him. This sets him to work.

Eighty miles from Abechir, we cross the British frontier with great enthusiasm. We have fought across more than 2,000 miles, and we have reached at least one of our objectives, for we have crossed Africa, from British administration to British administration.

We pause for a time, then continue towards Gereina (the first British outpost), and once more renew our struggle with sand and bush. We reached Gereina, within twenty-eight days of leaving Lagos. We had driven every day except three, and for the last 1,200 miles without a day's break.

Unkempt, unwashed, worn, weary and with parched, cracked lips, we look a first-class pair of rogues: our boys have hardly a stitch of clothing left between them. We are met by Colonel Gregg, standing alone on this outpost of Empire. He greets me: 'You are Gray,' he says, 'You must want some beer,' and after putting Bismark in hospital as quickly as possible, we taste cold beer, after our long weary trek of 1,200 miles. Nectar of the gods it seems.

Bismark had become worse and at one time looked like a dying man. His injury had already delayed us and materially added to our difficulties in the deep sand. It was during his illness, too, that we had our only two experiences of the natives being anything but very friendly. These were the only two occasions we slipped our revolvers into our belts, just to show we were not entirely without friends.

Chapter 5

We stay in Gereina two nights, the first stop of this length since Maidugari, and the third only since Lagos.

By stages from Lagos, Southern Nigeria, we have passed from one crude Western civilisation, from modern building to mud hut, but here, in contrast to the previous slow transition, the change from grass hut becomes violently perceptible.

We leave Gereina at dawn, as is our usual practice, and in four days, *via* Kebkebia, we make El Fasher. Beyond Kebkebia we get relief from the weary, dreary, dragging sand, for now we cross a mountain ridge. To say cross is a little mild; in fact, we bump and bounce the cars down the pass on the other side, and they withstand this as they have stood the bumps and crashes as we have dived through the bush, to avoid the worst sand. Our hoods are almost in ribbons, but they are still hoods.

We near El Fasher, or think we do, when we lose our trail, and where we should have wandered to goodness only knows, had we not have been pulled up by an impossible sand dune, with an impossible gradient. We slide and roll about on it till night closes in on our misery. Fortunately, a camel caravan joins us at our night camp, and we learn we are 4 miles (as the crow flies) from El Fasher. Yet we had been hopelessly lost.

Each night I used two hurricane lamps, attached to my car, to attract the attention of any wandering natives who were in our vicinity. We had to use every possible means of obtaining information regarding direction, water and, where possible, food in this trackless barren country.

El Fasher, at last, and the Union Jack and Egyptian flag. The Governor, Mr Pembroke, gives us a cordial welcome, as do the whole European community.

We now start the run from El Fasher to Nabuld, *via* Um Kedada, which for a distance of 250 miles proved the most arduous of all. At this stage, the quantity of petrol ceased to be a vital problem. The wonderful economy which became apparent as we progressed had allowed us to present 16 gallons to a French officer, in French territory! Water now became the goddess of the expedition.

Could we carry on and obtain, *en route*, sufficient water for the cars and ourselves, in this parched and sparsely populated country?

In Nigeria, we are punctilious in seeing all water was boiled, and should have felt aggrieved if we had not sufficient for each to bath, at the close of the day. Long before we reached this spot, we had become indifferent as to the boiling. We had now become indifferent as to the colour and taste, being content to allocate a quart of water to the triple duty to two of us: washing night and morning, and replenishing the radiators. We had been told of the water economy of the cars in the desert. Here is proof indeed.

We had a guide during the first 10 miles of sandbank and dunes from El Fasher and then lost our way; and, like the huntsman, we proceeded to pick the trail by casting around, and after a fierce battle with the sand for ten hours, night finds us at a bleak rest-house, only 35 miles from our starting place! During the next day of twelve hours, we put up a record for this area of 76 miles. This gives us new hope.

Chapter 6

The first event of the day – one of the cars caught fire, but was put out with handkerchiefs before any serious damage was done. This happened twice subsequently. Due to a valve held up off its seating, in one case, to match in another. To-day, too, for the second time, Jack Sawyer's bush shirt caught fire in the heat, but without damage to him. It seems almost unnecessary to point out that the metalwork of the car was so hot, due to the blazing blistering sun, that to touch it was to burn one's self.

This was to be our day of days. Imagine our amazement when we see a woman some distance away, and I notice on nearer approach that she has a water melon! I send Joseph to ask if she will sell it to us. She agrees, and on coming closer, shows me her ankles. Each has a large, rough iron shackle around, with a short connecting rod. Her ankles were bleeding, but she has managed to disconnect the rod, which gives freedom of action to her legs. She intimated that she wanted the shackles removed, and after a good deal of pulling and bending we managed to do this. After we had liberated her from her shackles, we carried her 120 miles in all, before we handed her over to the care of the District Judge.

I desired to keep the shackles as a souvenir, and asked to buy them. 'Me no sell, you good white man; I give them,' but I insisted in paying for them. Four hundred miles further on I was in some little trouble with a British officer who required the return of the shackles, as he had been notified there would be a court case, and they formed necessary evidence. I am hoping to get them back one day. One rarely gets the opportunity of giving freedom to a slave. And, what is it Jowett's say about this 'freedom'? The Jowett helped anyway.

Even now the day's adventures were not over. For the second time, my car crashed into a bush: the front axle being bent almost at right angles, and the car became unsteerable. Joseph and Bismark struggled with the steering gear, flattened and adjusted the track rod, and to everybody's surprise the car proved drivable again.

The next day, after a short run, we found ourselves at Um Kedada, arriving in a blinding sand storm – our first experience of this, fortunately. I do not think I ever saw a more dispiriting sight than Um Kedada, presented in that storm. Thank heaven it did not happen when we were out in the bush.

The next day proved to be one of our worst. Twelve hours' struggle with sand, and only 14 miles progress. The following day we do a little better and cover 47 miles. The next day we reached Wad Banda, took in water, and pushed on. Before proceeding far, we met four military lorries on our stretch of sand. They were on an experimental trip, four days out from El Obeid, and already one day behind their schedule.

To avoid them, I dashed straight into the bush, clambered over a steep sandbank, down which they had stuck. We had become accustomed to this sort of going, dodging in and out of trees with more or less no damage to ourselves. How they envied our nippiness in our little Jowetts.

Late that evening we made Nahud, and afterwards with better going made El Obeid, 130 miles from Nahud.

Chapter 7

We left El Obeid, aided by a police car, and got 11 miles out during the afternoon, with some difficulty, as the clutch in my car developed a slip. We therefore decide to reline my clutch at Areib, and then go on to Rahad.

After breakfast with friends of the road (a road construction official and a missionary), we make fair progress for 45 miles over cotton ground, which, though much better than sand, is nevertheless very bumpy, and long cracks have to be avoided at all costs. We spend the night at Um Ruaba, with the British representative, Mr Armstrong, after which we follow the railway line for 14 miles, and then turn north.

Seven miles covered, and we become conscious that we have lost all landmarks, but we are finally relieved to discover a small village of grass huts, a mile away on our left. Joseph the redoubtable is sent to ask for a guide, and soon we see a horseman galloping down on us. The head of the procession turns out to be the Omdah of the district, who insisted that we go to his village and have coffee with him. This we did, and pressed on him our desire for speed, and he provided guides.

Later, after many miles, and after we fail to find any signs of the track, I say to Joseph: 'You tell this guide that if he does not put us on the right road, within half-an-hour from now, I will shoot him.' The guide's lips quivered, and he showed every sign of dashing off into the bush. We went on until dusk, finally reaching a village the guide said he was seeking. It transpired later that we were not at the point he intended, but miles beyond, and, by good fortune, well in the direction we desired to go.

We were rewarded the next day, 1 May, by a quick run over hard ground to reach El Dueim. We seem now to have got back into civilisation, for we find Governor Nicholls with a flower and vegetable garden, the first we have actually seen since we left England.

Early next morning, under his direction, we drove our cars to the steam launch *Lord Connor* to get round an island, and thus cross the White Nile, to give us a road described as good, on the eastern bank of that river. With all the tugging and pushing, it is impossible to get the boat any nearer than 35 yards to the bank, but by the aid of trestles and planks, we manage to get the cars safely ashore, and there find a guide.

During the final stage to El Geteina, we came upon a motor car stranded, as it had for a week for want of petrol. We were able to present a 4-gallon tin – a truly amazing record to be placed to the credit of these cars, for in addition to the 8 gallons already given to the French officer, we had deposited 32 gallons with British officials to be picked up later, but we sailed into Khartoum with a surplus of more than 16 gallons.

In the early evening we reached El Geteina. Setting out at dawn the following morning, we expected to reach Khartoum, our goal, with ease.

We were mistaken. To our horror, almost in sight of our goal, my car absolutely refused to re-start after breakfast, we were unable to decide what the trouble was. We tried all sorts of things, and finally poured paraffin into the plug hole, without any clear knowledge of what the result would be. Strangely enough, the car started at once, and went as well as ever. For 10 out of the remaining 20 miles, the car went well. It then alternatively sped fast and hesitated, but she never stopped, and with a sick face I decided to drive the car (without stopping to investigate) right into Khartoum if it was at all possible.

I arrived in the Grand Hotel and the car stopped as if victory had been achieved, but it refused to start again, even to move 5 yards.

It didn't matter, the journey was completed, and we were quickly overwhelmed by the immense greetings of our friends.

Thus ended our expedition from Lagos to Khartoum, for we originally intended to finish there. We had beaten over 3,000 miles of the worst imaginable country on two British light cars, of only 7hp, which, we considered, proved the superiority of the British product. I cabled Jowett's the following day: 'Both cars arrived yesterday, I claim stakes. Cars have covered more than 3,000 miles in under seven weeks through a trackless country of rock, sand and bush. At one stage these cars carried all petrol and needs of four people for 1,600 miles. Each thus carried or dragged by trailer more than two hundredweights. These 7hp cars have been given a test never before applied to cars. We challenge the world of cars to beat this record under the same conditions of carrying supplies. This then is the triumph of the British light car. It was a romance to cross Africa; the Jowett has made it a commercial proposition.' – Frank Gray.

Chapter 8

On the following day I cabled again: 'Leaving for the Red Sea to-morrow.' Thus, after a few days' rest during which the cars were generally looked over, we decided to move on to reach the Red Sea, thereby completing the trans-continental trip.

It seemed such a simple job to do about another 500 miles, after struggling more than 3,000, but we were soon to find that we had embarked on as difficult and dangerous route as any we had covered. We were accompanied by a pilot car, supplied by the British Military authorities, for 10 miles. When Captain Haywood (in charge of the pilot car) left us, he urgently requested us to wire immediately we reached Kassala. 'If we do not hear from you in four days,' he said, 'we will turn out and search.'

A few hours later we realised the full meaning of his words, for having covered some 30 miles of good going, passing several wells, the track ended.

Apparently, we were going right by compass, but an error of one degree would put us miles out of our intended course. We ran into country that was almost impossible – rough land with high tufts of grass. The cars bumped from tuft to tuft, and every minute we expected those sorely tired cars to have their backs broken.

Ten miles we travelled in five hours, and no sign of an ending to this grass-tufted country. In the distance we espied a hill. We were looking for Jebel Geili, and steered for the hill, hoping it would prove the one we sought. When darkness descended, we were left in a morass of bumpy grass, without even firewood.

To add to our difficulties, we had a new staff, Bismark was still with us, but we had regretfully parted with Joseph, as his knowledge of languages would have been of little use to us in Eritrea. In his stead we had an experienced interpreter. We soon found he had not the bush-craft of Joseph, nor his gift to laugh in the hour of adversity. We also had an Arab lad of fifteen to act as cook and maid-of-all-work for the rest of the party.

Above all our other difficulties, we were short of water, and not withstanding my warning overnight, I found one of the boys using our priceless water for washing plates. I told him that if we did not find water soon, he would not live long under the blazing sun.

Now indeed we fully realised Captain Haywood's intention to put out search parties to find us. We started off with heavy hearts, being down to our last gallon of water. After covering 6 miles in three hours, we were delighted to sight a small cluster of Arab dwellings. We steered straight for it, and were welcomed by genial and good-looking Arabs.

They undertook to guide us to Jebel Geili, and to water (they had none to spare), then on to a track for Abi Deleig. Swiftly we got there, and found a policeman to act as guide for the next 60 miles. He was 6ft 4in tall and had never been in a car before, and could not get his stature at rest. He panted and groaned by my side, as we rocked and bumped over the ground, and nobody was more pleased than he when able to announce we had reached El Sofeiya.

Here we stayed the night and set out at dawn for Kassala. Again we lost the way, but saw a man on a camel. Both the little cars dashed across the bush to intercept him. He got frightened at our rapid approach and raised his spear. I, in the leading car, threw up my right hand as a sign of peace. All was well, and he put us on the right track for Kassala, where we were received by the Governor, at the last British outpost, before crossing into Eritrea, under Italian jurisdiction.

After two more days we cover 225 miles, and reach a point 8 miles east of Asmara and less than 70 miles from the Red Sea, our final goal. The going was good until within 20 miles of Asmara, where we started to climb the mountains which shelter the Soudan from the Red Sea. The Governor of Kassala had warned us of the danger of these mountain passes, with their shelf-like ledges, cliff above and precipice below. At first we smiled, remembering his remarks, but a few miles beyond Asmara we formed a very different opinion. For 6 miles we drove on a narrow shelf, appearing to get nearer to the top of the mountain, by easy stages, but at each hairpin bend in the shelf, with only a yard to spare, we saw the road still going up 2 miles beyond. We looked down and saw a 5,000ft drop into the green-blue abyss below.

Wondering what to do, we turned a corner and beheld three or four huts, a wide piece of land between two 1,000ft drops, and still more amazing, that wonderful railway – which will never pay – which the Italians have built in the face of all difficulties, and defiance of all rules of gradients and turns, from the port of Massawa. Here we halted for the night. For two months we had been praying for coolness. That night, on the mountain side, our teeth chattered with the cold.

We were off at dawn next day, the final day's run in our expedition across Africa. Six miles more on the ledges and shelves, and at a bend we saw – the Red Sea.

At Massawa, we were welcomed by the small boys of the town, and the only two Englishmen in the place.

We had crossed Africa from Lagos on two cars of 7hp only, carrying immense loads in the absence of advance dumps. We had averaged 65 miles a day, counting all rests, and covered almost 3,800 miles in less than two months.

Chapter 9

Our difficulties were not over. We had some trouble to persuade the officials we were not political agents, but eventually succeeded, and tried to get passages on a cargo boat licensed to carry twelve first-class passengers.

The boat was full up, but we got three steerage passages to Port Said, and that night, Jack Sawyer, Bismark and I, walked on the boat. The quarters below were too deadly, and we slept in the hatchway. Next day, the captain told us if we cared to pay we might have our meals with the first-class passengers. We declined (owing to our clothing being so rough after our journey) to dine in the saloon. Instead, we had a table on the captain's own deck, and his steward became ours.

Eventually we got a swift P&O boat, and so to home.

Of my companions, Jack Sawyer was just splendid. Without experience of the tropics, perhaps without experience of hardship, he nevertheless accepted with a smile all that came, and in a few days it was his spirit of youth and inspiration which made the journey possible. Bismark saw us through from start to finish, and is now with me. Joseph was, however, the tit-bit of the flock of us. He was the biggest rogue I ever met: he stole from me, and robbed Bismark; he got drunk whenever we got to a town, but it was he who was always at his best when the expedition was in difficulty. On reaching a native town or large village, he would get hopelessly drunk on native beer, usually with money obtained by me to buy food. This conduct he himself described as 'having a proper Christmas'.

In many places the natives had never seen a motor car before. Many were startled, and could not be persuaded to come near us at all. Some ran miles into the bush when they saw us. Others were, however, very interested, and the two things that amused them the most were to be allowed to look under the bonnet, and blow the horn. The electric light simply amazed them, and the exhaust note was as the music of their drums, charming.

The natives have extraordinary ideas about water, and I must admit we almost came to share them in so far as indifference to colour and taste, but it was, of course, very precious for many hundreds of miles. At one place where there was a stagnant pool of water, in the dried-up river bed, a friendly Arab begged us to accept some of his really good water, and I allowed him to empty one of our full tins of water and fill it from his pool. First of all he waded into it up to his waist, washed his face in it, waited while another native drove a herd of cattle through it, then filled our can. Some water.

When we abandoned Joseph, having to take a fresh interpreter for the new languages, he cried like a baby. We had deposited money with various British and French officers all the way from Kano, which Joseph could draw as he returned.

One officer remarked, 'That is what I call putting the carrots in front of him, and will make it certain he will return right back to Kano.' So to Joseph, then, may belong the credit of the first double journey across the hinterland of Africa. Joseph often reminds me of the concluding lines of Kipling's *Gunga Dhin*. A very lovable devil was our boy Joseph.

Chapter 10

A word by the makers of 'Wait and See'

We do not feel it necessary to make any further observations on the performance, reliability and splendid sturdiness of the cars. If you have read Mr Gray's narrative to the end, you will have formed your own conclusions – the only possible ones. They got there, that was what was wanted. But it would be saying less than is due if we did not refer to the amazing petrol consumption accomplished over some of the most terrifically difficult country in the world. That the cars frequently accomplished 45mpg, even with their heaviest loads, seems hardly believable. On the great trek from Maidugari to Khartoum, over which stage of more than 2,000 miles they had to haul heavily laden trailers, the average consumption was appreciably in excess of 30mpg not withstanding the hundreds of miles done in bottom and middle gears.

Wait and See pictured at the Jowett factory. Soon after this they were driven down to Southampton to be shipped to Africa. Frank Gray saw the cars for the first time when they were unloaded in Lagos! (JCC)

Mr Gray has indicated the dire necessity for water economy, and the fact that they managed to wash night and morning except twice, and replenish both radiators, using only 1 quart of water, is sufficient indication of efficiency in this direction.

His challenge to the world of cars, as per his cable to the Jowett Company, expresses his conviction that no other car, of whatever power, or country of origin, can accomplish this trip at an equal speed – if at all.

Who will now dare to question the superiority of a British car for the most arduous work to which it is possible to submit a mechanically propelled vehicle?

It was a romance to cross Africa; the Jowett made it a commercial proposition.

The first extract from other sources has only been seen by me recently, as in August 2005 the Jowett Car Club held an ex-employee's reunion meeting at the Bradford Industrial Museu where the VIP guest was Robert Sawyer, the nephew of Jack Sawyer, the second driver on the crossing, and a neighbour of Frank Gray. He donated a photo album of pictures taken on this trip. He also donated a transcript of a BBC Story Time radio broadcast entitled 'Across Africa by Car', which was broadcast on Tuesday 6 May 1969. Once again, it is an account by Frank Gray, but this account has much more interesting information in it, so I am reproducing it below. – NS

In the spring of 1924, when I represented Oxford City in the House of Commons, I was unseated on petition and with this event came an end to all the activities associated with Parliament.

I entered the quiet glade of restful idleness. I did not like it – and so quite alone, I embarked on a tour of Nigeria, the Gold Coast and Sierra Leone. The main object of this tour was to obtain commercial information. On my return to England I published a series of articles which displeased certain English Motor manufacturers, who claimed that their cars were in every sense suitable for the conditions prevailing in West Africa. In the course of correspondence, I suggested that two cars should be entrusted to me in order to carry out tests in Africa. One company accepted the challenge without qualification; obviously they were placing themselves at a disadvantage, since I had already expressed a very definite opinion that the British motor car was not suitable for Africa.

Now, since it might have been thought that I was more concerned to prove the truth of my words rather than the efficiency of the cars on such an expedition, the makers and I agreed on a sporting condition; that if I could drive the cars successfully from Lagos to Khartoum, a distance of 3,000 miles, then the cost of the two cars should be refunded to me. In this way I had a monetary incentive to get the cars through, and so my second tour of Africa came about and I gladly embarked on it.

A young neighbour of mine, Jack Sawyer, agreed to drive one of the cars. We had two 7hp Jowetts and together we left Liverpool on 24 February 1926. We arrived at Lagos, our starting point, on Saturday 15 March. The following Monday was a day of ceaseless activity, my engagements consisted of hiring personnel. I secured Peter, as cook and steward, and also a mechanic, one Bismark. It was no light task to secure a native mechanic and Bismark agreed to join the expedition on condition that he was taken to England for two or three months before being returned to Lagos.

The rest of the day I spent acquiring food and essential supplies and obtaining driving licences for both cars and drivers. In addition to this, I had to obtain permission to cross the Niger by way of the Jabba Bridge. Jack Sawyer had taken charge of the cars and that night, dirty, weary and angry, he reported that both cars were ready to take to the road the following day. At that stage they had not even been run in! And so before dawn the following morning we were up to take possession of the cars and the roads. Champagne, the English emblem of send-off, was produced, and a small and enthusiastic crowd gathered to wish us well on our journey. Two hours later we were off.

On our first run of 60 miles to Abeokuta there was a road made and plain to see. However, potholes and crevices were the order of the day and by the time we reached Abeokuta in the glowing heat, the need to go slowly had already impressed itself upon us. We stopped for lunch and then on for Ibadan, which is the largest native town in Africa. Altogether on this first day we had covered 118 miles – not bad going. After Ibadan, which we left the next day at dawn, the traffic was much less and the road direction much more hazardous and uncertain. In the early afternoon we reached Ilorin, a brief halt and then for the Niger River and the Jabba Bridge. Our journey took time however, night was approaching and we lost our way, we then experienced all the difficulty of night driving. Under the clear white moon of Africa the headlights had an entirely different effect from that produced in England; they simply created a series of uncertain rays.

At last it happened – one of the cars slid gracefully off the road and into a ditch. There were natives at hand – we heard them – but our headlights were quite enough to convince them that discretion was the better part of valour and so we were left to our own endeavours to get the car back on to the road. Fortunately, it was not much damaged, but much time was lost as we sweated and strove. We continued our progress slowly – it was as well we did, for later that night a European suddenly dashed out in front of the leading car, shouting that we were heading for a precipice. We found we had fallen in with the foreman of the railway, who had received a telegram advising him that we were coming, although he had expected us from a different direction! He sent for our host for the night, who, of course, did not expect us and there was an insufficiency of even water to drink. We were tired, jaded and unhappy, all had not gone well.

Preparing the cars prior to leaving Kano in Nigeria. (JCC)

After a night's rest things seemed a little better as we waited for a train to pass over the Jabba Bridge before we attempted to drive the cars over it. To do this we found we had to clamber up an embankment of 60ft and turn at the top on loose ground and then, with no manoeuvring space, to get on the sleepers and astride the rails. Eventually we managed to get both cars up and then over the long straight bridge across the Niger, which, in all its might, christens the whole area of country around. At the end of the bridge and by way of conquest of it by a car, we stopped, paused to look at the sacred mountain on our left, and also to take photographs. We then continued down the steep embankment and took up the road for Mowka. It was only twenty-four hours to Mowka, but we were glad to get there for thereafter the going was harder if less well-defined, until we were pulled up by the Kaduna River. This had to be crossed, and in anticipation of our coming, planks had been placed on two native canoes lashed together, and by this means we were able to cross one car at a time.

The far side of the river provided much easier ground and we had a nice smooth and swift run to the wonderful old city of Bida, where we were entertained at the residence of the District Officer. The next day we resumed our journey and soon reached Bernin Gwari. As we passed through the village we noticed two motorcycles at the foot of a hill, we scented Europeans, and explored on foot a winding path up the hill. At the top was a Government House and in this we found two young British political officers. 'Hallo,' they said, 'Where are you going?' 'To the Red Sea,' I replied. 'Good God!' they said, 'Come and have some lunch first.' After lunch we pushed on for another three hours and not long before darkness came we reached a rest-house and there we decided to stay for the night. The next morning we set out again and I found the right way – no other word can be used for it – a great source of excitement and I was never sure whether I was on the way to Kano, or travelling to be lost in the bush.

At long last, however, we arrived at the grand old city of Kano, with its 13 miles of wall and thirteen gates, wherein dwells civilisation not of the West but of the East, as it was known 2,000 years ago. At Kano, I decided to part with our boy Peter, since we only carried one boy in each car and an interpreter was essential for the rest of the journey. In substitution for Peter, I picked up Joseph, a Congo boy. Joseph claimed to be able to speak Hausa, Arabic, English, and French and also be able to act as cook and steward ... I tested his skill in English and, if his other efforts were no more successful, it occurred to me that we were likely to be lost in the very centre of Africa. It was also in Kano that we took delivery of and attached to each of the cars a trailer to carry supplies of petrol. The ability of the cars to carry loads was one of the tests we had to face. Our arrangements complete and all our essentials packed, on the morning of 25 March we set out, amidst a gathering of both European and natives to the accompaniment of a vigorous burst of cheering.

Five days later we had begun to cross Equatorial Africa – what a journey – there were dreary tracks of heat-exuding sand. In truth, there was no road, only a treacherous dry weather track. There were bridges, but these were only sand thrown over logs of trees. Although bridges might be avoided, dried-up river beds could not, and each one seemed more impassable than the last. We eventually reached Fort Kouserie, on the bank of the Chari River. Here we were met by two French officers and taken to a rest-house to await the morrow, when we should cross the river. After miles and miles of dreary sand, this river looked like sparkling sapphires, and although our cares were not yet exhausted, the drivers were.

Wednesday 31 March will always be well remembered by us. We said goodbye to our French friends and set out for the bank of the river Chardi, where we could get our cars on to the raft which the French Governor had kindly provided so that we might cross the river. We started and had gone half a mile and then found we were stuck; we could neither go backwards or forwards. In the boiling heat we were forced to unload all our gear and at 12 o'clock we were back in Fort Kouserie dishevelled and well-nigh disheartened.

But we received cordial comfort and sympathy from our French friends, together with the red wine from their country. Never before have I had such a high regard for French wine. We were

Nearing Khartoum, Frank Gray with his native guide. (JCC)

invited to lunch while a messenger was sent to get our raft to another place where it was thought we could cross the river.

With lunch over we gained the bank of the river and got one car and trailer on to the raft. We then had an hour's journey downstream to find a place to land. With the aid of fifty natives we got up the bank from the raft and one car was safe. We returned and the other car was placed safely on the raft, but it was too dark and we dared not attempt to go further. A whole day was thus spent in getting 2 miles! There was, however, a final compensation, for Monsieur Coppett, the charming Lieutenant Governor of the Province, insisted on our dining with him at once, dirty and travel-stained as we were. At the conclusion of the dinner we were found quarters at the rest-house.

There was a mild adventure here, for, on our arrival, late at night at the rest-house, we found an attractive native lady waiting for us. She seemed both surprised and hurt when we did not press her to share our abode. Had we been French, probably we should have done so…Ahem…

The following day it took some time to get clear. One car still had to be disembarked from the river raft, and then we waited until 8 o'clock for a French store to open, for it would be 1,200 miles before we should be able to buy anything except the produce of the country from the natives. One of our purchases was some French brandy, which smelt like elderberry wine, but tasted like port. This proved useful later in the journey when Jack Sawyer developed dysentery – a plentiful dose of the stuff satisfied him that he was not really suffering from anything, and made him feel that he would never like brandy again.

Several days later, during which we had travelled over loose and dreary wasteland, we came to a mountain range, then Guera. When we reached the centre of this range we pulled up at a pagan village. The chief with all his retinue came out and we were immediately surrounded by a large crowd. They were very friendly and we exchanged all sorts of favours and graces. I shook hands with the chief and thereafter we were his friends and they could not do enough for us. They ran for firewood, water, chickens, eggs and groundnut oil, and even a high signal of honour

Final preparations at Maidagari, as the trailers had to be filled with enough fuel and supplies to cover the next 1,800-mile section before reaching the railhead. (JCC)

this, some native beer. Our boys explained that this was a black man's drink and even Jack Sawyer was horrified when he saw me help myself to a pint and toast the King! I have had worse beer in England. We thus became great friends of the pagans, and as we retired to our cars to sleep we were conscious that under the white moon, at a respectful distance, sat two warriors, our guardians for the night.

The next day we encountered a misfortune, we had only gone 2 miles when the car that I was driving fell into a concealed hole and bang went the universal joint. At this point we had to face the fact that one car was out of action. However, we removed the injured parts and returned to the village to enquire whether any of the natives were skilled in the treatment of metal. A shrewd-looking native undertook the task. He produced a piece of metal in shape resembling a horseshoe nail, and about 2ft long in proportion. He drove the pointed end into the ground and this became his anvil. He had too a hammer and a pair of pliers. This appeared to be his total outfit and I protested against any attempt on his part to straighten cold metal. He laughed and produced an object made of baked clay, two cylinders centring into a third. Attached to each of the two larger cylinders was a goat's skin. With skill a boy worked these two skins; a small quantity of charcoal was put into the hole in the sand, and thus a furnace was provided with bellows. In an hour the craftsman had straightened the parts, (including the metal tube), absolutely true to fit the gearbox – an achievement which any English blacksmith might be proud of.

But now another misfortune overtook us – the redoubtable Joseph, our steward boy, managed to turn over a saucepan of boiling water over the body and both legs of our mechanic, Bismark. The injury was severe and Bismark was thrown out of action. We now set out for Um Dam with our invalid and drove all day. When we arrived at Um Dam we found there was no doctor to be had, but a very cheerful French Lieutenant entertained us and I called in a witch doctor for Bismark. Thus we of the West bow down to circumstances. Our reception at Um Dam had been a curious one. A horseman had seen us from afar and by the time we arrived the whole village

At the Atbara river bed during the dry season. (JCC)

had turned out to meet us, headed by a band with four strange instruments. They did not know us or our mission, but they gave us none the less a cordial welcome.

That night we narrowly escaped trouble with our boys. Bismark, worn out with his burns, and Joseph, jaded and wary, had ordered a large jar of local beer. Fortunately, the lieutenant who we had been dining with had seen fit to place a guard over the camp and cars. This guard refused to allow the beer to be taken in until we returned. Then it was never taken in and we were saved from the drunken orgy of our boys. It was, however, a grotesque sight on our return to see, under the white moon, poor Joseph gasping for beer on one side of the sentry with fixed bayonet and a big jug of beer and the would-be salesman on the other. Now came more days in which we covered 53, 78, 28 and 36 miles respectively.

During the last stages of French territory we sometimes managed as much as 14 miles in an hour, and at other times we only did quarter of a mile. We were growing weary and this in itself slowed up our speed, each day fighting alternately rock and sand. To escape the looser sand we ploughed our way through the light bush. Sometimes it was necessary to dig ourselves out or cut a way through. At all times we had a burning thirst and we could only touch the cars by putting handkerchiefs or cloths under our hands. We suffered the most at mid-day when the sun was at its hottest. Jack Sawyer observed to me, 'It doesn't matter when we start, what arrangements we make, mid-day always finds us digging our way out.'

Eventually we reached the British Sudan frontier, we had covered 2,000 miles and had at last attained one of our objectives – we had crossed Equatorial Africa. Thus, we reached Geneina, the first British outpost, twenty-eight days after leaving Lagos. We were unkempt, unwashed, and weary and parched and had cracked lips. We looked a first-class pair of rogues. But all our troubles and cares were at once removed by the cordial welcome of Colonel Grigg – the lone Britain standing solitary at an outpost of the Empire. Colonel Grigg greeted me, looking at my

Removing the shackles from the ankles of the stolen slave woman 140 miles from Umkedada, Sudan. (JCC)

worn, dirty and dishevelled appearance: 'You are Frank Gray,' he said. 'You must want some beer.' Oh, the bliss of getting back to civilisation – even for a day.

We rested in Geneina for a day and we needed it too. Joseph commemorated getting to British soil again and a day's rest by getting violently intoxicated. After spending two nights at Geneina we bade our host farewell and in four days, via Kebkebia, we reached El Fasher. There the Governor, Mr Pembroke gave us a real welcome and the whole European community did all and anything they could to help us. Shortly after leaving El Fasher we stopped at a military well and here one of the events of the day occurred. Events and adventures had become almost a daily occurrence, but this day was to be crowded with them. The first event was that one of the cars caught fire – but it was put out before any serious damage was done. Then Jack Sawyer's bush shirt caught fire in the heat, but luckily this too was put out without any damage to its owner.

While we were at the well we saw a woman carrying a water melon and coming up slowly towards us as though interested in our proceedings. This woman intimated that she was prepared to sell the melon for anything we were prepared to give, and then came closer to us and showed us her ankles – each had a rough iron shackle round it. The woman wanted the shackles removed, and after a good deal of pulling and bending, we managed to do this. She told us that her home was some 180 miles away and that she had been captured and carried off and confined as a prisoner. She had managed to escape and now she begged us to give her water at once and then take her on in the car. We consented and after a day and a night we were able to hand her over to the British authorities.

By 2 May we had almost reached our ultimate goal, Khartoum. We had covered almost 700 miles since leaving El Fasher and now we had reached a road which we hoped would bring us triumphantly and with ease into Khartoum. We were mistaken. My car stopped and absolutely refused to restart and, what was worse, we were unable to find out what was wrong with it. It

Nearing the end of the journey, in the Red Sea Mountains. (JCC)

was, we thought, cruel luck to be brought to a standstill after covering 3,000 miles when we were only 20 miles from our goal. We tried everything. Finally, we poured paraffin into the plug hole, without any clear knowledge what the result would be. It was a desperate performance and met with amazing results. The car started to go – that is to say, the car alternately sped fast and hesitated, but she never stopped and I with sick face and anxious heart was determined to drive to Khartoum if it was to be done. It was. I arrived at the Grand Hotel, our destination, and drove into the courtyard and the car at once stopped. But it did not matter – the journey had been accomplished and the sense of relief was immense.

After a few days' rest at Khartoum, during which time both the cars were thoroughly cleaned by the British military authorities, we now decided that we could move on to the Red Sea. We hastily prepared in a slap-dash way, to embark on the final stage. We soon found that we were embarking on as difficult and dangerous route as any we had covered and, after consulting with the British military authorities, we decided to take a route via Kassala into Eritrea to the Red Sea port of Massawa. To add to our difficulties we had new staff on leaving Khartoum, Bismark was still with us, but we had parted with Joseph. In his place we secured the services of an experienced Abyssinian interpreter, and we also engaged a young Arab boy of fifteen, who undertook to cook and valet for us. And so we left Khartoum and continued our journey.

Just before we entered Kassala the track on which we were travelling suddenly became a medley of tracks. In vain, like huntsmen, we cast around for the true track. We were lost. Our route notes said that Kassala which we sought could be seen 20 miles away. We discerned it was a black outline in the clouds, some 30 miles away. It was unmistakeable. We were making in the right direction, but we had no track. Suddenly we saw a man on a camel and both cars dashed straight for him to make enquires. He got frightened at our approach and raised his spear. Since I was in the leading car I felt rather alarmed. I threw up my arm in a gesture of peace, and all was well. The man became friendly and put us on the right track for Kassala, where we stopped for the night.

We spent the next morning in refitting for the short and final dash to the Red Sea through the Italian colony of Eritrea. The remaining distance was only some 350 miles, but experience had now taught us that difficulties were not to be measured by distances and so we re-provisioned the cars, allowing ample supplies of water, petrol and food.

The first town that we touched in Eritrea was Agordat. On arriving we left cards upon the Italian Resident Officer, who was out, but who had been advised of our coming, and left word that we were to await his return and to receive his hospitality for the night. This we desired to avoid, since we were consumed by the desire to reach, without any further delay, the Red Sea and to declare our adventures at an end. We therefore proceeded at once, without any intention of discourtesy, but unforeseen consequences were to follow. Passing through Eritrea without bringing ourselves in touch with the officials we found ourselves at the Red Sea unheard of, unheralded and with the meaning of our presence in the country unexplained. However, after calling at Agordat, we proceeded. We called at Karen, where we would have liked to stay, in order to study Italian enterprise there, but we pressed on. Our way from Karen was one large gradient, accomplished on the mountainside shelf. It was narrow – a track not for cars but for camels – a track which threatened terrible consequences if anything went wrong, and with little margin of space to avoid hurtling down 1,000ft below. The sun was going down and we drove into a heavy wet cloud. It was horrible. However, as it got darker, the shelf broadened into a wide space, and suddenly we came on a cluster of huts. Thank goodness, here was a place to spend the night in this weird mountain fastness, but the cold was bitter. The natives surrendered a hut to us for warmth. Our boys shook with cold – was this to be the last night of our journey? – We hoped so. We wondered what the natives who occupied the huts did and why they did it on this cold mountain height. Also, we wondered how they got food to exist. Our dinner was cooked on the only firing they could give us – goat manure – to which we added all the combustible material we could find, for we were determined to keep the fire going all night if possible. The next morning it was quite easy to get up at two thirty and be away by dawn. It was so cold that it would have been much more difficult to lie still. We renewed our journey on the shelf and each turn we made round the mountain side we saw the white cut of the track going up, and up and up. Eventually we got round one corner standing out into the skies and then we saw the sea. The five of us cheered loudly, it was as well that we did for we did not see it again for six hours. At long last level ground was reached, and then 10 miles separated us from our goal; Massawa and the Red Sea. As we regained level ground, we returned to the heat, but it seemed hotter than we had ever experienced before. We returned to sand also and indeed to all the old difficulties of picking up tracks. At last we reached a flat sand plain and across it we saw the outline of Massawa and the glitter of the sand.

We reached Massawa, traversed the prosperous looking town and reached the shore of the sea and the bungalow in which dwelt the only two English to find a home in Eritrea, and there we were cordially welcomed on the completion of our journey. But our difficulties were not quite at an end. We had got into and through Eritrea without formality and, indeed, without reporting ourselves to anybody. It now remained for us to get permission to get out again. I interviewed the Chief of Police to this end. He asked me a number of questions, but my answers did not satisfy him and he turned to a subordinate and said, 'I believe this fellow is a political agent'. Holding this belief, he then proceeded to cross-examine me for three-quarters of an hour. At the end of this interview the Police Chief said very nicely but firmly that he was afraid that it did not lie in his power to grant permits and that I had come to the wrong place. He said that I had better see the Government Officials. I then repaired to the Governor, a genial soldier with whom; fortunately, I had taken wine with earlier in the day when I had called to pay my respects. He at least I convinced of my bona fides and all seemed well.

The Italians were very kind and hospitable to us, but when we at last applied this for passages on a boat, they explained that they could not possibly allow us to go on this particular boat as there was no reasonable accommodation and they did not want us to form a bed impression of Italian shipping. We, nevertheless, did not want to spend any more time in the intense heat of Massawa if this could be avoided, so I sent Bismark to apply for steerage passages on a cargo boat.

He got them and we went on board at midnight, just before she sailed. We went to the steerage quarters below and found a medley of Italians, who had seen better days, and some Africans who hadn't. It was a veritable Black Hole of Calcutta. We could not stand it and went and slept in the hatchway. The captain sent us his compliments and informed us that if we cared to pay, we could take our meals with the first class passengers. After two days as glorified steerage passengers, swells by day and outcasts by night, we reached Port Sudan. A P&O boat was in port, so we got berths and sailed for England … Our adventures over.

The Wait and See story was also mentioned in T.R. Nicholson's excellent book The Age of Motoring Adventure 1897 – 1939 *published in 1972. This book had extracts from various adventurers' books on their own journeys in all parts of the world. This has a short extract from Frank Gray's* My Two African Journeys, *published in 1928, and is mainly to do with the rescue of the slave girl.*

Another excellent atmospheric book, The Romance of Motoring *by T.C. Bridges & H. Hessell Tiltman, published by George G. Harrap & Co. Ltd in 1933 is a really good read, and also features a chapter on the Wait and See story. Once again this is based on Frank Gray's reminisces, but in view of the fact that it would seem rather repetitive to publish these two accounts also, I have chosen to leave them out. It is interesting to note, however, that some seven years after the Wait and See crossing, nobody else had attempted it. – NS*

I cannot leave the Wait and See crossing without quoting this 2 July 1926 report from The Autocar, *although clearly the Wait and See story deserves a book of its own:*

Enterprise and Romance
A tale of a stirring pioneer journey across Africa on two British small two-cylinder cars

We are sometimes led to believe that all romance has gone out of motoring, that the glamour of excitement felt by the pioneer is a thrill that no modern road traveller is ever likely to experience. All such ideas fall by the way after perusing an illustrated booklet issued by Jowett Cars Ltd, descriptive of what may be fairly termed an epoch-making journey from the west coast to the east coast of Africa in two 7hp Jowett cars, recently performed by Mr Frank Gray and Mr John Sawyer.

The bald facts of the enterprise are that, landing at Lagos on 13 March last and leaving that place on 16 March, the cars reached the Red Sea sixty days later. The almost incredible difficulties encountered are narrated in this booklet, 'Across Africa by Car in Sixty Days'. The complete journey, so far as it is known, has never previously been accomplished by any individual.

It was necessary to carry all supplies of food, water, and petrol for vast distances, light trailers being attached to the cars for this purpose. One of the brightest features of the expedition would appear to be the unfailing courtesy of the natives, of both high and low degree, towards the travellers.

The whole expedition was a British triumph, and not only sheds lustre on the unconquerable pluck of Englishmen in pursuing successfully an extremely difficult enterprise, but on the stout construction and extreme reliability of two thoroughly British small cars.

To commemorate the successful conclusion of the journey, Jowett Cars Ltd gave a luncheon at Bradford on Friday last, when the Lord Mayor of Bradford held a reception, to Mr Frank Gray.

'I have two great qualities,' said Mr Frank Gray in a speech at that function in question; 'One is to be able to conceive adventures and expeditions with a total disregard for accuracy of detail, and the second is to be able to find a lieutenant with the fire, enthusiasm, and courage of youth, to extricate me from the difficulties into which my felicity of speech has led me.'

In these opening words Mr Gray spoke of his recent trans-African trip, and at the same time paid tribute to the driver of the second car, Mr John E. Sawyer, who was his sole English companion.

Mr Gray, an ex-MP for Oxford, contended some time ago that British makers produced the wrong type of car for overseas markets, and to his published views Jowett Cars Ltd took exception. The outcome was that Mr Gray purchased two cars of this make in order to attempt the crossing of Central Africa, without relying upon previously prepared sources of supplies and replenishments; in short, the expedition was to be self-contained.

The two cars were shipped to Lagos, where Mr Gray had his first sight and experience of them, but his companion, Mr J.E. Sawyer, drove one of the cars from Bradford to Liverpool.

Mr Gray confined his remarks to the object of the trip, which was to show that the British car, particularly the British small car, could face any kind of conditions without advance preparations. He paid special tribute to his companion, Mr Sawyer, and also to 'Bismark' the native mechanic, who was also present. The Lord Mayor of Bradford (Alderman Stringer) welcomed the adventurers and spoke of the appreciation of the City to those who demonstrated its products so successfully, and so far afield.

Jowett Cars Ltd are presenting to Mr Gray a silver model of his car in a desert setting, with native figures illustrative of incidents on the expedition.

Frank Gray dedicated his book, *My Two African Journeys*, to Jack Sawyer with the following rather touching quote: *To my young lieutenant Jack Sawyer who undertook to do so little and did so much, this book is gratefully dedicated.*

An expedition investigating the geology of the Nile, undertaken between 1926 & 1927
Dr K.S. Sandford and Mr W.J. Arkell

I was in correspondence with Leonard Cowell in early 1998, who told me about his father's 1929 Long-4 Jowett registered FR7132. Leonard was very interested in Egyptology and was a member of the Egypt Exploration Society, and gave me details of an expedition he had been reading about. This expedition was investigating the geology of the Nile and was undertaken by Dr K.S. Sandford and Mr W.J. Arkell, taking place between 1926 and 1927, the report being published in 1928.

Both these men worked for Oxford University, but this expedition was being funded by the University of Chicago.

The following quotes are direct from the published report, which I published in the Jowett Car Club's magazine The Jowetteer *in February 1998; it refers to the cars involved; the geology references have been omitted. – NS*

The plan of work necessitated covering as much ground as possible; camel transport had been used before, but though sure, is slow, wasteful of time, and involved unnecessary exertion. This year it was decided to sacrifice the reliability of camel transport for the more rapid, though more hazardous progress of motor transport. It had been intended originally to take two Ford trucks adapted to desert work, but a storm in the Mediterranean prevented an important letter from reaching its destination. On our arrival in Cairo we found neither cars nor servants at our disposal.

In the next three days a couple of cars were brought into service, a veteran Ford tourer with special back wheels and truck body, and a little 7hp Jowett. This proved to be a valuable asset; it carried as heavy a load as the Ford, and was admirably suited for long-distance reconnaissance work. It enabled us to investigate a much greater area than could otherwise have been covered. A driver-mechanic was found, and a cook. The latter was a portly Nubian of enormous bulk and stature; he deserted as soon as he saw the cars. This was fortunate, as he probably weighed a little less than a couple of hundredweight! The driver came to the rescue and introduced a friend and colleague who filled this onerous post of cook-mechanic to perfection.

The Survey Department in Cairo was kind enough to lend us water tanks, and we could carry a maximum capacity of 30 gallons for drinking, washing, and filling the Ford radiator – the Jowett never boiled and only leaked once (the Ford did both continuously). Our scientific equipment included the usual surveying instruments, less a theodolite, and the usual outfit of a field geologist. Our combined personal property occupied about 8cu.ft.

The first objective of the expedition in the season 1926–27 was to study the deserts bordering the Nile between Assuan and Luxor. Accordingly, our first task was to get the expedition and its personnel, stores and equipment from Cairo to Luxor, where Chicago House, the headquarters of the Epigraphic Survey of the Oriental Institute, was to be our home and base of operations. It would have been quicker possibly, and certainly less trouble, to entrain the automobiles and their loads from Cairo to Luxor, but if we had done this we should have been unable to carry out certain work that needed doing en route, and we should have found ourselves at Luxor ready to move into the desert with men, cars and equipment untried – an unenviable position. So the journey up the Nile Valley was done by road. Roads in Egypt are the banks of irrigation canals and ditches, and they follow therefore the needs of irrigation and not of getting from north to south in a straight line. Of recent years these canal banks have been made into excellent mud tracks in northern, middle and much of southern Egypt; and so, as far as we knew, the route to Luxor held no terrors for the motorist. We were disillusioned!

Having camped for a day or two in the desert west of the Pyramids of Gizeh to try out our equipment and to test the behaviour of the cars in the sand, we set out on the journey south, following the banks of the Ibrahimiyeh Canal. The first night brought us to the mouth of the Faiyum, the second to Minyeh where we were checked by the necessity for a complete dismantling of the Ford engine some miles north of Minyeh. We looked round (we were leading in the Jowett) suddenly to discover that the familiar cloud of dust which denoted the oncoming of the other half of our party (the Ford) was no longer following us. On returning we found our two henchmen with heads buried inside the almost empty hood, the rightful contents of which were spread around on the mud road. A connecting rod bearing and a main crankshaft bearing had burnt out, and spares had to be fitted at the side of the road. These matters having been put in order, we set out once more on the next stage to Assiut.

South of Assiut an unexpected obstacle, in the form of road repairs, delayed us and we covered only 70 miles in nine hours' driving. Western road repairs occupy only one half of the road at a time, while traffic proceeds unimpeded on the other half. A roller follows close in the wake of the road gang. Eastern methods are different! Trenches are dug beside the road and from these, gangs of men carry baskets of earth up the embankment from both sides at once and dump the contents on the road. Each basketful forms a hard mound of earth, which is no man's duty to spread out. The result transforms the road into a sea of earth heaps up to 3ft in height, a motoring surface far worse than a freshly ploughed field. These mud heaps raise the road level by 3ft or so, but each gang of men is given a definite strip of road to 'repair' and a yard or so is left to separate each strip from the next. The road was thus dissected by a system of trenches, and at short intervals the front axle thundered into one of these, sometimes burying the front springs and part of the radiator in the far side. Then followed digging, hauling and lifting and the rear wheels followed into the trench, or were left suspended in the air.

There were other pitfalls! Where the road was open, the sun soon dried the mud into a mountainous surface as hard as iron, but where a few plants or bushes shaded the road, the mud remained soft. These patches were usually only found by the Jowett (which led) sinking up to its running boards, developing a dangerous list to starboard, and having its other wheels clear off the ground. The nearest village had to be mobilised on such occasions to lift the automobile bodily on to the 'road' again. For hours at a stretch we were scarcely disengaged from bottom gear. The Ford boiled continually, and ominous smells arose from the ill-used clutch. The bodywork creaked and cracked and shed innumerable nuts, crowds of juvenile inhabitants yelled and pushed and ran beside us on the lookout for surreptitious joy rides on the running boards.

It was a very tired and dishevelled four who eventually arrived in Sohag that night. A broken spring on the Ford had to be mended, and many nuts had to be tightened or renewed on both cars. Meanwhile, we were kindly accommodated by the British manager of Barclays Bank.

The last stage of the 120 miles from Abydos to Luxor was accomplished easily in a day. The only problems occurred when the Jowett sprang a leak in the radiator, and the Ford parted company with a nearly red-hot exhaust pipe. At el-Mahamid the population, as usual, thronged round the cars as we walked in to see the stationmaster with a view to driving along the line. Having satisfied ourselves that no trains were due, and having telegraphed up and down the line that if any came through, they were to be stopped, we drove onto the track. The ballast was newly laid however, and consisted of fine loose gravel, so that we made a quarter of the speed that we had expected, never once reaching top gear throughout the 10km. We eventually reached es-Siba'yeh in safety, as one of the Ford's tyres had burst and had been ripped off.

The report continues at length describing the work being carried out at various sites, working southwards quoting similar difficulties with the 'roads' and landscape over a period of months. The expedition would end when the party worked its way back north to Luxor. There was no need to drive the long way north from Luxor to Cairo, as all the sites of interest to them had been visited on the way down, at the start of the expedition. The last paragraph of the report reads:

We turned westward and retraced our tracks through the hills and over the watershed arriving at the Nile Valley two days later. Fortune was kind to us after all, for it was on the very last day with 25 miles to go to Luxor, when both rear springs of the Jowett snapped simultaneously, twisting the rear axle out of alignment and allowing us to crawl crabwise into town. We had actually ferried across the Nile and within a few miles of Chicago House when the differential of the Ford gave out, such a noise issuing from it that our approach could be heard from afar. Neither car could have done another day's work in the desert without lengthy repair, but neither had to.

These exciting adventures were not solely in Africa, similar stories were happening all over the world, such as this following one taken from the July issue of the Indian and Eastern Motors *magazine. Granted, this almost seems tame, a 125-mile trip, in comparison to the previous exploits, but it is an interesting read nonetheless!*

From Mysore to Nilgiris in a Jowett
Mr M. Waine

A recent journey from Mysore State to the Nigiri Hills afforded one a splendid opportunity of testing the powers of the Jowett. There are few rides in South India more interesting than the one that runs from the capital of the State to Ootacamund and Kotagiri, for there is a continuous variety of scenery the whole way. The distance from Mysore to Ootacamund is just over 100 miles, and Kotagiri is about 25 miles further on. Leaving Mysore in the early morning it is possible to get up to Ootacamund by noon, and the rest of the journey can be completed in an hour and a half.

The first 15 miles brings you to Nunjungud, one of the great religious centres of the State, and especially connected to the Royal House of Mysore. Up to this point the road is in a moderate condition only, probably on account of the heavy cart and motor traffic into the city. The next 30 miles or so are a joy to the motorist, and he will find no difficulty in running at 25mph, a pace the Jowett with three up, does with ease. There are very few hills of any gradient, and these are all easily topped on the third gear. But after this the road enters quite a different type of country, for here we enter the dense jungles of Bandipur. Here we begin to tackle the real ghat, and the car has its share of pulling. But the makers of the Jowett call it 'The little engine with the big pull'. It is not, of course, claimed that the 7hp car can do what a twenty-five-horse American car can accomplish, and hills the latter may do on the top speed which the former must drop down to take. But the Bandipur Ghat will test most cars, and there are few that can manage to get up round the corners, for they are real hair-pin bends, without dropping into second. The whole ghat was done with ease on the second, and this at 12 to 14mph, not a bad speed for hill work.

We leave Mysore country and enter British territory. The whole run now is full of interest for we were passing through dense jungle, full of wild animals, and especially the haunt of wild elephants. Pray that we do not meet one of these angry gentlemen, for they are certainly not of a friendly disposition. Many motorists have had a scare passing through here, but there have been few untoward accidents. Unfortunately, for some reason not easy to understand, the British authorities refuse to keep the first section of 10 miles or so in their limits in a respectable condition, but they make up for it by keeping the ghat road and the one over the Downs in a first class state. At Tippukadu there is a road that leads up the Sigur Ghat, a much shorter way to the top of the Nilgiris than the one we shall take round Gudalur. But few are the cars that have dared to attempt this ghat, and some of those have come to grief. The Sigur Ghat is really not a practical proposition save for the motorists who are willing to risk their cars, for only the high-powered car can manage it. The Gudalur route, though longer, is much easier and is a delight all the way. From the town of Gudalur the road steadily rises for over 15 miles and it is one continuous winding road, but fortunately, the corners have been well done, and there are scarcely any that may be termed 'hair-pins', but it is a steady grind, and most cars have to do a fair amount of it in second gear, mainly for that directly above Gudalur. The American cars have to stop once or twice to cool their engines on this ghat, and almost without exception the water is boiling long before the top is reached. One of the unique features of the Jowett is the fact that, no matter how stiff the journey, the water never boils. The ghat is just too steep for top gear, and the greater part of it had to be done on second, but it was no hardship to steadily make one's way up at 12mph. After all, what are the gears put in a car for, save to use them. It is possible to get cars that laugh at nearly all the hills, but for general use, they do not appear to be so suitable as the other cars which are sturdy in all respects. In spite of the long grind there was no suggestion of the water boiling when the top was reached. Provided the connections of a Jowett are kept tight, there is no need to trouble about adding water for at least 200 miles. At the end of nearly 200 miles on this trip, it required about two cupfuls of water. This ghat road is a wonderful experience, if not for the driver, for the passenger. The former must give all his attention to the road, but the latter is free to view the glorious scenery on both sides. What a panorama! It is not easy to forget those great stretches of country, near views of which are continually being obtained as the car winds round the hillside. At one point one sees the road which makes a most picturesque loop.

After passing Pykara, where the new hydro-electric works are to be, the road reaches the Downs; this feature of the Nilgiris is what makes them specially attractive. The road is always in splendid condition, and a run along the open country is an experience, not soon to be forgotten. The Jowett revelled in this final section, and many times was found to be running gaily at 30mph, perhaps unwise on a road with so many corners, but it is so difficult to keep the car back when she appears to be enjoying it so much. Now we reach the last of the toll gates – this is the fifth – but who cares about a few rupees when spinning along a road like this. Ooty is within a few miles, and we choose the high road that leads over the golf links and drop into the town near the Club. The ride has been full of interest. What has it cost us? Well, in spite of the hill work, the Jowett has only used 2 gallons and we have not needed any more oil. The running cost seems almost negligible, and it is worth while paying a few pounds more for a car if you can save a considerable amount on every run. The difference is soon made up. At an altitude of over 7,000ft a car loses nearly a third of its power, but in spite of this, the Jowett faces the hills with evident pleasure, and there is no car anywhere near it in horse power, that can do any better. The latter part of the journey to Kotagiri was accomplished with the same ease as the one already described.

In reply to the question why he had bought an English car for work in India, a motorist answered, 'Because I cannot afford to buy an American.' His meaning was not that, if he was able to buy an American car he would have done so, but rather that he had considered an English car, in the long run, would prove far cheaper than an American. This point of view appears to be gaining ground in this country, and in many parts one finds that English cars, of moderate power are gradually ousting the cheaper well-known American cars, for, after all, it is not the initial expense that counts most. The advantage of an English car is in the running expenses, petrol consumption, tyres, repairs, oil etc. Hence the writer felt that from an economical point of view, apart from anything else, and there is plenty 'else' in a Jowett, the little car made in Yorkshire, and one of the most popular in the North of England. It well serves its purpose in India and is growing in reputation here.

Reminiscing
By Horace Grimley – Our debut into the world of motor racing
(As published in the Jowett Car Club Yearbook for 1970)

It was in late 1927 or early 1928 when one J.J. Hall, a 6ft tall, young lightweight-racing motorcyclist, purchased a long two-seater Jowett. He had motored this car around the Surrey roads and become impressed by its performance and reliability, with such a small powerhouse hauling such a large chassis and body, and began to dream up the possibilities of a hotted-up engine in a short chassis and a shell body. After searching the archives, Jim discovered a twelve-hour Class G record held by Merandez and Don at some ridiculously low figure. Although the 906cc capacity of the Jowett was the smallest in the class, he was convinced it could make a respectable showing.

The dynamic Jim came to Yorkshire to approach the brothers Jowett, and in due course persuaded Mr William to have a go. On what terms I do not know, but as a youth of twenty-two years with nothing but Jowett love in my cranium since joining the company straight after school at fifteen years of age, I was commissioned to build this 'Voiture de la course' to my own specification and almost single-handed.

Some two years earlier I had completed my apprenticeship, having served in the fitting shop, machine shop and tool room, after which time I was summoned to the office of the then general manager, Mr H. Mitchell, and told to take over the experimental shop. This was more or less a sound-proof cabin containing a small bench and vice and no other equipment. The Experimental Department had been set up some six months earlier, but this was the extent of it.

Our first requirement, if I was to improve the performance of the power unit, was a test bed. Using my acquired tool room and mill-wrighting and the help of a boy called 'Digger' by nickname, we constructed and grouted in a steel framework bed. Then we set about making our own 'Prony' brake lever arm with friction block, Salter spring balance, cotton rope 'well oiled', and flanged drum with a bib tap lipped over the edge to feed water in for cooling, and a scoop to take it out. This proved to work remarkably and if not strictly accurate, it proved consistent and provided a yardstick with which to check any improvement obtained in engine performance. Then came home-made 'flowmeters' manometers (U tubes) in great variety to enable checks to be made of quite small depressions in 'inches of water' as well as greater values in mercury. The local chemist came in very handy for these supplies of glass tubing, etc. to be shaped and fashioned on a home-made bunsen burner. A tachometer (rev-counter), belt driven as per the speedometer of that era, was mounted adjacent to the Salter spring balance and we were all set to start improving the engine performance.

It was established that the production engine, rated at 7hp, developed approximately 11bhp and maximum revs were about 2,500/2,750rpm. After eliminating restrictions to higher revs by strengthening distributor point's spring, valve springs etc., we eventually raised the revs to 3,500/3,750rpm and the output to 17bhp.

Some restrictions to aspiration were cleared from the inlet and exhaust ports in the process, but were still limited to casting discrepancies of the old one-piece cylinder with pancake head and awfully pocketed. And with valve caps torqued up by something like an old bed head frame key, creating a very unclean combustion space. I think the compression ratio in early days was something in the order of 4.6 or 4.8 to 1, and any attempt to increase it resulted in rougher running and some detonation.

My search for improvement led me to develop detachable head cylinders with increased port areas, and a much cleaner, but still 'L'-shaped combustion space. This permitted a 5.4 to 1 compression ratio with much enhanced performance, particularly at higher revs. We still had the bell crank shaped rockers, ' radius pads bearing on the very conservative cams, and operating the valves via solid tappets.

It was at this stage of development that the twelve-hour record was mooted. Naturally the partially tested but as yet unproven detachable cylinder heads were adopted, together with the lightened connecting rods – a row of diminishing holes drilled through the centre web of the H section from the big end to the small end. All surfaces were filed up to a smooth even section and strictly balanced as a pair, as accurately as available equipment would permit. Light thin section grey iron pistons were used. A very much lightened flywheel. (The standard flywheel at the time was of gas engine proportions, guaranteed to make almost any engine 'tick over' at about 200rpm.) A larger carburettor permitting the use of a 26mm choke tube, an increase of 7mm above the current practice, and suitably jetted.

The chassis was the standard two-seater frame, but with engine and steering mounting cross members moved about 18in rearward. I think my ideas at the time was to get more loading on the back axle, and to shorten the 1in-diameter propeller shaft tube whose companion flanges were coupled by Hardy Spicer rubber canvas joints. These were not conducive to vibrations at high speed. This change of cross member position weakened the front end of the chassis, so a tube tapped internally at both ends was mounted as a spacer between the front dumb irons and retained by elongated spring eyebolts. The front semi-elliptic springs were lightened by removal of the second lap and the rears used as standard. Four big Hartford shock absorbers were used as snubbers to this suspension and proved to be essential when leaping the punishing joints in the Brooklands track. A typical 'Brooklands' silencer was made up, which was purely a large expansion chamber with offset inlet and outlet pipes terminating in a large fish tail.

The body was a light aluminium shell formed on light wood members for scuttle, dashboard and back seat rest. The tail was an unsupported extension deriving support from its V-form shell.

The whole was mounted on a foreshortened two-seater frame, again somewhat narrowed down so that ultimately, it was not a single-seater but two people had to be awfully familiar to sit side by side. A small wind-deflecting celluloid cowl was riveted on the scuttle dash forward of the steering wheel to deflect the air stream over the driver's head. Wheels were the standard five-stud artillery type fitted with high pressure Palmer three-rib cord tyres.

The appointed day was chosen when old Mr Ebblewhite could officiate as timekeeper. I motored down to Surrey – loaded up with spare gaskets, etc., which eventually were arranged in the boot of Jim's long two-seater, which was used as the race tender. A day or so before the record attempt was to be made I had my first introduction to the famous Brooklands Racing Circuit. One or two warming up laps, then one or two at near top capacity of the car sufficed to learn the circuit and also to establish that at our conservative speeds, not much use of the banking would require to be made.

All other users of the track were advised of the record attempt, and although still continuing to use the circuit they always hugged the inside whenever we were approaching, allowing us to use our chosen line at all times. Practice over for the day, Jim would entertain me by showing me samples of his small motorcycle cylinders with inlet ports almost as big as the bore and polished like mirrors. Then we would shoot off in his two-seater, tearing round the leafy Surrey lanes in search of old world pubs with thatched roofs and where Jim invariably had to stoop and remain that way until seated to avoid bumping his nut on the roof timbers.

During these trips we planned our campaign; we would drive for three-hour stints, which would be a safe refuelling time, Jim starting the day at the drop of the flag by Ebby, I would take the second shift, Jim the third and I the fourth plus a lap of honour for good measure. How little we knew. We planned that whenever any trouble developed if Jim was driving, if he could reach the pits I would fix it then to prove it, I would take the remainder of Jim's shift. If he could not make it to the pits I would tear off round the circuit in Jim's two-seater, complete with tools, accessories, etc, to where he had stopped, fix it, take over again and complete his stint, whilst Jim returned with the two-seater to the pits. The ensuing troubles caused me to drive eight or nine hours of the twelve-hour effort.

The following is not necessarily in strict chronological order but covers some of the occurrences as they come to mind. We planned to motor steadily at 65mph, which speed, given no trouble, would give us a handsome lead on the existing record time, while at the same time steadily building up a reserve in the event of trouble developing. This speed was well within the capacity of the car.

The day broke bright and clear. A handful of Jim's acquaintances gathered at the pits, taking a minor interest in this stranger from the North with the still stranger opposed two-cylinder engine only filling a fraction of that long bonnet. Once Jim was off they dwindled away until Ebby up aloft and I in the pits were his sole supporters.

About two and half hours later whilst chewing a contemplative straw and acknowledging Jim's 'thumbs up' signal, I suspected I saw a feather of steam under his engine. This galvanised me into action. I leaped into the two-seater; started up and sat in readiness for a sign from Ebby should Jim be overdue on his next lap. Up to now he had been lapping like clockwork. Sure enough he was overdue and I raced off in the two-seater to find him pulled into the inside just approaching the railway straight.

A quick diagnosis established water all gone nearside head gasket blown – but why? There then followed a painful period of burned fingers from loosening off six head nuts, removing a hot head and gasket, and cleaning a steaming face with Jim passing my requirements like a well-drilled mechanic. Then new gasket on, head on, initial nip up of nuts, engine started momentarily. Everything apparently OK. Switch off; further nip up of head nuts. Then a gentle fill up of water from the can in the two-seater. Whilst filling up, we saw the apparent cause of the overheating. The front of the radiator block was a solid yellow mat of dead wasps; there was not an air hole through at any point. How to remove? Jim took a square of cardboard from the gasket packaging and whilst I did a final torque of the head nuts, he, using a corner of the cardboard, raked along every row of fins in the vertical tubes.

This we had to do twice more during the rest of the day. As arranged, I went off leaving Jim to return the two-seater to the pits and take over what should have been my duties at the next pit stop due in about fifteen minutes. This stop could have been avoided if we had carried fuel in the two-seater, or alternatively had Jim been able to limp to the pits; but these are the thoughts that run amok when things don't work out strictly to plan. This short interval and my next full stint seemed to pass without incident. Now beginning to feel more confident; Jim sunning himself on his back on the pit counter, grimacing at me lap after lap, as for me a little more bruised from this horrible track. Jim, from experience, was wearing a body corset. I, unwarned, had to depend on six coils of rope which were always slack after the first ten minutes bouncing.

Above: Horace Grimley at the wheel of the specially prepared Jowett sports, which had been lightened with mudguards removed and built on a narrower frame. He together with J.J. Hall broke the international G twelve-hour record at Brooklands in August 1928 at an average speed of 54.86mph. (JCC)

Left: J.J. Hall seated in the Jowett sports with Horace Grimley standing behind. (JCC)

Horace Grimley in a replica of the 1928 Brooklands record car which was displayed at the Jowett Car Club National Rally in Harrogate in May 1971.

Jim went away on his second shift and at about seven hours he was announced overdue, then, no, here he comes but more slowly and with a thumb down signal. He continued past the pits, his exhaust beat sounding peculiar, to complete another slow lap and then came into the pits. He explained that his speed had suddenly dropped from 65 to 51mph but he could not hear anything untoward. I loosened the bonnet and quickly checked distributor timing, examined both spark plugs, everything seemed in order. I leaped into the car, started up and did a lap to see what 'gave'. Same result – 51mph maximum. When I turned my head to listen she sounded to be running one cylinder; some doubt because this manoeuvre caused the air stream over the cowling to blow my eyes shut. Then followed lap after lap with pit stops between each lap, when plugs were changed, timing checked and rechecked, everything we could think of. We were now getting quite desperate and fighting against time. Finally in desperation I wriggled into the cockpit headfirst on my back to examine the wiring behind the switchbox. Here I found a low-tension wire loose, shaken out of its grub screw socket. Yelled for a small screwdriver, loosened back grub screw, pushed wire in, retightened grub screw, yelled for Jim to pull me out feet first, dropped into the driving seat and away. This time singing like an old sowing machine again, went straight up to 63mph.

The wiring trouble, which had dogged us and lost us so much time, was now right (why it caused this peculiar behaviour I have never known) but something else was now failing. Our previous 65mph lapping was not maximum, but 63mph was now all that she would give. Jim realised the improvement whilst I was finishing off his stint, but he also realised that we had lost an awful lot of time and the motor was incapable of giving more. A decision had to be made when I came in for fuel about the tenth hour. Whether we should cut our losses there and then, saving the remaining two hours costs, including Ebby's fees, or take a gamble that the car would continue at its reduced maximum to the end of the twelve hours, which would only pip the standing record time by something less than 2mph. I had to decide whilst giving the routine assistance at the pit stop. We went on; might as well be hung for a sheep as a lamb!

It had been surprising during the day, the casually interested people at the start had drifted away, and few had been present at our various tribulations. Odd ones had turned up at intervals, expressing surprise that this old crate was still running, but as the twelfth hour drew nigh, I realised from the track that there was quite a crowd gathering at our pit area where we had enjoyed almost splendid isolation.

Eventually I received the chequered flag but could not see Jim anywhere at the pits. I continued to complete the extra lap as arranged, and then saw Jim at the top of a flagpole which he had shinned up to watch me complete the last lap, such was the tension. The little crowd was on the track as I came in; I braked, put on the handbrake and began to climb out, then suddenly realised that the crowd was scattering. I looked down and the speedo was still at 45mph, so I dropped back into the seat and braked to a stop beyond the crowd, reversed back and announced to all and sundry that the car had been prepared for twenty-four hours and didn't want to stop!

Average speed for the twelve hours was 54.64mph, as near as I can remember. Perhaps someone has access to the records.

I must admit I was somewhat disappointed at the ultimate figure, knowing full well the car's potential, plus the fact that all our time loss was not strictly due to mechanical failure, but to unforeseen hazards such as wasps and loose wires. Still I suppose the biggest percentage of dropouts of the cream of European cars each year at Le Mans are due to unforeseen trivialities on cars upon which thousands have been spent.

Needless to say, within a very short time of our success Merandez and Don knocked our time into a cocked hat to regain the record, which as far as I know, they still hold.

Our lost performance was due to cracked valve seatings, the bridge between the inlet and exhaust valves on both cylinders. Raising the water jacket above ports and under the seatings cured this. Nevertheless the car in this condition brought me back from Leatherhead in Surrey via London and the old A1 to Girlington in Bradford, a distance of 240 miles in four hours twenty minutes.

One could motor in those days – if one had a motor.

The average speed quoted by Horace was 54.64mph, while J.J. Hall quoted 54.86mph, but it was rather ironic to me that Horace drove the 240 miles back to Idle at a higher average speed of 55.39mph! The record was broken again by Meranddez a short time later, but this was overseas, so Horace's British record remained intact. A modified 1936 MG, backed by the MG Owners Club, re-took the British record in 1986, but as Brooklands was never reopened after the war, their record will remain forever! – NS

A Jowett 12 Hours Record at Brooklands
By J.J. Hall
(As written for the *Veteran and Vintage* magazine in the late 1960s.
Hall was a regular contributor for the magazine at that time)

I don't think that in 1926 it entered anybody's head that the Jowett cars of that day could possibly go for any records at Brooklands.

I had been racing motorcycles at Brooklands for some years and wanted a cheap reliable runabout, and found it in the Jowett, a car with a tax of only £7 per annum, which did over 40 miles to the gallon and a good 50mph. It was simplicity itself, with a very accessible flat twin engine; the foot brake worked on a band round the prop shaft and could be relined in about ten minutes at a cost of about six shillings. All you had to do was to pull out two split pins, put on the new band, replace the pins and drive off.

During 1927 they brought out a sports model, the only difference between that and the touring model was the body, a two-seater made out of aluminium and weighing almost nothing, and a slightly higher compression ratio. I wrote and asked if they would like to lend me one, which they did. It was a snappy little affair with a maximum speed of about 60mph.

I had spent hours and hours perusing the record lists, which was the reason that I obtained immense quantities of world's class records on various motorcycles with very tiny engines as low as 73cc. I had observed that there never had been any records established in these classes, so with immense support from Vivian and Teddy Prestwick of J.A. Prestwick & Company, I had some special engines made up and, having persuaded the famous 'Ebby' (A.B. Ebblewhite), the official timekeeper, into his box, commenced to collect records by the dozen. After all, one only had to do four laps to collect four; the 5km, 10km, 5 miles and 10 miles. Then on 50km and 50 miles and 100km and 100 miles, one hour, two hours etc. All one had to do some weeks later was to go out again, go a little faster and break them all again!

Staggering advertisements used to appear: 'J.J. Hall smashes 22 world's records' – 'Once again J.J. Hall breaks world's records using R.O.P oil and petrol' which were factually correct but took the precaution not to mention in what class the records were obtained or at what speed, thus causing a good deal of umbrage amongst other professional record breakers who might spend endless hours trying to coax some 350cc masterpiece into reaching speeds approaching 100mph.

It was by careful study of the record list that I observed that the International Class G record for twelve hours for cars upto 1100cc stood at only 54.25mph, and was held by Kaye Don and D.M.K. Marendez on a 'Grand Sport' Amilcar. I had an idea that with a certain amount of tuning, the Jowett had a very fair chance of breaking this record, and I wrote to the Jowett's and told them so. They were extremely co-operative in the matter and built me a special car for the job. This, when completely stripped, weighed approximately 8cwts with a full tank. The bore and stroke was 75.4mm x 101.5mm, a special 30mm Solex carburettor was fitted, together with lightweight Hepolite alloy pistons. The chief departure from standard was the fact that the firm designed special high-efficiency detachable alloy cylinder heads, which raised the compression to 5.25 to 1.

The car was good for around 70mph over the flying mile, provided there was no headwind and lapped on a still day at 64-65mph, so in conjunction with A.H. Grimley, one of the development engineers, on 8 August 1928 we started off to see what we could do.

All went well for the first four hours. We were lapping at about 60mph and building up plenty of 'time in hand', but away went a cylinder head gasket which put us back again behind the record.

In another couple of hours we had picked up what we had lost and were again well ahead of time and pushed the lap speed up to about 62mph, but at that point another cylinder head gasket gave up the ghost. By the time the rescue gang had got round the track and put the thing right we were again behind time and things were getting rather tricky.

I remember Marendez and Kaye Don, having heard that a Jowett was having the impertinence to attempt their record, turned up at the track to see how things were progressing. At that moment they arrived a third cylinder head gasket gave up, which left us almost forty minutes behind time with only a few hours to go, so they went away feeling, quite justifiably, that their record was quite safe. From then onwards, however, the little Jowett got the bit between its teeth and we pushed the lap speed up to 63mph, and it completed the remainder of the twelve hours with no further trouble, breaking the record by a margin so fine that during the last hour I nearly had a heart attack wondering if another gasket would go. We put the record up from 54.25 to 54.86! In addition to the International Class G record we also broke the British record for the same period, which still stands.

On 17 October of the same year I established the 200km record in Class G at 98.9kph. It was a newly established distance and I was in such a hurry to get out onto the track before anybody else established it that I brought the Jowett out from my garden at Peaslake, where it had been standing for some time, placed a battery on the seat next to me – it was coil ignition – and went out without any mechanics in attendance. The result was that at 130km, when I found I was running low on oil, I had to stop at the timing box and ask Colonel Lindsay Lloyd, who was officiating, for permission to drive down to my shed in the paddock to get some oil, which he granted.

He remembered that record attempt for some time because, as usual, I was very hard-up and found I could not pay the timing fees, so left the car in the club's garage as security. It was quite remarkable the number of months that I garaged it free of charge while I was trying to find the money!

They were gay days.

This record also receives a mention in Bill Boddy's exceptional book Brooklands – The complete motor racing history:

In August the irrepressible J.J. Hall, aided by Horace Grimley, established the famous twelve-hour Class G record in a special Jowett at 54.89mph; Hall's car had a special 30mm Solex carburettor, Hepolite pistons and special detachable cylinder heads giving a compression ratio of 5.25 to 1. A two-seater body was fitted and the weight was about 8cwt. Three gaskets had to be changed during the run, but the Jowett could lap at about 65mph. From this evolved the production sports model Jowett, and racing had brought detachable heads to the famous flat-twin engines.

Another amusing anecdote I spotted about J.J. Hall, which has nothing to do with Jowetts, but is well worth including, is part of a lengthy article by Titch Allen of the Vintage Motor Cycle Club, which appeared in their 40th anniversary issue of their club magazine, Motor Cycling:

Graham Walker was having problems filling the 'Motor Cycling' magazine each week, and was growing very frustrated as he was getting no news from the industry or from the sport, so this was bad for him. From his own personal fund of memories he wrote some really nostalgic stuff, and encouraged his old pals to do likewise. One who emerged as a gifted storyteller was J.J. Hall, a large jovial character, who in the vintage days had scratched a precarious living at Brooklands breaking records that nobody else was interested in, or had even noticed. He broke records in strange and unlikely cars such as the Jowett 7hp flat-twin, an 8hp Omega JAP three-wheeler and funny little bikes that I have forgotten the names of.

He landed on his feet when the war came and as a captain instructing officers in the art of riding motorcycles at a secret location 'somewhere in the South of England' (Southend) he was free to ride around rural Essex. He evolved a jolly little game for his friends which took in two of his interests – pubs and bikes, old bikes as he had dropped out of bikes after the vintage scene. The game which could be played by an odd (very) number of players consisted of hunting for old bikes, and the drill was to seek out a rustic pub and after buying a few drinks for the yokels ask, 'Do you know of any old bikes round here?' This way, bikes that had been buried under hay barns, used with the rear wheel removed to power chaff cutters, or even to stop gaps in hedges were flushed out.

Their tongues loosened with free drinks and spurred on by the promise of more the locals clamoured to tell these mad foreigners where such worthless junk could be found. As generations of collectors were to find out long afterwards, farms were good sites to find old bikes.

Having climbed into lofts and lowered bikes down by rope, dredged ponds and shifted loads of junk, the players might have scored as many as half a dozen bikes, mostly veteran or early vintage in a week. There were extra points awarded if any of the players could get one of the bikes running.

The article then goes on at length about the club's forty years, but Jim Hall is not referred to again. Presumably he must have sold on these bikes, as he certainly seemed to find them in large numbers! – NS

W.S. Canney

Mr Canney wrote about his trials and rally driving in October 1975, but I cannot see that they were ever published at the time; it gives a good insight into how he prepared his cars etc. He started his letter saying that unfortunately all his press cuttings, route cards, diploma for climbing Post Hill etc., disappeared prior to his move from Yorkshire to the Isle of Man in 1968. – NS

You might have wondered how it came about that myself and Joe Hepworth were taking part in these competitions; this was at that time when no manufacturer was allowed by RAC regulations to take part in motor sport and in my case no one but Willie Jowett, Ed Shotton and myself was aware of these arrangements we had. They supplied me with a car which I tuned myself, at a special price, and unofficially supplied me with the parts or spares I required, I presume the same applied to Joe Hepworth, as he had made his own arrangements.

My contacts besides the Jowett brothers (mainly Willie) were with Teddy Gascoyne, the manager of the service department and Ned Tordoff, the foreman of this department. Ted eventually became the sales manager of Jowett Cars when the Javelin and Jupiter were being manufactured until the works were closed when Fords bought out Briggs Motor Bodies, which were based in Doncaster. He later went to Australia to, I think, manage the Roots Group affairs, and where I am sorry to say he later died. I often called into the factory when he was sales manager, and he gave me many details of the forthcoming Javelin, which was being worked on. Ned Tordoff eventually started up with another Jowett colleague in Bradford, and I saw him a few times in the after years, but again, he passed on. Both Ted and Ned were very good friends.

W.S. Canney in his Jowett sports, where the engine had been moved back by 18in, making what was said to be the first assent of Dalton Bank near Huddersfield; at its steepest part it was said to be 1 in 1½. (W.S. Canney/JCC)

W.S. Canney on the right in WW3584, his Jowett sports in dark blue, alongside R.S. Moorhouse in his Jowett sports registered VH1735 at Thrum Hall, the Halifax rugby ground, the track going around the outside of the rugby field. (W.S. Canney/JCC)

I even went to the factory very late on towards the end to see if I could get hold of the press cuttings appertaining to my experiences, as they had all these from a Press Agency. *(They were stuck into a series of scrapbooks, several of which do survive in the club archive. – NS)* I was told I was too late as they had all been dumped shortly before.

As regards tuning, in those days no one could get any information out of me, the same with Joe Hepworth, but I am not boasting when I claim to have got more power and performance out of a Jowett engine than they were able to at the works. We had what we called an orange box saloon, about 1927 or 1928 I think, to which I fitted an engine tuned by myself. At the same time Jowetts had a similar car extra-specially tuned for the sales manager, Ed Shotton, of which they thought to be invincible. It was the habit at 5.30 p.m. for the director's cars to be brought to the front of the factory ready for their departure. On one occasion it so happened that Mr Shotton and his staff were leaving the works. His car was standing alongside our similar car; as we were approaching the cars I casually said to him that I thought I could beat him from the bottom of Idle up to the works, which was a distance of perhaps of nearly a mile. He looked at me with surprise and said, 'Do you think you can beat me?' to which I said, 'Yes!' He immediately turned to his assistant, Bill Smith, and said, 'Get into my car Bill, go down to the bottom of Idle, get side by side and race back up to the factory.' This we did, and with quite a few people standing waiting and watching. I was approximately 100 yards ahead by the time we passed the works, so needless to say I was rather pleased with myself. The first person to congratulate me the next time I was at the works was Ben Jowett.

In those days no special tools such as reamers were available so everything had to be done by hand, and I must have spent hundreds of hours on individual engines, scraping and polishing ports etc. I had specially cleaned-up connecting rods and beautifully machined the journals, turned up to a minimum of metal and drilled, this was done by Hepworth & Grandge for me. I had special Terry valve springs and on these used to put distance pieces to strengthen them, but I had to watch that the springs could close properly. As regards the pistons, I think it was $7/16^{ths}$ of an inch I had built on these, or should I say pistons made that came this distance further up the cylinder. I think the compression ratio was in the region of 10 to 1, so much so that (this was with the solid cylinder heads) a piece of brown paper on one engine I did could not be pulled out when the piston was at the top, so you can imagine the stress on the crank etc.

The acceleration was so vicious that special timing gears had to be made in steel, as the standard gears being of cast iron, could not stand the strain, the teeth being stripped off like dominoes. I tried some of the cylinders with detachable heads with a similar compression ratio, but they could not match the non-detachable cylinders. Also, the detachable heads were made with, I think, six studs and again, these could not stand the pressure and the gaskets would regularly blow, so that when these were fitted to production cars, I think they added another stud, although the compression was lower.

For a long time I ran the car on an alcohol fuel Discol PMS2, for it was thought the engine would blow with petrol, and it was only by accident that I found that it would run on an Ethyl or Benzol mixture, when Willie Jowett and Joe Hepworth took my car to Kettlewell to try it up Moorend and ran short of alcohol, and rather than leave it there they decided to put in some mixture and were able to drive home. Nothing at all was done to the flywheel, so this was perfectly standard.

I remember Joe Hepworth inviting me up to his home to have a run in his car, and he described it thus: 'You put your foot down and something hits you in the middle of your back and you wonder what it is.' This really was a sensation.

Another thing I did was to fit a clutch stop, by doing this I could change gear like lightning, and in freak hill climbs I was usually two car lengths away before any one else had started. As you will know if you have driven one of these, it is a work of art double declutching and waiting to engage second gear. Incidentally the lads at the factory could not manage this at all, but it served me to good purpose. Another thing I did was to have a solid back axle, but it was a work of art driving with this on the road, as you could not run round corners, but thanks to the transmission footbrake, I was able to skid the car round them. I don't know whether you have studied the gear ratios of the Jowett to four-cylinder cars, I think top gear was about 3.5 to 1 and second was definitely 7 to 1 and bottom 14 to 1, whereas no other car could pull such high ratios particularly in second, the usual thing being 10 to 1 and often a bottom gear of 18 or 20 to 1 even with more powerful engines.

Another peculiar thing with my tuned engines, although I tried KLG, HS1 racing plugs and other brands of racing plugs, but my engines would only run satisfactorily on standard AC plugs. I also tried magnetos against coil ignition, but I did not find this of any advantage.

Sometime in 1928 at the beginning of the dirt track craze, four motorists were asked by Blackpool Motor Club to go unofficially, for they had not got an RAC permit, to give a demonstration on the Squires Gate Trotting Course, which was an oval sand track of about ¾ mile round. There was an Essex, a 30/98 Vauxhall, Myself and a Morris which the Huddersfield agents had copied the layout of my Jowett. I think there were about 6,000 people there, but after several escapades with the Morris, I managed to turn my Jowett over, and was unconscious for three days before coming to in the Victoria Hospital in Blackpool.

There was also great rivalry between myself and the aforesaid Mitchell Brothers who had copied my Jowett design on a Morris Oxford chassis, and it was a great day when I climbed Post Hill, but they failed half way up the hill when carrying 56lb weights on the back of the chassis to try and get grip, but to no avail. I well remember my first attempt up Dalton Bank in Huddersfield, whose pimple was 1 in 1½ gradient, and I failed with my rear wheels spinning thinking I needed more weight on the back. Joe Hepworth was watching and said, 'Never mind more weight, that won't help, go home and get some more power out of the engine, you will still find the wheels spinning, but they will spin you out and up to the top of the hill', I found this to be perfectly true.

Unfortunately in those days there was not much to be won in the trophy line, even then the Leeds Motor Club and the Huddersfield Motor Club packed up owing me various cups or medals, but anyway it was a happy time.

I did not mention earlier that I had to carefully balance my wheels to get maximum performance and was able to get 52mph in second and over 70mph in top gear, which in those days was a very fast speed, for we used to think of 60mph for motorcycles as almost unbelievable speed.

I cannot think of much else to tell you, but there are most likely many incidents I have forgotten about. Of Miss Worsley, I must say that she was a great sportswoman, for at our last meeting at the Yorkshire Aeroplane Club at the Sherburn-in-Elmet grass track meeting, we were both in the final run-off for the Silver Rose Bowl. As the starter dropped his flag, my engine stalled, and she only had to run round the track to pick up the prize, but she refused to do this, to give me an opportunity to rectify my fault. After a second start the same thing happened again, and still she refused to go, although I wished her to go on each occasion, as it was her only chance of winning, but after the third attempt, with the same trouble persisting, I refused to hear of her stopping again and indicated to her that she had to do her lap of honour and take her prize, which she reluctantly did. I later found that my trouble was the battery holding down plate had fallen across the terminals and caused a short circuit.

I forgot to mention that I had a large intake Solex carburettor on each cylinder, and I dread to think what would have been the cost of fuel if it had been today, for indeed, it would drink fuel like a dry camel.

The Jowett 907cc Sports-registered KW3400
Victoria Worsley
(Taken from *The Jowett Car Club Yearbook* of 1971)

The years 1928 and 1929 were perhaps the highlights of my life, because in the spring of 1928 I bought the Jowett Sports two-seater, the most wonderful car I have ever owned. Being a Yorkshire woman, I longed to have a Yorkshire-built car. Also, I had watched the performance of Jowetts in the few trials I had driven in, and saw that they were in a class apart when it came to rough stuff.

The two Mr Jowett's were charming and co-operative people. They agreed to build this car, which was finished in polished aluminium and had detachable wings. These wings were of minimal size, just large enough to meet with road regulations, but all the same Ken Smeeton, one of my best navigators, refused to drive with me through Newark on cattle-market day, when the debris flung up by the wheels was apt to be particularly distressing. The car had, of course, no differential, which enabled it to grip on impossible surfaces, and to eat up any hill it encountered. The 25 to 1 low gear ratio took care of any gradient. The car had no doors, so the driver merely stepped into the driving seat over the side of the car, leaving a muddy imprint on the squab.

It was a crude vehicle by modern standards, but it went where it was asked to go, and never let me down. In the two years I owned this car I drove it in thirty-one different events, to the great disapproval of my family, who expected me to be brought back on a five-barred gate on every occasion. I even raced it at Brooklands, though it was most unsuitable for speed events, its top speed being a debatable 71mph. Jimmy Hall was most helpful on my first visit to Brooklands, and was one of the few speed-merchants who didn't raise his eyebrows at the idea of a Jowett appearing on the track. However, his friend Philip Brewster was extremely scathing and cast aspersions upon the dicing potential of the car.

As I drove proudly away from Idle just before Easter 1928, having just taken delivery of the Jowett, shielding my streaming eyes from the reflection of the sun off the polished aluminium bodywork, I was determined to tackle the three stiffest Reliability Trials in the country at that time – the Colmore Cup, the Travers trophy and the Victory Cup. Little did I know what I was letting myself in for? These trials were primarily intended for motorcycles, but included one class for any cars with owners sadistic enough to enter them.

I was also mad keen about Hepolite Scar and Dalton Bank, both freak hills built on West Riding slag heaps. Rosedale Bank was another freak hill on the North Riding Moors, and I had a mind to have a bash at that also. These hills were more or less unscalable by cars, as the surface was loose and the gradients varied between one in two and one in three. Rosedale also had 'grips' across it, guaranteed to do a mischief to any rear axle. They all presented an irresistible challenge to a Jowett owner. Money was my big headache. I was living at home in Yorkshire, helping to look after my widowed father and acting as his chauffeur. He very generously gave me a dress-allowance, in order that I should appear less oily and grubby when I went out with him; almost every penny of this allowance went on the Jowett. I had to find entry fees, tuning and running expenses, as well as accommodation for trials held some distance away. Jowetts very kindly undertook tuning and servicing at a very moderate charge and also kept a spare engine for me, in case of emergency. Most events took place at weekends, so did not interfere with my chauffeuring duties. Many years later I met Mr Wilson, who was the chairman of what was then the Yorkshire Centre of the Jowett Car Club. He reminded me that he had found me, sitting disconsolately in the car, while all other competitors were hurrying in to an enormous tea. When I explained I was too broke to pay for my tea, he, out of kindness of heart, offered to stand it for me, for which I was eternally grateful.

The very next event I entered the new Jowett for was a climb of Hepolite Scar. I had already made the assent in a Salmson, but it was a poor effort, and I hoped to improve my time in the Jowett. Paralysed with nerves and sick with terror, I managed to do this, and, when I arrived insane with excitement, at the summit, there stood the two Mr Jowetts, waiting with happy smiles on their faces.

My hero in those days was Mr W.S. Canney, a modest, fair-minded young man, who drove his Jowett much faster and infinitely better than I did. I think he was the uncrowned king of Hepolite Scar.

The Travers trophy, the toughest of the big three trials, was organised by the Newcastle Motor Club, and attracted six car entries in the winter of 1928. The course was 160 miles, and the trial was held on one of the worst days on record. A bitterly cold and piecing wind with all the venom of the Steppes behind it drove showers of finely powdered snow into one's eyes. The Jowett was, of course, an open two-seater, and scorned either hood or side curtain. There were only two small squares of glass as windscreens. I remember great chunks of ice clinging round the radiator cap, while huge chunks of frozen mud ricocheted off my purple face. Time after time we competitors were taken through water-splashes, rugged rocky paths, up hill and down dale in what the papers called 'an exacting test of human endurance and of metal'.

The Jowett behaved magnificently and won a bronze medal, but Sid Bryant, my unfortunate navigator-mechanic, suffered agonies of cold and was never quite the same again. We fitted chains to the rear wheels for the worst sections. One of them came off on a deserted river-bed, and was flung up into a blasted oak, where it hung like a gibbet, but there was no time to get it down again, and it is probably there to this day, scaring un-suspecting wanderers silly. Though my gallant and honourable navigator was frozen solid, he had moments of frenzied activity when he had to leap out and push the car through some especially adhesive mud. The moment the wheel got a grip on something solid the car leapt forward, and everyone knows what happens to the valiant pusher on these occasions. I often wonder why anyone is insane enough to be a passenger.

Trials in those days set an average speed of 20mph throughout, but it was really a case of getting through at all rather than getting through at speed. If that Jowett could get a grip with one of its back wheels, it would pull up any hill, regardless of surface. The clearance was terrific, too, and it would leap over boulders without a second thought.

I entered for the Travers Trophy a second time in 1929, though understandably enough I had difficulty in finding a navigator. But eventually Walter Skelton, actually an ex-gardener but a good man with a spanner as with a lawn mower, was prevailed upon to enter the passenger seat. This time the weather was kinder, and the Jowett won the Bradford Bowl, for the best performance by a car. My cup of happiness overflowed.

But wait. My boring conscience compels me to admit that the Jowett was the only entrant in the car class, so had to win the Bowl if it finished the course. A loyal newspaper called *The North Mail*, however, restored my flagging ego by writing 'Miss Worsley's Jowett ran splendidly and really won the Bradford Bowl, as apart from merely collecting it.' A nice newspaper that, and I took it for several years afterwards. I tried my hand a few times at grass and dirt track sprints but the car was not built for that sort of thing. I was too inexperienced and kept rolling tyres off, though once I had a remarkably tough inner tube, which took me over the finishing line into third place.

The Jowett was really in its element at Freak Hill climbs and tough Reliability Trials. It did well on Rosedale Bank and also climbed Dalton Bank, a 1 in 2.2 horror with a sliding surface, on the second attempt. According to *Civil and Military Gazette*, Lahore, India, the car stopped on the first attempt, and made a sensational slide backwards for 30 yards. No English paper was heel enough to print this but, like Sid Bryant, my navigator, I have never been the same since.

Victoria Worsley in her Jowett sports registered KW 3400 climbing Hepolite Scar on 6 April 1928; she managed to climb the hill, but did not win an award. (JCC)

Victoria taking part in the Travers Trophy which was organised by the Newcastle & District Motor Club on 14 April 1928; she won a bronze award. (JCC)

Victoria climbing High Oak Hill in the Victory Cup Trial on 9 April 1929, she was awarded the P.J. Evans Cup for the best car performance. (JCC)

My last event in this wonder car was the Irish End-to-End Trial in July 1929, in which I gained a bronze medal. It was a most enjoyable slaphappy event, held in glorious weather and the rules were as elastic as the smiles of the scrutineers. There were no tiresome breathalyser tests to spoil the fun in those days.

What I most remember about the Jowett was coming to some Test Hill during a trial and assessing not how I should get up through the stranded cars at the side of the track, but how fast I could make it, and how efficiently. Insufferably conceited that Jowett made me. I wish I had the car now.

Competitions entered in KW 3400:

1928

Date	Event	Result
6 April	Hepolite Scar	Climbed hill, no award.
14 April	Travers Trophy Tria	Bronze award.
21 April	Dalton Bank Hill Climb	Climbed hill, no award.
5 May	Middlesbrough & District Reliability Trial	No award.
19 May	Pickering Freak Hill Climb	Exhibition climb.
28 May	Half-day Ladies' Reliability Trial	2nd Car in class.
16 June	Rosedale Bank Hill Climb	2nd Car in class.
19 June	JCC High Speed Trial (Brooklands)	Silver Medal.
5 July	Skegness Speed Trials	1st in handicap race.
14 July	Bournemouth Rally	No award.
21 July	NW London Club, Coventry Cup Trial	Gold medal.
25 July	JCC Yorks. Centre Greenwood Cup trial	Won cup.
28 July	Grass Track Races	No award.
5 & 6 Aug	York – Edinburgh – York Reliability Trial	Silver Medal.
25 Aug	Cyclecar Grand Prix (Brooklands)	Finished.
1 Sept	Grass Track Racing	3rd in class.
8 Sept	Lowestoft Speed Trials	2nd Car in class.
29 & 30 Sept	JCC Night Trial	1st Class award.
14 Oct	Cyclecar Club Championship Trial (Brooklands)	Silver Cup.
7 & 8 Dec	NW London Club London – Glos – London	Gold Medal.

1929

Date	Event	Result
16 Feb	Sutton Coldfield M.C. Colmore Cup	Silver Medal.
16 Mar	Birmingham M.C. Victory Cup	Evans Cup for best car performance.
29 Mar	Leeds £200 Trial	Gold Medal.
1 April	Hepolite Scar Hill Climb	Failed.
6 April	Shelf Moor Hill Climb	3rd Car in class.
9 April	Travers Trophy Tria	Bradford Bowl for best car performance.
4 May	Dirt Track Races	Also ran.
20 May	Grass Track Races	1st and 2nd.
8 July	JCC High Speed Trial (Brooklands)	Silver Medal.
15-18 July	Irish End-to-End Trial	Bronze Medal.

The Jowett Car Club held its tenth International Rally at Cheltenham Spa on 21 and 22 June 1975. Victoria Worsley was asked to contribute an article for the Rally Programme *(priced 15p!). She wrote a much-shortened account of her exploits detailed above, which I also reproduce, as it all sounded such splendid fun! – NS*

The most arduous, yet enjoyable, Reliability Trials for which I entered the Jowett were in 1929, which must seem ages ago to most of my readers. The stiffest of all was the Travers Trophy, which was primarily meant for motorbikes, but had a class at the end for cars, which few owners were foolhardy enough to enter for. The course by then was well churned up by the motorcycles. I won a bronze medal for that, being the only car in the competition. One kindly paper said that I won the award, not merely collected it. I think I am proudest of that medal than all of the others.

The previous year I drove in the Victory Cup, also incredibly tough going, and there I won the Evans Cup for the best car performance. Once again I was the only car entrant and was extremely proud of getting round the course in one piece, which only a Jowett could have done.

My other exciting events were climbs of Hepolite Scar, a man-made slag-heap which went up at an angle of one in two and a half, my lovely little Jowett climbing it with ease. There was never to my mind any car, which approached the Jowett on the rough stuff. Whenever an inch of tyre could get a grip, the car sailed up. I don't think the car ever failed on a hill in any trial I drove in. It was the car, not me, that did it. It was a specially built model with aluminium finish and detachable wings and mudguards and windscreens. The engine was undefeated, and I wish I had the car now!

The Hon. Mrs Victor Bruce

In 1974 the Hon. Mrs Victor Bruce was asked to test drive the new Ford Ghia Capri at the Thruxton circuit on its first appearance to the general public. At the time she was seventy-eight and a half years old, but she was still able to reach 110mph in it, the fastest she had ever driven. She had been involved in motor racing and record breaking on land, sea and in the air during the 1920s and 1930s and was something of a legend. This renewed interest in her prompted her to write her excellent autobiography Nine Lives Plus *in 1977. As Jowett enthusiasts know, she and her husband owned a Jowett Kestrel, and it was used in various events, but sadly they are not referred to in her book. I am sure this is due to the incredible life she had, where other much more daring escapades are detailed. I will detail just a few of her earlier non-Jowett adventures to set the scene, before listing her Jowett involvement. – NS*

The honourable lady was born on 10 November 1895, the only daughter of Laurence Petre, the squire of Coptfold Hall in Essex, and was named Mildred May Petre, she had five brothers. One of her brothers, Louis, bought an 8hp Matchless motorcycle and sidecar at a cost of £120. 'I was delighted with the very sight of it, I remember saying to myself, just imagine, eight runaway ponies! Naturally I asked Louis if I could ride it, but he replied, rather loftily, don't be childish, you're a girl. Soon afterwards, however, he went to Germany for a few months and asked me to look after it for him, by polishing it. I fear I interpreted his instructions a little too liberally; I felt he would want me to exercise it for him too!'

Soon after she was racing up and down the lanes in Osterley Park and around Hounslow at breakneck speeds and enjoying every minute of it. She had her hair tied back with red ribbons, likewise her collie dog, Laddie, who travelled with her in the sidecar. 'To my delight I found that I could push my speed up to between 55 and 60mph, which in 1911 was like breaking the sound barrier today. To lighten the bike and to get a few extra miles per hour out of it, I took the baffles out of the silencer. I don't know whether or not this ploy succeeded, but to me the roar of the engine was exhilarating, and it certainly made me feel as if I was going faster.'

Soon after she was pulled over by the local policeman who wanted to know what she was doing on the bike, under age, as she was only 15¾ at the time. She was the first girl to appear in a magistrate's court on a charge of speeding at 67mph. She was banned from riding a motorcycle for a year and had to pay six shillings court costs.

The Honourable Mrs Victor Bruce with an unlikely pair of vehicles – the first is a Bradford-registered Jowett Kestrel which she used in the 1933 RAC 1,000-mile trial. Later in the year she and her husband drove the car continuously for seventy-two hours round the Montlhery track in Paris, covering 2,775 miles at an average speed of 38.54mph. The other is a Fairey Fox aeroplane, which was probably the highest-powered privately owned plane in the country in 1933. (JCC)

She married Victor Austin Bruce, a grandson of the second Lord Aberdare, at the time he was a test driver at AC Cars, winning the 1926 Monte Carlo Rally in one. This led to her first big motoring challenge, the 1927 Monte Carlo Rally; at the time the couple were living near the AC factory in Thames Ditton.

'The managing director, I expect, became tired of my repeated requests to borrow a car to enter in this trial. After refusing many times, he suddenly said, 'Yes'. S.F. Edge was his name, and a great sportsman he was. I decided to start from John O'Groats; my passengers were three: Bobby Beare, motoring editor of *The Daily Sketch*, the engineer and my husband Victor. I had met Victor at the AC factory; he was a member of the AC works team and raced for Mr Edge. He had won the 1926 Monte Carlo Rally, the first Englishman to do so. I drove to Perth but we decided not to stop for food until we reached Blair Atholl, as we were anxious to be done with the mountains before nightfall.'

After leaving the first official control at Glasgow they carried on southwards and 50 miles north of Carlisle they hit fog, which was to persist for the next 300 miles or so. With a sigh of relief they reached the Doncaster control, by which time Mrs Bruce had been driving for sixteen hours solid, with the three men as passengers. It had been wrongly reported to the press that she was intending to drive the whole way to Monte Carlo single-handed. So to cut a long story

The Honorable Mrs Victor Bruce in her flying days in the 1930s.

short, that is exactly what she did, winning the *Coupe des Dames*. So husband and wife had won it in successive years, so 'we were all very happy that day'.

Mr Edge was delighted with this result, as his cars had won two years on the trot, but he was to have another trick up his sleeve. He suggested that she should carry straight on into an official distance trial over 8,000 miles which took the four of them down the leg of Italy, across the Straights of Messina to Sicily and from there by ship to Tunis in Northern Africa. They then drove along the African coast to Tangier, cross the Straights then returning to England through Spain. This trip was completed and was an incredible achievement, as the roads, particularly in southern Italy, were very poor.

'We were not to return straight to England however, Mr Edge had suggested that we might show that the car was still in fine fettle after all its gruelling journey, by running it for 1,000 miles round the Montlhery racetrack outside Paris. We aimed at an average of 60mph. This done – without problems – we made our way back to London. The press, particularly *The Daily Sketch*, showed great interest in our achievement. When I wonder why I had driven all that way without relief at the wheel, I think it was perhaps because I wanted to take the opportunity of showing how easy the AC was to drive. Perhaps, too, the press's mistaken statement at the beginning made me feel that driving single-handed was expected of me.

Whatever the reason, Mr Edge was pleased. He had arranged a lunch for us on our return, at the Hotel Cecil in the Strand. In his speech he said, 'She's earned that little car. It's outside. I've given it to her'. When we drove back to the AC factory at Thames Ditton, there was a surprise waiting for us there too, a tribute which meant a great deal. All the workers, the men and women who had built the car, were waiting outside the factory to welcome us home.

By October 1927 Mildred was looking for a new record to break, she had heard that a team had taken a Chrysler car round an American track for a week or so, covering 10,000 miles at an average of over 60mph. She also heard that a British team driving a Sunbeam were planning to attack those records in the spring of 1928, so she wanted to get in first. The record attempt would have to be undertaken again at Montlhery, as she would not be able to use Brooklands as the locals had complained about the noise, so no night driving was allowed. Mr Edge had agreed to 'hot up' an AC open sports for her; they removed the mudguards etc. to lighten the car. She would drive with her husband, Victor, in shifts of six hours; they hoped to cover 15,000 miles during the ten days and nights.

By the time the car was ready it was early December before the attempt could be made. It was very cold and foggy, with hard-packed snow and ice on the circuit; it was in fact the coldest winter on record at that time. 'I drove a trial lap to get the feel of the track and at once found it very different to Brooklands; it was much smaller, of course, only a mile and a quarter round. As I went high on the banking, I felt as if the track was bearing down on me. It was like the well-known fair-ground-act, the Wall of Death, and it made me feel dizzy, almost sick. Then it was Victor's turn for a trial run, I said nothing to him about the strange dizzy sensation I had known because I felt it would pass in time; and when he had finished his run he was quiet too. He had probably had the same sensation, but kept quiet about it in case it worried me'.

The weather was atrocious throughout the attempt; they covered over 15,300 miles in the ten days and nights at an average speed of over 68mph and broke no less than seventeen world records.

The honourable lady continued to enjoy herself during 1928 with racing at Brooklands and sand racing at Blackpool; she also entered the Alpine Trial, driving from Milan to Munich over the Alps, a distance of 1,100 miles. Soon after this she was approached by Alvis to join them as a works driver, which she accepted, as it was her opening to drive against the 'big names' of the day. She was soon driving at Brooklands with her new teammate, John Cobb, against the likes of Malcolm Campbell. 'Brooklands is today no more, but I well remember the track; it was 2½ miles round, and very bumpy at high speed. In one race, my dashboard split and the steering wheel dropped down. But as usual, even if my car came to grief, I survived.'

By June 1929 she had a new record in her sights, the world record for single-handed driving for twenty-four hours. She had managed to talk W.O. Bentley into lending her a race-prepared 4½-litre Bentley which had been driven by Tim Birkin, but was to be driven at Le Mans the following month by Earl Howe. 'Switching from a David-sized car to a Goliath caused me no concern, nothing seemed to!' Before the record attempt started she took the car on a practice lap, and as the bonnet was so high she could not see ahead properly. When she came into the pits some cushions were quickly located and put on her seat! As the car was so powerful she had to be careful not to get too high on the banking, as there was a strong chance she could have gone over the top. After a few laps she settled down into a steady 107mph which was more than enough to beat the record, but also slow enough to keep her safe on the banking. 'The bumps that hit me so hard in the AC in 1927 were even worse in the bigger, faster Bentley. They pounded me, battering my shoulders and restricted my breathing. I was so near the top of the banking, so the car had to be held very firmly, constantly it felt like it wanted to leap off the top of the track, especially at night when I had to drive by feel. I knew I could not lose concentration for a second.'

She broke the record, even though she had an enforced delay of fifteen minutes after drinking from a water bottle in the pits, which had BP petrol in it for the spirit lamp. BP picked up on this in their advertising, saying it kept the car and driver going for the full twenty-four hours! 'The twenty-four-hour single-handed record I set at Montlhery on 7 June 1929 has yet to be broken.'

Following this success she was encouraged to tackle new records, but this time on water. She had stopped one day to watch speedboats racing on the Welsh Harp at Edgeware, and decided she would buy one! She called her new 12ft-long boat *Mosquito*, which was fitted with a special Elto Quad engine which was capable of pushing the boat along at 40 knots. After using the boat for a few weeks in races she asked herself, 'why not cross the Channel in the *Mosquito* and create a record for the fastest time?'

So on 15 September 1929, that is just what she did, but with a slight difference! She had arranged for a man from the Automobile Association to record her time as she rounded the buoy in Calais harbour. 'I hailed him Vive La France! And in a mad moment, turned and headed for home, as I knew that if I stopped the engine I would never start it again! I now had in mind the record for the return journey, and just hoped that I had enough fuel!' The sea was much rougher heading back to Dover and the little boat took a terrible pounding and the bolts holding the engine in place started to break loose. 'My luck – and the bolts – held just long enough, and through the mist the indescribably welcome sight of the white cliffs of Dover. The return journey had taken me one hour forty-seven minutes, which was the fastest by any outboard boat to cross the Channel and back.'

Then in October 1929 she went on to win the record for the longest distance covered in a non-stop period of twenty-four hours, but this time she was using a much larger boat. The following January she took part in the Monte Carlo Rally again, but after that she set her sights on aviation records.

'I had an urgent appointment in London at 1 o'clock on a typically wintry summer day, and found myself walking down Burlington Gardens, with an hour to spare with nothing to do. Such things nearly always lead to me spending money – if I have any. On this occasion it led to much more, for what did I see in a shop window, but a full-sized aeroplane for sale. I had never seen one in a shop window before, and never have since for that matter. I passed by and came to another shop with a pretty dress in the window; it was easily the best I had seen in years, and soon I was inside trying it on. The dress sealed my fate, as it did not suit me, and I wandered back towards the shop with the aeroplane, with still half an hour to go before my appointment.

Perhaps the sales assistant had seen me looking in the window, as there was now a ticket on the aeroplane with the words 'Bluebird Honeymoon Model – ready to go anywhere.' I said to him, 'Could it fly round the world?' His reply was 'Of course madam!' She left the shop, saying she would think about it. By the time she got home she had made up her mind to buy it and took a pencil and drew a line round the world, as she had already planned that she would fly round the world in it! The fact that she had never flown before was only a minor setback, she took flying lessons and within a couple of months she had her flying licence and she was on her way! To cut a very long story short, she managed the flight. For her final leg over the Channel she was met by Amy Johnson and Winifred Spooner, the two most noted lady pilots of the time, who escorted her back to Croydon airport, where large numbers of well-wishers and press were waiting to greet her, as her epic flight had captured the public's imagination.

Returning to Jowett, the honourable lady owned a Kestrel; I must confess I am not sure why as it was not the sort of car she was used to previously! In 1933 she entered the car in the RAC Rally in the less than 10hp class over a course of approximately 1,000 miles. She was eighty-seventh out of a class of 106, so qualified for a finisher's award. She must have been impressed with the reliability of the car, as it could not have been its speed! She and Victor took the car to Montlhery in the same year to attempt the longest non-stop run. The car was driven continuously for seventy-two hours; the little car had to pull a trailer that carried a 100-gallon tank of petrol. The total weight of the car plus trailer was 1½ tons, but this would reduce over the seventy-two hours as the petrol was consumed. The petrol was pumped into the car, which had to run at over 15mph to make sure an adequate supply was delivered. As in the ten-day endurance test, she and Victor drove in six-hour shifts, which allowed them plenty of time to eat and sleep. The only difference being that on this occasion they had to switch whilst still on the move. The optimum speed for doing this was 6mph, so they had to get a move on, as the carburettors would be soon starved of petrol if they dilly-dallied. Filling the car with oil caused other problems however, as the crankcase pressure blew oil back out of the engine over the person filling it and everything else in the immediate vicinity!

Needless to say the Kestrel was travelling much slower than the Bentley was, so problems on the banking were not an issue, as the car would hardly have ventured onto that area at all. There were no mechanical problems and the plucky little Kestrel covered a distance of 2,775 miles at an average speed of 38.54mph. This will have seemed like a picnic to Mildred after averaging speeds in excess of 100mph in the Bentley four years earlier, where she covered nearly as much distance in twenty-four hours!

This record was noted in Lord Montagu's excellent book Lost Causes of Motoring *published by Cassell of London in 1960, and which ended with this wonderful quote: 'It was a triumph of patience one feels, rather than mechanical endurance!'*

In John Bullock's excellent book Fast Women, *published by Robson Books in 2002, he states that: 'When racing Mildred refused to wear overalls or slacks, but was always dressed in a smart blouse and skirt, with a pearl necklace. She is quoted as saying to a surprised interviewer in this wonderful off the cuff comment, "Don't call me a woman's libber! I don't approve of that sort of thing. I was a girl among five brothers and have always tried to remain feminine".'*

Motoring: The Golden Years, A Pictorial Anthology
Compiled by Rupert Prior
(Published by H.C. Blossom Ltd, London, 1991)

This rather charming piece by Mrs Victor Bruce was written in 1933 and entitled 'Good driving or good racing driving is not a matter of sex', and was published in the above book, but I have not been able to find out where it originally appeared. At this time she owned the Kestrel, which had lovely mudguards, even though she does not refer to it in the text! – NS

Many male motorists I know start a 'moan' about the women drivers whenever anybody driving does something silly or thoughtless on the roads. They immediately give off their war cry, 'I bet that's a woman'; quite often when they arrive opposite the offending car they discover the driver to be a man, but this fact does not soften their judgement of the woman driver.

I often wonder how many men who teach their wives or sisters to drive – I do not include other men's wives or sisters, because a man, strange to relate, usually has so much more patience with friends than with members of his own family – do the job properly, and how many just teach the woman to steer and scramble through the gears, so that it is a relief to get her into top gear, so much so it usually stays there too long, with the horror of changing down.

Another thing which the male motorist sometimes overlooks is the fact that a few years ago women more or less all started to drive together, so that there was an enormous number of women on the road making the usual beginner's mistakes. On that quite a lot of male drivers based their opinion of the woman motorist – despite the fact that today on the roads one usually finds the woman to be a perfectly normal driver.

Running Boards in Favour Again
Women motorists will be glad of the return to favour of the running board. Recently I have covered a good number of miles in two different motor cars equipped with running boards rather than just steps. I could not help but notice how clean these two cars have remained whilst being driven about in all kinds of weather.

One of them was a cream and black Armstrong Siddeley sports saloon, which has amazingly good 'mudguarding', and keeps its spick and span appearance even after a week of driving in our changeable climate. Very little dirt gets on the body; and most essential of all, the screen keeps clean, an item that has not been found on other recent designs. Numerous cars that I have driven in bad weather get their windscreens into an appalling mess, with the mud being thrown up by the car due to ineffective mudguarding. Even the best of windscreen wipers cannot clear mud off the windscreen.

The other car, which, by the way, has reverted to running boards, is the new MG Magna, last year this car was without. The appearance of the car is actually improved by the extra mud protection provided by the running boards, for the sweep of the wings, one line from the front to the rear, is a delight to the eye. And, of course, such a car keeps much cleaner, a thing which a woman owner-driver who does her own weekly wash down will appreciate.

Gears Still Not Used Effectively

Nearly every week I drive up Reigate Hill, and a thing that surprises me is the fact that very few drivers seem to get the best out of their cars climbing this famous 'test hill'. The majority of drivers wait until the engine is dying before changing down, and the result is they lose revs and in the end have to drop down into an even lower gear than that which was necessary.

They do not seem to realise that to change early when the engine is still revving comfortably will mean that they can climb the hill on a higher gear than if they lose all power by letting the engine labour. Apart from which, of course, it is much nicer if the engine is turning over nicely. As the easy-change gearboxes become ever more popular, drivers will get the full benefit from their gears.

Chapter 2

Post-War Rallies and Races

During the war Jowett were busy making munitions for the war effort, but their dynamic managing director, Charles Calcott-Reilly, was already planning for replacement Jowett models as early as 1942. He advertised for a new chief designer with a view to starting work on the new car straightaway. One of the applicants was Gerald Palmer, a young engineering draughtsman who was working for MG at the time. It would appear that Gerald was not impressed with his trip up north to Bradford, and returned to MG. That could have been the end of the story, but Calcott-Reilly was most impressed with him! He made a special trip south to see Gerald as he was sure he was the man for the job. He offered Gerald a salary of £500 and a free hand to design the new car; this was an offer he could not refuse and he took the job!

The result was the stunning Javelin, which took the Motoring Press *by storm when it was launched in 1947. The well-known Yorkshire rally driver, Tommy Wise, spotted the potential the Javelin had as a rally car so approached the Jowett factory with a view to entering a car in the first post-war Monte Carlo Rally in 1949. It seems only fitting, therefore, that the first reminiscence in this section should be that of Gerald Palmer, who drove with Tommy Wise and Cuth Harrison in his brainchild, the Javelin, in its first competitive event. – NS*

1949 Monte Carlo Rally
Gerald Palmer
(Taken from the book *Auto-Architect: the Autobiography of Gerald Palmer*, assisted by Christopher Balfour, published by The Magna Press, 1998)

In November 1948 it was announced that the famous Monte Carlo Rally would definitely be held in January for the first time *post bellum*. We at the works had never viewed the Javelin as a rally car as it had been designed purely as a utility vehicle. It was a well-known Yorkshire sportsman, Tommy Wise, who saw its potential and he persuaded the management to sell him the latest prototype, which he entered into the rally with T.C. (Cuth) Harrison as co-driver. He very kindly asked me to join them as second co-driver, 'It would be a salutary experience for you as the designer,' he said to me. I jumped at the opportunity, and the experience has remained a vivid memory with me ever since then.

The British section of the rally started at Glasgow, the authorities having provided all competitors with petrol coupons to drive from home to the start and down to the South. Our first stop was at Tommy's house at Guisley, where our wives fuelled us up for the night section to Folkestone. Over the Channel the 'wicked' French had laid on a champagne party at Calais, perhaps to delay the naïve British entry? Suddenly Tommy yelled, 'We're an hour behind schedule'. I shall never forget that journey across the atrocious roads of Northern France to Luxembourg.

They wouldn't let me drive as they said I would treat the car too gently. So it was bang, bang, bang from one pothole to the next pothole, me in agony wondering what would break first on the car. But we made it to Luxembourg with minutes to spare – and the car in one piece. The route then led north to Holland (Nijmegen, Amsterdam and The Hague) through Antwerp and Brussels to Paris, where we arrived at about 9 p.m. on the third night with the control under the Eiffel Tower.

The enthusiasm of the French populous was extraordinary and my recollection is of cheering crowds lining the streets of every sizable town, waving and urging you on. It was an all-night stretch through France until the dawn came up at Lyon; and with it the dreaded fog. Tommy drove through it but we were obviously losing time, so on turning east towards the mountains and clear weather we had to make it up. I took over on the long straights down to Sisteron and Digne, it was flat-out. 'Faster,' yelled Tommy from the back seat. 'It won't b----- well go any faster,' I yelled back to loud laughter from the two of them; me wondering if the engine would survive.

Cuth took over at Digne and we came up to the first pass, the Col des Leques, which was not high but difficult with lots of hairpin bends. Cuth yelled, 'Shall I let her rip Tommy?' 'Yes,' came the reply, and I immediately groped for the door exit handle as we approached the first bend at a madly high speed. Cuth literally threw the car round that bend in a four-wheel drift, me having kittens wondering what would break. I suddenly said to myself, 'this chap knows what he is doing' and was completely calm as he repeated the performance at every bend. I timed him over the pass and we averaged at 40mph! Phew! I had never experienced this type of driving before, and was never surprised that Cuth became one of our top Grand Prix and rally drivers in later years.

And so into Castellane and down to the coast at Nice and on to Monte Carlo. The car and I had survived and we had lost no marks on the road section. A few hours of rest and relaxation followed and then came the eliminating test, which was a high-speed hill climb up the Mont des Mules. Tommy made one or two practice runs and was satisfied that he would be well placed. He made his two climbs, made good time and was confident. To our astonishment when the results were posted up, Gatsonides, the Dutchman in a Hillman Minx was placed first in the 1.5 litre class, and we were third in class and twenty-seventh overall in the rally. I said, 'I don't believe it, let's go and look at the detail figures,' but there was not time before the prize-giving, so Gatsonides was presented with the Riviera Cup and £75 prize money by Prince Rainier and we got a miserable £35. We then rushed to check the detail times and I found a simple arithmetic error had been made in our result. A protest was immediately lodged, which had to be upheld by the rather confused and red-faced officials. 'Ah monsieurs,' they said, 'This is the first rally after the war and we are out of practice'. The revised total put us way ahead at the top of the 1.5 litre class and fourteenth overall. The Riviera Cup was grabbed back from the hapless Gatsonides and given to Tommy, but he had quickly disposed of his £75, so they had to make it up to us. Another Javelin driven by Ron Smith and Horace Grimley, was twenty-second overall and third in class. Three other examples (Turner, Hume and Miller) were among the later finishers.

As a postscript to the rally, I had hoped to have a day or two basking in the sun. Not a bit of it! We left that evening and spent the night in Aix. Setting off again at the crack of dawn, we eventually bedded down 500 miles later, near midnight, at Amiens. I well remember that all the hotels were closed. We saw a light on in a basement shop; Tommy just walked in to find an astonished baker at work. He managed to persuade the chap to give us beds either in his own or his neighbour's house. Those who remember the state of the French roads in 1949 will agree that that was a good day's motoring. The car came through in tact, which was a great relief to me. It was a real privilege to have driven with Tommy Wise and Cuth Harrison – they were two fine Yorkshiremen.

No company could have wished for greater publicity at the debut of a new model than this win in the Monte Carlo Rally. It was followed in July by an equally spectacular win at Spa in the Belgian 24-hour race. Anthony Hume, who had also driven a Javelin on the rally, had then read the Export Report by the Belgian journalist, Paul Frere, in the 23 February issue of *The Motor*. Frere noted the Javelin stand at the Brussels Show had not attracted much attention, concluded that the car was too little known and suggested running a team of three cars in the Touring Class at Spa. This led to Anthony to ask us to enter a team. We decided that there was not enough time to prepare three machines, but that we would lend one production car to be driven by Anthony and Tommy Wisdom.

This was prepared in accordance with our service bulletin recommendations for competition, which involved stripping the engine and with careful reassembly, raised compression, larger carburettors, higher gear ratios, racing tyres and stiffer shock absorbers. The car ran like clockwork, needing no repairs or adjustments. It won the 2 litre Touring Class covering over 1,500 miles at 65.5mph and covered a greater distance than any other 1.5 litre cars (both sports and touring), and the much larger 4 litre touring cars. Other rally successes followed, so that the car was beginning to be known by its semi-sporting qualities, rather than its utilitarian qualities, which were the original design objectives. This was disturbing to me since it might lead to its getting a reputation for unreliability. I knew there was a lot of development work still to be done. (Apart from the use of Javelin mechanical units, including the torsion bar suspension, I had nothing to do with the Jowett Jupiter. Von Eberhorst's steel tube frame was an idealistic layout for a limited production sporting car but was not easy to manufacture.)

With the successful launch of the Javelin, the very favourable press reception it received, and the fact that my name was so closely connected with it as the designer, I found myself the recipient of a certain amount of acclaim in the industry. I was getting known! Therefore, it should not have surprised me when it was whispered in my ear by a mutually friendly trade representative that my former company in Oxford might be interested in re-employing me in a design capacity for some of their future projects. My immediate reaction was one of surprise and elation. I had fulfilled my contract with Jowett and had produced for them a worthy successor to their pre-war range of cars, which with vigorous development and competently produced, should have a sales life of several years before major changes were necessary.

As I could see no future design project in view at Jowett, and as I was a designer not a development engineer, I felt justified in pursuing the approach from Oxford and fixed up a meeting with the Nuffield Deputy Chairman. The concept team had already been dispensed with by the Lazard people with Peter Reilly dismissed and the helpful Steven Poole pushed into retirement.

Unfortunately, after I had left, the development and production of the Javelin did not continue as I had hoped. The gearbox was a salutary example. There were no serious problems with the boxes built by Meadows. Then, to save money, Jowett decided to make their own, which jumped out of gear. There was insufficient pressure to keep the sliding dogs engaged when in top gear, which I think was a consequence of the worn state of Jowett's tooling. At Vauxhall there had been a similar problem with gear shapes cutting very slightly tapered dog teeth. These tapered teeth caused an axial load thus forcing the gears out of engagement.

Gerald Palmer
Obituary
(*The Independent*, 16 July 1999)

Jowett's slogan 'Take a good look when it passes you' was aimed at those pottering along in pre-war Austins and Hillmans.

Fifty years ago, a previously parochial car company from Bradford was impressing buyers with a stylish, roomy and fine-handling new saloon. It was not so much a Brunelesque engineering feat as a carefully planned consumer product – rather like the Renault Megane Scenic today. The Jowett Javelin was a sensation, and Gerald Palmer designed it. The Jowett company, however, went bankrupt in 1954. 'Of course I was sad when Jowett failed,' Palmer recalled. 'The Javelin was my brainchild and it still had useful life left in it.'

When he was twelve and growing up in Bulawayo, Palmer created his first car, a rakish plywood-bodied machine based on an old Ford Model T given to him by his father – Rhodesia's chief railway engineer. Palmer senior wanted him on the railways but the young Gerald opted instead for an engineering apprenticeship with the truck-maker Scammell back in England, where he worked for five years.

He then met Anthony Fisher, the founder of the Institution of International affairs. Fisher agreed to put up £1,000 to back a speculative venture to manufacture the perfect small sports car, and Palmer formed the Deroy Car Company to make it. The Deroy prototype that emerged was a stylish two-seater roadster, powered by a small, four-cylinder Scammell engine. 'I named it after a Portuguese villa,' said Palmer. Alas, for all its handsome looks no further backing materialised. But the Deroy brought Palmer to the attention of MG boss Cecil Kimber, and he was offered a job running the company's drawing office.

One day in 1942 though a small advert in *The Automobile Engineer* transfixed him. It said 'Wanted chief designer for a motor manufacturer'. The car company turned out to be Jowett, and Palmer was just the man they needed.

The visionary Jowett managing director Charles Calcott-Reilly had ensured that the company gained plenty of war-time contracts; yet he also realised that Jowett would need to afterwards offer a tough, modern saloon car oozing export appeal – not the primitive two-cylinder contraptions it had thitherto built. Recruiting Palmer was his masterstroke. For Palmer, too, it was a dream; a blank piece of paper and a mission. Few designers since have had the freedom to plan the entire car, body, engine, interior, everything. The only parts he didn't design were the gearbox and back axle.

Although they agreed, recalled Palmer, on a 'six-passenger family utility', the result was Britain's most sophisticated family car. For one thing it featured unitary body/chassis construction. Then there was supple torsion bar suspension all round, independent at the front, precise rack and pinion steering, and a passenger compartment in which even those in the back seat sat within the wheelbase, giving excellent ride comfort. Palmer redesigned the traditional Jowett flat-twin engine, adding two extra cylinders and enlarging it to 1,486cc. *(NB. Jowett did have a pre-war flat-four engine from 1935, but Gerald's engine was a completely new design. – NS)* The wind-cheating teardrop-shaped body was as up-to-the-minute as anything from the technically more adventurous Italy or Germany.

Light, aerodynamic and high-geared, the Javelin could cruise at 80mph, with excellent acceleration, and the critics loved it. Palmer himself helped take the car to a class win in the 1949 Monte Carlo Rally. Jowett's slogan 'Take a good look when it passes you' was aimed at those pottering along in pre-war Austins and Hillmans.

Palmer appreciated that 'showroom appeal' was just as important as good road holding, performance and space utilisation. He said, 'I had quite a good feel for "eye-able" shapes yet, really, the Javelin's was dictated by the position of the passengers, luggage and engine.'

The public got a sneak preview of the Javelin at the motor industry's Golden Jubilee parade in London on Saturday 27 July 1946. It poured with rain, explaining why few noticed the prototype Javelin on the sidelines. Jowett's other slogan, 'One day – it has to be yours', began to ring with a pitiful irony because only a handful of cars had reached British customers by 1949.

By then, his task done, Palmer had been lured back to MG, to mastermind the new MG, Riley and Wolseley designs. He became a director of Morris Motors and the guiding light behind such classic models as the MG Magnette ZA, the Riley Pathfinder, the MG TF and, in part, the MGA. However in the Nuffield Group (Morris/MG/Riley/Wolseley) with Austin to form the British Motor Corporation, Palmer found his work bedevilled by company in-fighting. His talent and energy were largely ignored by warring BMC bosses.

At Jowett, meanwhile, things were going disastrously wrong; it was a typical British case of being brilliant at designing things and awful at making them. Owners loved their cars when new but many were dismayed when, for instance, engine crankshafts broke. A protracted boardroom hiatus and Javelin parts supply problems all helped to force the liquidation of the firm in 1954. In six years just 23,307 Javelins were built. *(It was, in fact, only 22,700. – NS)*

By 1955 Palmer had left BMC for Vauxhall, becoming assistant chief engineer of passenger cars; he stayed until 1972. 'It was interesting to see how American companies compared to British ones, and General Motors was a highly professional organisation,' he said.

Palmer could not resist the chance to buy (as several tea-chests of parts) the Mercedes-Benz GP car that won the 1924 Targa Florio. A defining moment of his life was driving this fearsome car to Italy and opening the 1974 Targa Florio by doing a complete lap of the circuit in it. 'It goes like a bomb,' he said.

His autobiography, *Auto-Architect*, written by Christopher Balfour, was published last year.

Gerald Marley Palmer, car designer: born London, 30 January 1911; married 1939 Diana Varley (deceased; one daughter); died Oxford, 23 June 1999.

TOMMY WISE

I have not been able to find any direct quotes from Tommy Wise, but I could not publish a book on Jowett racing personalities without a reference to him, as he was one of the greatest characters connected with Jowett. I am pleased to say, however, I found this interesting potted-history about him, which was published in 1957. There are a few other short notes I am also including. – NS

'Pen portraits of Northern Sporting Personalities'
written by Francis Penn
(From *Autosport*, 22 November 1957)

My first recollection of Tommy Wise was in 1947, when as a very 'new boy' to photo-journalism I covered a big northern trial run by the Yorkshire Sports Car Club. Inquiring where I could obtain a good action picture, I was introduced to Tommy Wise, the organiser, and was gently led to the most fiendish trials section I have ever seen – a 90 degree grass bank on to which cars could only stay put by sheer speed. The inventor chuckled down my ear, 'This should fix Harrison and Co.!' It did! Since then I have photographed many of the 'Wise enterprises' which can always be relied upon to make the 'picture of the day'. Seriously though, I am proud to present one of the great names of the North. Tommy has been and is a racing and rally driver, trials artist and organiser par excellence. Commencing his sporting career back in 1933 'mudplugging' with a V8 Special purchased from Sydney Allard for the then large amount of £120, this car, known as the Spider, ran in all the big trials of that era and was probably the forerunner of the Allard.

From 1933–39 Tommy specialised in these 'big heaps', but had a top price limit of £17 10s; with these he won at one time or another all the 'Majors'. One of his feats was driving the first car to climb 'Red Roads' – the 1 in 1 horror at the Camberley tank testing ground. After the war, during which he was on 'hush hush stuff', he restarted in 1947 by organising the first Yorkshire 4/44 Trial. In 1949 entered his own Javelin in the Monte Carlo Rally, and accompanied by Cuth Harrison and Gerald Palmer (the Javelin's designer, who has never been the same since), won the Coupe de la Riviera for 1½ litre cars, this being the first occasion in which British names had featured in the prize list since 1935. The same year he did the Lisbon Rally with Mike Wilson, and south of Paris 'lost a pot' on the Javelin, finishing on three to take a class

Tommy Wise at the wheel of the 1950 Le Mans Jupiter, registered GKW111. Tommy was to purchase this car from Jowett's and entered it regularly as a privateer on a regular basis in the early 1950s. (Len Thorpe)

Tommy Wise in action at the 1950 Le Mans. (Louis Klemantaski/JCC)

second! In 1950 Tommy Wise bought the ex-works Jupiter, prepared the car with some works assistance and entered for Le Mans. ★ As the co-driver was Tommy Wisdom, the car was called *Sagacious Two*. The result of this effort was a 1½ litre class win at 75.8mph beating both course and lap records which had been held by Astons for the last three years, and against such competition as Simca, Porsche, MG, Osca etc.

In the winter of that year Tommy organised the first 'Yorkshire Rally' which, after covering the event, was christened by the writer the 'Yorkshire Mille Miglia' by which name it is better known and about which at least three verses have been written:

If you are looking for excitement and you really want some fun –
Do the 'Yorkshire'!
Though your motor may be 'jiggered' and your shock absorbers done –
Do the 'Yorkshire'!
It's a night-and-day adventure with a chance of snow and ice,
It's a rally you can enter with your own family device,
It's a glorious adventure for a death-defying dice,
Do the 'Yorkshire' my boy do the 'Yorkshire'!
– By H.C. Mason (the others I shall quote nearer the day it next happens!)

Again in 1951 Tommy drove at Le Mans, this time in a works 'bolide' which blew up! In the RAC Tourist Trophy he drove his own Jupiter and was second to Hadley in the works car which won by thirty seconds. In the Alpine he was, together with Mike Wilson, thrown into jail after making best times on the Stelvio and Falsarego. In 1952, a Coupe des Alpes was lost through the failure of a gearbox washer; after this Tommy retired until last year when he fell for a modern trials special and by adopting big car technique (self described as brute force and b....y ignorance) won the Yorkshire 4/44, his own trial. Personally watching the event I remarked at the time that 'the old hand has lost none of its skill'.

Tommy Wise, born at the turn of the century, is married to Pat, has a boy and a girl, all of whom share his sporting ideas. In business he is boss of the Scarborough Main Ford Dealers, his hobby is gardening and his favourite transport is a much modified Zodiac. Tommy likes Le Mans best as a circuit. His club has been the Yorkshire Sports Car Club, whom he has served 'long and well' and his suggestion for the improvement of our sport is 'Better sportsmanship by the younger generation'.

Tommy Wise's ambition is twofold, to win a Coupe des Alpes and to see the cover of *Autosport* always green. The incident questions brought first a complaint that 'Mike Wilson stole my thunder' but gave as his second funniest 'After Le Mans in 1950 the sight of my black and oil-drenched face with two eyes staring out, when I looked in the mirror at the finish – coming out of White House Corner the oil cooler of the Jupiter when just on 100mph, completely blinding me, so that I only just managed to stay on the road.' Most disappointing – the 1952 Alpine when the gearbox washer packed up leaving only two gears.

★ *This was incorrect, the 1950 Le Mans Jupiter GKY111 was entered by the factory, but they did sell the car to Tommy at a later date. He did two Alpine Rallies in the Jupiter as a private entrant, with Mike Wilson as his co-driver. – NS*

A short letter written by Tommy's son, Tim, was published in Classic & Sportscar *magazine in August 2007, which gives a bit more insight into his father, which I reproduce below:*

Le Mans or bust

It is perhaps only a matter of time before somebody writes in saying they have seen a Jowett Jupiter running around the north of Tenerife (*Lost and Found*, March).

Well, the car is mine and now wears Spanish historical plates. I brought it here in 2001. If you cast your mind back to 1950 (all right then, look it up), you will remember that the Jupiter won the 1500cc class at Le Mans, the first of three consecutive wins. The *pilotes* of that car were Tommy Wise, my father, and Tommy Wisdom and the car was called *Sagacious Two*, which was written on the bonnet.

In 2000, the Jowett Jupiter Owners' Auto Club (and *grand fromage* Edmund Nankivell) organised a trip to Le Mans to celebrate fifty years since the win. I bought my car sight-unseen through *mon ami* Howard Bryan, who has done the Rally of the Tests in his ex-works Jupiter, and we managed to get it through the MoT just in time for the trip, despite it having lain in a garage in Blackpool for twenty-eight years. We got from York to Le Mans and back with no reverse gear.

Father bought the Le Mans car, GKW111, and continued racing and rallying it with the rotund and redoubtable Mike Wilson of BARC Yorkshire fame. He also used it as his road car – how often do you see pukka racers doing the school run today?

I remember being collected from school in one of the '51 Rallye Monte-Carlo team cars, GKY106. On the way back the lights failed and we went off the road, through a hedge into a field. Not being able to find the original hole in the dark, father had to punch another hole in the hedge to regain the road!

How about an article on the competition life of Jupiters in the '50s? I am sure Ed Nankivell would help. Great magazine, keep it up!

Tim Wise
Puerto de la Cruz, Tenerife.

Sadly, Tim died in Tenerife in 2008; after typing up his letter I was going to contact him to ask if he had any other reminiscences about his father, but sadly I was too late. – NS

1949 Monte Carlo Rally
Harry Schofield

Motor sport had been dormant for a long time when, in November 1948, Robbie *(Robbie F. Ellison, the Jowett agent for St Annes on Sea – NS)* rang up to say that Ronnie Smith had got an entry for the first post-war Monte Carlo Rally in January 1949. Ronnie had no suitable car, but Robbie had one of the first Jowett Javelins and he agreed to let Ronnie enter it provided that I accompanied them as co-driver. We had no time to do any serious modifications to this brand new design and we had practically no petrol, although we managed to get it run in and get almost 1,000 miles on the clock before we set off for Monte Carlo. For the rally the Government had given us a supplementary ration – presumably to show the flag! There was a colossal entry for this first post-war rally, with all types of vehicles competing. We were in the Jowett team of three Javelins, Tommy Wise piloting one together with Cuth Harrison and the car's designer, Gerald Palmer. The second car was piloted by Tony Hume with Horace Grimley, the Jowett development engineer, with John Eason-Gibson, the journalist as navigator. I think it would do a lot of good if every designer was made to compete in a rally to experience the idiosyncrasies of their brainchild, the way Gerald Palmer did.

The run through northern France and the Low Countries was exceptionally cold, in fact the efforts of our puny heater failed to stop ice forming on the inside of the windows. Nevertheless we were garbed in teddy bear suits and flying boots so we managed to keep warm. Our progress towards Monte Carlo was somewhat of a triumphal procession, everywhere we found that the rally was greeted with terrific enthusiasm and the British cars in particular were feted. In Amsterdam, Brussels and Paris we had the benefit of a police escort mounted on motorcycles. The experience of hurtling through these capital cities whilst all traffic was halted and the thunderous applause from the crowds, out to make the most of the spectacle after the long drab years of the war, was most exhilarating and now unrepeatable. In Liege and Rheims the controls were manned by the local motor clubs who also provided pilot cars to guide us out of the cities. I had my work cut out to keep the 1939 BMW, which was my guide, in sight, as the cobbled streets of Liege were covered in ice. Motoring down the deserted Grands Routes of France through the third night of the rally was particularly hard on the eyes. The trees lined these roads continuously produced a flickering cinematographic effect that necessitated a change of driver every hour. However the trying night ride was more than compensated for as we climbed up into a glorious dawn on the Savoy Alps. On the decent to Monte Carlo Ronnie lost the car on an icy corner, but we were able to do a quick beat out of the slightly damaged wing and still finish with no loss of marks.

We left the Jowett in the *parc ferme* and went to our hotel which has since been converted into Radio Monte Carlo; there we tumbled into bed to recover some of the three night's sleep that we had lost. Next morning we recovered the car, which started immediately, and then we drove over the inspection ramp where the seals were checked, after which we adjourned to the competitors' cocktail party in the Jardins Botaniques.

The eliminating tests consisted of three circuits of a secret route which had to be covered at the highest possible speed, but also at exactly the same average on each circuit. Here we made

Line-up of the team of Javelins taking part in the 1949 Monte Carlo Rally, the first running of the event in the post-war era. From left to right are Gerald Palmer – the designer of the Javelin, Gordon Wilkins – motoring correspondent and Tommy Wise. Tommy Wise, Cuth Harrison and Gerald Palmer all drove in the Javelin registered MNW444.

a mistake in not aiming for a high enough speed, but nevertheless we finished in third place behind Maurice Gatsonides' Minx. However, as Tommy Wise took first place and Hume and Grimley finished just behind us, we had secured the *voiturette* team prize. It was infuriating; however, to realise that had we been a bit more adventurous we could easily have been placed above the Hillman.

The final dinner at the Sporting Club was a most magnificent affair and proof that a banquet for 300 people can also be a gourmet's meal perfectly served. Our return journey up the N6 was horribly cold as the *mistral* was blowing hard.

In effect the rally had been subsidised by the French Government, for they had issued to each competitor a colossal number of petrol coupons. These surplus coupons were openly purchased at Monte Carlo and their value could be appreciated by the fact that our fortnight on the Continent, due to this hidden subsidy, cost us no more than £25 each. Nor did we economise; for example we had lunch at the Roy Rene in Aix-en-Provence where Winston Churchill normally stayed. The first night en route home was spent in the Hotel d'Europe at Valance and on the following day we had intended to reach Paris. The ultimate goal of a good car designer is that the vehicle will disintegrate immediately after crossing the finishing line. Gerald Palmer did not quite achieve this, for our big end bearings lasted to Villeneuve sur Yonne. However, we located a small garage where the local mechanic, after his enthralled inspection of a new British car, fitted a spare set of shells whilst we waited. Meanwhile the garage proprietor plied us with cognac and regaled us with stories of the part he had played in the local resistance group. His stories became more and more lurid as the contents of the cognac bottle diminished, and we were relieved when the car was completed. By that time we had reached the point of him brandishing his revolver to emphasize his heroic deeds. In his enthusiasm he had just loaded it and we did not trust his aim, so we made our excuses as rapidly as possible and reached the Hotel du Poste at Sens where we had a magnificent meal.

Next day we halted for a short time in Paris, whose streets were almost deserted in the freezing cold, and then crossed on the night boat to England. Our journey home was comparatively uneventful, though some of Ronnie Smith's driving through London was nerve shattering. He rarely dropped below 50mph as he zigzagged between the tramcars that infested the area. A week later there was a celebration dinner at the Great Northern Hotel in Bradford where Jowetts gave us presentation tankards. Of course our slight success went to our heads and we decided we must enter the 'Monte' in the following year. Meanwhile Robbie had entered the car, registered JTJ300, for the Alpine Rally, but as this event took place in July, I felt my commitment at this time of year must be to the family. Perhaps this was as well for the Jowett retired on the second day; the fan had gone through the radiator.

Neither Robbie nor I felt that we could submit our lives to the hectic driving of Ronnie again, so Walter Mason made up the crew for the 1950 event.

1950 Monte Carlo Rally
Harry Schofield

In this year's event the crew was made up with Robbie, Walter Mason and myself. Once again we started from Glasgow and continued without incident until we reached Nevers on the second night of the rally. As we left Nevers snow began to fall heavily, and to make matters more difficult it started to freeze at the same time. We ploughed on passing many cars in trouble. Soon we appeared to be approaching an illuminated Christmas tree; in actual fact this was a short but steep assent, which was littered with vehicles that had spun to a halt. Robbie brought his old mud-plugging experience to bear and stormed the hill, bouncing madly to maintain adhesion. But halfway up some clot who was attempting to fit chains had left open the rear door of his Austin Princess. The Javelin shut it very firmly indeed. After which Robbie made a very clever detour through an adjoining field and we escaped the blockage. Only three cars from the Glasgow contingent got through this melee, the other two being the Allards of Cyril Potter, who later crashed, and Sidney Allard himself. Incidentally, had Sidney not have run out of petrol in Nice, he would have won the rally outright. As for ourselves, Robbie continued to drive until Lyons, meanwhile as the snowstorm was dense as a London fog, we navigated by hanging out of the nearside window. At the Lyons control we were still on time – just and here we became silly druggers. We were carrying some Dexedrine tablets issued by Jowett's medical adviser, which were supposed to keep us awake. I made the mistake of taking a couple of these, which certainly kept me awake, but which inspired a *joie de vivre* that was artificial. In Lyons I had taken over the controls and as the snow had ceased to fall I was hurtling down the Rhone Valley in a series of controlled slides, approaching Train l'Hermitage. I lost the Javelin on a right-hand bend and we collided with a tree. We hit this poplar with some considerable force, following which everything went dead and silent. For a moment I thought we had reached the next world; in fact the accumulation of snow from the branches of this large tree had descended on us, completely covering the car. Robbie had sustained a cut forehead, so we trudged back to the village, roused the local doctor who stitched him up. Then Garage Moderne turned out in force, recovered the car and after breakfast at Papa Chabert's Hotel we mournfully inspected the damage. The front offside suspension was completely demolished and our rally was obviously over. However I did glean some slight consolation when the official Bentley *(it was a Rolls-Royce – NS)* driven by Mike Couper came to grief on the same corner later that morning. Mike rang Rolls-Royce who flew out a new wing and two fitters to patch the car up so that it would be in time to compete in the Concours de Comfort for which it had a special entry. The road section had to be completed for this award but without any time penalty – the Rolls-Royce, though two days late, carried off the cup!

Our damage was much more serious so Robbie rang up Idle and they arranged to fly out a new suspension assembly the next day. Walter Mason got a lift down to Monte Carlo in the repaired Rolls-Royce, and having seen them off, we caught the *rapide* to Lyons. We soon learnt that *rapide* in France means anything but a fast train; in fact it took us all morning to get to Lyons, where at the airport we ran into difficulty. We were obstructed by a little Gestapo-like customs officer who refused to release the parts without the payment of an astronomical amount in duty, which we did not possess. Eventually with the help of the Automobile Club de France, we obtained our spares by signing endless papers and promising to produce the damaged parts after the repair was completed. By this time there was no train back to Valence, but we discovered an ancient Citroen bus whose passengers were chiefly farmers returning from the market with purchases ranging from livestock to furniture. The driver, a full twenty stones of Gallic joviality, announced to his passengers: '*Viola Les deux Anglais avec la Bomb Atomique!*' The bus relapsed into roars of laughter and though they had no English and we little French, we had a hilarious and amicable journey back to Tain.

Papa Chabert, realising that we were on a currency allowance, offered to keep us for £1 per day each until we had repaired the car, such was the popular esteem for the British immediately after the war. I would add that this hotel proudly sported a Michelin star, and though we had no choice, there was no hardship in the fare that Chabert served. During the day we worked at the Garage Moderne helping to rebuild the Javelin, and each evening after dinner we donned flying jackets and walked across the bridge over the Rhone to drink Verveine Du Velay as an antidote for the sub-zero temperature. On the Saturday we were taken by Jean Barrou, a local coachbuilder, in his new drop head Simca coupe up into the hills where we met a gallant little old lady who had sheltered many escaping servicemen during the war, passing them down the line to Spain. Then, about ten days after the accident we drove the battered Javelin home.

During the next two years we entered the Javelin, which had been somewhat modified, in various local events. On one Lancashire Automobile Club 'Rough Ride' we holed the sump but as the damage was immediately below the oil pump, we found that by maintaining about 3,000 revs the pump overcame the pull of gravity, thus we were able to finish. On the Lake land Rally the starter solenoid packed up and even though Robbie had to lie beneath the car to operate the starter for the eliminating tests, we still achieved a first-class award. The classic aim is to finish – there is no future in giving up. In the next Monte Carlo Robbie drove a Jupiter and he won the voiturette class. Louis Chiron, having tried the Jupiter, said that had he been driving it he would have expected to win the rally outright! The following year Robbie, disliking the open body of the Jupiter, had a special coupe built by Farr's of Blackburn. Once again there was a heavy snow fall and the Jupiter plunged off the road into a ravine, putting paid to his efforts.

In January 1949 I managed to get a Javelin for myself, this was an ex-staff car. At the time anybody who obtained a new car had no difficulty in selling it for a profit of between £400 and £500, and in consequence there was a covenant scheme introduced to prevent this black market. Hughes and Bolton were fined £100 for purchasing a three-month-old Humber, even though they had bought it through the trade. There was an enquiry regarding my Javelin, but as the makers had slipped it out 'through the back door', nothing happened.

The Jowett was a most enjoyable motor car; it was far ahead of its time in its suspension and bodywork, though I was plagued with teething troubles to which the flat-four engine was subject. Nevertheless until I disposed of it in 1955, it gave me as much pleasure as any car I have ever owned. Thank heaven the perfect car has not been made yet; when it is we shall turn away from it in sheer boredom!

Harry Schofield

In this article Harry Schofield refers to Mike Couper, who drove Bentleys in the Montes of 1949, '51, '52 and '53, and, as he quite rightly says, he drove a Rolls-Royce in 1950. If you read on I refer to Mike Couper and his book Rallying to Monte Carlo *in the section relating to Raymond Baxter. In this he states that a temporary wing was fabricated locally, but it was a new suspension unit that was flown in and fitted in Nice. I know this does not affect Harry's story, but I mention it as a point of accuracy. – NS*

1949 Monte Carlo Rally
Maurice Gatsonides
(Taken from the book *Rallies and Races: Gatsonides' Adventures* by William Leonard and Maurice Gatsonides, originally published 1951)

Maurice Gatsonides was a famous Dutch rally driver who had a very long rallying career, and was also a very prolific freelance journalist on motoring topics. He is probably best known to the modern motorist as the designer of the dreaded 'Gatso' speed cameras! He wrote about all his races in great detail in the above-mentioned book, but sadly his two Jowett drives are not detailed, as this book was written just prior to them. I have reprinted the account of his 1949 Monte Carlo entry, which I feel is of particular interest – he was in fact driving a Hillman on this occasion, but was heavily involved in our story! I am also reprinting several other articles he wrote for Autosport *magazine etc. as they include fascinating period advice for the would-be rally driver. – NS*

It was not until 1949 that the Monte Carlo Rally reawakened from the deep sleep it had been in throughout the war. It had taken an additional four long years before the political situation had become conducive to the staging of such an event once again. Four years before foreign exchange, and other restrictions relaxed sufficiently so that Mr Anthony Noghes felt confident that it could at last take place. During those four years many enthusiasts at home and abroad had been restless indeed, spending as much time recalling the good old wild and carefree days, when car spares were ten a penny and the costs of damage to the cars incurred in numerous incidents on the glorious rallies from Athens and Umeå were hardly counted. Damage of all kinds was most liberally handed-out by the Holy St Christopher in those pre-war Monte's, which at that time were indeed Grandes Epreuves de Tourisme, and of which that fascinating name of the most important of all rallies – although it was not actually quite the hardest – was truly deserved on the bumpy desert roads of Greece, or the barren ice-fields of the North. In 1949 all of that was no more. The Iron Curtain was in place, effectively cutting off for the time being our former motorsport friends in Czechoslovakia, Poland, Yugoslavia and the more distant countries which had now come under communist rule. Only Prague could still be used as a starting point, apart from which the rally was restricted entirely to Western Europe. The shortening now of the pre-war 3,600km distance also excluded Umeå, and so, beforehand, it could be seen that the rally was likely to be little more than a rather tough pleasure trip or perhaps just a classifying test after a 3,000km run. This could be seen in the quality of the entry list, which appeared to be rather too civilised in parts, with all kinds of people who would not have known what to do in the ordinary map-reading trial, now thirsting for some post-war adventure. That didn't stop us from having great pleasure making careful preparations for our trip to the sunny south. When I say 'us' I mean my faithful rally mate Klaas Barendrecht and myself, who were keen to know how far we would get with our new Hillman Minx. I had of course tuned it up somewhat, and although only of 1185cc it had become quite spirited, albeit a rather thirsty little Minx, for that little acceleration and top speeds was duly represented on the fuel bill.

Although this time we were denied the extra points and the adventures of a Balkans' start, it was with considerable pleasure that we left in convoy for Monte Carlo and the start. It was indeed quite a procession as in addition to the Minx and our luggage car, a Chevrolet, we had joined up with a 1.5-litre Riley, crewed by Gijs Polle, Henk Luyting, Han Van Splunter and Captain Adriaan Van Splunter. They did not mind at all competing together in one car, but the Riley was less than happy about the situation, its undersides almost touching the ground under the weight of the four men and plenty of luggage. I had advised them not to go four-up, but they did not want one of them left behind. On arrival at Monte Carlo however they realised it could not be done, and so drew lots for someone to stay behind. The unlucky Henk Luyting sportingly accepted the decision, and despite not being able to speak French, did enjoy his enforced stay in this casino town. The Riley crew gained a lot of experience on the journey from Holland to Monte Carlo, as we let them find the way by studying their maps in front of us. This is a recommendable procedure.

Once there we found that atmosphere peculiar to rallies. All the pre-war aces were present again, and that was reason enough to organise many festivities, although even all those pleasures were not able to take our attention away from the great event about to take place. And when, on that glorious night, it became our turn to start, we immediately had the unique feeling once again of actually being in the rally. It is a strange feeling brought on by the knowledge that human beings and machines are about to be severely tested along the 3,000km route lying ahead. For the next few days 1001 things were waiting to spoil the broth, and you can be absolutely sure that some will come right to you. But against that that you know you can count on your team-mate throughout the forthcoming tiring days and sleepless nights. And above all there is that adventurous tingling inside you, and the adventure is beckoning both novice and veteran alike. Then there is the hope that you will make good, so that at the end on that dirt-streaked muddy bonnet which you have seen in front of you for seemingly endless hours, there will be hung a laurel trophy, a trophy that will never be won by the fait-hearted.

It was exactly twenty-three minutes past midnight when with a pleasant exhaust rumble our Minx shot away into the dark night. It was unseasonably mild weather, and so I was only lightly dressed, which is always stupid in a rally, and this time resulted in me catching cold which nearly caused our failure. Climbing from Grasse into the Maritime Alpes we quickly realised that the roads were already slippery with ice, so we had to be careful now not to end the rally, and indeed ourselves prematurely, as a drop into a ravine can quickly shut a lot of doors behind one, sometimes even that of the family grave.

It was not without a dark foreboding that, when topping a slope, we saw a fierce burning. 'That's one burning,' we said simultaneously, and down went the accelerator of the Hillman as we raced forward to offer first aid. We went faster and faster, but the red glow always seemed to be one mountain further ahead. It was a relief to our helpful souls to find out in the end that the expected burning wreck was the Northern Lights playing a trick on us. Later though, a little further along we could exercise our desire to always give help, when alongside the road we saw the stricken Delahaye of Yvonne Simon and Germaine Renault. The engine of the Delahaye was not receiving any petrol, and of course we searched diligently for the trouble in the hope of getting the girls going again. In the end we fitted a complete new fuel pump. Germaine and Yvonne, who had their eyes on the Coupe des Dames, were frightened out of their wits that some other competitor might see them receiving male assistance and give the game away. Each time another car approached they went into a chorus of French yelling and played 'hide and seek'. However, without petrol they would definitely not win the cup, although it later proved they would not anyway, for it went to Holland's Duchess Van Limburg Stirum. It was noticeable to us, by the way, that there was very little urge in other male drivers to assist these damsels in distress. The whole affair cost us eighteen minutes, and we had to dice like mad to arrive at Digne on time. There had been no time left to refuel our car, so after checking in at the control, we went back to a pump situated just before there. After refuelling we turned round and drove past the control again, causing some shouting from those who had not realised what we had done, and who thought that only those stupid Dutch could miss a well-marked control point!

At Grenoble we had plenty of time again. From there we carried on via Annecy (oh, sweet memories of the sunny Alpine Rally) to the frontier, but before crossing it we stopped for ten minutes at the monastery La Grande Chartreuse, which was another sweet memory itself. It was regrettable, and certainly not advisable, to combine the liquid produced there by the monks with the driving required for the rally average. At Geneva we met the Florence starters, who had not had things particularly easy. At some forsaken Italian spot several trucks had collided and completely blocked the snowy road. British crack drivers including Tommy Wisdom, Donald Healey and Geoff Imhof had been stuck there and lost so much time that they were forced to drop out. Meanwhile we were beginning to find that it really was winter. To save weight we had no heater in the car, and were now learning something of what it must be like on an Antarctic expedition.

We continued to Strasbourg via Bern, where a couple of over-zealous French officials nearly spoilt everything for us. At the control we went as usual to the restaurant where the control was situated, and where hungry and thirsty souls are being revived. As on this section we had gained some time we parked the Hillman Minx between the 'parc ferme' and the control post, which was not in accordance with the ideas of the officials who said that as we had not arrived we should hand over our route card. However as we had gained more time than the maximum average allowed I kept tight hold of the card, and pointed out that I had not crossed any line or been in the closed park, and therefore had not officially arrived as yet. The Frenchmen got quite cross, threatening us with all sorts of recriminations, including disqualification. But we stuck to our guns, and so the situation developed into one of those lively discussions, which make life in France so attractive, and we eventually won the argument. On the second night of the rally we went from Strasbourg to Luxembourg over roads which only in France seem so long. At Thionville we were cheered up when we saw in our headlights a big Swiss-registered Kaiser standing horse like, with its four wheels across a dry ditch. How it got there was not clear, neither was how it would get out of the situation, which is always the troublesome part. We couldn't solve it, for our Hillman simply wasn't suitable for such tractor jobs. It was certainly a peculiar sight for one could walk underneath it, which of course we did.

At Luxembourg we learned that the starters from Britain were late. But we started on time for our trip now though the Ardennes, which with their winding and undulating roads keep the sleep out of your eyes. Our lights swept over the ruined houses of Bastogne and La Houffialize, where the Americans held out against the furious onslaught of the Nazi regime. At that moment we remembered the time not so very long before, when the noise of exhausts of the big GMC American trucks, full of tired but brave GI's echoed against the walls of these Ardennes villages. Even as a rally driver, one suddenly felt very small indeed.

Black ice was encountered on the road just before Liege, but the slippery conditions did not kill our joy. We usually hurried whenever approaching Liege because at the Motor Union de Liege Klaas and I always enjoyed looking at the photographs taken there during the pre-war Liege – Rome – Liege rallies, from which we have such sweet memories. Our friend Maurice Garot and his staff almost overloaded us with sandwiches and drinks. It was all very cosy, but the time soon came for us to be hurrying onwards to Holland, through Vise and Venlo we made our way to Amsterdam. We were followed by several competing French cars, and also the Tatra of our pre-war friend Formaneck. We were able to assist the Czech crews and officials with their language difficulties etc., and built up much goodwill between us. (This goodwill was to prove beneficial the following year, resulting in me driving a Czechoslovakian-entered Aero Minor in the Le Mans 24-hour race.) It was daylight when we arrived in Amsterdam, and I saw my son Tommy, who was with his rally step parents (my wife Ciska was waiting for me in Monte Carlo), had risen early to encourage his dad. At the control point at the Apollo Hall the Van Splunter brothers told me they were pulling out due to clutch failure on the Riley. I advised them to immediately get in touch with the Riley importer, who managed things for them so quickly that the Riley arrived at the Brussels control dead on time. Over the very slippery Dutch roads – two French ladies managed to land their car in a ditch near Utrecht – we went on to The Hague, were the Klaas' family was waiting for us with a car full of food. Also there was our friend Theo Van Ellinkhuizen who seemed to have brought the whole countries egg production, and so much salt that we had enough to keep our screen ice-free for the remainder of the rally. No less than eight men from the Hillman importer in The Hague were there to lubricate and wash our Minx, before we rushed off to the Belgian frontier. There, at Wernhout, the customs officers with whom by this time I was quite familiar, promised us a brass band if we should return with a prize. At Brussels we had a few minutes to visit the Gatso stand at the Motor Show, and shake hands with Jan Apetz and his three assistants manning the stand.

We reached Reims with still more time in hand, and were able to enjoy a warm welcome by the Automobile Club de Champagne, which did honour to its name. Over long straight roads, but with many climbs and descents, we went to Paris, where many competitors had difficulty in finding the control in the centre of town, and arrived too late.

From Paris Klaas took the wheel for the first time on the long stretch to Monte Carlo, and in the bitter cold we faced South for a stage which not for the first time held a few unpleasant surprises. These started at Nevers, where the always badly organised control was besieged by a crowd of rally drivers whose nerves were badly frayed due to tiredness, cold and discomfort. It was a proper push and elbowing party in the narrow passage as everyone was attempting to get his road book stamped in time. It became even more unpleasant when I began to feel sick with fever, shivering like a dog. I felt colder than an ice-cream; sitting shivering under a rug I damned the rally and its organisers. Back on the road my stomach continually showed signs of a desire to turn itself inside out. My feelings of wanting to vomit grew worse when Klaas became hungry for eggs. If I remember correctly he had eaten thirteen of them, and I had to hide them from him. Wow, under those circumstances does a hard boiled egg smell! All the time I was praying to heaven that he wouldn't get an appetite for smoked eel sandwiches. I prayed in vain. But when he asked for a smoked eel sandwich I simply felt too rotten to grab a monkey wrench. However, those eggs and eels seemed to have given Klaas wings, as he skilfully drove the Hillman right across the Massif Central to Lyon. Just before Lyon came another 'treat' in the form of thick fog which quickly froze to the windscreen. Although I know the town very well we passed the control on the Saone quay three times before eventually finding it in that pea soup. We didn't even see the river, and continued round and round having no idea where we were. Even Klaas' resilience came to an end, and with the courage of the condemned, I took the wheel for the last lap. A miracle (aided by a Pervitine pill) happened. Bitter necessity stopped my stomach from further acrobatics, and feeling lots better I began the difficult task, and difficult it was!

Immediately outside Lyon the windscreen wipers froze to the thick layer of ice on the screen. We took the right-side wiper off to give the other a little more power, and using our salt managed to keep two small spots free of ice. It was a hell of a job driving to schedule, and was sometimes only possible in that freezing fog by keeping the wiper going with our heads out of the side windows. This way we passed many competitors who then tried to hang onto our tail, and so we came to the Rhone Valley, which lay below us under a thick layer of cloud. Above this, at the top of the hills the sun was shining, but we had to get down through the clouds to the valley below, a decent which for us was like blind-flying in a car. It was something which I was not keen about having to do ever again, although many times in the future we were faced with a similar decent. It was not until the control at Valence that our sufferings were at last behind us, and it was only a fleabite to Monte Carlo. Across the Col de Cabre we flew to the Dinge time control, and then over the Col des Legues via Grasse to Monte Carlo. Before the finish our wives were waiting for us with the Chevrolet luggage-car on the Moyenne Corniche. We put all that we could spare now into the Chevrolet, in order to arrive at the closed park with the Minx as lightly loaded as possible in readiness for the classifying test. Sunny Monte Carlo smiled at us, but as I was suffering from some form of reaction following my temporary revival, I went to bed with a shipload of quinine in my stomach in the hope of being somewhat fitter for the test.

I had already had a brainwave about this test even before the start in Monte Carlo. The particulars issued about the secret circuit stated that it was 17.1km long, and that it had to be driven three times, and that enough petrol for 75km had to be in the tank. The first time round the circuit was for reconnaissance and not timed. The circuit was split into three sections respectively 3.5, 3.5 and 10.1km, and on the second and third times round the 3.5km sections were timed in 10ths of a second, and had to be covered as quickly as possible, but also in equal times. The larger section had a larger margin, which did not influence the penalties. In bed I had been thinking where that route might be. After studying a detailed map I reached the conclusion that it had to be Mont des Mules. As the Minx was of course locked away in the closed park, we went to the Mont des Mules in the Chevrolet and practised diligently in every curve. My intuition hadn't deceived me as the time controls were almost within a yard of where I thought they might be. I decided – again to save weight – to drive the test unaccompanied, ours being the only crew out of the best 100 finishers from the road section to do this on the test. However, it was a decision which I'm afraid did rather upset Klaas, but saving weight was vital if I wanted to have any chance against the much faster Lancias, Jowett Javelins and some other potential winners in the same 1.5 litre class. I took with me my precious piece of wood with the three chronometers attached, which I would have to handle myself during the test. Well during the practice lap I did the most difficult of the two special 3.5km sections in four minutes and ten seconds, and so I decided to set myself at four minutes and eight seconds in the actual test.

There isn't really much to tell about it – I succeeded beyond expectation. With my hands and eyes being distributed equally over the steering wheel and the clocks I started, and away went the little side valve Hillman; I can only remember that I drove as never before. The faster I diced through the curves of the Mont des Mules, the more the French public enjoyed it. The first and easiest of the two 3.5km sections I did in three minutes twelve seconds, and so stopped before the line. I waited until the chronometer showed four minutes and three seconds and then drove off again across the line. This was repeated in the following 3.5km section, and then again the next time around. When it was all over I had made 4 minutes 7 seconds, 4.8, 4.7 and 4.8. I was well satisfied with that, as to judge by what the others were saying it was plain they were not consistent. It was late in the evening before the last test had been completed by all the qualifiers, and not until late the next day before the results – some of which would unfortunately later prove to be incorrect – were announced. You can be sure that I am not usually a tearful type, but when the news came through that the team Gatsonides and Barendrecht in a Hillman Minx had won first prize in the 1.5 litre class I went out alone to swallow a lump in my throat. This you will see was one dream fulfilled. Probably not so very important, but at the same time absolutely marvellous, as I was so proud to have done this in a class in which our car was somewhat prematurely considered to have no chance at all. We were presented with a genuine-silver cup by the Prince of Monaco, together with a decent sum of money. With our French friends the Angelvins, who had won first prize in the 750cc class, for celebration purposes we exchanged the money for champagne in the Sporting Club.

The next day however not only our heads whirled (champagne), but that also of the rally organisers (protests). It had just simply rained protests! Soon it became apparent that the organisation of this first post-war rally was considerably flawed. With every new protest lodged, competitor's names went up and down the results list in great leaps. The calculations were almost completely wrong, and practically every protest was accepted. Some who claimed they had been classified too low went up ten places on the list.

Next morning, after we had loaded our luggage and enjoyed a last coffee before departing, we received a phone call from Anthony Noghes informing us that the Jowett Javelin driver, Tommy Wise, had protested against the decision in the 1.5 litre class. We were told that we would have to hand the cup back, and I think it was darned lucky that the money was already spent. Noghes had been forced to agree with the important leading official Charles Faroux who had decided in Wise's favour. When we told him that it was not right to ask for the return of a prize already given out, after consulting a no longer valid copy of the Code Sportif (dated 1937, instead of the revised edition of 1939) Faroux still maintained that the trophy had to go to Wise.

The use by Faroux of the wrong edition of the Sporting Code was only found out later by the Dutch sports marshall Jan Van Haaren, who, unfortunately for us, had already left Monte Carlo for Holland on the day after the results had been announced, and so was not able to act on our behalf when the protest, which according to the regulations was too late, eventually came. (In the regulations for every international event the procedure is clearly noted, giving competitors usually a period of six to twenty-four hours within which to enter a protest following the publication of the provisional results, after which the results cannot be changed.)

Some weeks later at home in Bentveld we heard from our Automobile Club that they had received a letter from Anthony Noghes in which he openly stated that his decision had been wrong, saying 'But now it is really too late'. But we did not wish now to appeal at the French Automobile Club, because although Wise had lodged his protest outside the time limit, it transpired that he had indeed made the best test.

I do enjoy reading about the same event from more than one person's viewpoint, as clearly people remember things so differently. Reading Gerald Palmer's account, it gives no hint of their protest being lodged too late to be valid, and they may have been blissfully unaware of the turmoil behind the scenes. It was clear, however, that Tommy Wise was the rightful winner by posting the best result in the speed trial. It would have been a real shame had his appeal not been upheld due to his lateness in lodging his protest. Maurice Gatsonides was a true sportsman of course, and was the first to say that Tommy Wise had posted the best time. – NS

Maurice Gatsonides drove in his second Le Mans race in 1952 with a works-entered R1 Jupiter. Originally Gatso chose a Fiat 1400, but later secured a drive with Singer. However, they withdrew at the last moment. He was offered a drive in the third R1 Jupiter with his fellow Dutchman Count Hugo van Zuylen van Nijevelt. In this picture Gatso is seen negotiating the Esses in front of the Hadley/Wise R1, both being caught by the big Cunningham C4. (*Autosport*/JCC)

Gatso in the pits during the 1952 Le Mans, where he had been experiencing problems with the clutch. Gatso had to retire after seven hours and twenty-three minutes with a broken crankshaft. Five days after the race Gatso wrote a detailed letter to Jowetts with some recommendations regarding the clutch. He did, however, like the Jupiter, saying, 'In spite of my bad misfortune, this Le Mans race will remind me of a very pleasant car with excellent road holding and cornering capabilities, which enabled me several times to pass bigger and much faster cars in the bends.' (*Autosport*/JCC)

Gatso cornering wide during the 1952 Le Mans with a Porsche in front and the Bert Hadley and Tommy Wise R1. (*Autosport*/JCC)

Another view of Gatso R1 followed by the Hadley/Wise R1 in the 1952 Le Mans. (LAT/JCC)

1953 Monte Carlo Rally
Maurice Gatsonides
(Taken from *Autosport* magazine dated 5 December 1952, giving
advice to would-be entrants for the 1953 event. – NS)

Are you going on the 'Monte'? Some practical suggestions on the experiences of a famous rally-driver, for competitors in the great winter classic

In this article I would like to discuss all the futilities appertaining to a rally, futilities which one is apt to overlook, but which may grow out of all proportion during the event.

My first advice is to start your preparations as soon as possible, both on the car and the rest. I am firmly convinced that the only way to obtain a good place in the final results is to start work on a Monte Carlo Rally car during the first few days in November. Not more than a month later, work on the other formalities should begin.

Firstly, the choice of a team, it goes without saying that this team should be composed of motor-sporting enthusiasts who can drive fairly well, and who can get on well together. Team members should put up with each other, especially when sleep and fatigue are beginning to tell, and they should always be cheerful. Morale in the car must never be in doubt, even when everything goes wrong. Quarrelling in this small, confined space is intolerable, and many times after doing a rally together, even the best of friends have been known not to speak to each other for years. In direct connection with this fact, it is a wise precaution to put all agreements clearly, in writing if possible, particularly anything to do with finance!

Talking about finance prompts me to say some more on this subject. It is clear that every team makes its own arrangements, but for those interested it may be useful to know something about the arrangements made, as a rule, in Holland, but which are also in use in France. Usually the car is the property of the entrant. He completes his team with one or two co-drivers. We always pay equal shares of all rally expenses, including those for the preparation of the car. There are items such as insurance, entry fees, fuel, meals and hotel expenses for the trip to the starting place, rally and the trip home again. Sometimes the owner also stipulates that an amount for the depreciation of the car is included, and this is perfectly reasonable. The car will not suffer more than on a long distance foreign trip and the normal depreciation per mile need not be exceeded.

It may be superfluous to remark that each team member should see to it that his health is in perfect order. All organs that should be tested from time to time, such as eyes, teeth, a rupture and other weak spots which everyone knows for himself, must be looked at, and if possible, put right, even by an operation.

I strongly recommend paying for all meals during the rally, as well as for fuel, out of the common purse. However, to avoid trouble later on, costs of hotel, meals, and drinks and so on, after the finish in Monte Carlo, should be paid separately. I won't try to give more detailed costs, as they may vary widely with personal desires and tastes, but the following is a rough estimate: total costs of a Monte Carlo Rally, the preparing of the car, hotel and cost of living for three men, both in the starting place and at Monte Carlo, could be done for about £250. (I know some teams will not be able eke out a dreary existence at double the sum!) An important item is hotel costs in Monte Carlo, where at least a week is spent. Although running the risk of displeasing the owners of sumptuous hotels out there, I would advise you who have to make do with a small sum, owing to foreign currency restrictions, to frequent the smaller ones. There are no escalators, maybe, no gold-braided menials to revolve the revolving doors for you, but when living in one of the small hotels, many French Francs will be saved. The tales about vermin in those small hotels are completely untrue and the beds are always clean and comfortable. When all is said and done, sleeping quarters are a necessity, but for most of the day one is out and about to look at Monte and its lovely surroundings in weather which is always far to be preferred to a British or Dutch January.

What I said about sleeping arrangements also goes for meals, too, only more so. There are small restaurants where, 'mine host' disappears into the kitchen when you enter, while a boy is sent running to the butcher and the grocer as soon as you have ordered. Invariably the food is more often than not prepared with far more care and devotion than is the case in many big establishments, and costs less than half the price – and for a few shillings you get plenty of the *vin du pays*.

Talking about food and drink reminds me of the important fact that team members should lead separate lives – at least for several weeks before the start. This is self-evident, but it often happens, and I am no exception, that one works on the car for nights on end, or that a sudden disaster has to be met with hard work. As regular sleep is so important, see to it that each night you stay some extra hours between the sheets, and this advice for pre-rally days is equally valid for the rally itself. 'What the blazers does Gatso mean? You will probably say. But I firmly maintain that during the rally you should eat and sleep as much as possible, whenever you get the chance - for instance, when a precious hour is saved at a control. A substantial hot meal is then indicated, while the team-member who is not scheduled to be behind the wheel for the next few hours, may partake in a good glass of wine, so that he may sleep soundly as soon as the car moves off.

When not driving, try to sleep! It may be absorbingly interesting to see what happens outside, to note which fellow competitor has finished up in the ditch, or simply to admire the surrounding landscape, but all those interesting scenes are for the man at the wheel only, and the others should sleep. It is, therefore, to equip one of the front seats with a back that can be let down. This means that a wide front-bench should be replaced by two separate seats. I know that many experienced rallyists violently disagree with me and that in many three-man teams one man only is allowed to sleep, while the driver relies on the navigator to find the way. The roads on the continent are not as difficult to find as all that. When the driver memorises the names of some places and preferably some road numbers for a stretch to the next control, it is almost impossible to get lost. During the Monte the roads are always lined with policemen, especially at junctions and cross-roads, to indicate the right way – at all hours of the day and night.

To be able to profit from the above advice it is necessary to trust one's co-drivers at the wheel explicitly. Keep this in mind when composing your team. It is also necessary that each team-member has his (or her) special task. One of them controls the money and has to look after refuelling. Another looks after the oil, water and tyre pressures, whilst the third, usually the skipper, is responsible for timekeeping, the road book, the map-reading for the next run, and when his turn has come to give the wheel to a team-mate, he also transfers this work to him. The decision what to take along is up to the skipper, too, of course.

Before the start one should practise assiduously the changing of the wheels, the fitting of the snow chains, the handling of the unditching-gear, and all other things that may have to be done en route. The first practise may take place on the clean floor of a nicely heated garage, but it should be repeated many times under the most difficult of circumstances, and if necessary a trip should be made to snow-clad mountainous country, where these activities should be carried out at night on a steep slope. Even driving a car into a ditch or putting her into a snowdrift may help to put the crew wise about the use of shovels, wire-mesh matting, etc. I can hear you swearing at me when you have overdone things and the car is immovable in the pitch dark! I can really enjoy this, but nevertheless, a spot of real trouble is the best preparation.

Clothes are important, too. In 1937 I saw two Frenchmen start from Umea in a splendid Delage. A famous Parisian 'maison de couture' was responsible for their dress and headgear, which were in perfect harmony with the interior decoration of the car, while a comfortable bed with spotless linen was also installed. It looked just fine and may have been practical, but in my experience your oldest suit, in which you always feel comfortable, is the ideal wear. On top of that a one-piece waterproof-flying suit, to be had at any army surplus store, should be worn, together with fur-lined flying boots, good warm gloves and a ski-ing cap, or ordinary cloth cap. If necessary you can crawl under the car in this outfit, without worrying about the dirt or water. At the wheel I always wear soft slippers, which can be abandoned for the flying boots in a matter of a few seconds.

Talking about dirt and water reminds me about washing and shaving. At the controls the lavatories are often bursting with competitors who want a wash and brush-up. It is, of course, very refreshing to have a wash, but from experience I know that a dirty skin can better cope with the big differences in temperature of working in the snow below zero and sleeping in a heated car, than a clean one. My team members only wipe their hands and face with a clean cloth during the run, or, at most, cleanse them with Vaseline, but our 'wall-paper' is never cracked or worn-out at the finish, but we could be cleaner!

Changing drivers is another item of interest. There are many methods. Some teams stop punctually every two or three hours to let a co-driver take the wheel. I do not like this system. The best principle is to let one man do a complete stretch between two controls, while the co-drivers sleep. At the control all members of the team have to put their signature in the road-book, and everybody has to be awake then, the wheel may be given to the next man. Stopping en route to change drivers should be guarded against, and then only when circumstances necessitate this, for example, when the driver gets sleepy. He should immediately wake up a co-driver and not try to carry on. It is far better to take a nap and wake up fresh for the next spell at the wheel. Also, when one is late, the roads are iced or the weather is really bad, the wheel should be given at once to the driver who is best accustomed to these road and weather conditions. If one man is assigned to this task, and then he should be excused from long spells in the first days of the rally, so he is fit for the special kinds of trouble, which one can be sure to meet in the last eighteen hours of the Monte. If no special man is assigned to the job of driving under difficult circumstances, then it should be done by the owner of the car or the skipper of the team, to avoid reproaches in the case of a crash. But it also means that he should be spared in the beginning, and that he will have to leave the wheel to his co-drivers. Psychologically speaking, this is the best way to make the co-drivers feel at ease, they drive all the better for it. And never should there be any criticism of each other's driving methods.

Although I am well aware that in this article I have only touched lightly upon a few of the hundreds of problems, and although I know that many will disagree with my points of view, I sincerely hope that aspiring rally-drivers will be able to profit from these few lines.

Certain advice I have kept to the end of this article: however many commercial or other motives are involved, the proper spirit of the team should be kept, and it should always be remembered that our mutual hobby is a 'sport' and nothing else. Many a rally has been lost by bickering amongst the members of the crew, leading to distrust and consequently errors of judgement and in navigation. A happy crew is more often than not a successful one!

(I must confess that it would have slipped my mind to go to the dentist and also have my hernia operation done unless I had read this first. On this occasion Maurice was driving a Ford in the rally. This was his best year in the event, as he won it outright, so clearly, he knew what he was talking about! – NS)

Monte Carlo Rally 1953
Maurice Gatsonides
(This is another interesting article Maurice wrote for *Autosport* published in
the issue for 16 January 1953, with lots of good tips for any would-be
competitor's preparations for the Monte Carlo Rally)

Roulette De Monaco ... It's a gamble ... The fortunes of the 440-odd competitors in the Monte Carlo Rally depend on the weather

Just before Christmas, through a partly flooded France in abnormally mild weather, we drove down to the City of Roulette and Baccarat, the City, which has forever given its name to the most famous of all Rallies. It looked as if the North Pole had moved, for here on the beautiful Cote d'Azur of the Mediterranean, we huddled shuddering about the stove, if one was lucky enough to possess such a thing. People here are more prepared for the heat than the cold.

On the other hand, this abnormally low temperature had an advantage for Rally-drivers-to-be, of whom many spent their Christmas holidays there. Their object was to do some reconnoitring on the 74.5km Col de Braus Circuit. Last year almost the complete stretch was snowbound. This had not happened in thirty-five years according to the natives, who proved friendly, but who still cannot be taken seriously. This wonder of last year has not, so far, repeated itself to the same extent now, but the Col de Braus, the Col de Castillion and the small road in between has quite a layer of snow. This part covers the third, fourth and partly the fifth stretch of the circuit, this fifth being the most difficult of the six stretches into which the circuit is divided. In addition to a great number of Renaults we also saw quite a few British and Italian cars attacking the mountains a trifle quicker than they would normally do so, to slither down the slopes on the other side. Chances are, however, that the test will be done with hundreds of spectators, basking and picnicking in the sun, on spots where now more than 3ft of snow keeps them away.

The very fickle winter weather strongly puts its stamp on this historic Rally. That was what I thought, when, on my way from Clermont Ferrand through Le Puy and Valence to Grasse; I closely studied the different alternative routes. As I said before, the weather was abnormally mild then and only on some of the roads of the Massif Central, situated over 3,000ft high, were some patches of snow to be found. I talked to lorry drivers, bus drivers, to garage people, police officials and municipal authorities and to many others, but I really learned nothing new. Only the number of roads which one can take when the shortest routes are snowbound, which added to, because I was shown routes which necessitate such enormous detours that I had never thought of trying them.

Last year only twenty or so competitors managed to reach Le Puy and Valence on time. I have made a basic map of this part of the route, from which you will see there is a wide choice. The factor 'Luck', which cannot be overlooked in any competition, plays a very important role in the Monte Carlo Rally, especially the choice of route in this part of the country. The official Rally route is, 'St Flour to time control Le Puy over the N-590; from there, along the N-88 to Yssingeaux were the N-103 is taken to St Agreve, then the N-533 to Valence'. The 'Service des Ponts et Chaussees' (the service responsible for the upkeep of roads in France) has the task of clearing this road as soon as possible in the event of snow falling. With a heavy snowfall this is a tall order as the road climbs to over 3,000ft and is tortuous in places. In how far it should be recommended in these circumstances to take the low road ('an' I'll be in Monte afore ye!') which has fewer bends but is longer, I cannot possibly tell, nor can I give any advice, too many unknown factors being involved. The only remark I can make is that the secondary roads designated with a 'D' or 'CG' followed by a number, are not cleared of snow soon, and are, therefore, not to be recommended in case of snowfall.

Starters from Monte Carlo are unexpectedly up against an additional difficulty. As a result of a landslide the Col de la Croix Haute is closed. The organisers had to substitute the N-85 for the N-75 in the official route. This N-85, known as the Route Napoleon, is 8km longer (5 miles), for which ten extra minutes are allotted, but the road is very undulating and tortuous between Gap and Grenoble.

Another landslide, above Monaco, has made the Moyenne Corniche impassable for a short stretch. It is, therefore, not possible to take the 'upper 100' who are admitted to the decisive Col de Braus test back to the starting point, without sending them right through the Principality. A solution was arrived at by leading the last few miles of the circuit along the Monte Carlo Beach and by having the finish on the Sea-Boulevard. This also simplifies the returning of the cars to the parc ferme, which is only slightly further along the same Boulevard.

Spot them by their numbers – British starters from Glasgow *(NB. I have only listed the Jowetts from the list. – NS)*:

128 F.E. Baker & F. Marchant (Jowett Javelin)
134 A.R. Foster & G. Holdsworth (Jowett Javelin)
143 F.D. Dundas (Jowett Javelin)
178 Leslie Brooke & Bill Pitcher (Jowett Javelin)
194 C.A. Leavens & Mrs J. Leavens (Jowett Javelin)
222 Frank Grounds & Jack Hay (Jowett Jupiter Saloon)

Overseas drivers include:
Marcel Becquart of France in a Jowett Jupiter saloon
K. Erichsen of Germany in a Jowett Javelin

Be Prepared – For bad winter conditions
Maurice Gatsonides
(This interesting article from *The Motor*, 30 December 1953, would have assisted both the ordinary motorist and rally driver alike. – NS)

Suspecting that real winter cannot be long delayed, we asked Maurice Gatsonides, the noted Dutch competition driver, who won the 1953 Monte Carlo Rally in a Ford Zephyr, to give his views on the best way to tackle motoring under winter conditions.

It goes without saying that the first advice is 'Be prepared'. See to it you are not caught unawares by the sudden onset of winter conditions. Of course, this 'Be prepared' is meant for the car in the first place, but also for the driver himself.

To start with the car it is quite often possible to prevent or correct successfully a skid, which is one of the commonest causes of an accident. To diminish the chances of a skid, the car should be in perfect alignment, the springs should be equally strong on both sides of the front and rear axles, and the shock absorbers be perfectly adjusted and, of course, perfect adjustment is even more important for the brakes.

Not only should the steering be without play, but it should also be light and easy. Heavy steering may be as dangerous as are worn king-pin bushes or other worn vital parts. In both cases there is no 'feel' in the steering wheel. It should be possible to steer with two fingers. If the road is suddenly covered with black ice and the adhesion between tyre and mother earth is practically non-existent, it is important to feel exactly how much adhesion is left, and also to feel exactly when the adhesion diminishes or disappears. If you don't, you might feel something else which might be quite painful!

Our modern brakes, although working on the hydraulic principal, may still pull the car to one side. This can be checked, like other faults, by doing brake tests on a perfectly flat and horizontal road. Tyres should be equally worn and at the correct inflation pressure, and the car itself should be evenly loaded.

The most important thing with which to increase adhesion to the road surface is the tyre. There are many makes with anti-skid treads; some of them are quite good. Generally speaking, a tyre with a soft rubber tread is less liable to skidding than a tyre with a hard tread. But the soft tread wears away sooner. Everyone should choose for him or herself whether to spend a bit more on tyres, thus increasing safety, or to take some more risk, thus chancing far greater expenses sooner or later.

Generally speaking, longer lasting tyres with hard-wearing treads are more liable to skid. The greater the rolling resistance is, the greater the friction and therefore wear. There is a simple aid to increase this friction; an aid that can be used on partly worn treads also, viz., the Adersol grooves, used already before the war by Tecalemit. Small, parallel grooves of $^1/_8$in depth are cut across the tread, close to each other with a fast-revving buzz-saw. This procedure is cheap if the special Adersol apparatus is used. However, the life of the tread is shortened considerably. Not only is rubber removed but, when driving, heat is generated through friction between the strips of rubber and through friction between the tyre and the road. But the latter gives the better adhesion, which we value so strongly in winter. If I am right, this procedure was called in England 'pneu-gripping'. Tyres may be pneu-gripped three or four times until the saw touches the canvas. In this way a tyre with dangerously bald tread may still be quite useful.

For driving on soft snow, such a tyre with thin tread is of no great use. Under these conditions knobbly tyres are best. A good precaution to be taken in winter is the fitting of soft rubber tyres with thick pneu-gripped treads, but not the special scramble or trials tyres, which are generally too hard and can only be used in heavy snow or mud. Moreover, they are very uncomfortable for normal touring.

The life span of the canvas of our modern tyres far exceeds that of the tread, and tyres can be retreaded several times if the canvas has not been damaged. Before starting work on a tyre a good retreading factory first checks the canvas. Usually soft rubber is used, and the soft rubber diminishes the chances of skidding.

One of these factories arms the treads with a great number of wire 'claws,' which are said to give extra road holding. Of course this tread cannot be pneu-gripped, as the saw will cut through the steel.

As a general instruction I would say; always keep your tyres at the right pressure, but only deflate by 20-25 per cent (according to the weight of the car) when running on iced roads. Therefore, a good tyre pressure gauge with a clear scale should always be in the car.

Experts will disagree on the use of chains. Personally, I consider them a necessary evil and I only use them when all other devices to proceed on snow have failed. I hate them on ice because they very easily start a skid. They also interfere with the balancing of the wheels, which is very important on modern cars.

I would like to enlarge on the subject of 'Skidding.' It is very useful to learn to skid a car, by intentionally forcing it into a skid. It really is important to be used to skidding, so that you can keep a cool head when the skid happens unexpectedly. Road and traffic permitting, there is nothing wrong with skidding your car intentionally. At first it should be done when going slowly, but soon the speed may be increased. Try to regain control of your car when skidding. The best way to practice this comes only in very cold winters, when a frozen lake on which the ice is thick enough to support the weight of the car can be used. When doing this, you will soon realize that the car is no longer controllable, but goes straight on when the brakes are applied. The front wheels are locked, and the car does not steer anymore. When the brakes are released, however, the car can be steered again, unless the skid has developed into a 'tete a queue' or a complete pirouette.

If you want to practice skidding methodically, you should fit bald tyres to your car. Once you have conquered that funny feeling in your stomach you will like skidding, and this, in turn, gives you the necessary self-confidence. Now you know how to react when your car skids unexpectedly. There are thousands of drivers who would not dare to use their precious cars for anything as dangerous as a skid, and a voluntary skid at that, but I am convinced that it is in their own interest to give it a try. That my advice is right is the fact that, especially in your country, many official bodies and institutions, such as the police and public transport companies, send their drivers on a special course on skidding on a track especially built for that purpose.

The motto 'be prepared' is far more important when driving on slippery or iced roads than in the case of normal driving. You should reckon with every possible move of visible – and even invisible – traffic, many hundreds of yards in front of your car. The faster you drive, the further you should look ahead. In this way you can prevent the need of a sudden pull on the steering wheel or for stamping on the brake pedal. All these sudden movements and quick reactions result in a skid. In my estimate, you should look at least twice as far ahead when driving on iced roads as under normal conditions.

To mention another important point; the electrical gear. It goes without saying that this should function without a hitch, and it should be entirely dependable in winter. Not only should the battery be in perfect condition, but it should also be remembered that the dynamo only has a limited output, so you cannot go on using too many electrical gadgets indiscriminately. There are many accessories such as radio, defroster, fog lamps, kerb lights, heater and ventilator, cigarette lighter etc, and they all draw their energy from the dynamo via the battery. Both components are of limited capacities, limited because of weight and size. The driver should realize that the current available should be used wisely. How often do you see a car with blazing headlights, a couple of fog lights and a flame-thrower into the bargain? Of course it is just downright silly.

In fog, headlamps and a flame-thrower hinder the man behind the wheel because of the glare, and the best way to proceed under these conditions is with one or two good foglights. Not every light bought as a foglight, can rightly be qualified as such. A good fog light should give a broad, flat beam with a sharply defined line were light and dark meet. The best way to test this is to throw the beam onto a light-coloured wall; there should be a sharp edge to the flat-top beam.

The best fog lamp is no use when the front glass is dirty. Mud and even tiny drops of water, which act as tiny lenses and disperse the light, may strongly impair the efficiency of the beam. It is recommended to fit foglights close to the ground, as fog is less dense close to the ground. Oncoming traffic, too, will be less hindered by the light.

Although the problem of white and yellow lights is just as individual problem as the wearing (and not wearing) of special night spectacles, my personal opinion is that yellow light is far more agreeable when driving in fog or driving in snow for hours on end. Yellow light is less dazzling, anyway, for oncoming traffic. And here I would like to point out that dipped lights under Continental traffic regulations are less dazzling for other road users than dipped lights in the UK, where the filament is placed slightly out of focus. On the Continent, the filament is screened at the underside by a U-shaped cap, and although Continental dipped lights do not throw a long beam, oncoming cars suffer practically no dazzle at all.

Now even when your car and yourself are prepared in the best possible way, you should never forget this saying, which is of double importance under winter conditions: 'Don't drive faster than you can steer.'

Maurice Gatsonides
Obituary
(From *The Independent*, 22 December 1998)

It is taken for granted now that leading rally drivers are full-time professionals who make a handsome living from the sport. This was not the case between the wars and in the years just after the Second World War, when most rally drivers were keen amateurs who drove for the fun of it and were happy if a manufacturer provided a car for them and covered their expenses. Maurice Gatsonides deserves the credit for breaking the mould as he was probably the first full-time professional.

He was born in 1911 in Gombong, Java – in what was then the Dutch East Indies – where his diplomat father was posted. His parents then returned to Holland where he was educated. He joined KLM and qualified as a commercial pilot but left in 1935 to open a motor business near Haarlem.

An enthusiasm for motor sport led him to start rally driving. His first major event was the 1936 Monte Carlo Rally in which he drove a Hillman Minx saloon, so beginning a long association with British cars. His first important success was in the 1939 Liege-Rome-Liege rally driving a Riley Kestrel; he finished fourth. This event was run in late August and there were fears that the war would start before the competitors had completed the course. During the Second World War, Gatsonides built up a profitable business making charcoal gas generators which kept cars and commercial vehicles running in occupied Holland where there was no petrol. This was a useful cover for his work in the Dutch resistance, helping escaped prisoners of war. When the war ended he resumed his motor trading activities and also tried to become a car manufacturer at his garage at Heemsteede. He built a car using a Ford V-8 engine and other Ford parts which was called the Gatso or Gatford. This had startling aerodynamics with a cluster of lights on the front and covered occupants with a perspex canopy. The Gatso did not prosper, as it was undercapitalised and Ford components were hard to get. Gatsonides now had agencies for Studebaker and the British Hillman and Humber. He took a Studebaker on his first major post-war rally, the 1947 Alpine Trial, and when the Monte Carlo Rally was revived in 1949, he won an award with a Hillman. The following year he was second overall with a Humber Super Snipe, a most unlikely rally car. While the Monte had the glamour and the publicity, to the real rallyist success in the Alpine was the true criterion of a leading driver. The Alpine ran for a week in high summer over the toughest Alpine passes; the aim was to win an Alpine Cup for finishing without losing any marks. In 1951, Gatsonides was offered a works Jaguar XK 120 for the Alpine and Bill Mackenzie, the motoring correspondent of the *Daily Telegraph*, went with him as navigator and co-driver. The Jaguar broke down on the last day with a water leak when a cup was in sight; afterwards Mackenzie said he would never go with Gatsonides again, it was too frightening. In the 1952 Alpine he again used an XK 120 and this time secured a cup. His great win though, which secured him a permanent place in rallying history, was the 1953 Monte when he drove a Ford Zephyr; afterwards he admitted that he had taken the easier route over the Massif Central, but despite this had lost time and his winning margin was only three seconds. The Monte always had a strong element of chance and in 1954 Gatsonides was paired with another former winner Marcel Becquart in a works DB 2/4 Aston Martin. They had a huge lead but lost it when Becquart missed a secret control and they fell to seventh place. Gatsonides also tried his hand at motor racing, but he was a steady long-distance driver rather than a wheel-to-wheel racer, so in his four appearances in the Le Mans 24-hour race he treated it more as a fast rally than a race; he was placed twelfth with an Austin Healey in 1953 and eleventh with a Frazer Nash in 1954. He also drove a Triumph TR2 in the 1954 Mille Miglia, the legendary Italian open road race. He was nominated as a co-driver of a Maserati in the 1952 Dutch Grand Prix but the car fell out so he never had the chance to match his abilities against the grand-prix drivers of the day. In 1954 Gatsonides switched his rallying allegiance to Triumph and stayed with the British firm for the next four years, gaining Alpine Cups in 1954 and 1956 and many minor places. During this time, he also had successful outings with Porsche and DKW. By the end of the 1950s a new and younger generation of rally drivers had emerged, so he gracefully moved away from the front-line events but still kept active driving Citroen ID19s in the Mobil Economy Runs, rallies which required rapidity with a light throttle foot. He won the Mobil event in 1958, and scored a hat-trick between 1964 and 1966. Gatsonides retired as an active competition driver in the mid-1960s but showed his talent in a new and very profitable field. He had considerable skill as an electrical and electronic engineer and developed two devices which have had a great impact on British motorists. First he invented the familiar timing device for catching speeding drivers, using two parallel rubber tubes set a short distance apart which operate pressure switches as vehicles cross them. His second device was the Gatso flash camera which is now a familiar feature on road junctions throughout Britain, apprehending drivers who jump traffic lights. Maurice Gatsonides was a man of great charm who had many friends in Britain; his son is now managing director of the Gatso electronic companies.

Maurice Gastonides test-driving the prototype R4 Jupiter in the wilds of West Yorkshire in 1953. Only three of these cars were made before Jowetts ceased trading, two of which still survive. Here Maurice is outside a local hostelry having a pint of best before setting off again … happy days! (JCC)

Maurice Gatsonides, rally driver: born Gombong, Java 14 February 1911; married 1941 (one son, and one daughter deceased); died 29 November 1998.

1949 Spa 24-Hour Race
By Anthony Hume
(As reported in *The Motor*, 31 August 1949)

And Thus it Came to Pass... The story of the entry and successful running of the Jowett Javelin in this year's Spa 24-hour event

'The Jowett Javelin stand in the Brussels show obviously did not attract much attention, in spite of a sectioned car displayed. This lack of interest does not seem justified for a car offering at the same time a good performance, a spacious body with excellent luggage room, and a good design all round. Its new price is not extravagant either, being between the Fiat 1500 and the Lancia Aprillia. The main fault seems to be that the Javelin is too little known, and successfully running a team of three cars in a Touring Class at the forthcoming Spa 24-hour race would probably make all the difference in the world to the sales of the car over here.'

The above paragraph having given me furiously to think, I approached my good friends at Idle with a view to having to persuade them to enter a team of Javelins at Spa. After many discussions on the subject, it was decided that, while it was not possible in the time available 'properly' to prepare a team of three cars, a production car would be loaned to enter for the race in conjunction with Tommy Wisdom.

The car was prepared at the works strictly in accordance with the bulletin issued to owners desirous of entering their cars in competitions, and involved stripping the engine, very careful refitting, smoothing the heads and gear parts, raising the compression slightly, fitting large Zenith carburettors, fitting new gears with higher intermediate ratios (in our case, giving maximum speeds of: 1st 24mph, 2nd 40mph, 3rd 64mph and top 86mph, with Dunlop Racing 5.150 by 16 tyres), and stiffer shock absorbers.

We removed the radio and heater to save weight, thereby incurring the wrath of Tommy, who said he had been looking forward to a really comfortable race at last, with his feet up in front of the fire, the radio playing and a nice box of cigars at his elbow.

We eventually left England with the race car, another Javelin as tender and a trailer full of spares and equipment.

Our team consisted of Charles Grandfield, the Chief Engineer, as Chef d' Equipe, Horace Grimley, head of the Experimental Department and my partner in the Monte Carlo Rally, Arthur Illingworth, foreman of the Experimental Department, Tommy and myself. I would like to stress particularly that, apart from Tommy and myself, no one had any experience whatsoever of running a car in a race. I mention this because I wish to say here and now that no drivers have ever had better control or pit handling than we had during the race from the Jowett boys. Dunlop Mac had offered to be in our pit during the first pit stop in order to be in a position to offer his invaluable advice in case of necessity, but, in his own words, he stayed on in order to pick up a few tips himself.

Charles had asked me to let him have details of any equipment peculiar to racing, and I mentioned large funnels and racing jacks, while saying these jacks would be impossible to use on the Javelin owing to the body hang. Nothing daunted, the boys produced the most ingenious compromise I have ever seen; in effect, half a normal racing jack with a protruding shaft at 90 degrees, which fitted in the socket of the Stevenson jacking system, pressure on the handle then lifted one side of the car complete in one go. When I say that to change two front wheels (five stud fixing), take on 15 gallons of fuel, top-up oil and water, clean the screen, and change drivers, took four minutes dead during the race, it will give an idea of the efficiency of the equipment and pit work.

Our plan of campaign had been to run at a comfortable speed for the first twelve hours, review the position taken, and if there appeared to be a chance of a place, decide then whether to speed up or continue at our normal speed. However, a few practice laps showed that the car appeared perfectly happy lapping at around 70mph, so a snap decision was taken to run under close pit control, getting signals every lap, and driving accordingly.

Our maximum speed, 86mph, was limited to that figure by valve bounce setting in at 87mph, and we reached our maximum very shortly after the beginning of the straight, hence any speeding up had to be done by braking later and cornering faster. As it turned out the car ran so well that we were never pushed, and still don't know what our maximum lap speed may have been. The cornering capabilities of the car may be judged by the closeness of our best lap speeds (approximately 74mph) to our maximum, and then the fastest bends there was little to choose between the Javelin and the race leaders. Another advantage we had was the excellent vision in fog given by the short bonnet. We used the fog patches for passing faster cars, and were very annoyed when it lifted.

The start of the race was productive of one of the funniest episodes I have ever seen. The cars were parked diagonally, fairly close together and just before the flag dropped, Tommy, who was taking the first spell, discovered that the car on his right, Marcel Masuy with a BMW 327, 80 coupe had left-hand drive, and that with both doors opening together it was impossible for either driver to enter the car. After a moment of shocked horror Tommy suggested that, as Masuy's car was undoubtedly so much faster, he should enter first and pull away. His Gallic courtesy to the fore, Masuy insisted that, as his extra speed would doubtless enable him quickly to overtake the Javelin; nothing would satisfy him but that Monsieur Visdom should have every advantage. This, I fear is what the wily Tommy was angling for, as he thereupon hurled himself into the car, disappeared like a rocket, and was never seen again during the course of the race by the gallant Masuy.

Another interesting incident, in which Tommy was involved, was when he passed the pits with his arm out of the window, briskly slapping the door panel. This caused furious discussion among the pit staff as to the meaning of this cryptic signal, and for his next pit stop every preparation was made for a major overhaul. When he arrived, frantic questioning ensued to elicit the answer that it was merely a gesture of affection for 'this nice little motor car.'

The race as a whole was (for us) completely lacking in any incident or excitement, apart from my clumsiness in getting my hand trapped in the glove box handle and breaking a finger in its extraction. The car running like clockwork, not one repair or adjustment being made in the course of the race. Our finishing laps being made at our fastest speeds, as we had been speeded up to pull well ahead of the leaders in the 4 litre Touring Class.

At the finish the interest and admiration shown in the car by all the Belgian crowd, many of whom had never heard of the marque before, testified to the good judgement shown by the writer of the paragraph at the head of this article, and I would say any manufacturer with confidence in the performance of his vehicle will obtain far more benefit from the running of a car or cars in an event such as this, than he will by expending ten times the amount of expense involved in other forms of publicity.

For myself, I offer my grateful thanks to 'The Motor' for the idea, to Jowett Cars for their foresight and whole-hearted assistance, and to Tommy and the wonderful little car for my most enjoyable twenty-four hours.

1949 Monte Carlo Rally
By Tom Wisdom
(Taken from the *Daily Herald*, 31 January 1949 ... Monte Carlo, Sunday)

Row in 8 tongues at rally

Arguments in eight different languages have been going all day as 300 motorists rained protests on the organisers of the Monte Carlo Rally.

Two different lists of results already have been issued. Another – and that is only provisional – is to be published tonight.

But since protests are still being drafted, amid violent altercations there is still a fourth list to come. The trouble is that the time-keepers are new to the game, and with a record number of competitors, there have been many errors in working out the results of the worlds most difficult motor trial.

The chaos tonight can be judged from the fact that one competitor has protested at being placed too high! Geoffrey Imhof, a London radio manufacturer, first protested that he had been placed too low at fifteenth. The organisers agreed and made him third. 'Too high' protested Imhof. 'I was seventh.' Anthony Noghes, president of the organising committee, tore his hair and muttered, 'Mad Englishman'.

One thing is certain Jean Trevoux, a Frenchman, who has already won this event twice, is the outright winner of the event driving a Hotchkiss. When the other results are finally agreed upon, the British cars will have done exceptionally well.

The light car class was won by a Hillman Minx*, and the smallest car in the event – the new Morris Minor – finished second to the Dutch-driven Ford V8 in the women's cup competition. The Morris Minor driven by an all-women crew, ranked third in the baby car class.

* NB. This was the Hillman driven by Maurice Gatsonides; Gerald Palmer lodged an objection, as clearly, the marks had been added up incorrectly. This put the Wise/Harrison/Palmer Javelin first in class, with Gatsonides second in the Hillman and R. Smith's Javelin in third. – NS

The Javelin of Anthony Hume and Tom Wisdom in the pits during the 1949 Spa 24-hour race, this was a triumph for Jowett as the car won the 2 litre car section even though it would have qualified for the 1½ litre class. The car was in fact the fastest saloon car in the race irrespective of engine size. (Louis Klemantaski/JCC)

1949 Spa 24-Hour Race
(Daily Herald, Sunday 12 July 1949)

An ordinary touring saloon car, entered for the first time in a motor-race, beat all other contenders in the Touring Class in the 24-hour Grand Prix, which ended here this evening. It was a Jowett Javelin 12hp saloon. It beat bigger Italian, French, German and American cars to average 105.15kph (65mph), covering 2,534.5km in twenty-four hours over what is regarded as the most difficult circuit in the world. And there was thick fog for four hours on the mountainside this morning.

The car was driven by Captain Anthony Hume, general manager of E.R.A, the racing car builders. Apart from changing a set of tyres, it was never touched – except to take in petrol.

Of the thirty-six starters, twenty completed the course, with the Jowett Javelin nineth in the general classification. The Belgian motorist appreciates a lap of over 70mph on the mountainous Spa circuit, and the Javelin did this frequently – coupled with 20 miles to the gallon.

In the last minutes Luigi Chinnetti (Italy), who had led the sports car class from the start, shot into a bend at Stavelot to find the crowd all over the road. He jammed on the breaks of his Ferrari, skidded on the sun-melted tar, spun round and crashed broadside into a house. A woman was pinned between the car and wall. Chinnetti, unhurt, leapt out and rendered first-aid to the woman, who had a broken leg. He then jumped back into his battered car and went on to win the Grand Prix at an average speed of about 78mph.

The HRG team, captained by Peter Clark, won the King of the Belgians' prize for the first complete team to finish.

NB. It is interesting to note that the second driver of the car was in fact Tom Wisdom, who was the motoring correspondent for the Daily Herald. *In his report, above, he makes no mention of his involvement – obviously he was too modest. It was just as well that an un-named colleague of his wrote this short piece in the same day's paper, as he was happy to name Tom Wisdom:*

1949 Spa 24-Hour Race
(Daily Herald, Sunday 12 July 1949)

Drivers of the Jowett Javelin (made at Idle in Yorkshire) which won against all-comers at the 24-hours motoring Grand Prix of Belgium were Captain Anthony Hume and the motoring correspondent of this paper, Thomas H. Wisdom.

By averaging at 65.34mph for the twenty-four hours over a difficult and dangerous circuit, these two gave a valuable boost to Britain's export car sales.

I heard from Wisdom yesterday, and he told me that the little car behaved perfectly. For him the race had two big moments and one embarrassing one. The big moments were passing the Italian Ferrari at 140kph and taking the notorious Burneville corner at 85kph when a black cat walked in front of his car. The secret of motor racing, he said, 'is to keep your fingers crossed and to watch out for black cats!'

The embarrassing moment came at the end when the president of the Automobile Club of Belgium publicly kissed him on both cheeks!

Opposite below: Another view of the Anthony Hume and Tom Wisdom Javelin in the 1949 Spa 24-hour race, just passing a Renault garage at speed. (JCC)

1950 Le Mans
By Thomas Wisdom

Britain's little Jav has big win – Record in 24-hours race starts rush to buy

Le Mans, Sunday … Britain's newest car, the little Javelin Jupiter, marked a great victory today in its first race, the 24-hours Grand Prix d' Endurance.

The Jupiter won the light car class and broke the fifteen-year-old speed record in this most famous of all French motoring events. And it surprised the experts from five nations by averaging 77.1mph for the twenty-four-hour grind round the 8-mile Le Mans road circuit. This new car was shown at the last Motor Show and in New York, was driven here by myself and Tommy Wise, a Harrogate competition motorist.

We had a no-trouble run despite competition in the light car class of the swiftest French and British racing cars. There was a melêe on the first lap, a big American car crashing into a sandbank at the Mulsanne turn. There was heavy fog during the night, a torrential rainstorm that made the roads like ice this afternoon.

The little car with only a nominal 12hp and with the famous 'flat four' engine pioneered by the Bradford firm, clocked 100mph on the straight and put in one lap on the twisting circuit at an average of over 80mph. (The previous record for the light car class was 76mph.)

Briggs Cunningham, American millionaire, who brought over two Cadillac's from America to challenge the Continental aces and brought them home in tenth and eleventh positions, came to me after the race and ordered a Jupiter on the spot, he owns thirty-two sports cars.

Then Harry Ainsworth, well-known European motor agent, told me that the speed and reliability of the Jupiter demonstrated today would result in many sales abroad.

Tommy Wisdom passing the pits area in the 1950 Le Mans. (JCC)

Touring Abroad – A practical guide to carefree motoring
By Tom Wisdom
(Published by Odhams Press Ltd, 1960)

This is an extract from chapter 29 'A-rallying we will go', from this excellent book, which is such a good read. This does not refer to a Jowett drive, but it gives such a good feel of the times, and I could not resist using it, particularly as Tom did drive for Jowett, with particular success in the 1950 Le Mans 24-hour race, where he scored a class win with Tommy Wise in a Jupiter. – NS

There are motor rallies and rallies: some grim, formidable affairs, severely testing professional driver and skilled amateur alike. And there are 'jollies', which offer fun, and a chance of winning something, to the tyro on holiday.

Among the tough jobs are the rallies qualifying for the Rally Championship of Europe. The annual round starts in January with the Rallye Monte Carlo, the event that attracts most attention in Britain, even among non-motorists. A month later comes the Italian Sestriere Rally. Then at the end of April the fans go to the Low Countries for the delightfully named Rallye des Tulipes. May brings the West German Rallye d'Allemagne, and the Greek Rallye du Soleil de Minuit – or the Midnight Sun – and the French Coupe des Alpes, are accommodated in June. The Yugoslav Rallye Adriatique is held in July, and the Finnish Rallye de Mille Lacs in August. The Belgian Liege – Rome – Liege event, which neither starts in Liege nor goes to Rome, is held in September, as is the Norwegian Rallye Viking, followed in October by the Rallye de IAC du Portugal. Then back to Britain for the RAC Rally in November. And what does your keen rallyists do in December? He can go to Ghana for the Rallye Kumsai. Or prepare for the 'Monte' in January, or both!

The holiday motorist who wants less exciting and less dangerous fun, plus rally companionship, will doubtless prefer the 'jolly', run perhaps by municipality, or one-make club, or by interests anxious to advertise a wine district, or scenic beauty, or gastronomic attractions.

Little more than 20km south of the western end of Lake Geneva is the delightful old town of Annecy, which has its own beautiful lake and which is a fine starting point for numerous excursions in the Haute-Savoie. Annecy, a health resort in its own right, is the centre for a popular annual rally arranged by the London Motor Club in association with the Motor Cycle Club de Mont-Blanc and the Auto Club de Mont-Blanc. The main event, the Petit Rallye, is limited to 220km, with the trials and road checks. There is a hill climb at La Clusaz and a driving test in the Annecy Casino gardens. There are numerous prizes for production cars of different classes, and 'special' cars.

Another motoring 'jolly' is the Languedoc Rally, with night stops in Epernay, Vichy and Carcassonne, taking your own time. You stop a couple of days at Andorra, where there is a magnificent barbecue party, before seeing Sete. Here is a braking test and a regularity test in which you circle the town three times trying to keep a precise average of 45kph. After four nights at Sete, the party breaks up. Many of the competitors make for Spain or the Riviera.

Riffling through some notes of the 1938 Monte Carlo Rally, I got a painful jolt on how costs have risen over the last twenty years. We accept (because we have no option!) the monthly and annual rises in prices without too much emotion, and then suddenly we are confronted with the accumulated effect in one generation.

On this trip of 2,275 varied miles, I teamed up with Colonel F Stanley Barnes, 'the gaffer', a racing driver of note, now a renowned engineering consultant, and his brother Donald, a brilliant driver who put the first British car past the post in the 1937 TT race. Our car was a new Vauxhall Ten, which we entered privately, i.e. it was not a works' entry, and its cost, with extra equipment, was less than £200. Our start was from Stravanger, which we reached by boat from the Tyne. On the way, at Newcastle, I bought an exciting novelty, an electric razor, which with a variety of sockets and plugs to meet the wide range of electric systems on the Continent, cost less than £1. This was the device, which blew the ship's fuses, an occurrence from which the Captain derived a minimum of pleasure. I am afraid that several other fuses went in the course of this journey and Donald occasionally showed lack of enthusiasm for holding the bared ends of the razor cable, when we did not have the right plugs.

I regret all this, but it is the price of progress. I was not the first pioneer to proceed by the harsh method of trial and error.

We had at first to average at 26½mph at the controls, which were some 200 miles apart. This speed, of course, had to include all stops, for petrol, repairs, meals and rest. Father south, before the race across the Alpes Maritimes, the average speed was increased to 31mph.

After a nightmare trip over the mountains, snow and ice, we were escorted by police the 300 miles across Denmark. Our convoy averaged more than 60mph in the country and 50mph through towns and villages, and even tough racing drivers found it hard to keep the high-powered police cars in sight as they roared along with sirens shrieking and lights flashing. At Hamburg we got our clothes off for the first and last time in the four days and four nights' dash across Europe, and revelled in a hot bath. Lucky Stanley and Donald stretched out on their beds for an hour, while I had to write my story and telephone my newspaper. It was not worth while trying to rest in the brief time available from hanging up to the resumption of the journey.

Such little time as there was taken up by a very beautiful German girl, who persistently examined me on what was the real purpose of a journalist travelling across Germany at that particular time. She may have been a full-time Nazi agent. More probably she was one of those characters, painfully common in Germany in the few years before the balloon went up, who hoped to pick up some information of military or political interest in order to ingratiate herself with whatever Nazi group they associated. She seemed unable or unwilling to accept that an English journalist could be a genuine rallyist. She was, as I have said, very beautiful, but I was too weary to appreciate her charm or to get annoyed by her tenacity.

All the way through Germany, Holland, Belgium and France we had but one complaint. We left behind us a trail of half bottles of beer and wine, because we never had time to finish them. Nearly out of petrol at Grenoble we had a frantic scramble to change a pound, before we could persuade the petrol depot man to fill us up.

My wife 'Bill', who had driven in another team, begged a lift home with us after we had spent a few days in the sun. We had a successful 'tour gastronomique', making up for all the repasts we had missed. This time we scrupulously finished each bottle.

'The gaffer', who kept very accurate records of all the spending, sent me a memo recently, in which he stated 'with a car then worth perhaps £150 we drove home from Monte Carlo to Boulogne – and we did live properly, lunched, dined, wined, good beds, the lot! Including all car running expenses, and excluding only cigarettes, the total cost per head, for the full trip of almost three days, was just inside £5. Quite a thought today!'

Desmond Scannell, for nineteen years secretary of the British Racing Drivers' Club, bubbles with stories about rallies abroad and has a knack of implanting a vivid picture on one's memory. He partnered Stirling Moss in the Monte Carlo Rally for three successive years, in two of which they secured a second and a sixth. It was in the 1952 event that they screamed into Le Puy, amid the enormous volcanic peaks of the Massif Central. Stirling was driving their Sunbeam Talbot. After a most hectic dice from St Flour they reached the town with eight minutes in hand, but desperately short of petrol. They slid to a stop at the first petrol pump they saw. It was one of those ancient devices into which petrol was pumped by hand up to twin 5-litre glass containers, from which it descended, by gravity.

After a time, in response to urgent calls, an ancient crone emerged, but slowly. However, after frantic cries of *Vite! Vite!* She was replaced at the creaking pump by a younger female.

Des went with the crone into the *bureau* to pay for the fuel. No sooner had he approached the car than the impetuous Stirling, whose patience was exhausted, engaged the clutch and started to move off, oblivious to the fact that the nozzle of the heavy hose was in the tank.

To the accompaniment of screams from the female attendant, the pump began to assume an alarming angle and, thinks Des, would have toppled over completely had not the surface been too slippery to give reasonable wheel adhesion. It took a few minutes to restore calm. They reached the control just in time.

The chief Scannell picture in mind, however, is that of him making the world record standing start – not on the track but across a level crossing. He had arrived, and tooted the horn impatiently. An old woman, who apparently had something in common with the first lady of the pump at Le Puy, emerged from a nearby cottage after a time, put her ear to the rail and then slowly opened the gates. Not quite convinced of the infallibility of her method, he revved up, glanced nervously and quickly each way and leaped, rather than drove across the lines. This was in Ireland.

The Route Napoleon, in the French Alps, continues to provide excitement to the Monte Carlo Rally competitors. To this day it is occasionally reported that a peasant, in the steep gorges below the road, finds a gold Napoleon, a relic of some loot-laden mule which missed its footing a century and a half ago. In Castellane and Digne they will sell you one at a pretty steep price. But, as with Roman coins I saw made in a Cairo 'souk', and afterwards buried in the desert hard by the Mena House Hotel, to be 'discovered' by an excited tourist, I mistrust their authenticity. It is, I suppose, all good clean fun!

I suspect Napoleon had a pretty hard time, sleeping in every one of these hostelries which line this famous route. If his itinerary was completed in the reported time, then I reckon he spent twenty minutes of darkness at each of the hostelries, refuges, hermitages and Hotels Napoleon.

On the eve of the 1959 Monte Carlo Rally I wrote, 'At the ripe old age of fifty-one I am off again on the Monte Carlo Rally. At precisely 2.18 tomorrow morning – a time when the human frame and mind are at their lowest ebb, when courage and hope are hard to summon – I shall start my sixteenth rally. This time a three-day, two-night, 2,200-mile jaunt over mountain roads, which, they assure us, are flooded in the valleys and either blocked by snow, or covered with sheet ice over the peaks. A *fairly* tough assignment, in fact. Which may be the reason why friends, over the last few days, have been giving me pitying looks, while murmuring; "Really you aren't thinking of doing it again! After all, though doubtless you think you can keep on, you must also think of *anno domini*, and all that".'

It is no good pointing out that Tazio Nuvolari, greatest racing driver of all time, was still racing at fifty-eight, that Sir Malcolm Campbell, when fifty, broke the world speed record at 301mph, that Donald Healey did 200mph at fifty-eight, and that grand old man Fred Bennett, at the age of eighty-three, drove through hail and snow on a veteran car run to Brighton, at the wheel of his first car, an open Cadillac of 1903.

No, my friends have decided that the Monte Carlo is too much for me, despite the fact that I have been assiduously practising and training for some forty years and think that motoring is the only thing I do well.

My first 'Monte' was in 1934. Donald Healey and I started out from Athens in those long ago days, when it really was something. There weren't any proper roads in the Balkans, and the goat-tracks were usually worse than driving across the fields, while rivers had to be forded, since there were no bridges. Cars were not only unreliable but had open bodywork. There were no heaters, no windscreen wipers and de-icers or washers. You were cold lonely travellers in a frozen land.

No man willingly went abroad in the depth of winter and not only for fear of packs of prowling wolves.

In those days the rally went on for five days and four nights. It was tough alright compared with the modern rally which, between you and me, is kids' stuff, a piece of cake for the condescending youngsters who have all the benefits of civilised motoring which their fathers (and betters) pioneered.

They are never out of reach of garages, teams of mechanics, of a chain of petrol pumps, in cars that won't go wrong, in this modern age of over-organisation.

In 1934 you were jolly lucky to borrow a bullock team to tow you out of the ditch, or come across a blacksmith who would hammer out a new spring from abandoned and ancient pieces.

But even today, and especially at the advanced age of fifty plus, you need to be fit. My plan is 100 per cent no smoking, no drinking (alcoholic), and moderate exercise.

How to keep awake? Remember, even in these softy times, the rallyist is on the road for a little over sixty hours with, in the usual two-man crew, no rest apart from catnaps when the going is good. Keeping awake for goodish periods is a matter of long, long practise. Some believe in banking-up sleep – going to bed early and rising late for weeks before a rally starts – while others adopt the opposite plan – stay up late and get up early. In fact make yourself do without sleep. The younger generation seems to prefer the latter plan. At least, the Crazy Horse, one of the naughtier of the Paris night-spots, seems to have been extremely popular with the British contingent starting from this gay city. Incidentally, few competitors rely on 'keep awake pills' except in an emergency. This rally isn't dull enough to let you sleep.

But age (and experience) does make you more careful. Certainly, I don't take the chances I took thirty years ago. At the half-century you rarely recourse to 'Leaning out of the window', a motor-racing term denoting that the driver is really going flat-out, chancing his arm. The expression is derived from the hazardous game played by schoolboys; an older version of 'Last across is a sissy!'.

The two-wheeled equivalent is 'ear 'oling', from the motorcycle and sidecar racers, and these feats are indulged in only by the young and very brave.

The over fifties in this rally, like past winners Sidney Allard, Louis Chiron, the Dutch champion Maurice Gatsonides and, I add modestly, myself, motor fast and surely we pride ourselves that as well as years we also have 'know how'. But we shall see. A niggling reminder is that in 1934, at the age of twenty-seven, we finished second, and have never equalled that since!

Tom Wisdom became the chief executive with the British School of Motoring (BSM) and wrote a couple of books for them. The first was on how to pass your driving test called, Good Driving – The BSM Way, *first published in 1961, the second was* High-Performance Driving For You, *first published in 1966. There is an interesting section inside this second book entitled 'Motoring on Mountains and on Ice and Snow' which I found of particular interest, so I feel more than justified in reproducing some of it here. – NS*

Heights worry me normally, yet I find motoring through mountain passes on roads with great drops and no barriers one of the real joys of motoring. I lose my fear of heights – just as one does on an aeroplane – in absolute bliss of both forcing and nursing my car up the steep slopes, round rocky hairpins, through the black tunnels and down the narrow roads that seem to fall away in front of you.

I think it is the demands of this kind of motoring that makes me love it so much, because I also like driving in other conditions which have a reputation of being difficult. I like driving on ice and I like driving on snow, which is just as well because often there is plenty of it on the mountains I like so much.

Ice, snow or mountains present an acceptable challenge to one's driving skill, and it is a challenge which can only be taken by those who possess some skill.

A few years ago it was essential to drive through mountain passes if one wanted to motor about Europe, but those tremendous tunnels they have built through the Alps make it unnecessary nowadays so perhaps future generations of motorists will live and die without knowing the pleasure of guiding a car through some of the most spectacular motoring country in the world – the mountain passes.

Mountain motoring is, I think, a sort of modern mountaineering. It is the best driving fun left for motorists. The Alpine passes of Switzerland, Austria, Germany, France, Italy and Spain allow the motorist to see some of the most beautiful and terrifying aspects of nature. Often, gazing at Alpine peaks through the cold, clean upper air with its invigorating champagne quality, I have puzzled over the creation of mountains. Their billions and billions of tons of rock, upper caps of ice and the snow, always look heavy to me, but geologists tell us that they floated, because of their relative lightness, to the top of the bubbling, molten surface of the Earth as it cooled, and who am I to quarrel with the geologists?

At the same time I am amazed to think of the engineers of more than 2,000 years ago who thrust winding paths up over the mountains. Particularly I think of the great Carthaginian general, Hannibal, who brought his army and his elephants over the Little Saint Bernard Pass (or was it, after all, Mont Cenis?) from France to Italy, leaving generations of historians to puzzle how he got to France first and where he crossed the swift waters of the Rhone.

Today Mont Cenis is one of the finest passes and it used to be the quickest way from the west to Italy. Several times I have covered the 750 miles from Le Touquet, the air-ferry terminal, to Brescia, starting point for the Mille Miglia, in a day. And I was able to test some excellent cuisine on the way.

In the past forty years I think I have driven through every well-known pass and some of the little-known military ones. At the top of the terror list of passes – and I admit they frightened me too, although I enjoy them all the same – I put three, the Gavia, and the Vivione, in Italy, and the Isoard in France. I cannot say which frightened me the most.

The Gavia
The Passo di Gavia, 8,600ft, is a narrow dusty road, which connects, for military purposes, Bormio with Ponte di Legno on the road to Merano. This pass has been used for International Alpine Trials and a few years ago an Italian general named Enzo Marchatti, viewing the mountain manoeuvres of his troops, became so excited at the sight of the speeding skidding Alpinists on the Gavia that he fell out of his helicopter. He landed, fortunately, in some branches of small trees and was borne to hospital bruised but alive.

The Gavia and the other two passes provide spectacular routes for the brave but they are not the places to learn mountain motoring. They are narrow and without barriers. The surfaces are loose gravel, dust or mud, perched on ledges over quite dreadful chasms.

The driver must keep his eyes ahead, otherwise, I am assured by passengers he would stop, get out and walk! This may be an exaggeration but, nevertheless, it points one of the lessons in mountain motoring. Watch the road and not the drop!

Such passes, little used, are not typical. The views normally make you forget any difficulties of the climb. To see from the summit of Furka the sunlight glint blue in the glacier where the Rhone starts is stupendous. The Rhine flows from a sister glacier just over the mountain and the view of either repays the arduous climb and even more difficult decent.

The Stevio
The finest of all the passes is the 9,050ft Stevio; from Trafoi you round the hairpins on a wonderfully engineered road that climbs to snow. The view on a clear day is out of this world.

At the beginning or end of the season it is well to inquire from the chief village whether the road is open. It is annoying to chase up the lower slopes to find a sign saying *Col Ferme*. There are times when it is quite impossible to drive up the mountains and if you try you may slide off.

The mountain hairpins can be tricky, especially in a big car, and they should be approached wide, taking full advantage of the width of the road. Then, having adjusted your speed and changed to the appropriate gear – usually first or second – swing the wheel hard over. If you make a mistake, stop before you hit the wall or go over the edge, reverse and have another go!

Be careful of tunnels, other than those superb new ones that join Switzerland and France with Italy. The others can be tricky, even to an experienced driver; poor Raymond Baxter of BBC fame found this out a few years ago when he was rallying along happily on a good mountain road in bright sunshine. He came to a tunnel and forgot to remove his sunglasses, which is why he did not notice that the sides of the tunnel were wet and so was the road. The car slid and bounced of the walls a few times, but fortunately did not suffer any lasting damage. Moral: expect changes in conditions inside tunnels.

As I pointed out earlier, it is easier to go up a mountain than down one. Descending requires more skill and it would be very embarrassing to decide at the top that you were not competent to drive down again. The nights are cold up there.

A common mistake when descending is excessive use of the brakes. This will make them 'fade', although modern disc brakes are less likely to do so. Instead of braking change down as you approach the corner – it is impractical to be in top on a mountain – and before the corner change down again if necessary. This will result in the engine doing most of the braking and it will help to steady the car. It is in this respect, by the way, that many of the automatic gear-boxes fall down. Their 'thinking' isn't good enough for mountains.

Bear in mind that most corners, particularly *lacets* (shoe laces or hairpins) have loose or slippery concrete surfaces which should be treated with care. Approach slowly under full control and then accelerate away.

In the rare and frightening event of another car coming round your corner in the opposite direction on the same bit of road as you, don't attempt to dodge if there is a precipice at either side; take the oncoming car head on and you will be less likely to go over the edge and, therefore, more likely to survive.

Some of the lessons on mountain driving are useful for driving in Britain when there is snow and ice about. One is that sometimes hills are impossible to go up and dangerous to drive down if the surface is slippery. So if you are making a journey in slippery conditions spend a few minutes pouring over your maps to see if you can choose a route with no hills.

Driving in snow

Generally speaking snow is fairly easy to drive in. Fresh snow found if little-used gives reasonable grip and braking distances are not increased dramatically. Packed snow, usually found on not so busy roads, can be tricky. Bear these points in mind when you are planning a route – but most important of all – remember that the busy main roads are the first ones to be cleared or treated with salt or grit.

Never reduce tyre pressures for driving on snow or ice. I know that this is a contradiction of the old advice, but it has now been shown that your grip can be better on hard tyres. It pushes the tread pattern more firmly through the snow or against the ice and helps your grip. The only time I reduce my tyre pressures is for mud, which is just as slippery as ice. I really don't know why, but soft tyres do give a better grip in mud. If anyone doubts me I can assure them that on Safari Rallies I have been stuck helplessly in mud with normal tyre pressures and have been able to drive away when I have reduced the pressures.

Slippery roads

All slippery roads call for gentler use of the controls, steering wheel, brakes and accelerator. This means that you must go more slowly and plan farther ahead more than usual. Fierce sudden movements will cause skids or loss of control through locked wheels, particularly when braking. Many people in fact like to use 'dab' braking on slippery roads because of the danger of locked wheels. In 'dab' braking you pump at the foot-brake. The wheels do lock, but only momentarily, with each dab, but the loss of braking by this method is counteracted by the fact that each time you have a fraction of a second of maximum possible braking power, which comes just before the wheels lock.

It is always advisable to use the highest gear possible for the speed when driving on slippery roads because then you are less likely to have skids by acceleration. You will also find that hills normally taken in second are best taken in third.

Stirling Moss is a master at driving on ice and he was once chased and eventually caught at a closed level-crossing by a police patrol car. The roads were icy and Stirling was accused of driving dangerously 'because we couldn't catch you'. His name lowered their spirits somewhat and they withdrew the suggestion when Stirling pointed out why they could not go at his speed. They were driving on the most slippery part of the road – the middle. He had his nearside wheels in the gutter where most of the road grit had collected and this improved his grip.

Snow chains can be useful providing you know how to fit them, but in our climate I think a good set of tyres is the best all-round answer. In rallies nowadays we use studded tyres for really icy conditions and they are used widely in Scandinavia in winter, but they are not really necessary for most parts of Britain.

Starting off can be one of the worst problems when there is snow or ice about. Sand, grit or sawdust under and around the driving wheels is always a great help. In a real emergency you can scrape some grit off the inside of the wings and scatter that around with the same effect. If you cannot get the car moving forwards, try reversing, and if you can move just a few inches try going forward again. Sometimes you will find that you can move away. In a front-wheel-drive car try turning the steering wheel a little so that the wheels are at a different angle, this may help. In a rear-wheel-drive car keep the front wheels straight.

My own favourite method of getting rolling on ice is a set of snow mats, which are developed from the sand mats we used in the Western Desert during the 1939 war. They are foot-wide strips of sacking about 10 or 12ft long which are laid out in front of the driving wheels. The car has to be manhandled onto them but once you are you can drive away. If the mats are tied to the rear bumper with string they will follow you along the road and can be removed at the first suitable spot for stopping.

A good method of getting moving is to use the starter motor to ease the car out. This method won a contest for the 'quickest out of a snowdrift' in Canada. You remove the sparking plugs, engage first gear, and press the starter. In a car with that great boon, a starting handle, you can use that instead of the starter motor and wind the car out. It works in flood water too.

Black ice

Black ice is more dangerous than ordinary ice because it is virtually invisible and often is in patches so you may come upon it unprepared. If you do, remember your skid drill. Normally you only find black ice when the temperature is below freezing point, which is why one of those devices which warn you of outside temperatures are also useful. You know to be careful if the temperature is within two or three degrees of freezing. This also warns you when your windscreen is likely to start getting ice-covered.

I have found this a great help on the Monte Carlo Rally. The device has warned me that the temperature is dropping to the danger point and I have turned on my windscreen de-icer. This has kept my forward vision perfect while others have had theirs obscured by ice, so I have been able to overtake much faster cars or else found myself leading a convoy.

Iced up windows can be a problem even when parked and the best way of preventing them is to use newspaper as protective covers. Failing that, use a plaster scraper to get the ice off – and off all the windows. You might also avoid parking with the hand-brake on, if possible, because the linings can freeze to the drums. Frozen door-locks can be annoying and can be dealt with by warming the key until it melts its way into the lock. Then hold the flame of your lighter or matches at the end of it and the whole lock will gradually de-ice. Be careful not to burn your fingers!

A nasty piece of freezing happened to a friend of mine last winter. His car was parked in the freezing cold for some hours and he could not get it rolling afterwards, so he went to the boot to get his emergency equipment – and found that the lid-lock had frozen too.

Tom was still very active in motor sport as far on as 1966, and The Motor *wrote this excellent article about him and his adventures in the Monte Carlo Rally, which are detailed below. Tom did not drive a Jowett in the Monte but he did in the following events: the 1949 Spa 24-hour race, 1950 Le Mans 24-hour race, 1950 Dundrod TT, 1951 Le Mans 24-hour race and the 1951 Dundrod TT. – NS*

People and Cars – Tom Wisdom – Twenty-three Times into the Monte Breach, Dear Friends
By Dennis May
(*The Motor*, 15 January 1966)

Tom Wisdom co-won the light car category in his first Monte Carlo Rally, thirty-two years ago, and has, he says, been working steadily down the lists ever since. This, if literally true, would be a record for descalation, because the '66 event will be his consecutive 23rd. But it isn't literally true – respectable class placings, even a win or two, alternate with the ah-wells on his Monte dossier; and for his money anyway, as for Charles James Fox's, the greatest pleasure in life, after winning is losing. So the struggle availeth.

The obvious sometimes has to be stated and Wisdom states it; the rally isn't what it was. And in 1934, when he was a starry-eyed beginner, no doubt the same was being said with equal truth by the first-edition people who'd competed in 1911.

In the small '30s the rally had a serious mission to perform, *viz*, to hasten the development of immature and fragile cars, and incidentally it was terrific fun. It has now performed its mission but to some extent it must still be fun, otherwise why would a veteranissimo like Wisdom (he'll soon be sixty) keep coming back for more?

Variety has been the spice of Tom's Montes – variety in cars and fellow travellers both. His cars have ranged from a Ford Eight to a Straight-Eight Daimler about half a parish long and so ponderous with all its kitchen stove type equipment aboard that technically it wasn't a motor car at all (Heavy Locomotive perhaps?).

The worst of starting your Monte career as co-driver to Donald Healey, as Wisdom did in 1934, is that any subsequent change is bound to be for the worse, unless you prefer losing to winning. Nevertheless, he counts himself lucky in his rally mates. These, befitting his own status as a lifelong newspaperman, have included such prominent verbalists as Courtenay Edwards of *The Sunday Telegraph*, Jack Hay of *The Birmingham Post* and Gregor Grant of *Autosport*. Then there were sundry celebrities of the motorcycle world, like the old-time Norton works rider, Norman Black, T.T. lap record wholesaler Jimmy Simpson, world champion sidecar tamer Cyril Smith, International Six Days' Trial captain Alan Jefferies and Ron Watson of Watsonian Sidecars. By Kipling's *If* test, Tom gives motorcycle people a high rating; mostly they are tough, resourceful, and chirpy in adversity, with a habit of doing things above and beyond the call of duty. Cyril Smith typified this spirit when he partnered Tom in a Healey with one arm in plaster, the result of a racing crash.

That Straight-Eight Daimler gave Wisdom one of his pleasantest Monte surprises. When the makers delivered it to his doorstep, he and his companions, Lord Selsdon and Tony Hume, decided they must have been crazy in the head to bespeak such a colossus of roads. Their starting point was Lisbon. This was the year (1952) that Mercedes made a comeback to rallying, also using the Lisbon route. With drivers like Caracciola and Lang in the Mercedes, and the added strength of Alfred Neubauer bossing the whole operation, the Daimler crew spent the tee-up period developing king-size inferiority complexes, heightened by hearty Teutonic laughter as such absurdities as the limousine's dowager type electric division. As it transpired though, the car's enormous weight proved to be its salvation in one of the most arduous rallies of the series; where lesser machinery skated perilously over the abounding ice, the Daimler graunched through it and fastened a grip on the earth's undercrust. Thus aided, Wisdom-Selsdon-Hume found themselves hitting 100mph in places, and actually overtaking the whole Mercedes team on sections south of Paris that to everybody else were almost bankrupt of traction. Thereafter the jolly *Herrenvolk* sang a different tune, suddenly remembering the Daimler-Benz kinship and practically promoting the British car to German nationality.

The smallest and lowest-powered car Tom ever drove in *Le Rallye* – the Ford Eight – produced its fair share of rigour. In it, in 1939, he and Mike de Belleroche, an Odhams Press man, like Wisdom, braved the dreaded Athens itinerary – just like their cheek. With its souped-up engine the little Ford was not short on guts; but realising that there was no such thing as au revoir to lost revs, only adieu, the partners just drove flat out until rpm sagged in top, then smacked 'er in to second with the foot still hard down, then finally in to bottom. Thus goaded, the car pogo'd and aviated along for mile after interminable mile, obedient to the Law which says a vehicle does not stop while actually airborne. When oil escaped from its rear main bearing into the clutch, quantities of fire-extinguisher fluid were procured and the off-duty driver stayed on duty pumping the stuff into the bellhousing through a hole they had drilled for the purpose at a wayside garage. The Ford made it to Monte and won its class.

If a good rally passenger is a man who is not afraid when being driven very fast over ice in a snowstorm on a pitch-black night, Wisdom isn't a good rally passenger and never was. Even good drivers frighten him a bit under these conditions; he prefers not to stare the potential accident in the face, so unless he's busy with map reading or something, he adopts an eyes-left attitude and 'watches the scenery'.

For his age he's pretty good at fighting off sleep after abnormally prolonged periods of enforced wakefulness. Nevertheless, and excusably for one in his late fifties, he's beginning to find the sleep/awake ratio by a two-man crew a mite too much for him; after twenty-two Montes he'll take on the extra organisation that triplication involves, rather than face a possibility gruesome twosome.

Correction to something we said earlier; the rally three decades ago, had two serious missions in life, not just one. The second was to open up benighted regions to easeful tourism. This, of course, it has done, or helped to do so, as Tom underlines with his recollection that the AA's 1934 advice to Athens starters included these words: 'North of Larissa it is advisable to take to the fields as the roads are so bad.'

It was from Athens in '34 that an experienced Donald Healey and the youthful and totally inexperienced Tom Wisdom set forth in the former's Triumph Ten (nick-named the Roller Skate on account of its small size and contrastingly enormous balloon tyres) on the drive that this light car was to win.

The 1935, effetely opting for a cat with a roof, unlike the little Triumph, Wisdom spliced into a Chrysler crew, again starting from Athens. He didn't get through, but neither did anybody else. A surviving photograph of this bid shows him riding one of the bullocks' postilion fashion, that had been hired and enharnessed near Larissa in a vain effort to extricate the stranded Chrysler.

Cars with roofs were the exception rather than the rule in the Montes of the low '30s, of course dressing up like a sewage inspector, Sidcot-suited, polymufflered, high-booted, was all in the game. Car suspensions hadn't gained independence and consequently the quality of ride over atrocities that passed as roads, was somewhere around strappado level. Such heaters that existed were rudimentary and anyway there was no point in cooking up a fug merely to let it escape into the atmosphere.

As pieces of engineering the cars of the day, as we see it now in hindsight but didn't realise it at the time, were half-baked, or three quarters at most. Mechanical failures from the minor to catastrophic were the common lot of almost all, with the scales tipped heavily in favour of Messrs Wilco, the resourceful fixers. Natural hazards and obstacles were there to be overcome and if *you* did not overcome them, the chances are somebody else would. When floods washed a river bridge away, or the just wasn't a bridge when you needed one, you hired a barge and pressed on regardful…

Now, obviously, all that is changed. Wilco can be your middle name but lose time and you've had it, finally. To win a modern Monte, says Wisdom, you need to be as brave as Bond, a superb driver, backed by faultless organisation, accompanied by a master navigator/mathematician, blessed with a car that's as good as the best in the act. You will then travel in perfect comfort, leaving your overcoat at home, and although you may die a good many mental deaths en route, your physical death is less likely that it recurrently seems.

You will be doing nothing to improve the breed of the automobile – all that belongs in the past tense. But you will still be having fun, up to a point, and with luck, may even stay on good terms of friendship with your co-driver(s).

Wisdom does not *steel* himself – he just does what come naturally. During the preliminaries to the 1934 *kampf*, he and Donald Healey has a serious talk on the subject of what to do, or omit, by way of preparing themselves physically and mentally for the big ordeal. 'We came to the conclusion,' he recalls, 'that it wasn't advisable to disturb our routine by taking regular meals, going to bed early, practising teetotalism – that kind of thing. So we just went on living in night clubs and avoided giving our systems any unpleasant shocks. I don't know if this approach is the best one, but it hasn't let me down and I shan't change now.'

CHARLES GRANDFIELD

Charles Grandfield was manager of the Jowetts Experimental Department and was responsible for the development of the Javelins and Jupiters that competed in rallies and races such as the Monte Carlo Rally, Spa 24-hour race and Le Mans. He and Horace Grimley were heavily involved with the testing and developing of these cars, as detailed below:

1949 Spa 24-Hour Race
Charles Grandfield
(Published in *The Jowetteer*)

Feeling very much as newcomers to motor racing, the decision was taken some weeks ago to enter the Jowett Javelin in the Touring Class of the Belgian Twenty-four Hour Road Race to be run at Spa in the Ardennes on 9 and 10 July.

Mr Tom Wisdom, Motor Correspondent of the *Daily Herald* and *Sporting Life*, and Captain Anthony Hume, both well-known and competent drivers, expressed eagerness to drive the Javelin in this event, and were therefore nominated as drivers.

The car in the terms of the regulations had to be perfectly standard with only slight modifications allowed in the interests of safety. These consisted of stiffer shock absorbers, two bucket seats instead of the standard bench seat, and oil cooler. The authorities also allowed us to increase the compression ratio in order to take advantage of the fuel they were providing. This was done by Messrs Hepworth & Grandage making special pistons which had a smaller cavity in the piston's crown. The remainder of the tuning consisted of meticulous attention being given to every mechanical detail in the car, especially with a view to eliminating friction, so that as much as possible of the engine's power would be available at the road wheels instead of being used in turning the engine over.

We were of course inundated with advice and criticism from those so-called 'experts' in the know!

We must 'run on at least 10:1 compression ratio',
'The brakes will fail',
'The bearings will run',
'The axles will seize',
We must 'fit a petrol tank as big as the car'....etc.
All these, however, were, we hoped, side-stepped with politeness – although as the day for sailing approached, the latter commodity seemed to be getting into rather short supply.

At last, however, the car was ready, and after a few circuits of Sherbourne Aerodrome we felt that it was as good as it could be. It was motored from Bradford to the Francorchamps circuit at Spa under its own power, accompanied by a tender vehicle and trailer with enough spares, I felt, to keep the service manager happy for weeks to come. The above part of the journey was quite uneventful, except for the unholy delight taken by HM Customs in checking all our spares for illicit export. Consternation was expressed that only three quarter-inch BSF bolts could be found, whereas our list plainly stated four.

The circuit at Spa is situated in most beautiful country and there was a real air of Continental gaiety pervading: flags, sunshine, fast motor cars, arguments over entry money, petrol, regulations, and everything else.

At 4 o'clock on Saturday afternoon, however, everything was in order, the forty-four cars were lined up at one side of the track and their drivers opposite on the other side; all eyes on the starter's flag. The flag dropped and amid the melee of thrashing legs, Tommy Wisdom emerged, threw himself into the car, and was away in the first dozen.

All eyes in the Jowett pit eagerly awaited the appearance of the car, and after eight minutes being taken to traverse the 9½-mile circuit, it appeared to be going extremely well, accompanied by 'thumbs up' signs from the driver.

The pit personnel now settled down to the manipulation of stop watches and recording the progress. This, we found, could be quite exciting, especially when three cars or more passed us in a bunch, when strange oaths were heard as the wrong watch was stopped, or some belated foreigner walked across our line of vision.

The Javelin continued to run with monotonous regularity, and after the first hour established a small ever-increasing lead in its class. As the hot afternoon changed into a beautiful cool evening the Grandstand lights came on, and one realised the thrill which is part of the Continental 24-hour Grand Prix racing *(sic)*. The cars flashed by with lights ablaze, disappearing as two small red lights up the distant hill, with the crackle of exhausts.

Drivers were changed at four-hour intervals and the car filled up with petrol, oil, and water. At these events it was obvious that the Jowett's mechanic – A Illingworth – was something of an athlete, as displayed by his agility in leaping over the pit counter and the 'snap' with which the change-overs were carried out, especially as only the driver and one mechanic were allowed to work at one time. We were reaping good rewards in valuable seconds saved by not having to make any adjustments to the car, as a result of the careful work weeks before at Idle, and this state of affairs continued through the race.

During the hours of darkness our only casualty occurred when Captain Hume was struggling with a jammed glove box lid and broke his finger. He continued driving, however, until the end of his shift – a very commendable performance indeed.

At last Sunday morning came, accompanied by very thick fog on the high ground of the course, but our drivers seemed to possess some uncanny sense, since our lap times were very little reduced in comparison with other cars, and by the time the sun came up we were well ahead as leaders in our own class and running only one lap behind the leader of the 2000-4000cc Touring Class.

It was decided at mid-day to increase our lap speeds in order that we could beat the 2000-4000cc class; this was done after a valiant struggle lasting an hour, Mme Simon driving the leading Delage in the big class, gave us her best as we continued with our trouble-free motoring to win the event at 4 o'clock at an average speed of 65.5mph, having covered 1,573.92 miles, which meant we had covered a greater distance at a higher speed than any other touring car irrespective of size.

After drinking champagne, eating and collecting our prize, the Equipe Jowett motored uneventfully back to Idle. The engine of the car was stripped down and everything was found to be in perfect order, so it has now been reassembled with no new parts being required in preparation for future events.

Charles Grandfield
Obituary

This obituary was written by Bill Boddy, no less, the legendry motoring journalist, who was editor of Motor Sport *for many years. In fact he still contributes even though he is now well into his nineties. He is also the acclaimed author of several books on Brooklands, and is acknowledged as the world's authority on the subject. This obituary was published in the July 1998 issue of* Motor Sport. – NS

Charles Grandfield, Manager of the Jowett Company's Engineering Department, and who was responsible for the Javelins and Jupiters that competed in rallies and races such as the successful 1949 Monte Carlo and 1950s long-distance races at Spa and elsewhere, has died aged 84. After working on Rolls-Royce aero-engines from 1937 up to being called up. Grandfield was mentioned three times in dispatches, and was de-mobbed a lieutenant-colonel. Until 1947 he was with Sir Roy Fedden, developing the stillborn sleeve-valve aero-engine before going to Jowett's in Bradford.

There his work embraced improving Bradford vans and overseeing the competition Jowetts. Excellent results were eventually obtained with lightweight Javelins and sports Jupiters. At this time the proprietor of Motor Sport, the late W.J. Tee, was the enthusiastic owner of at least one Javelin and a Jupiter. We got excellent help from the company, both with the cars and the articles I wrote about them.

Apart from the competition cars, Grandfield devised better gearboxes, resin-fibre body panels etc. on the production-car side, and was involved with the Farina-Jupiter project. He is mourned by his wide circle of friends, the Jowett CC whose vice-president he was, and ourselves.

HORACE GRIMLEY

I was in correspondence with Victor Grimley, Horace's son, for a period during 1999 and 2000. I personally think that Horace is the unsung hero of Jowett from the very early days, right through to the closure of the company in 1954. Horace did in fact stay on at the factory after then, working for International Harvester, the tractor manufacturer who took over the premises at Five Lane Ends in Idle, Bradford. Victor sent me an excellent letter in January 2000 where he recounted his boyhood memories of his father. I published this in The Jowetteer *in April and May 2000 and quote parts of it again here, as I believe he deserves a large space in this book, as he drove on many occasions and was the driving force in the pits in such events as the Spa and Le Mans 24-hour races. – NS*

John Grimley married Hettie Jackman and produced Albert Horace Grimley, who married Elsie Muriel Clayton, and produced me, Victor Moreland Grimley. I married and produced Vandon Grimley, who, I believe, is now a member of the Jowett Car Club, or at least had some contact with them. *(He was a member then and still is. – NS, Dec. 2008)*

Dad worked for his Uncle Willy (William Jowett) with two others in the Experimental Department for a pittance of five pounds a week, the level of which rose but little as the years passed. Willie Jowett felt that Dad should be shown no favouritism lest nepotism be suspected; Dad had to accept the conditions...at least he had a job in the harsh economic climate of the 1930s... but made him strive to become as useful to the firm as possible, being his only route to better levels of remuneration.

He did just that; much of it was self-taught. I well remember his prowess on the centre lathe, milling machines and ancillary machine tools, all driven by unguarded heavy leather belting from overhead shafting running down the length of the Experimental Shop. I recall too how he could wield hammer on anvil, next to the blacksmith's health, brilliant red sparks flying up into the trunking as the noisy motor blew pressurised air through glowing coke, producing virtually any shape from a block of raw steel. I can still hear the hiss of the quenching bucket and see Dad's perspiring brow. He was just as skilled with sheet metal; I have watched him form a mudguard by hand over a timber jig, almost without blemish and only requiring a final polish. On the fitting bench, he would make and assemble virtually everything he needed for the prototype car currently in hand. In the 'office' hung engineering drawings, many of them his own, representing the components he was about to make.

This was how all Jowett prototypes were built, piece by piece, by hand, in the confines of the Experimental Shop, strictly off bounds to all but a few men who worked there under Dad's guidance. There was Harold 'Digger' Metcalfe and Tommy Laycock, the original stalwarts, later joined by others whose names are lost to me. Almost always there would be an engine on test on the 'dynamometer' in the corner, reading power outputs on a huge white dial surmounting the whole rig. Dad would religiously record readings as changes were made to pistons, piston rings and valves. Different cylinder head contours, piston crown contours, compression ratios and all manner of fine adjustments would be tried and recorded, until Dad was satisfied that a unit was producing optimum output for the purpose intended in its future use as a power source. At this stage in my life, my Dad was no less than a magician in my young mind, as I accompanied him frequently on Saturday mornings to the Works, so witnessing at first hand his latest achievements.

He could sing too. Father John Grimley (my esteemed grandad whom I loved), was the choirmaster and organist at Brownroyd Methodist Chapel and all the family, myself included, passed in turn through the Sunday School to the main church. The delights of Handel's *Messiah* were committed to memory and brought to bear anywhere, provided that more than one voice was available. It just so happens that there were such voices amongst the Jowett team; the Experimental Department never needed to resort to 'Music While Work'.

Sometimes, early on cold winter Sunday mornings, the La Roche (this was a prototype four-cylinder in-line car which was under test in 1935, of which two were made. It was badged as La Roche to avoid panic by Jowett owners at the thought of the scrapping of 'The little engine with the big pull' *(See page 48 of my book* Jowett 1901 – 1954 *for a picture and more details of it – NS)* would motor along through Skipton, Threshfield and Cracoe, past Kilnsey Crag and on up the River Skirfare to Hawkswick village in Littondale, where Uncle Willie (Jowett) had shooting rights over Hawkswick Moor. Here, in Cockshott's field at the side of the river, was 'The Hut', built by Willie as his 'shooting lodge'. Dad had two privileges, rarely granted by the Jowetts; firstly, he was allowed to partake in the twelve-bore activities over the moor; secondly, he was allowed to use the other La Roche registered KY4695 (a registration plate indelible in my memory) as his personal transport. I believe that, later, the car became Dad's property, probably through his own wit at spotting a second anagram, using his Belle Vue School French.....'l'Horace.' No doubt he deemed it more profitable than 'Chorale' *(La Roche was said to be an anagram of chorale – a slow and dignified hymn...NS)*. After each shoot the two Jowetts (Uncle Willie ran his own Kestrel) loaded with guns, spaniels and gutted rabbits for the whole family, returned triumphantly to Wool City.

Now this La Roche had been another subject of Dad's technical development. At the time, Bradford Corporation were experimenting with pre-selector gearboxes on their buses. Jowetts thought they might, as always, keep up with the times, and a Wilson pre-selector box was installed in Dad's car. It incorporated a rotating drum marked 1-2-3-4-R, mounted on a stalk to the left of a steering column. In advance of the need for any gear change, one's left hand rotated the drum until it clicked into the required position (pulled firmly outwards to the left for reverse); then the 'clutch' pedal was depressed, whilst engine speed was modified by the throttle pedal, and released again quite quickly to engage the required gear. Also a 'fluid flywheel' allowed the car to remain stationary whilst 'in gear', the drive being taken up smoothly with opening the throttle. However, this was not a clutch in the normally accepted sense; the box housed a series of circular 'friction bands' that gripped around corresponding drums, transmitting power through the gears in accordance with the selection made. Much later on, during my early driving lessons with Dad, I was well-schooled NOT to use it – not even to think of it – as a clutch in the usual sense. The habit so formed rendered me liable to release the clutch pedals on future years rather too quickly, with juddering results – a habit that was difficult to break. This was, of course, the first step to fully automatic transmission, towards which some progress was made, but the idea was dropped and never pursued by Jowett again.

Long before I was of an age to engage in the above 'official' driving lessons, and before my legs would reach the pedals, Dad used to sit me on his lap, give me the steering wheel, and let me drive us home to 11 Portwood Street, Daisy Hill, from Grandma Grimley's house in Girlington. This only took place after dark, when passers-by could not easily detect the double-headed driver in the strange black saloon. On one such night I was happily negotiating the bends in Duckworth Lane, past the Bradford Royal Infirmary, when the headlights picked out a police constable walking towards us on the off-side pavement. As the beams penetrated the policeman's eyes, Dad reached with customary rapidity, more fearful for his license than the welfare of his son, and ejected me sideways from his lap. The action confirmed the solidity of the Jowett coachwork as my tender left hip met the nearside door handle. It hurt, but I understood, and if I had moaned the privilege might well have been withdrawn.

One last La Roche memory; motoring to Filey for a week under canvas for Dad's favourite 'fishing off the Brigg' holiday, we were towing the trailer full of equipment. Having stopped to re-fuel with Cleveland Discol at one and a penny a gallon, we had just left the garage and had reached about forty five on the speedo, when Dad had to brake for some obstruction. At that moment a whirring object overtook us on the off-side. 'That's my wheel' shouted Dad. It was. The trailer was down on its haunches; its off-side wheel entered the hedge almost a hundred yards in front of us. Dad spent the next hour with his extensive tool kit, I was sent back to pick up the six wheel nuts scattered along the road. Not entirely successful, we reached Filey with only four.

When the Second World War came, car production ceased, Dad wanted to volunteer with everyone else to join one of the armed forces. This was denied to him by Ministry order requiring certain key engineers to be retained to organise the conversion of the factory for war production. It was soon accepted that Jowetts might now become a prime target for German bombs and a team of 'fire watchers' was formed, under Dad's control, to sit on the factory roof every night in steel helmets with stirrup pumps at the ready. Dad quickly realised, having seen the glowing fires on the horizon in Leeds, that these primitive arrangements could never be effective against a concentrated incendiary attack. He negotiated with the National Fire Service and obtained trailer pumps and water tankers to be distributed around the factory, then underwent intensive training himself with NFS before forming the Jowett Cars Fire Brigade from volunteer workers. On Saturday mornings he could be seen – and heard – as their new Fire Officer, drilling his smart squad, marching in military style in the main factory roadway, in which activity they were later to win several competitive events. He often secretly arranged for controlled fires to be actually started in various locations around the factory, so the new fire brigade could be put to the test in readiness for enemy action, though it never came to Bradford, with the exception of two stray incendiary bombs believed to have been inadvertently dropped by some German bomb-aimer with finger trouble.

Another small contribution to the war effort was made when spare land at the foot of Spion Kop, the slag heap at the end of the factory site, was converted to form allotments, cultivated as part of the 'Dig for Victory' campaign. Dad had one of these and the Experimental Shop became a sorting and distribution centre for fresh vegetable produce alongside the abandoned prototype cars still remaining in the building. Only restricted work was still being done on engine development for the Bradford van until the first whispers of Javelin began to permeate the atmosphere.

Long before the hostilities ceased, new faces were entering Dad's world. I remember several early sessions at our house between Gerald Palmer, Dad and other members of the residual experimental team, discussing the very early stages of Javelin development, notably the flat-four engine, the torsion bar suspension and the column-mounted gear lever. At every stage of Gerald's pioneering, Dad's small team were unknown to the world outside, secretly converting his ideas into solid state in the 'little shop' at the far end of the Works. On many occasions such effort extended through the night and Muriel Grimley, my Mum, exhibited tolerance beyond belief. It was fortunate that Mum and Dad were very close, or this period could have rocked their marriage.

The war was finally ended and some pressure was applied to advance the Javelin development as quickly as possible. Dad would bring experimental cars home, the dashboard bristling with gauges mounted on temporary brackets. Looped wires and copper pipes communicated top and bottom radiator temperature, crankcase temperature, oil pressure at various points in the lubrication system and other tell-tale signals from which he could deduce engine performance in a most detailed and specialised way. A car arriving at number 11 in this guise was a sign to me that he intended to drive through the night, when little traffic would be on the road. Using my persuasive powers, I would beg to occupy the passenger seat, and there would begin the most thrilling experience of my young life. His aim would be to put the car through the most punishing of tests that man could devise, and the Yorkshire Dales were the best place to do it. Dad was entirely fearless; he could make that Javelin leap like a lion, and fast driving was his forte. Even since my later days as a naval fighter pilot, I have never been able to drive a car like that. The narrow, snake-like road along the Wharfe through Kettlewell, Starbotton and Buckden was a favourite stretch, offering (in those days) every conceivable type of surface. Drystone walls flashed past, so dangerously close to the wings, as the engine growled with that unique Javelin fury under full throttle, and the headlights picked out the next tight bend. The speedo ranged between fifty and eighty, where sane folk used thirty and forty. The best braking test often came uninvited after rounding a fast curve to be confronted by the white silhouette of a sheep in the middle of the road, only yards distant, its eyes glistening with the reflection of our beams as we came to rest at its feet. My job was to immediately dismount through the haze of tyre smoke and 'shoo' it away; then off again through the night, engine, torsion bars and every other component under stresses unlikely ever to be encountered elsewhere, myself experiencing indescribable excitement that my school pals could never know. Oh, how that man could drive; if you want one word – it's tenacity. And how did he ever read those gauges at such frenzied speeds? Yet when we were home he accumulated enough information to formulate the next day's work on the car.

There is one more Javelin episode I would like to relate. We had gone eastwards from Bradford, making for Harewood Avenue, one of the longest straight stretches in the County. It was of sufficient length to enable absolute top speed to be reached. The needle had reached seventy five and Dad's throttle foot was still on the floor. Suddenly there was a loud thud and a flurry of feathers, followed by a complete blackout of the windscreen. A pheasant had flown across and struck the car just above the grill, deforming the nose and releasing the bonnet catches. Up came the huge cover, right across the screen and Dad hit the brakes. It took him a long time to straighten out the tortured metal, mainly with his thumbs, sufficiently to re-fix the bonnet in place … I always knew that Horace Grimley had the strongest hands in Yorkshire … but it had ended the speed trials prematurely. Both he and I were both disappointed. Who says pheasants do not fly in the dark?

By the time that the Jupiter was 'leaping to fame' at Le Mans, I had started to lead my own life, which distanced me from home and my parents. Whilst I do remember odd occasions when our paths crossed, Dad and I no longer enjoyed such a close liaison as we had when I was younger. My memory is mainly of the different models arriving at No 11, receiving little more than a cursory glance from me as I left on my AJS motorcycle, by then totally engrossed in my own other world. So I can only say, 'I remember vaguely' the Jupiter Le Mans and 'Monte' cars or the R4 and CD models, up to the time when tractors replaced all of this … and broke his heart.

Let Horace Sing!

In 2004 I was sent a selection of pre-war Jowett adverts from the late and much-missed Jowett historian, Ted Miller, who set up, and was the driving force of the North American Jowett Register. He had single-handedly tracked down a very high proportion of all Jowetts exported to the USA. One of the adverts he sent was in the typical floral border and entitled 'Let Horace Sing', which I was sure had to be a reference to Horace Grimley, as he was well known for having a good singing voice. I wrote to Victor again, sending him a copy of this advert, and this was his most entertaining reply. – NS

Dear Noel, it was good to receive your letter enclosing a copy of the *The Autocar* clipping. Yes, I suspect it was deliberately published 'on the skew' as part of the typical tongue-in-cheek light hearted attitude that always pervaded the Jowett Company, especially in its advertising. This endeared them to so many folks in itself, quite apart from the esteem in which the cars themselves were held.

With regard to the content 'Let Horace sing!' it could well have been a reference to the 'Glee Club' of which Dad was a long-term member. Our branch of the Grimley's were all blessed with some degree of musical ability of one sort or other and Dad was no exception. He played piano and violin and his rich bass voice excelled in both solo and choral performances. Much of this was learned at Brownroyd Methodist Chapel (now demolished) in Ingleby Road, Bradford, just south of Girlington. It was later practiced at the Jowett Cars Glee Club that met frequently at the Idle factory canteen (now also demolished).

His own dad (my granddad, John Grimley) was for many years the Choirmaster and Organist at Brownroyd, but my own childhood performances were limited to dabbling on the harmonium (the pedal-pumped wind organ) located in the Sunday Schoolroom below ground level under the main chapel. The only merit there was when Grandma called time and silence was restored as I was dragged off to Sunday lunch!

Your opening wish that I'm 'keeping well' was well received. I am in fact now a cancer survivor, having contacted the devilish disease in both my mouth and throat. Fortunately it was all (rather painfully) surgically removed and burned out by radiotherapy, leaving me somewhat disfigured and struggling with (again painful) dental reconstruction, but with a renewed and blessed lease of life, so thanks for asking. The answer has to be, 'Yes, I'm great thanks!' (Surprising though how you value that which you have lost – like teeth!)

So Noel, I'll get off, back to my studies; I'm quite mad of course, taking a GCSE in German at the age of seventy-three. But it's rather good to be the hairiest old student in the college and still better at it than some, fifty years older!

Perhaps there's a streak of Uncle Willie Jowett in there somewhere?
Best wishes with the Club.

Vic M. Grimley (son of Albert Horace!),
Chichester, April 2004

Sadly Victor lost his brave battle against cancer in February 2006, but his son, Vanden, told me that his father did pass his GCSE in German before he died. – NS

Let Horace sing!

If Larwood and the Selection Committee can't come together, put Bowes in. He's a Yorkshireman. Put Clarke in, he learned his cricket in Bradford League. So did Sutcliffe. (Did you know that Jack Hobbs used to play for Idle? Well, he did, and we're very proud of it here).

And now, seeing that we have to pay for this space, that's enough of Test Matches.

You can, however, have a test match any time you like, and free of charge.

The Jowett is the roomiest and most comfortable light car made. (It has a wheelbase of 8′ 6″).

It is the cheapest to run, the most reliable, the most economical in upkeep.

It is as nice-looking as the next.

Test our assertions by trying one for nothing.

Prices from £150   Tax £7

JOWETT CARS LTD., IDLE, BRADFORD

Spa, 1949

The Spa Javelin was in fact driven from the factory to the race. Horace Grimley and Charles Grandfield travelled in convoy in two Javelins. This second Javelin towed Horace's camping trailer, which was filled with spares. It was thought the run to Spa would be a good test-drive for the car! At Spa the bumpers etc. were removed to lighten the car prior to the start. I always think these Jowett successes were even more remarkable as everything seemed to have been done on a shoestring budget. Not like some of the larger racing concerns, who would have had the cars transported there, plus an army of pit crew mechanics etc.

As regards the pit crew, Horace and the rest of the team were complete novices at the job. Ingenuity however cannot be bought and Horace clearly had this in abundance and took to the task like a duck to water. So much so, that The Autocar *wrote in the following week's issue, 'In racing 'experientia docet' is sometimes belied in more ways than one. For instance, at Spa last weekend, from all accounts, there was a striking contrast between the preparedness and good organisation of the Jowett pit, manned by an inexperienced but thought-taking staff, and the relatively haphazard atmosphere in quarters dripping in 'experientia.'*

Clearly this was Yorkshire ingenuity at its very best. Nice one Horace! – NS

Monte Carlo, 1951

A rather nice little anecdote regarding Horace Grimley is detailed in the excellent book, Jowett Javelin and Jupiter – The complete story, *by Geoff McAuley and Edmund Nankivell, published in 2003 by The Crowood Press, relating to the aftermath of the 1951 Monte Carlo Rally:*

For winning the 1500cc class, the Ellison/Robinson Jupiter collected the Riviera Cup, the Coupe Cibie for the class, the Calculateur Road-ex Award for the class, the Stuart Trophy and, with Ken Wharton, the Tyresoles Challenge Cup (for the best performance by a member of the Monte Carlo Rally British Competitors' Club, irrespective of tyres). The top three Jowetts together won the *l'Action Automobile* Challenge for the highest three placed cars of the same make in the 1500cc class.

Ellison and Robinson donated the cup to Jowett, and were promised a replica each. Expenses for the rally could be claimed back but had to be submitted to Norman Snell, the Company Secretary, who was noted for his stinginess. Horace Grimley warned Ellison, '…put your expenses up a bit, because Snell will knock them down again.' When the replica cups arrived they were two inches high!

Test Driving the Prototype Jupiter GKU764 during April 1950, drivers were Charles Grandfield and Horace Grimley

This account was by way of an internal memo dated 20 April 1950, dictated by Charles Grandfield, with copies being sent to Mr Woodhead, Mr Poole, Mr Mayall, Horace Grimley and Reg Korner. This memo was in fact the late Reg Korner's carbon copy and was barely legible, it was deciphered by John Blaze and published in the Jupiter Owner's Auto Club magazine By Jupiter *in issues 3 and 4 1993.*

I have decided to include this, as Horace Grimley was heavily involved with the testing of the car and this report. Also, as Charles Grandfield was instrumental in the racing of the Jupiter, and was in the pits with Horace at Le Mans in 1950. Clearly, without this research work being carried out on GKU764 the Jupiter GKW111 would not have been ready for the 1950 Le Mans race; also various mechanical alterations were made in time for the race, which helped in the record-breaking run. GKU764 was in fact chassis number EO/SA/5, exported to Canada on 19 July 1950. It had the straked front and rear wings which did not appear in the production cars, due to the cost of manufacture. The car has since been restored to her original specifications and now resides in Cornwall. – NS

ROUTE – Bradford, Huddersfield, Oldham, Manchester, Northwich, Chester, Wrexham, Oswertry, Welshpool, Llanfair, Newtown, Llanidloes, Dyffrun, Devilsbridge, Yspytty-yetwyth,

Horace Grimley at the wheel of the race-ready 1950 Le Mans Jupiter at the Jowett factory in Idle. The car would later be driven by Tommy Wise and Tom Wisdom to the first of three consecutive class wins at Le Mans. (JCC)

Another shot of Horace Grimley (left) with Roy Lunn (right) standing behind the 1950 Le Mans Jupiter. At the demise of Jowett in 1953 Roy went to work at Ford in the USA and worked on the Mustang. He was to see success at Le Mans again with the GT40. (JCC)

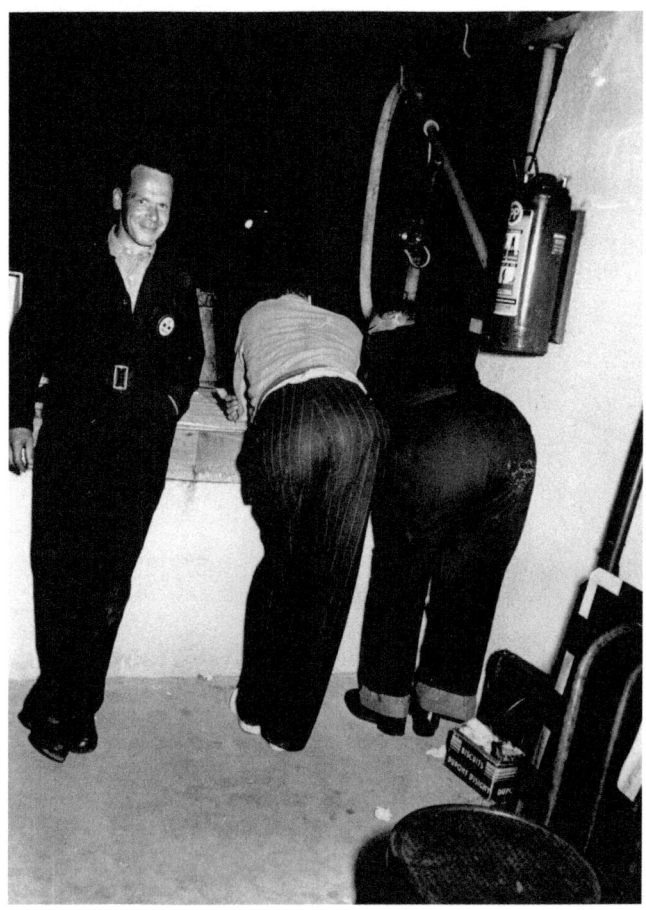

Horace Grimley in the pits area at Le Mans in 1950 together with a couple of other Jowett bums! (JCC)

Tregaron, Llanpeter, Llandovery, Brecon, Abergavenny, Chepstow, Beachley, Austferry, Bristol, Bridgewater, Watchet, Lynton, Barnstaple, Bideford, Bude, Camelford, Launceston, Okehampton, Exeter, Lyme-Regis, Dorchester, Wimborne, Romsey, Havant, Arundel, Brighton, Hastings, Rye, New Romney, Hythe, Folkestone, Dover, Dunkirk, Hesdin, Abbeville, Rouen, Alencon, Le Mans, Tours, Chateau-Roux, Limougs, Uzerche, Souillac, Cahore, Montauban, Toulouse, Carcasson, Rabonne, Sete, Montpellier, Mimes, Avignon, Montelemar, Valance, Lyon, Macon, Chalon-sur-Saun, Auxerre, Paris, Beauville, Abbeville, Boulogne, Calais, Dunkirk.

6 April 1950 The test commenced at 11.10, the weather was fine and we arrived at Llandovery at 19.30 hours, having covered 252 miles at a running time of six hours and twenty-three minutes, representing an average speed of 40.5mph.

7 April We left Llandovery at 8.53 and motored South East to the River Severn, which was crossed at Austferry. We then continued motoring along the coastal roads through Somerset, Devon and Cornwall, finally going inland from Bude to Exeter, where we arrived at 19.00 hours, having covered a distance of 319.2 miles in a total running time of 7.06 hours, representing an average speed of 45mph.

8 April We left Exeter at 9.12 and continued by the South Coast road passing through Dorchester, Wimborne & Brighton to Dover, where we arrived at 18.55 hours, having covered a total distance of 285.85 miles in an actual running time of six hours fifty minutes, representing an average speed of 42mph.

9 April	We crossed from Dover on the night ferry and left Dunkirk at 8.51 hours, when we motored due South via Abberville and Rouen to Le Mans where we arrived at 18.05 hours, covering total a distance of 307 miles in an actual driving time of six hours twenty-nine minutes, representing an average speed of 47.5mph.
10 April	The morning was spent investigating the race circuit and in concluding the necessary negotiations for accommodation for the Race period. A number of circuits were made of the course, and we left Le Mans at 13.40 hours whence we continued motoring South via Tours and Limougs to Cahors, arriving there at 22.30 hours, having covered a distance of 348 miles in six hours twenty-seven minutes representing an average speed of 54mph.
11 April	We left Cahors at 8.35 and headed for the Mediterranean Coast via Toulouse and Carcasson. We struck the coast at Sete and proceeded North via Avignon to Valance, arriving there at 19.45 hours, having covered 393.6 miles in eight hours two minutes, representing an average speed of 50mph.
12 April	We left Valance at 8.45 and continued motoring North via Lyons and Chalon-sur-Saun to Paris, where we arrived at 18.30 hours, having covered 405.2 miles in eight hours forty-eight minutes, representing an average speed of 46mph.
13 April	We left Paris for the coast at 13.40 hours and travelled via Beauvais and Boulogne to Dunkirk, arriving at 19.30 hours, having covered 223.2 miles in four hours fifty-five minutes, representing an average speed of 45mph.
14 April	We crossed from Dunkirk to Dover on the night ferry and left Dover at 6.55 hours. Some time was spent at Albermarle Street *(The London showrooms – NS)* and we then proceeded North to Bradford, arriving there at 16.00 hours, having covered a distance for the day of 318.9 miles in seven hours fifteen minutes, representing an average speed of 44mph.

It will be observed from the above that the lowest daily average speed for the whole trip was 40.5mph, and the highest was 54mph, giving an average speed for the whole journey of 46mph, which means that the car must have been driven at almost its maximum speed for very large stretches of the journey.

The total mileage covered was 2,888 miles.

The total amount of petrol used was 93.485 gallons, giving an overall fuel consumption of 31mpg

The amount of oil used was 0.75 of a gallon, giving an overall oil consumption of 3,850 miles to the gallon.

The weight of passengers and luggage carried on the car was 450lbs.

OBSERVATIONS – The points requiring attention noted in the last paragraph of the previous report had all been rectified prior to commencing this test. *(NB. I have not seen a copy of the notes from the first test drive, so am not aware of the remedial action which was carried out after it. – NS)* During the above running, the following additional points have been noted:

1) In spite of the steering castor having been increased to something in the order of 4½ degrees there is still surprisingly small amount of return action on the steering. It is also noted that a considerable number of road shocks were being transmitted to the steering rack and pinion. It is felt that the rack must be positively located against radial movement since not only would this prevent a large amount of pinion shock, but would also stop any tendency towards the rack and pinion binding due to the rack being rotated and forced into closer mesh with the pinion.
2) The near side rear bumper bracket creates considerable noise due to it fouling the rear mud-wing and some clearance is necessary around this point.

3) The fan unscrewed and fouled the radiator at Chester. It is imperative that the new design of fan which is not located on a screwed thread is introduced as soon as possible on both the Javelin and Jupiter, since the present method of attachment is neither good from a balance or security angle.
4) The car is much better to handle with the hood down, although this will be further considerably improved when a bench seat has been fitted.
5) There is a slight suggestion of propeller shaft vibration at 80mph, and some attention should be given to that point.
   It will be necessary when these cars are being produced in the factory for particular attention to be paid to the prop shaft balance and it will be probably advisable to acquaint Messrs Hardy Spicer of this fact.
6) The suspension is infinitely better than on the Scottish section of the trip and it is considered that the increased bump clearance is now satisfactory. It is felt that the bump rubbers at the rear could do with being a little stiffer.
7) As a result of the better suspension, it has been noted that the tendency to break away on a corner is much improved due to the better adhesion resulting in the suspension change.
8) The gearbox is not satisfactory in third gear, and tends to slip out on a very long pull.
9) The lights on the oil and water gauges are far too bright and diffuser strips are necessary around these instruments.
10) The RAC badge fouls the front wing on lifting the bonnet, the paint will require re-touching and the bonding strip renewing locally due to this.
11) It is apparent that from the limited amount of use the hood has already had, that the method of securing it to the body by a number of 'Lift the Dot' fasteners is not satisfactory, approximately fifteen of these have to be released in order to collapse or erect the hood and it is felt that the hood should be permanently fixed to the body with a tonneau cover over the top of it.
12) The engine is very susceptible to the type of fuel used and the degree of tune carried out on it, it will be absolutely necessary to run it on a fuel of not less than 78 octane if anything like a good performance is to be obtained. The most effective mixture was found to be 30 per cent Benzole, the remainder being standard pool. On the Continent, however, there is a leaded fuel available known as 'Supercarburant' which is very satisfactory and gave no sign of pinking, although it was felt the power was not quite up to that obtained with the Benzole mixture. It should be borne in mind, however, that the engine was tuned on the test bed to a Benzole mixture so that an equivalent power could probably be obtained on a leaded fuel if the engine was tuned for it.
13) The extended drip channels on the front scuttle fouled on the bonnet radius and tend to squeak.
14) The degree of tyre wear would appear to be fairly consistent all round, although the rate of wear for the car is high, which we put down as being due to the high speed cornering which has been carried out. This would seem to be borne out with our experience at Spa where we completely wore out two sets of tyres in twenty-four hours of fast motoring.
15) The rear over-riders require reducing in length underneath the bumper, since they foul on the slightest slope.
16) There is a suggestion that the oil temperature, which has remained low throughout the test, is not an accurate indication as there may be cavitation at the end of the cooler where the take-off point is. A check should be carried out on our test bed to make sure that the thermometer bulb is in the correct position.
17) It is felt that the steering wheel could be considerably improved; it is heavy and shows a tendency for the spokes to creep in the rim when subjected to high loads. The particular wheel fitted to the car required checking to see that no breakage or weld between the spokes and the rim has occurred, also that the wheel hub is not fretting on the steering column key.

18) The driving position for the taller driver is not ideal. There is a lack of support under the knee and some thought must be given to improving this. It is felt that the scuttle could, with advantage, be taken 1' or 1½' further forward, so that the steering column could be inclined at a more acute angle which will have the effect of lifting the wheel position relative to the driver's lap and will allow more freedom.
19) The security of the hood would now appear to be quite satisfactory and it would also appear that the effect of having the hood down is to reduce the maximum speed by approximately 4 or 5mph.
20) The maximum speed obtained on this run would be something slightly in excess of 90mph, and the effect of fitting the 4.5 to 1 ratio axle does not appear to have been at all beneficial, in fact, on the long and straight roads of France it is considered that the 4.1 to 1 ratio would have been more suitable. This condition will apply in America and it is recommended that the production versions should be fitted with an axle of 4.1 to 1 ratio.
21) The 9' brakes have proved very satisfactory throughout the test, and on this part only one brake adjustment has been necessary. It is therefore considered that no fears may be held on their account prior to our change to the 10' version.
22) The front of the rear wing requires a stainless steel guard since it tends to be very badly chipped by stones thrown from the front wheels.
23) The accelerator pressure is considered to be too high, especially at full throttle openings, and it is advised that the ratio of the throttle linkage should be revised to give a lighter pedal pressure, which will result in a lighter throttle return spring being fitted.
24) It is apparently essential that the steering rack is lubricated at approximately 1,000 miles intervals, and it is considered essential that this lubrication should be in the form of oil and not grease, since this introduces such an excessive amount of drag which acts as a deterrent to any return action to the steering geometry. The clamping ring fractured at approximately 1,000 miles, and this component requires stiffening.
25) An occasion arose to change the tyres on the front wheels and it was apparent that the balance of the wheel and tyre assembly is very important since after fitting the front wheels with a pair of unbalanced tyres it was found with speeds above 70mph the vibration from the out of balance force in the front wheels was most disturbing. It will be necessary for Production Department to procure some form of wheel and tyre balancing equipment and all cars must be sent out with completely balanced front wheel assemblies.
26) Whatever type of seat is fitted, it must be designed so that it cannot come off the runners. On one occasion, the seats at present fitted came off the runners and much valuable time was spent in re-fitting them.
27) A slight amount of play has developed to the off side rack ball joint, the reason for this should be investigated.
28) The rear of the body is too flexibly mounted and it is apparent when travelling over bad French roads that the tail of the car is moving about in an uncontrolled fashion. A type of mounting must be provided at the rear, which limits the movement of the tail, as the present soft rubber bobbins are not satisfactory.
29) Before any other car from this Company is sent on a Continental tour, it is essential that the headlights are converted to Continental dipping. It is bad enough to use white lights, but this combined with incorrect dipping is tantamount to suicide at the hands of a French lorry driver.
30) The rubber gloves surrounding the rear bumper brackets require securing by Bostik compound to the body.
31) There was a tendency after 1,000 miles for the brakes to grab, and the shoes need investigating in regard to this.

32) The hood front support frames when in the folded position fouls the back of the front seats when these are in the rearmost position. This caused serious damage to the trim of the back of the front seats. This point requires rectifying on the car before the bench seat is fitted.
33) The operation of the horn relay was erratic towards the latter part of the journey, and this component obviously requires attention.

Summarising the above points, I would say that the test has on the whole been very satisfactory and the car, considering it is a prototype has done extremely well. The main points that require attention are:

1) The steering assembly from the angle of positive location for the rack and lubrication of same, and the method of securing the housing in the frame.
2) The hood so that it is easier to erect and there is not so much messing about with fasteners etc.
3) Flexibility at the rear of the body.
4) The introduction of the bench seat, with the possibility of setting the steering column approximately 1' nearer the centre line of the car.
5) Make sure the oil temperature indicated is accurate, since at the moment it appears to be abnormally low.

If the above points are attended to on the car in question, it is quite allowable for this vehicle to go to America as a demonstration car, and it is expected that these points can be corrected in the next ten days.

I think it would be advisable, however, to inform our American agents that the two cars they have should not at the moment be sold, but should be regarded as prototype demonstration models.

A complete re-designed steering rack and pinion should be sent out as soon as possible for the car they already have, together with information regarding the alteration to the rear suspension of the body. Also information should be provided as to the re-setting of the front torsion bars and the shortening of the shock absorber distance piece so as to give greater bump clearance.

With the above points incorporated, I would consider we should go right ahead and build 25 cars. During this period, alterations to the body will be put in hand so as to ensure that future cars have the wider body with the more comfortable disposition of the steering wheel. Design and experimental work is in hand covering all these points.

Horace died in 1971 and his obituary appeared in the October 1971 Jowetteer *and was short to say the least, and to me he deserved a much larger write-up:*

It is with deep regret that I have to record the passing of one of our Vice Presidents, Mr A. Horace Grimley.

Horace Grimley was with Jowett Cars from 1921 to 1954, 28 of those years were as Chief Experimental and Development Engineer. He then stayed on with the plant, transferring to International Harvester Co. of Great Britain until he retired this year. Horace Grimley was at the centre of all that evolved from the Jowett Company and in fact was one of the pillars of the Company.

On behalf of the Club the Committee extends to Mrs Grimley and family, their deepest sympathy and condolences in respect of their bereavement. 9 October 1971.

A more detailed tribute from Norman Snell, the Company Secretary of Jowett Cars Ltd was also published in the Jowett Car Club Yearbook *for 1971:*

The news of the sudden death of Horace Grimley must have come as a shock to all those who knew him, as he had apparently made a good recovery from the operation he had undergone earlier in the year. He was looking forward to celebrating both the recovery from illness and his recent retirement, and had every reason to expect many happy and peaceful years after the stress of fifty years in industry, but it was not to be.

The whole of his working life was spent in engineering – all in one factory but with two companies. He came to Jowetts from school and after initial training spent the remainder of his time with the company in experimental and development work. He was involved in the making of all models produced by the company from the early 1920s to the cessation of production in 1954, and when the company moved to Birstall he remained with International Harvesters to deal with design and production of tractors. During the war he took on, in addition to his ordinary work, the control of the works Fire Brigade, which he made into a most efficient unit, winning many events when competing with other industrial brigades, but which, fortunately for the company, never had to tackle any major outbreak at the factory. This duty meant that, together with the chief ARP officer, he spent weeks on end at the works, and must have been almost a visitor to his family.

He rendered yeoman service when during the early 1950s he became a member of the Works Production Committee, which consisted of the senior executives, and met once a month to discuss production and service problems and to decide on the action to be taken to overcome them.

Horace always gave of his best, but was far happier doing the job than talking about it, but when the need arose he could present his views in a clear and concise manner. He was one of the kindest and most helpful people I have ever known.

He will be sadly missed by his many friends and not least the club. His knowledge of Jowett products was equalled by few and surpassed by none.

Things improved, however, in 1989, when Harry Brierley, who at the time was the club's technical information officer, wrote a potted history of Horace for the May 1989 Jowetteer:

The subject of the Horace Grimley Award was discussed at the EC meeting in April and I was asked to prepare something for *The Jowetteer* in view of the fact that a good number of the members had never even heard of the name. This month I will write solely about Horace and return to the subject of the award next month.

It seems to me desperately sad that although we made quite an effort to perpetuate the name of Horace Grimley in the founding of an award, we have clearly allowed his name to slip from the memory in quite an unaccountable way. I suppose it may be a penalty of being a man of considerable humility. Nevertheless Horace Grimley was probably the most important figure in the Jowett saga – even more so than the Jowett brothers themselves.

He was in fact a nephew of the brothers and joined the firm straight from school in 1921. He remained with them through to the closure of Idle in 1954. So, not only did he encompass the days of the twin, but also the post-war cars. He was barely out of his apprenticeship when he was given the job of developing the humble little 1926 seven to break several twelve-hour records at Brooklands, one of which stood until quite recently. It was no small feat of engineering to wring lap speeds of 65mph out of such a car. The previous holders of the class twelve-hour records, Kaye Don and Captain Marendez (who died at the end of 1988 aged ninety-one), regarded the whole affair as impertinence!

Horace became development engineer and head of 'Experimental'. During the war he was also the factory fire officer, an office he regarded with great glee. Obviously he had a great respect for the old twin engine but he was a realist, and regarded it as incapable of further development after the war. In this he was proved quite correct in experiments on the CD. He approached the post-war cars with the same dedication as he did with the twins. Although suffering rather badly from travel sickness, he took part in a number of major rallies. If I remember correctly, Bill Robinson remembers him as being an expert at changing tyres on the back seat of the Javelin. He also drove a Jupiter at Silverstone, where for most of the race he was second to Clark in an HRG. In future years he believed he was second to Jim Clark, but no one had the heart to tell him that it was not that Clark! He was co-driver with Tommy Wise in a Monte Carlo Rally, and of course, was to be found with the works cars at most major events.

It used to be said that it was Horace Grimley who first devised the sort of quick lift apparatus which is now general on racing tracks, but I do not know if this is really so. He was certainly an ingenious practical engineer and our president (Gerald Palmer) once described him as the best development engineer in the North of England. He ran a Javelin for his own transport, this a left-hand drive probably because of the amount of Continental driving he did. The car still exists in the hands of Jack Mitchell who hopes to restore it one day. *(The car is still waiting; Jack sold it in 2006 in a very poor state, so it will need a great deal of work. – NS)*

He also involved himself in Club affairs and always attended the National Weekends, sometimes a concours judge. He gave questions and answer sessions to Sections which often degenerated into fascinating talks, although he denied any ability as a speaker! I remember his detailed description of the investigation of overheating in a Javelin. He went on holiday towing his caravan with thermocouples inserted all over the engine and the cooling water supplied from 5-gallon drums on the back seat.

I met him mostly at National weekends, but as I am Technical Information Officer, I used to write and ask his advice when I got stuck on matters, like how the hood on a 1922 car was fastened down. I always got a friendly, exact and helpful reply. He was a very self-effacing man, and it was typical that in the well-known picture of the 'Experimental' staff with the first Jupiter, he appears just down on the left-hand side. At the close of Jowett Cars he was very emotional, as one would expect from his total involvement with the firm. He joined International Harvesters but found an organisation on the American mould, where to be unassuming and modest is not a recipe for success. There is a testimony that he was not at all well treated and was unhappy but, characteristically he stuck with it.

He retired through ill health of a type brought on by stress in 1971. He had a stomach operation not long afterwards, but although he seemed to be in much better health after it, he died suddenly.

I have talked to many people who knew him and talked to him about the many he knew. No one has ever said a critical word of him nor he of them. If we forget all that he did for us and Jowett Cars, it would be a disgrace.

Then in the July 1989 issue of The Jowetteer *there was another tribute to Horace from Duncan Laing:*

I was pleased to read the tribute to Horace Grimley by Harry Brierley in May's edition of the *Jowetteer*. He is too often the forgotten man in Jowetts.

I first met Horace in September 1952 when I was asked to be one of the drivers for the MIRA tests. I had joined Jowetts under Charles Grandfield in October 1951 as the first of three graduate apprentices that he had taken on.

The MIRA tests were carried out at the Motor Industry Research Association's test track near Nuneaton. In 1952 the bank circuit was under construction and we used a triangular circuit on what had been a wartime airport. The tests were to prove the series 3 engine and three Javelins were driven twenty-four hours a day at an average speed of about 60mph. After five weeks or 40,000 miles, similar tests were carried out on three Jupiters.

Horace was in charge of the whole programme and we lived in caravans at the side of the track. There were nine drivers – three per car and three mechanics I think, and another graduate apprentice, John Brace, who looked after all the data and logging etc.

I do not think I have ever met such a knowledgeable automobile engineer as Horace. When not driving, during my working hours, I spent most of my time with Horace and John in the headquarters' caravan discussing and analysing the results.

That was when I was a young, inexperienced engineer and appreciated these discussions. Every topic John and I raised, Horace knew about and had very often tried or tested.

The tests were carried out scientifically and strictly under Horace's control, but he was such a pleasant person that it was like one long picnic. The tests were very satisfactory and each engine did as I remember 40,000 miles without trouble – and this was the object to test the Series 3 modifications. We did have gearbox problems but I am in no doubt that Jowett's gearbox problems were a direct result of poor quality control during manufacture, which had been transferred from Henry Meadows to Idle.

One incident near the end of the tests was on a wet Sunday afternoon when one of the drivers rolled his Jupiter. Fortunately he was unharmed but the car was badly damaged. I suggested to Horace that as we were there to test engines, we could transfer the Jupiters engine into one of the Javelins. He liked the idea and suggested it to Idle, but the feeling was that the tests had already cost the earth and as the 'Javelin GT' was not marketed the tests could not be justified. A pity.

After the tests I worked in Service at Clayton, then at Experimental directly under Horace and finally in the Drawing Office. I used to get a lift home at night from Horace in his LHD Javelin to my digs in Manninghan Lane. Here again Horace's conversation was always interesting and informative.

It is typical of the man that he never once mentioned that he was related to the Jowett brothers.

I left Jowetts in October 1953. By this time the supply of bodies from Briggs had dried up and the last Javelins were being assembled from bodies which had been lying outside the factory for some months.

I know how disappointed Horace was, but he never lost his dedication to the company. To me Horace was Jowetts.

BILL ROBINSON

Bill Robinson was the proprietor of Mill Brow Garage, Dalton, Cumbria, and like several other garage proprietors, competed in Jowetts in various events including the Monte Carlo Rally. – NS

Tulip Rally 1949
Bill Robinson
(Taken from an unidentified newspaper clipping. – NS)

Furness team still in the Tulip Rally

The only Furness team still left in the Tulip Rally of Holland reached the finish at Noordwyk yesterday without loss of marks – one of sixty-four teams to do so – and so will compete in the braking and acceleration tests today.

The team comprises of Messrs. Bill Robinson, Les Hall and Tom Ward. Mr Robinson's father, Mr Herschall Robinson, of Dalton received this message late yesterday afternoon: 'Arrived in Noordwyk safe. No loss of marks. Keep your fingers crossed for tomorrow.'

The other Furness team – Messrs Towers Leck, Bert West and Tom Iddon, driving a Jowett Javelin, as was the Robinson team, went out with engine trouble this side of Paris on Monday.

Bill Robinson poses with his Javelin prior to the start of the 1949 Tulip Rally. (JCC)

The 1950 Monte Carlo Rally
Bill Robinson Remembers
(Originally published in the Jowett Car Club publication *Jowett Sport* No. 5.)

The following recollections have been taken from a tape-recorded interview between Bill Robinson and Mike Cheavers. On this 'Monte' Bill was using his own Javelin. It was only when he turned to Jupiters did his entries become 'works assisted'.

JTJ34 was a standard Jowett Javelin with the small headlights; it was a 1948 model, fitted with a few spotlights and louvers on the bonnet, which were fitted for the previous Monte.

The run from Glasgow to Dover was uneventful, thence to Boulogne and Paris. Before we got to Paris we started having bad misfiring and we thought it was ignition trouble, and changed the plugs, but it was no better. In Paris we spoke to Bob Ellison, another Javelin competitor. He said he thought it was the distributor, and he had a spare one, which he let us borrow. As soon as we left Paris we pulled into a very well lit garage and changed the whole issue, but by Nevers the car was performing so badly that I was afraid of doing some damage to the transmission. By now it had started snowing, and we had checked in with time to spare, so we took the carburettors off to find both chambers half full of water. How it had run under these circumstances I just do not know. Taking out one of the jets I dropped it in the snow. With frozen fingers and only the light from torches it was eventually found and the carbs put back together after which it really went well.

After Lyons we came to a little village called Die (pronounced Dee) where there was quite a crowd when we arrived, due to a competitor's car and a lorry becoming jammed while trying to pass each other in the narrow street. It was impossible to get round because on one side of the road, behind the houses, was a cliff and on the other, a river. However, just on entering Die, I noticed a bridge crossing the river, so I reversed up and crossed the bridge. I then asked a man, in our very good French, if there was another route. Following the directions given, through snow that was 2ft deep, we crossed a field, in the top corner of which we saw a 'bridge'. Well, this bridge, believe me, was enough to give anybody a heart attack! It was a flimsy wooden structure across the river, which must have been 30 or 40 yards wide. It turned out to be a cattle crossing, but my friends, Towers and Tommy assured me it was OK. I backed up for about 50 yards and took a run at it; I'm here now so I must have got across it!

There were a series of down hills after Grasse with corners all looking the same, and the only way I could pull up was by running into the gravel at the side of the road – either side. I was doing this regularly until I came to one in particular, which I found did not allow me to get into the gravel because there was a dip on the right-hand side and an outcrop on the left. In front the ice was like polished glass and I couldn't stop. We almost managed to get round it, but then the back end started to slide towards a drop of several thousand feet. The car started sliding slowly round and the back nearly caught up with the front! I thought we were all going over the top. I was on full lock left, and suddenly the wheels right on the edge started biting into a little bit of gravel and the car came round. Towers, who was sitting in the back, said 'well held Bill!' We had not got very far when Tommy, who was sat next to me said, 'Tell you what, there's a bit of a funny smell in this car' and Towers in the back said very quietly, 'It's all right for you two b******s in the front, you can only smell it, I'm sat in it'!

After that things got a lot better and we came into Grasse and eventually on to Monte Carlo. Unfortunately we were a few minutes late, and were outside our time. With all the bad luck we had experienced, we had just not made up enough time.

Bill's local paper, The Mail, wrote an article on his entry before the event; this is what they said:

Monte Carlo Rally 1950
Bill Robinson

Three-Man Furness team in Monte Carlo Rally

At 5 p.m. on Sunday entry number 117, a Jowett Javelin with already 35,000 miles under its bonnet, will slide over the start line in Glasgow in the twentieth Monte Carlo Rally with almost 2,000 miles of treacherous mid-winter roads to traverse before reaching its goal – and with it will go the good wishes of the many motoring enthusiasts in the Furness district for its team of three drivers, all from Furness.

The team, competing against most of the crack drivers of Europe, comprises Mr Bill Robinson of Mill Brow Garage, Dalton, Mr Towers Leck, public works contractor, Springfield Road, Ulverston and Mr Tommy Harrison, local manager of Edward Box & Co Ltd.

It is one of 75 British teams out of a record total of 308 starters.

The object of the rally is to cover the 1,951 miles from Glasgow to Monaco – the rally is organised by the AC de Monaco in conjunction with the International Sporting Club – at a set speed from control to control which are about 250 miles apart. Slowest average speed must be no less than 50kph (about 31mph) and the fastest speed allowed is 65kph (about 41mph). No allowances are made for stoppages for food, repairs or mishaps, marks are knocked off for any delays, and competitors may not carry on any saving of time from one stage into the next, except on the final lap.

Apart from Glasgow there are five other starting points Lisbon, Oslo, Stockholm, Florence and Monte Carlo itself, with the most tortuous and dangerous stretch near the end where competitors have to drive down the Rhone Valley – almost perpetually fog-bound, and thence over a succession of passes in the Easses Alps which are likely to be frost-bound and almost certainly deep snow.

Bill Robinson at the start of the 1950 Monte Carlo Rally. (JCC)

At Mr Robinson's Dalton home I found the team of three putting the final touches to the preparations for the four days and three nights of non-stop driving which are then followed by acceleration and braking tests on the Wednesday afternoon – when they are due to arrive in Monte Carlo – and regularity speed tests on the Friday on a 10½-mile mountain circuit above the principality's only city.

The car is the one which Messrs Robinson and Leck used in the Tulip Rally of Holland last year, and included in the mass of kit is de-ditching gear and two spare wheels as well as fur-lined suits for the team.

'We have prepared for the worst and are hoping for the best' said Mr Leck adding that he thought they had prepared for every eventuality.

The Furness trio are to leave Dalton at about nine o'clock on Saturday morning so that they will be able to hand the car – a standard model – over to the scrutineers before 5 p.m. at Glasgow.

Once started their route and check points are Doncaster, Folkestone, Boulogne, Luxembourg, Amsterdam (via Liege, Benlo and Arnhem), The Hague, Brussels (via Antwerp), Rheims, Paris, Nevers, Lyons, Rhone Valley to Valence over the Basses Alps to Digne, Grasse, Nice and finally Monte Carlo, where the Furness team is due to arrive at 4.20 p.m. on Wednesday.

Interesting point regarding contact is that the rally is to be reported on from point to point at regular intervals by the BBC Light programme, so that Messrs Robinson, Leck and Harrison's progress may be noted from that programme, although the commentators might dwell on the big names in the event.

The final broadcast – at 9.10 a.m. on Saturday week – will give the final placings in the rally, and it might be that the local team will figure in that broadcast – they certainly will not in the first programme which takes to the air at 5.15 p.m. on Sunday, just eight minutes after they cross the start line!

Monte Carlo Rally 1951
Bill Robinson

French went wild with excitement – Mr Robinson reports on the Monte Carlo Rally
Back from his successful Monte Carlo Rally trip, Mr W.H. Robinson of Dalton, reports two highlights, the first when he crossed the St Julien Pass by mistake, after having been warned to keep clear of it, the second when he overhauled a more powerful car during the speed test on the Monaco circuit.

On Tuesday Mr Robinson left for London to take part in a television broadcast on Wednesday with his co-driver Mr R. Ellison of St Annes.

The crossing of the St Julien Pass on the Puy-Valence section saw Mr Robinson blaze the trail for the other competitors, as his car was the first over the pass.

The previous control had warned them to avoid the more direct route over the pass, as snow drifts were known to be upto 13ft deep.

However, the wrong turning found the car headed over the pass following a track made by a cart, and by rushing some of the worst parts in order to keep going, the car was safely through.

Worse conditions, however, were encountered in the section from Digne to Grasse, for a while the road over the pass had been covered with firm snow, here the roads had between six inches and a foot of icy slush, and it was difficult to keep going.

'It was really tough there,' commented Mr Robinson, 'and had the average speed been any higher than it was (31mph) a lot of the competitors must have been knocked out. Many of them just managed to make the controls in time. Had the rally been just a little later things could have been very difficult for the snow was very heavy, with flakes the size of dollars, and there was a gale of a wind. Had the drifts had time to build up we would have been in trouble'.

On one occasion, passing a point where another driver was cutting his way out of an entanglement of fallen telegraph wires. Mr Robinson could hear the wires breaking as he forced his car through; fortunately no damage was done to the car.

In the final speed test on the Monaco circuit Mr Robinson started half a minute behind a four and a half litre Delahaye – three times the power of his Jowett Jupiter – but passed him on the fourth of the two minute laps. As he did so the French supporters went wild with excitement.

Mr Robinson is uncertain of the exact number of prizes he and Mr Ellison won, their principal prize was The Riviera Cup for winning the 1500cc class to which they added the manufacturer's team prize for their category, the Monte Carlo Drivers' Club prize, shared awards with Ken Wharton for the best British entry and other awards from trade interests.

And a later report reads:

Provisional placings in the Monte Carlo Rally made Mr W.H. Robinson, the Dalton driver, winner in his class and sixth in the entire rally, tying with another for the honour of being the highest placed British entry.

Mr Robinson, who started in Glasgow driving one of the three works Jowett Jupiters in partnership with Mr R. Ellison of St Annes, gained the praise of the critics in the handling of his car in the final test on Sunday, when the best 50 competitors took part in high speed tests over the tortuous Monaco Grand Prix circuit.

Publication of the provisional results followed completion of these tests and they showed that the rally had been won by France once again, by Trevoux in his Delahaye, who won outright in 1949 and tied for top place in 1939.

The next four places went to a Portuguese driver in a British car, an Eireann driver in a British car and two all French entries.

Then came the Ellison/Robinson Jowett tying with K. Wharton (Britain) in a Ford. This high placing among the much more powerful cars gave Jowett first place in the class for cars upto 1500cc.

Second place in the class went to G. Wilkins and R. Baxter driving another of the works Jowetts, they were placed ninth in the rally as a whole.

News of Mr Robinson's success delighted motor sports circles in Furness particularly members of Furness and District Motor Club, of which he is a member.

Results as quoted in *The Motor:* Class Results … 1500cc

1) R.F. Ellison & W.H. Robinson (Jupiter) 6th in general category.
2) G. Wilkins & R. Baxter (Jupiter) 10th in general category.
3) L. Odell & R. Marshall (Javelin) 26th in general category.

Riviera Cup (1500cc category) R.F. Ellison & W.H. Robinson (Jowett Jupiter).

Alpine International Rally 1951
Bill Robinson

Rally made road racing look easy

The Jowett car which Dalton Garage proprietor Bill Robinson and St Annes driver Robb Ellison were driving in the Alpine International Rally was almost a casualty in the first lap before it was put out with a stone through the radiator towards the end of the second leg.

During the first leg from Marseilles to Monte Carlo, as they were negotiating (by sliding round) one of the hundreds of hairpin bends, the rear off-side wheel of the car slid over the edge of a precipice, and for a split second hung sickeningly there, before the car moved forward again.

Comment of the experienced British road-racers on this year's Alpine was that the Italian Mille Milliga 1,000-mile road race with a reputation of being the fastest and most dangerous in Europe was 'chicken feed' compared to it.

Proceeding more cautiously after their narrow shave, the northern pair finished at Monte Carlo with a minute to spare.

Things went well for Robinson and Ellison on the second stage, but on the 5km stretch that had to be completed flat out, they got a very bad start as an Italian lorry driver pulled across in front of them. However they got away after vital seconds had been lost 50 yards inside the checkpoint, and averaging 80mph, at times touching 90, they gained third place in their class.

This was between Turin and Begram on the Italian autostrade, but a little further on a stone through the radiator shattered the fan and burst the radiator hose and pump. Toilet soap was stuffed into the holes in the hose, and they pulled into a garage, but language difficulties made their task hopeless, and though they got into Cortina they were well outside the time and were disqualified.

One of Bill Robinson's memories of the trip was the 70mph dash through Turin with the police waving them on, although the streets were congested with traffic and tramcars. Driving at that particular juncture he had not the time even to hoot his horn, Mr Ellison had to lean over to do that!

1951 British Empire Trophy, Douglas Isle of Man
Bill Robinson
(As detailed in several reports in *The North West Evening Mail*, 7 June 1951)

When thirty-eight-year-old Bill Robinson, Dalton Garage and coach proprietor, roars away from the starting line in the British Empire Trophy Race next Thursday, he will be driving a car largely designed by himself and built to his own specifications.

The car, a sleek green saloon, started life as a Jowett Jupiter, but in place of the usual rakish open two-seater body, Mr Robinson designed a saloon coachwork which he claims, will boost its speed and give greater acceleration. Nearly three months of work in the body shop went into its construction before the finished coachwork arrived back at the garage.

Bill, who lives at Garden Lea, Dalton, has already made a name for himself in rally circles. He won the 1500cc class and tied for sixth place in the general classification in the gruelling Monte Carlo Rally, and in the recent Tulip Rally he came seventh. He has also entered the Alpine Rally.

In next week's rally he expects to cover a course of about 130 miles and will compete with some of Britain's crack track and road racing drivers including the veteran Reg Parnell, Sydney Allard and Bob Gerrard and the brilliant young Stirling Moss.

Keen followers of the sport feel he has a good chance in his class.

13 June 1951 Robinson to have four-lap 'start'

Practising in the Isle of Man last night for the British Empire Trophy race which will take place on the Willaston circuit on the outskirts of Douglas, tomorrow, and in which he is driving a 1485cc Jowett Jupiter of his own design, W.H. Robinson (Dalton) completed several laps, his best being covered in four minutes nineteen seconds at an average speed of 53.92mph.

In tomorrow's race Robinson will start with a handicap advantage of four laps and will have to cover thirty-one circuits of the 3¾ miles course, a distance of 116 miles.

14 June 1951 Robinson in good form for today

W.H. Robinson of Dalton who is driving a 1485cc Jowett Jupiter in the British Empire Trophy race over the Willaston circuit on the outskirts of Douglas, Isle of Man, this afternoon was in good form when an *Evening Mail* representative spoke to him at the conclusion of the final practice runs last night.

'I have had a few spots of trouble,' he said, 'but I think they are all over now, and I am keenly looking forward to the race'.

Just as he was about to start practicing last night he experienced some delay through a fault in the petrol pump, but soon put it right and covered eight laps, the fastest being completed in four minutes nineteen seconds (53.92mph) thus exactly equalling his best performance on Tuesday night.

Fog covered large sections of the circuit last night, and most of the sports cars entered for the Empire Trophy had their headlights on.

The fastest amongst these cars was made by D.A. Clarke (1971cc Fraser Nash in three minutes twenty-six seconds – 67.78mph).

Spectators included Sir John Cobb, holder of the land speed record, who is one of the stewards of the meeting.

The Empire Trophy, following races for the Manx Cup and the Castletown Trophy, will begin at 3.45 p.m. today. The twenty-nine cars will be despatched in a mass start and the race will be over thirty-five laps of the 3¾-lap course.

Cars upto 1500cc capacity, which includes Robinson's car, will receive four credit laps, and cars up to 3000cc one credit lap.

15 June 1951   Robinson went out on the eleventh lap

W.H. Robinson, of Dalton, who yesterday drove a 1485cc Jowett Jupiter saloon car of his own design in the British Empire Trophy race over the Willaston circuit on the outskirts of Douglas, Isle of Man, had the misfortune to experience an engine seizure about a third of the way through the race and had to retire.

The race which was on a handicap basis was over thirty-one laps of the 3¾-mile course for cars upto 1500cc capacity, thirty-four laps for cars upto 3000cc capacity and thirty-five laps for cars over 3000cc capacity. Robinson was one of ten drivers who received a credit of four laps.

Robinson had averaged about 54mph for nearly 40 miles of the 116-mile race when it was announced that he had stopped on his eleventh lap.

The winner of the race was Stirling Moss (1971cc Fraser Nash) who with one credit lap completed thirty-four circuits in one hour fifty-seven minutes and thirty-eight seconds at an average speed of 67.27mph.

Five cars were involved in a pile-up at the Nursery Corner, Onchan, and one of the drivers, D. Clarke (Fraser Nash) was taken to Douglas Hospital where it was found that he had escaped with superficial head injuries.

1951 Alpine Rally
Bill Robinson
(North West Evening Mail, 7 July 1951)

Bill Robinson, the Dalton garage proprietor, left last night in the scarlet Jowett Jupiter two-seater which he drove to triumph in the Monte Carlo Rally, to take part in the Alpine Rally which starts next Tuesday. He will be partnered this time by Bill James of Barrow.

The Alpine Rally starts in Marseilles and the competitors drive to Milan on the first day. After that they travel to Cortina in the Dolomites, tackle the Dolomite Grand Prix course, return to Cortina and then go up to Innsbruck. From there they travel back to Chamonix and then on to Cannes.

In expectation of a gruelling drive, the Jupiter is carrying a 'double issue' of tyres and tubes.

(North West Evening Mail, 13 July 1951 – Robinson's clean sheet)

Bill Robinson of Mill Brow Garage, Dalton, who is driving a Jowett Jupiter in the Alpine Rally, reached Milan without loss of marks.

ROBERT ELLISON

Robert Ellison was the Jowett agent and garage proprietor from St Annes on Sea and drove in the Monte Carlo Rallies of 1949, 1950, 1951 and 1952. In the 1949 event he used his Javelin registered JTJ300 with Ronnie Smith and Hartley Schofield. They finished third in class and twenty-second overall. In 1950 he used his Javelin again with Hartley Schofield and Walter Mason. In 1951 he teamed up with Bill Robinson of Mill Brow Garage, Dalton as part of the works team of three Jupiters, where they won the 1500cc class, winning the Riviera Cup, coming sixth overall. In 1952 he teamed up with Walter Mason in the Farr-bodied Jupiter registered MTJ300. The car crashed near Le Puy and had to be recovered by a team of oxen. It still managed to reach Monte Carlo but too late to be classed as an official finisher.

Monte Carlo Rally 1952 ... Jupiter MTJ300
A brief history told by R.F. Ellison to Bill Jackson
(As published in the *Jowett Car Club Yearbook* for 1971)

In about May 1951, Charles Grandfield of Jowetts told me that they were not entering the 1952 Monte Carlo Rally, so if I wished to enter I would have to find my own car, but they would assist me with parts.

So I obtained a Jupiter chassis from them and approached Farr's of Blackburn to build a body for me. (Mr Farr senior was at that time President of the Lancashire Automobile Club.) It had to be a fixed head coupe; soft tops not now being allowed. The foreman body builder and myself made out some drawings and they proceeded to build the body.

They made a good job of it, but it was too heavy and they took too long to finish the work. The short tail with two spare wheels in it caused them some trouble, provisions for tools and spares was made in the doors. An extra 10-gallon petrol tank was fitted behind the seats; these seats were only light-weight things about the car. They were in frames from the spare Le Mans car (Horace Grimley found these) with Dunlopillo inside and upholstered in cloth, very comfortable. A bench seat upholstered in leather was also made (the car was later sold with this fitted). I belicve Marchel lights and Michelin tyres were fitted and a competition engine from Jowetts. (A standard engine was fitted when the car was sold.)

The car was sprayed a rich maroon, a first-class job, and the car looked very well. Incidentally, the rear window was from a Humber Hawk, the glass and the rear body panel was shaped to suit.

The car ran well, was quiet, no appreciable wind noise; steering column chatter, prevalent on many Jupiters, was absent; it was, however, rather too heavy, so acceleration was down slightly. The maximum speed, however, was about 95mph, according to the speedo.

The car competed in the 1952 Monte Carlo Rally, Walter Mason, a St Annes solicitor, was co-driver.

We had an uneventful run through England, Wales and Northern France, however before Nevers snow came down very heavily so we fitted the spare wheels, complete with chains. (I had never used chains before in rallies, I would probably have done better without them.) However, near Saint Fleur, I over slid the car on a downhill right-hand corner and as there was no bank or wall we went over the edge, turning over twice and finally coming to rest on a ledge about 8ft wide. The roof was pushed down and the screen was broken, otherwise the car seemed OK and we were completely undamaged. We had dropped about 30ft down a near vertical bank, so we decided we could do nothing about the matter and we would wait in the car until daylight.

However, we had just settled in when a great shower of snow and stones etc. descended on the roof, followed by the front end of a Traction Avant Citroen, with the wheels doing apparently 5,000rpm over our heads. We abandoned ship with great haste, helped to push the Citroen back on to the road, then, as two more French cars made a forced landing just over the Jupiter, I decided to try and save the Jupiter from annihilation and waved all cars down to a safe speed with our large torch. An English crew came past very slowly in large Rolls and thanked me profusely in rather flowery French.

Meanwhile, my comrade had gone away to make a sortie to round up some natives if any could be found. He came back in about half an hour later, having found a village and café with natives and a local brew, a cross between Rum and a Cognac. Walter said he found it was quite palatable after the first half-dozen. He brought me some hot coffee laced with this brew; it had a considerable effect.

Just as dawn was breaking natives started to appear, and as far as we could make out from gesticulations and their local dialect, one of their members had gone to get the gear to extract the car. We assumed a tractor, but when the gear did arrive it was six oxen! The owner of the oxen attached them to the front of the Jupiter with a chain. He flicked the ear of the leader with a long wand (there was no bridal or such contrivance), then slowly walked them up the near vertical bank and the car followed, all in about one minute flat. We suitably imbursed the natives and then proceeded on the coldest run in my life, no windscreen, about 15 degrees of frost and 3ft of snow.

We went to a body builder I knew at Tain L' Hermitage, they immediately set about straightening the car, fitting the screen etc, while I fixed the bent steering. The car was ready again in about twenty-four hours, so we went on to Monte Carlo, arriving a day late, but we went on to the prize giving and reception.

Back in St Annes we fixed the car mechanically and Farr's body builders finished the body repairs and completely resprayed the car. I ran it for a while and then decided to sell it, putting it back into standard form again. The extra fuel tank was taken out and a production engine was fitted again.

A St Annes businessman bought the car for his daughter, Miss Audrey Cook. She ran the car for twelve to eighteen months and then her dad sold the car. Since then I have never heard of the car until contacted by Bill Jackson.

Bill Jackson was the press officer of the Jowett Car Club at the time this account was written in 1971 (the position I have held since 1984). The car is still in first class condition and was owned by Frank Cooke for many years. Sadly, Frank died in October 2008 and his daughter, Sheila Rigg, now owns the car. – NS

JOYCE LEAVENS ... and details of six rallies in which she took part

These rally reports were prepared for me by Joyce Leavens, after I had been in correspondence with her regarding her rally days. I published some of these in Jowett Sport No.6, but this is the full collection she sent me. She competed with her husband and her brother initially, but also made up a ladies team with Nancy Mitchell and Bea Norman, which proved to be very successful. She would later team up as navigator with Nancy Mitchell as driver in the works Ford team. – NS

The Monte Carlo Rally 1950

Berry Leavens (real name Charles), bought our first Jowett Javelin in 1949, which was registered JLJ323, in duck-egg blue. The first rally we entered was the 1950 Monte Carlo Rally. We were lucky to be accepted as only a limited number of British entries were allowed. It was our innocent effort to take part in the 1949 Monte in a motor caravan (designed by ourselves from a war-time Humber wireless truck) had produced a promise for an entry the following year.

Being new to the game we enticed my brother, Hal O'Hara Moore, to make a third in the team. That was just as well as the whole event turned out to be a terrific adventure. The task was to cover approximately 2,000 miles, with stops at controls, at an average speed of 33mph.

We started from Glasgow, number 77, with Berry driving, at 4.27 p.m., on Sunday 22 January. I caused a certain amount of interest, being one of the few ladies taking part, and was dubbed by the press 'The Farmer's wife' (Berry and I were farming in Dorset). The drive to Dover was reasonably uneventful apart from some ice in places and fog in the Midlands. Mostly we kept at a steady 55mph, as previously decided between ourselves.

The Luxembourg control was the joining centre for the routes from all the different starting places. It was a bedlam. Crews waiting to check out; others clamouring to check in quickly so as to go and get food; only two glamorous girls to cope with the lot!

Driving through the night to Amsterdam it was cold and frosty, but the car was not pulling well. The engine kept slowing down, and then picking up again. The other two blamed me for bad driving, but that wasn't the cause. Eventually we stopped and Berry got out and had a look under the bonnet. He slipped on black ice, but could not find anything wrong. After a few more miles of the same trouble he had another look under the bonnet, and this time he found it. The carburettor was covered in hoarfrost so that the petrol couldn't vaporise properly! Fast driving pulled the cold air in to freeze on the carburettor, but each time the engine slowed down its warmth thawed it. Closing the radiator muff completely solved that.

Paris, the following evening, and prepared a lavish buffet in a building like a small palace. Champagne, coffee, sandwiches, croissants and fruit were heaped on us by more glamorous females, who were in great contrast to the grubby tired-looking rally competitors.

Then off again, this time police motorcyclists were laid on to lead the cars two by two out of Paris. Ours must have been jet-propelled. In his wake we shot through the city, twisting and turning through the traffic, which miraculously opened up for us, frequently touching 70mph, and crossing red traffic lights without a qualm, amazingly without hooting or siren. At one moment a women was crossing the road as our motorcyclist roared up. She took one look, and then stood stock still with hands over her eyes. He shot past on one side of her and we on the other! At the outskirts of the city we drew up alongside the second car to find the driver, like Berry, completely exhilarated with the thrill; his poor passengers and ours were ashen white and almost fainting.

Light snow was falling at Nevers when we left at 1.24 a.m. on Wednesday 25th. We checked out of the control then let the tyres down to 22lbs all round. It was my turn to drive, with Hal resting, but I was not used to the slippery surfaces and after one or two wobbles and a nice skid, Hal was easily persuaded to take over. He was much more used to driving in snow than either Berry or I, soon after the fun began. Snow was falling quite heavily, but nothing daunted Hal, who drove as fast as he could see, seldom less than 40mph, often well over. We passed car after car with no tendency to skid as long as the wheels were being driven and the torque kept on. In one village we caught up with an enormous lorry almost completely filling the narrow street. A rally car was endeavouring to pass it on the left without success. Did Hal slow down? No! He merely edged the Javelin over the right-hand side climbing up onto the pavement. We passed the lorry and the houses with only fractions of an inch to spare, just squeezing back onto the road in time to avoid a flight of stone steps jutting out onto the pavement in front of us.

For several miles all went well, until we came to the foot of a long steep hill dotted with red lights. They were the tail lights of lorries and cars stuck in the snow all across the road, so we couldn't get through. Then we had to stop and put on the chains, an awkward job as we were tired and fumbly. Meanwhile space had cleared in the road ahead and Berry was sent ahead on foot to see if we could get on. Starting off again and not wanting to stop on the hill, Berry had to run and jump into the back, being hauled in through the open door as the car caught up with him. Our troubles were not over as the chains kept flapping against the mudguards. One by one the tensioners snapped, which meant stopping to remove them, continuing with chains only and no tensioners. Then some time later a clank, clank, made us stop. One of the chains had broken off and wrapped itself round the rear axle. Unwinding this and loosening the catch of the other chain, which had iced up, was not an easy or quick operation. The result was we checked in at Lyons twenty-seven minutes late.

Once more we set off; by now it was getting light and the snow had stopped falling. The road was bumpy and rough and it was not long before the car decided to perform a dance sliding from side to side across the road. It was a puncture! Were we getting cheesed off? With bleary eyes we changed the wheel and continued on to Valance. Entering the narrow streets of one of the villages on the route a policeman encouragingly waved us on then hastily slowed us down again. There was a right-angled turning to be negotiated. I, now driving, did my best to round it by changing down and accelerating, but instead of flicking neatly round the corner the Javelin merely slid straight ahead on the slippery surface towards a very solid looking brick wall facing

The 1950 Monte Carlo Rally: Hal O'Hara Moore driving, Joyce Leavens is passing out the passports from the front passenger seat at the Dutch border. (Foto Borgers/JCC)

us. Everyone watching shouted in horror. We waited for the crunch of crumpling coachwork, but nothing happened. A pile of snow in front of the bumper had saved us by half an inch from hitting the wall. Colour returned to our faces. Backing away we could see the imprint of the car in the snow pile, it was just like Tom and Jerry!

At Valance we found that we had lost one hour and thirty minutes. Here everyone said we would need chains for the mountains, so we had to go to a garage. They had none of the right size but managed to repair ours. Stupidly the man welded the wrong links, so that when it was laid out it was found to be twisted and had to be redone.

This time we learned from him the correct way to fit chains; lay them out flat on the ground, run the car onto them, let out the air, do up the chains and tensioners, then blow up the tyres to their normal pressure. From then on we had no more trouble with them.

The last section of the rally led over the mountains through Digne and Grasse. It was snowing again; everything was white except where some of the rocks remained uncovered. In the half-light, and being very tired after seventy-two hours, it was a ghostly drive. We kept seeing people crossing the road, and once distinctly a ship on the bank. All an illusion of course, but very bewildering.

Further on one of the rally cars had skidded into a ditch, the drivers were looking very cold and dispirited. Wisely or unwisely we stopped to help them out with the shovel and tow rope we packed in the boot before leaving home. This time loss added to our previous penalties unfortunately made our arrival at the final Monte Carlo control too late to qualify as a finisher. That was a great disappointment, especially as it meant not taking part in the acceleration and braking tests, at which Berry was adept.

Thoroughly exhausted we vowed we would never enter another rally. But after a short rest and clean up in the hotel we joined the other competitors comparing notes.
Then it was 'When is the next one?'

The Tulip Rally, 1951

Our first Tulip Rally, in 1951, started from The Hague. The competitors were welcomed by a bevy of Dutch girls dressed in colourful national costume. They presented each team with a bottle of Bols (Dutch gin) decorated with a revolving windmill, a keyring and a miniature Dutch cheese.

Berry Leavens, Hal O'Hara Moore, and I set off in our Jowett Javelin registered KRU40, which we had driven over from our home in Dorset. The first part of the route was straightforward; we travelled fast along main roads to Paris. Then south to Limoges, Bordeaux, Sete, and inland to Clermont Ferand, which we reached in the dark the second night of the rally.

After refreshments we were given several sheets of instructions for the next stage, called 'The Route of the Thousand Bends'. This was to take us up Mont Dore, the Dom, and along the twisty mountain roads east of the Rhone valley. These instructions consisted of columns of small plans of road junctions with arrows indicating which way to turn. The poor navigator sitting with a torch, swaying about as the car swung round bends and hairpins, one eye on the road, one on the paper, just couldn't make sense of the diagrams. We soon discovered that at each road junction a 'Tulip' shaped arrow, fixed to a tree or something pointed the way to go. In the dark these were not easy to spot or interpret. The navigator gave up trying to follow the printed plans, so both passengers had to keep their eyes skinned so that the driver could maintain speed and concentrate on the road. This really was a hectic drive, up and down, twist and turn, through woods, onto high open plateaux, down a river valley and flashing through hamlets.

At one village we passed a hump back bridge sign, but couldn't see a bridge. Further on an excited group of people with lanterns waved us to go faster. As we sped past them at about 60mph there was a sickening crunch to the springs of the car, and we realised that the sign had really presaged one of those open gutters crossing the road, as happens in Continental countries, but not in England. Fortunately the Jowett withstood the shock better than our systems, but the locals loved it!

Day was breaking as we pulled into a time check control at the end of the 'Thousand Bends' without loss of time. Berry was exhausted after his night session at the wheel, driving as fast as possible all the way. The gear lever on the steering column must have been used a thousand times, without any complaint.

Through the day Hal and I took turns at the wheel journeying north through Epinal and Nancy to Luxembourg, where all were given a splendid meal before setting out on another mystery route in the dark, following more of the tulip arrows. Berry drove again; he was always good at the tricky sections, handling the car with confidence and skill. The navigator in the front seat, which in the Jowett was a bench type, needed extra strong leg muscles to keep steady; (no seat belts in those days), but even then suffered a number of bruises from being thrown about so violently.

Having had some experience in following the tulip arrows we again completed this section without trouble, actually with exhilaration. Arriving at the time check we had no idea where we were on the map. 'Go to Liege', replied the marshall when we asked for directions; so we set off northwards hoping for the best. Some way on we emerged into what seemed to be a racetrack, with white railings. 'Left or right?' called Berry. 'Hold on,' answered Hal as he leaped out of the car and looked at the stars. 'Left,' he commanded, having oriented himself with the Pole star, knowing that Liege was still north of us. Further on a sign post pointed to Liege some 50km ahead. We reached it still in the dark, the race track turned out to be part of the Spa circuit.

From there to Nijmegen, Utrect and The Hague to end up at the Parc Fermee in Nordwijk, our destination, without time penalties, about 2,000 miles in seventy-two hours, no mean accomplishment with all those hairpins and corners on twisty B roads.

I have forgotten to mention one trouble that occurred at Bordeaux, the ignition switch on the dashboard failed to work when we turned the key. However, our mechanically minded genius was not dismayed. Hal disappeared underneath the Jowett with a large screwdriver in his hand to short across the terminals of the solenoid, while the driver manipulated the controls. This caused much interest to the public standing by; they hadn't seen such an operation before.

Actually it was fortunate that the solenoid was not under the bonnet, as it was in most cars. Once in the Parc Fermee at each control it was against the rules to open the bonnet, or to be towed. But there was no rule that prevented one from lying underneath the car!

Some time later a fellow competitor who had seen what we were doing told us to lift up the carpet by the navigator's feet and we would find a solenoid knob there, which only needed pressing to connect up with the battery. That was much simpler and proved to be a great blessing at the end.

A couple of other excitements cropped up during the rally. The first was at night. A white light kept flashing on the dashboard causing considerable alarm. It was intermittent and only visible to the driver, so the passenger couldn't help to locate it. After a long time we discovered the cause; moonlight reflecting on one of the chromium fittings.

The second occurred in the daytime, there was a leak from the carburettor. A small screw had worked loose and disappeared, so that petrol could trickle out. Somehow Berry found a similar sized screw, I think it was from the fabric lining of the car, which just fitted and stopped the leak. Otherwise we would have had to find a garage and so lose time.

The day after the arrival at Nordwijk the cars were inspected to see that none of the engine or wheel seals had been tampered with, and that there were no electrical faults. When the marshall asked Berry to start the engine, of course Berry had to bend down to press the solenoid. 'Why do you do that?' enquired the marshall, 'Doesn't your ignition key work?' With incredible inspiration Berry replied, 'That is our thief-proof protection; no one can start the car from the dashboard'. The Dutchman was impressed at such an ingenious idea!

The final eliminating test was ten circuits of the Zandvoort race track; this was run in the reverse direction in case any of the drivers had previous experience of it. The race took place in classes according to the category and cc rating of the car. Berry did well in coming in second in the 1000 to 1500cc class; first was the Peugeot which although the same cc it was always a little faster than the Javelin, both on the straight and on the hill climbs.

We received a large cup as second prize for the saloon class 1000 to 1500cc, a great reward for all that effort, presented after a wonderful celebration feast arranged by the hospitable Dutch.

The London Rally 1952

This was a rally designed and organised by Geoff Imhof and assistants. All the competitors congregated at a meeting point in Wales, where they were given a list of map references of control points. They had to work out their own routes between these control points and clock in at a specific time, already calculated, and based on the shortest route at a given speed. I don't now remember what it was, probably about 27 or 30mph. All this took place in the dark, the navigator had to pinpoint the map references, spot the best route there, and watch the time by the light of a torch. Some crews had more sophisticated methods; ours was by means of an illuminated magnifying glass.

Berry was always the driver on these occasions as his speed, accuracy and instant reactions to my directions were superb, though I did try to describe the bends and turns in good time ahead. Once a car in front of us was driving fast straight on and I spotted a concealed turning to the right which we had to take. 'Sharp right,' I commanded and Berry just made it. The other car had swept past it and we never saw them again.

Another time along a narrow lane bordered with high banks we caught up with a slow competitor, who would not let us pass, in spite of our hooting. There really wasn't room for two cars abreast. Berry noticed a wider part ahead where another lane branched off, slammed his foot on the accelerator and shot past the astonished driver. As we said afterwards, the Jowett just picked up her skirts and flew!

Practically none of the routes from one control to the next included main roads. They were often hardly more than tracks marked on the maps with the lowest grades. One of our best efforts was the occasion when we drew up behind another car at a gate. His passenger got out to open the gate for him to go through, and then he stopped for her to get back aboard again. In the meantime I got out to close it again after Berry had followed on, but I couldn't do so, as the other car had not left enough room to draw clear of the gate. When the leading vehicle slowly ambled on I shut it quickly and hopped in like lightning. We were now on a farm track edging a ploughed field, some 200 yards ahead was another gate! Again my old man's determination leapt into action. With tremendous courage he swerved into the ploughed land and hurtled past the sedately driven obstruction, roaring ahead to reach the gate first. When we entered rallies we always did our best to get on!

At the final stop we found that we had lost a minimum of marks, and actually at the prize giving in London some time later we were awarded the prize for best husband and wife team.

The following year we again entered the rally, full of high hopes but an unfortunate encounter with a rock on one of the Welsh tracks over heath land. It was a rounded rock sticking up in the middle of the track, the same colour as the mud and unseen until we bounced on it. It cracked the sump, allowing oil to leak out. Remembering that we had a packet of chewing gum in the glove compartment, I was put to chewing it into a sticky mess. Berry then dived under the car to push the masticated substance into the crack and top up with oil. This enabled us to continue on our way, but the operation had to be repeated every twenty minutes until we could reach a garage to effect a reasonable repair. Needless to say, although we completed the rally we finished far down the list.

In spite of all our difficulties we thoroughly enjoyed all our rallies. They kept us alive, looking forward to the next one.

The Lisbon Rally 1952

Jowett Javelin KRU40 was entered in the Lisbon Rally as a ladies team. Me as entrant, with Nancy Mitchell and Bea Norman from Dorchester, as co-drivers. (Later on Nancy and I joined together as a ladies team for the Ford works, Nancy as driver and me as navigator.) The Javelin was given the rally number 2. Before starting I took a course in the engine, electrical and braking mechanics of the car, to be prepared for all emergencies.

There was little to report until we reached the French-Spanish border at San Sebastian. Here we were told that the towns along the coastal rally route were suffering from tremendous flooding, the result of heavy rains. The first place we reached had muddy water about six inches deep in the main road. People were scurrying about carrying belongings out of their houses and cursing the rally cars, which were streaming through throwing up waves of water.

After this we were diverted on to a road avoiding the floods. It led inland out of the range of our maps, so we had to navigate more or less by instinct. Signs were few and far between with names of towns not mentioned on the route card, which we had obtained from the AA.

Making for Oporto in Portugal we kept heading westward as much as possible along roads often barely more than a rough gravel tracks. It was dry barren country where small children wrapped in brown blankets herded flocks of goats and sheep, their homes a collection of ancient houses on a hilltop, huddled together within an encircling wall as a protection against marauders.

That night, the second since starting from London, we came to a junction of five roads with no intelligible signpost. Here again a knowledge of the stars enabled us to find a westerly direction.

Having covered about 300 miles of this scantily inhabited land we found ourselves in wooded foothills leading to the Portuguese coast. Here the road twisted and dipped along the sides of narrow valleys. Before dawn we passed many people walking singly or in groups carrying large baskets of market produce on their heads, or leading domestic animals. One woman had a pile of plates on her head; another balanced a baby in her basket!

Joyce Leavens used her Javelin to make up a ladies team in the 1952 Lisbon Rally with Bea Norman and Nancy Mitchell. They had a successful rally, winning the Coupe des Dames finishing eleventh in class. Joyce would later team up with Nancy Mitchell as a works ladies team for Ford. Left to right: Bea, Joyce and Nancy. (JCC)

Before entering Oporto we had time to fill up with petrol, check the oil, water and brakes. After a good breakfast we were on our way again to the final stage. Shortly before the finish at Lisbon we stopped to check the electric's and brakes again to be ready for the final tests, and to have a quick feminine tidy-up so we arrived looking bright and fresh to the cheers and photographs of the awaiting crowd, with no marks lost.

The eliminating tests, held the following day, included an acceleration and braking test and a three-lap speed circuit of 2 or 3 miles round the houses. Only two people were allowed in each car for the latter test; Nancy Mitchell drove and I was the navigator and time-keeper. Once again, having a bench seat in the Javelin made it no easy job to watch the road and the clock when hurtling round street corners at break neck speed, and slipping along the seat and bumping the driver! (Later on, when Berry and I did rallies together in the TR2, I fastened myself in with a thick leather strap round the back of the bucket seat.)

It was an exciting and hair raising experience. People lined the roads cheering and waving as we swept by. We arrived at the finish and congratulated each other on a well-performed effort, and waited impatiently with Bea to hear the official times. Much to our joyous surprise we found that we had won the ladies prize, the Coupe des Dames, and were heartily congratulated by everyone. The Jowett Javelin ended up eleventh in its class.

Home going was uneventful but more comfortable, along better roads, with a night stop on the way.

It may amuse you to know of one unusual incident that occurred on the way home. Bea Norman had left us in Paris to visit some friends there. Nancy and I continued to High Wycombe where she lived. I stopped only long enough to deposit her there and then set off by myself to Chesilbourne in Dorset. It had been a long trip back and I was tired, so I drew up in a lay-by to have a sleep. An hour or so later I woke up feeling much refreshed and set off once more. There was no traffic on the road for quite a long way, but then ... imagine my surprise when I saw a Jeep coming towards me on the wrong side of the road! With holy indignation I stopped and it stopped, we were almost nose to nose. I got out and said to the driver, 'What on earth are you doing driving on the wrong side of the road?' He looked at me amazed – after my sleep I thought I was still in France. 'Oh goodness,' I exclaimed, 'It was me! I've been on a rally in France and thought I was still driving on the right, I am sorry!' With that I scuttled back to the Jowett and shot off before he had time to recover – this time correctly on the left, with no further incidents.

The 24-hour Endurance Race at Spa, Belgium, 1953

This race was quite a different event from a rally. As usual Berry had taken the Jowett up to Bradford for a complete overhaul. The works had always been good to us, giving the Javelin a full check up before each rally, for only a moderate charge.

With John Jesty from Doncaster as our mechanic, Berry drove the car over to Francochamps from home. John worked in one of George Hartwell's garages. I had been taking part in the Rallie des Alpes with Nancy Mitchell as the Ford works Ladies Team, and met up with Berry and John at Spa directly from that.

The day before the race began competitors gathered at the track to find their way around and establish their pit stops. After a briefing, everyone had a period of practice runs.

We had entered as a husband and wife team, but it was strange to be around so many professional drivers such as, Jackie Stewart, Mike Hawthorne and the Italians. The Jaguars, Mercedes and the Ferrari's were in the Formula One class, other cars were in the lower cc range, and there was a class for saloon cars which the Jowett was one.

Our decision was to drive for two hours at a time, with Berry starting. John would record the laps and have everything ready in the pits in case repairs were necessary. With that settled Berry set off on his practice laps. These were very important as they provided an opportunity to study the course and find out what speeds were possible for each corner. 'Maximum speed is 74mph, so don't go over that,' he said when he returned. Then it was ready to go so off I went looking out for landmarks for gear changing, watching the speed and noting the types of corner. Then about three-quarters way round the engine developed a nasty knocking noise, so I slowed down and cruised to the pits, with a horrid feeling in my stomach.

Tragedy! One of the con rods had bent, but luckily it had not gone through the piston. The three of us worked all night to strip the engine and replace the rod. Berry and John were wonderful in their determination to put it right. With a full set of spare parts, John being an experienced engineer and Berry adding his knowledge of engines, the job was finally done, leaving time for a rest and some food before the start of the race at midday.

Crowds were watching enthusiastically as the cars pulled away for the twenty-four-hour run. John timed the laps on a stopwatch and counted the laps as the car came round each time. Something had happened in the pit next to us where Pirelli tyre mechanics were on duty. Either their race car had not turned up, or it had dropped out very quickly, because they offered their services to us, which we gladly accepted.

At my turn I was advised to start fairly slowly until I had got my eye in, as we had to be very alert to watch out for faster cars coming up behind. The Jowett was behaving well and I was very careful not to exceed the 74mph limit. It was a lovely course with several long straights, a number of 'fast' corners, a couple of sharper ones and a hairpin followed by a chicane leading downhill to the starting line.

Berry and I carried on in turn through the afternoon and evening. As I was nearing the end of one of my shifts at about midnight, rain began to fall. Coming up to one of the sharper corners I noticed headlights behind me drawing rapidly nearer. In a flash one of the Ferrari's passed me on the apex of the corner, so close that inadvertently I jumped in my seat. The jerk on the steering wheel sent the Jowett off course sliding the front wheels off the road onto the edge, only a foot away from a steep drop down. Instinctively I turned inwards to prevent the car hurtling into the abyss. Before I could regain proper control it shot across the road and hitting the opposite bank with a mighty thud, which shook me out of my seat, (no seat belts then), and caused me to bounce back towards the precipice. Somehow it came to a standstill facing forward, not quite overhanging the void.

For a moment I wondered if I was dead, as my helmeted head had banged hard against the dashboard. Then gathering my shaken wits together I clambered out of the passenger's door and found that the boot had sprung open and the spare wheel was careering down the road behind. With the one thought of preventing any of the race cars from colliding with it I dashed after it, catching it just before the next competitor swung round the corner.

Sadly the poor Jowett's near side front wheel and mudguard were too badly buckled to carry on the race. You can imagine our team's desperate disappointment, especially as we were doing so well up until then. Later in the pits several competitors came to commiserate with us. Mike Hawthorne, one of the Ferrari drivers, said that Villoresi should not have passed so closely, but the Ferrari's really had no brakes. After that all in our pit went to sleep for the rest of the night!

At the end of the event we three got lifts back home and Berry arranged for the AA to collect the car and deliver it to the Bradford works for repair. That was the end of our rallying for some time.

The Monte Carlo Rally 1954

This time Berry and I had decided to have a few days reconnoitring the route through France in the Jowett, timing the difficult sections down to our chosen starting point at Monte Carlo.

There were two different routes over the Massif Central between Le Puy and Valance. One was shorter but higher and more twisty, and tricky if there was snow on the ground. The other was lower, longer and sometimes subject to mist in the valley. It really was a toss up to choose, but both needed to be traversed at top speed.

The Javelin had been fitted with special snow tyres, which had little metal points in the tread for gripping well in snow. They were also efficient on normal roads. On the third morning of our recce it was raining as we set out from Digne for the last section of the Alps Maritime down to the coast. The road wound up through the mountains to Grasse and then began the decent to sea level. Driving down a fairly steep slope the car took control and gently slid sideways into a shallow ditch, turning over onto its side against a rocky bank. The tyres had no adhesion however much the steering wheel was turned. It wasn't really a skid, but was partly due to the rain water running down the road and the reverse camber. The metal points were of no help in such wet conditions.

So there we were, Berry at the bottom against the door and me collapsed on top of him; the alarm clock which we had with us for time keeping on top of me! Oddly enough I couldn't reach the passenger's door to open it, but fortunately a few moments later some French people came along and pushed the car upright. It was not badly damaged, apart from some dents and a queer feeling of lopsidedness. But when we tried to drive it we found that the nearside wheel was out of place. Our friendly rescuers kindly offered to contact the nearest garage, so it was not long before a breakdown van came to tow us in for repairs.

1952 *Daily Express* Rally, where 'Berry' and Joyce Leavens were entered. (JCC)

Another view of the Joyce Leavens car in the 1952 Lisbon Rally, with Bea Norman on the passenger side and Joyce on the driver's side. (JCC)

Some urgent telephoning to England was necessary for spare parts, as the rally was due to start in three days. Magically the repairs were carried out in time and we arrived at the start with twenty minutes to spare!

The rally itself was uneventful, which included some timed hill climb sections for a change, which would sort out the entrants by the times being included in the penalty points. The one real excitement was the route over the Massif Central, which had had a covering of snow since our recce. It was in the dark; we came up a hill a little way behind another competitor. A group of excited youngsters with torches sitting on a bank were waving us straight on behind the other car. The tyre tracks in the snow were leading straight ahead, suddenly I shouted to Berry 'Turn right!' He did! There was a hidden road, which was the correct one. The 'straight on' wasn't a road; it was an opening into a field. Those little wretches had enticed several cars to go that way and become stranded! What a relief we had not been caught likewise.

At the finish we had done reasonably well but were not among the prize winners. As usual the Peugeot was ahead of us.

The return home journey was not without trouble, it was extremely cold all that day and night. Our finances had almost run out, having had to pay for the repairs. Just before dark we used up the last of our French money for petrol. It was enough for us to reach the French coast with a little left over in the tank. At 2 a.m. ascending a hill the car coughed and stopped, it had run out of fuel! The petrol must have been too cold to vaporise properly and was being used neat. So now what? We couldn't run the engine to use the heater, we had no hot food or drink, just a rug and a tin of self-heating soup, which we always carried but never used. Somewhat warmed by the few mouthfuls of soup, which is heated in the tin by a chemical reaction, we huddled together in an effort to keep warm, but were actually getting colder and colder all the time.

At about 4.30 a.m., it was still dark, but we could hear a car. As it passed I pressed the horn and the car stopped. Blessings from above, not only was it a British competitor returning home, but he had a can of petrol on board, which he generously poured into our tank! We were grateful! Thus refuelled we set off once more with no further worry, as we were able to cash a cheque when we arrived at Dover.

Jowett Javelins in the Monte Carlo Rallies of 1950 & 1952
By Stanley Sedgwick
(From a chapter called 'Borrowed Plumes' taken from the book *Motoring My Way*
by Michael Sedgwick, published in 1976 by BT Batsford Ltd, London)

Although not exactly lent to me, I feel justified in regarding my participation in the Monte Carlo Rallies of 1950 and 1952 in other people's cars as falling within the description of 'borrowed plumes'.

I considered myself honoured to be asked by the Jowett Company to be the third man in one of the three Works Javelins entered in the 1950 Monte Carlo Rally and eagerly seized the opportunity to compete in this great event.

The Monte Carlo Rally had been revived the previous year after a ten-year gap bracketing the Second World War, and was passing through a transitional phase when amateur owner-drivers could still take part with a good chance of doing well. Manufacturers had not yet really got into the act with professional drivers, expensive pre-rally reconnaissance and immense support teams. Some manufacturers, realising the publicity value of success in International Rallies, were assisting private owners with the preparations of their cars and others were participating with works-prepared cars, but with one or two exceptions their drivers took part on an 'expenses only' basis.

Left: The Spa 24-hour race of 1953, driven by Berry and Joyce Leaven; with John Jesty as their mechanic. (JCC)

Below: Disaster strikes the Leavens' Javelin in the 1953 Spa 24-hour race following a high-speed overtaking manoeuvre by Villoresi in a Ferrari. Mike Hawthorn told Joyce that in his opinion it was the fault of the Ferrari for not giving them enough room. (Van Bever/JCC)

I travelled by train to Bradford in early January to meet those responsible for entering and preparing the cars and other team drivers. 'My' car was in charge of Horace Grimley, a member of the factory staff, the other co-driver was Reg Phillips, a well-known trials driver. One of the other Javelins was manned by seasoned competitor John Eason Gibson and Reggie Minchin, who was responsible for supervising the operations of the Metropolitan Police Motor Driving School at Hendon. The third Jowett in the team was that of Tommy Wise and Mike Wilson.

In the event, that year's Rally turned out to be one of the hardest since the series started in 1911. Out of the 283 starters, 101 failed to reach Monte Carlo at all. Of those that arrived in the Principality, 62 were outside the time limit and only 5 of the cars finished the course without loosing any marks for lateness. The reason for this tinning of the ranks was, of course the weather.

We started from Glasgow at tea time on 22 January in the company of sixty-four others, facing 2,000 miles of night and day motoring to the Cote d'Azur to be covered at 31mph plus, including all stops. Patches of ice on high ground in Scotland and the North of England presented no difficulties and it was a cheerful boat load of competitors which left Folkestone the following morning for Boulogne. In Northern France, Luxembourg and Holland the roads were dry – fortunately so as the temperature had been below freezing all the way from Glasgow. We felt it couldn't last and at Controls we heard rumours of snow in Central France. Sure enough by the time we reached Nevers snow was falling, slowly and relentlessly, as if it was in no hurry and would go on forever.

I can't remember how late we were, but the maximum lateness allowance of three hours at the end was being whittled away. Between Valence and Digne conditions remained the same, but seemed somewhat less daunting in daylight. The Jowett Javelin flew along, with Horace Grimley driving it in masterly fashion. The speed in which he went up and down these slippery mountain roads was really something. Reg Phillips, no doubt accustomed in trials to pointing the car only vaguely in the direction of travel, drove with commendable speed. Frankly, I was pretty scared at times and I fear that my co-drivers must have been irked by the pace, which I deemed to be my fastest in the icy conditions when entrusted with the wheel.

Despite the most valiant efforts – particularly on the part of Horace – we fell further and further behind our scheduled time. We arrived in a rainy Monte Carlo without mishap and were placed ninety-sixth. Tommy Wise and Mike Wilson finished forty-fourth. The Eason Gibson car had gone off the road in an uncontrollable slide when cruising at about 50mph where the average motorist without the competitive urge would be driving 10mph. Later the windscreen wipers ceased working in the most trying of conditions, all of which resulted in his Javelin reaching the Finish Control one-minute after it had closed.

The rally was won by the Frenchmen Becquart and Secret in a 1939 3½ litre 'Paris-Nice' Hotchkiss, followed by Gatonsides' Humber Snipe and three Simcas. (It says a lot for the quality of the Hotchkiss car, for this make of car had won the rally six times in the 1930s.)

The rally had proved to be a severe endurance test for crews and, as a contemporary motoring journalist put it, 'a searching eliminator of inefficient cars.' The Jowetts gave us a fast, safe and comfortable journey and we were impressed with their performance. It was a very tired and worn crew, which left the Javelin in the parc ferme and made for the hotel.

When I telephoned Con before falling into bed for a long sleep to tell her of our safe arrival, she told me that a friend of ours had been 'successfully delivered of a son'. Next morning I sent the joyful mother a telegram, which tells its own story; it read 'Congratulations, I nearly had a baby too.'

Two years later a private owner of a Jowett Javelin, Bob Nelson-Harris invited me to join him as a co-driver in the 1952 Monte. This time there would only be two drivers. Again we chose Glasgow as our starting point and this year, too, turned out to be one of the most gruelling 'Montes' on record. It will live in our minds as Sydney Allard's year, as he won the rally in a car of his own construction – a Type P Allard Saloon – being the first Englishman to do so since Donald Healey won in 1931.

The weather and road conditions presented no problems on this side of the Channel and all was going well on the other side until we approached Bourges where it was snowing hard. The road from Le Puy down through the Rhone Valley to Valence was very bad. The N7 was narrowed by deep snow, and cars were involved in crashes and ditchings; many were fitting chains; others pushing in the hope that wheels would eventually secure a grip on icy gradients. Only seventeen cars were on time at Valence. Sydney Allard, with co-drivers Guy Warburton and Tom Lush, was among them, but not so Mrs Allard and her two sisters driving in a similar car. They had skidded off the road in the Rhone Valley and hit a kilometre stone. Sydney's rally number was fifteen higher than his wife's which meant the ladies left each Time Control quarter-of-an-hour ahead of Sydney. Going like the clappers on black ice, Sydney recognised his spouse's car stationary on the snow-covered verge. He slowed down, wound down his window and yelled, 'You all right?' Back came his wifely reply, 'No.' Quick as a flash; 'Pity,' retorted Sydney, winding up the widow and accelerating away without actually coming to a stop. Of such determination and dedication to the task in hand are Rally winners made!

The atrocious conditions persisted in the mountains to the East of the Rhone. One stretch of road was a shambles. Crews were taking hours to get out of ditches; others were stuck on hills and many were baulked by fellow competitors unable to get going. Ken Wharton's Ford went straight on at a corner, through a gap in the wall and dropped into a ravine, landing on top of a crashed Citroen, which itself was on top of another car.

And it then happened to us. Bob was driving at a commendable speed on the frozen snow when the car side-slipped into an invisible snow covered ditch on a left-hand hairpin bend and bumped into a wall. It was beyond our human strength and our aides to get the Javelin back on the road, so I trudged through the night in knee-deep snow to rouse a farmer, who unprotestingly (and suitably rewarded) brought a pair of oxen to the scene. The two beasts were hooked up to the car and, on the command of their master, leaned forward and loped through the deep snow recovering the Jowett with no more effort than drawing a cork out of a bottle. Throughout the rescue operation competing cars were speeding past in the dark, our presence adding to the hazards on the slippery road, and our own position being somewhat dangerous. Inspection revealed that the front suspension and steering had been bent and further motoring at competitive speeds was out of the question. We drove slowly to the next town, being at pains not to impede more fortunate competitors and, after effecting repairs, continued our journey to Monte Carlo too late to rank as a finisher.

It was disappointing not to be among the finishers, but no disgrace, for more than half of the 328 starters met the same fate, and only fifteen reached Monte Carlo without penalty.

The highest placed fifty cars on the road section were required to compete a couple of days later in a Regularity Test at 50mph round a 50-mile mountain circuit inland from Monte Carlo. Either the route or the speed – I forget which – was changed and I spent the 'rest' day before the Test reworking all of Sydney's pace notes. The British contingent was overjoyed when he drove the Allard into the Palace Square to receive the winner's laurels from Prince Rainier.

An incident on the non-competitive run home stays in my memory. About 150 miles south of Paris we took pity on a lonely figure thumbing a lift on a deserted stretch of road in very heavy rain. We sat him between us on the bench-type seat, the rear compartment being 'loaded to the gunwales', and at once regretted it, for we were enveloped in an aroma of garlic which persisted and increased all the way to Paris. I detest the smell of garlic and my discomfiture in the code a code accommodation of the Javelin can scarcely be imagined.

My Monte Carlo Rally experiences in the Jowett Javelins gave me a healthy respect for these great little cars. They were easy to drive; willing performers and the road-holding qualities had to be experienced to be believed. What a pity that production ceased two years later.

1950 *Daily Express* Rally
Mary Farrington

I bought my Jupiter; a 1952 example registered JBE4, in February 1985, and still own it today. The car was first registered in Scunthorpe in January 1952 and was supplied to the Jowett agents there, Marshalls. I wrote to the local paper in Scunthorpe in 1997 to see if they would publish my standard 'Jowett information request', which I altered slightly to mention my car in particular. This they did and I was contacted by Mary Farrington of Brigg in Lincolnshire telling me about her Javelin. This produced another unexpected snippet of rallying information that I would not have found out about otherwise, so I will reproduce her letter below. – NS

Thank you for your letter and the copy of *The Jowetteer*, which I found most interesting, I am glad my information was of some interest to you.

I have to say you are stretching my memory as regards to the *Daily Express* 1,000 miles Rally, as it was a long time ago. I know we left Harrogate on 8 November 1950, and that one of the more famous people taking part was Ian Appleyard *(in his Jaguar XK120 registered NUB120 – NS)*.

We drove down to Dover via the east coast, where we were greeted by girls giving out doughnuts and hot drinks; I found the doughnuts very indigestible so early in the morning! Soon after we checked out and drove back up to Chester via the Midlands, and we had a short rest-stop there. Soon after we were off again on the night section through the Welsh mountains, which included Bwylch-Gaves and carried on through Ross-on-Wye to Bristol and then to Torquay. Here we had to do the usual tests, such as driving between cones and backing into spaces etc.

After two damp and cold nights a bath and bed were most welcome but, being young, we were up to enjoy the dinner and dancing in the evening. So in effect we had been up for three nights! We were presented with a plaque for coming fourteenth out of 856 drivers, all of whom were amateurs.

The car was bought new by my husband and I from Rounce & Sons Ltd in Scunthorpe and was registered ECT720, the rally plate number for this event was 138.

Mary's car had a Lincolnshire registration that ran from July 1949. The Jowett agents in Scunthorpe were Marshall's Garage, so they must have supplied the car to Rounce & Sons for Mr and Mrs Farrington. – NS

GORDON WILKINS

Gordon Wilkins was a very prolific motoring correspondent for many motoring publications and journals, in particular The Autocar, *and was in the class-winning Jupiter with Marcel Becquart in the Le Mans 24-hour race in 1951 and 1952 and he was in fact one of Jowett's most successful drivers, winning several other events which are detailed below:*

Foreword to the 1951 Monte Carlo Rally

Horace Grimley and Charles Granfield undertook another test drive and reconnoitre, this time in the 1950 Le Mans class-winning Jupiter GKW111 a couple of weeks before the 1951 'Monte'. By this time the car had been altered into standard trim, this included the strakes on the front and rear wings. They had written up a report of their findings along the route to assist the works team of three Jupiters. They were:

239 Gordon Wilkins and Raymond Baxter.
253 Tommy Wise and Horace Grimley.
255 Robert Ellison and Bill Robinson.

This report formed the basis of an article that appeared in The Autocar *on 19 January, just four days before the start of the rally. There were several pictures of GKW111 in heavy snow, particularly in the Le Puy Valence section. Luckily the snow was not as bad two weeks later when the rally was underway. I would guess that the report was put into an article for* The Autocar *by Gordon Wilkins, as he was a journalist with the magazine at the time and was in one of the works Jupiters with Raymond Baxter. – NS*
The Autocar *article reads:*

On Tuesday next, 23 January, starting signals will be given by timekeepers at Glasgow, Lisbon, Monte Carlo, Oslo, Palermo and Stockholm to 362 crews who will be starting on Europe's big winter Rally. During four days and three nights they have to cover a difficult route of about 2,000 miles from each starting control, maintaining an average speed of 31mph, with no time allowances for eating, sleeping, refuelling or repairs; they are due to arrive in Monte Carlo at intervals from 6.34 a.m. on Friday 26 January.

A full list of entries and a map of the routes were given in *The Autocar* of January 5. As the number of applications is far in advance of the number of competitors who can be handled, the number of entries to be accepted from each country was established in advance on the basis of previous rally entries, and Britain, which has always strongly supported the rally, although British drivers have succeeded in winning it on only two occasions, has the second largest contingent with seventy competitors against ninety from France.

This year the National club of each competing country was given the task of selecting the entrants from the available applicants, so the rally has more than ever the air of a classic international contest between crews and cars chosen as the best representatives of their countries.

Sixty-five of the British competitors are starting from Glasgow and the route is complicated for them by a diversion to Llandrindod Wells before they catch the boat from Folkestone to Boulogne en route for Belgium and Holland.

All routes converge on Bourges, from where the route goes via Clermont Ferrand over the mountains of the Massif Central to Le Puy and Valence. After that the rally joins the route of last year's event via Gap, Digne and Grasse.

If the weather is bad, the top placings in the rally will almost certainly be decided on the section from Clermont Ferrand through Le Puy to Valence, which has been specifically included by the organisers this year in the hope that the winner will be found on the road section and not in eliminating tests in Monte Carlo. The section begins easily enough with well-surfaced main roads, but it becomes narrow, winding and rough as Le Puy is approached and between there and Valence there is a great deal of climbing and descending over narrow tortuous roads with precipices yawning at the roadside to discourage any attempt to slide the corners. The photographs on these pages were taken on this section only a fortnight ago when conditions were such that it was virtually impossible to maintain the average speed required.

Le Puy is only a passage control, but the lateness at Valence will be penalised at the rate of 10 marks per minute. A failure to pass through a time control means exclusion from the rally, but competitors of various nationalities have noted that failure to get the road book stamped at a passage control costs only a penalty of 50 marks. If there is really bad weather for the Le Puy section, it would not be surprising to find a number of people arriving at Valence without the passage control stamp in their road books, for there are other ways round, and it might be an investment to sacrifice 50 marks rather than risk being stuck for an hour or more on a mountain road.

A few British competitors have been able to investigate parts of the route and these photographs were obtained when one of the Jowett Jupiter team was carrying out a brief reconnaissance in the first week of January, but the Frenchmen have an undoubted advantage which will pay rich dividends if conditions are anything like last year. Becquart and Secret, last year's winners, revealed in an interview how they were glad to see snow falling, for, being residents of Savoy, they felt they were almost unbeatable in difficult conditions on the mountain roads they knew so well. Louis Rosier, champion racing driver of France is another competitor who benefits from local knowledge, as he lives in the Clermont Ferrand area and they say he has almost worn grooves in the Le Puy road. If the mist comes down, as it can quite quickly, few even amongst the Frenchmen will be able to hold him.

The subsequent section through Gap and Digne to Grasse may be just as bad. Three weeks ago it was completely covered in snow and at the top of the Col de Cabre the snow was 6ft deep. The snow plough had been able to clear a track wide enough for single-line traffic on the Col de Leques and on these roads buses and coaches show a very strong disinclination to be passed. Such conditions can be heart-breaking for tired competitors trying to maintain the required average speed, and in the event of two cars colliding, complete chaos can result. In the words of one of the French competitors who was over the section at its worst just after Christmas, 'It will be more like the Retreat from Moscow than the Monte Carlo Rally.'

From Le Puy onwards the mere repetition of the names of the passes to be climbed conjures up visions of endless work with steering, brakes and gearbox just when the crews are becoming really tired, to say nothing of the cars. The Col de Pertuis is 3,300ft high, and there is a decent to 2,800ft at Yessingeaux before climbing again to 3,400ft at St Agreve.

There is another road to the south which by-passes this section and is almost 10km shorter. It would be a tempting alternative but for the fact that it is rough and rises an extra 500ft. At Christmas it was blocked by snow. The official rally distances are based on the Yessingeaux – St Agreve route.

Soon after Valence comes the Col de Cabre (3,800ft) which was only just practicable with chains when *The Autocar* staff tried it; then the road descends for a fast run to Gap and Digne. Then come the Col de Leques and those of Luens and Valferriere, followed by the Pas de la Faye, all rising to well over 3,000ft to block the road to the sea and (they all hope) sunshine.

The special nature of this year's event, with its limited hand-picked entry, has spurred the French on to special efforts to maintain their record of victory. Renault and Simca teams and many of the others had all been over the route in force before Christmas and it was said that at least one car had been overturned in the process. The star teams were due to tackle the route again in their actual rally cars in the first days of the New Year.

1951 Monte Carlo Rally
Gordon Wilkins
(This article appeared in *The Autocar*, 16 February 1951 under the heading:
'No snow on our boots – A driver's impression of the 1951 Monte Carlo Rally')

The revs rose to a scream in second gear – the finishing line flashed by, the cotton thread broke and we could cut, brake, park the car and relax the tension built up over four days and three nights motoring. We had checked in on time in Monte Carlo and had just completed the vital acceleration and braking test in 24.5 seconds; nearly two seconds slower than all three Jupiters had achieved in practice, but still not bad on a water-logged course. Now to relax and enjoy the luxury of doing nothing, and doing it slowly while waiting our turn to unload the baggage and put the car in the *parc ferme*.

It was easy to relax the body, but flashing through the mind like an endless newsreel were scenes from last night and those breathless early morning hours. Fighting against fatigue and driving with the fingertips to control incipient skids on the miles of ice over the notorious mountain sections from Clermont Ferrand to Le Puy and Valence. Vainly trying to sleep while Raymond Baxter took the car over the snowbound Col de Cabre and rushed on, making up time over slippery roads through the Grasse to Digne.

Taking the wheel again to plunge into a snow storm and fight for wheel grip in deepening snow on the Col de Leques. Debating whether to lose time by fitting chains or press on and take the chance of getting stuck. Deciding to take a chance, and then juggling a way with spinning wheels past other competitors who had made the same decision and got hopelessly trapped in the snow. The decent to Castellane and the slide through the snow covered square in a tightly packed bunch of cars which nearly demolished the cine camera on the corner, and gave a lensful of action. Then up over the Col de Luens, the Col de Valferriere, the Pas de la Faye and the Col du Pilon. They are all names on the route card with height figures rising to 3,800ft, but in retrospect they merge into an endless succession of very slippy snow-covered hairpin bends, of desperate efforts to get past slower cars, of slides on the edge of dizzy drops as we dodged trucks and snow ploughs, and somewhere a fantastic struggle with coils of wire from a line of demolished telegraph poles.

Then the dash down the treacherous lower slopes from Grasse in blinding rain, a quick refuel at Nice, a check of all electrical equipment and the never ending run along the tortuous Lower Corniche to clock in at Monte Carlo with a minute in hand. Finally, screwing together every remnant of skill and concentration, using every rev the engine would give and using all the brakes one dared in the acceleration and braking test on a course that was swimming in water. But there was Donald Healey telling us we had all lost time by braking too gently and the sun was already peeping through the clouds to dry the course for the later arrivals. Soon little wisps of steam were rising from the track and tyres were beginning to squeal as the later arrivals crammed their brakes on really hard. The Lisbon starters were still to come and would do the test on a dry course. A Lisbon winner seemed certain and for a gloomy period, as one car after another crashed over the recording strip with locked wheels it seemed as if Lisbon starters would monopolise the final test, to which only the best fifty performers in the brake test would be admitted.

But no, it did not turn out quite like that, and the British contingent from Glasgow had their fair share of success, but these were the agonised speculations which occupied tired crews during the excessively long wait outside the *parc ferme*.

From the time the first car arrived at 8.07 a.m. it was an hour and a half before any competitor recorded less than twenty-five seconds. The Hillen and Schade (Ford) did it, followed by a procession of Simcas and Ken Rawlings (Vanguard). During the next hour and a half only two big cars managed and there was another long wait until soon after midday, when Vard and Waring with Jaguars and Ellison and I with Jupiters broke '25.' The course was drying off nicely when a Citroen from Monte Carlo did it, then Mrs Stanley Turner's Alvis clocked 24.7 and Trevoux came in with his unbeatable 22.6. From then on it was plain sailing for the remaining Lisbon finishers, five of whom recorded less than 25 seconds. Against this background, Colin Vard's run in 23.1 seconds on a waterlogged course stands out as a magnificent effort.

The vital importance of the acceleration and braking test arises from the method of marking. On the 2,000-mile road section, drivers had to average 50kph (31mph). They could maintain a higher speed upto 65kph (41½mph), and at each control, cars arriving early were put in a closed park. The crews could then rest or relax until the time equivalent of 50kph average was reached.

With Raymond Baxter and I, the time margin usually went making recordings for the broadcast reports of the rally, but we did manage to get about one hour's sleep in Lille, Amsterdam and Brussels. As hotels seem to have a habit of charging the same for an hour in bed as for a full night, sleep cost about a £1 an hour, but seemed well worth it at the time.

Competitors checking in before the minimum time fixed, or after the maximum time, were penalised, and in the interests of public safety a competitor who had driven too much too fast could be excluded at the request of the national club of the country in which the incident occurred.

Time early or late on the road section carried penalties at the rate of 10 marks per minute but the time taken in the acceleration and braking test was at the rate of a half mark per second or 30 marks per minute.

The final test, to which only the best fifty were admitted, consisted of six laps of the Monte Carlo Grand Prix circuit, at 3.18km (1.98 miles) per lap. The last four laps were the most important, as the times recorded were used to decide the results on the formula:

$$R = \frac{T + 1.2 (E_1 + E_2 + E_3)}{10}$$

Where T is the time of the fastest lap in seconds and E_1, E_2 and E_3 represent the difference in seconds between this and the other three laps. Time taken on the circuit is therefore penalised at the rate of only 6 marks a minute and irregularity at the rate of 7.2 marks per minute. This shows why even Chiron, going extremely fast and with great regularity on the circuit, could not make up for an indifferent performance in the acceleration and braking test.

No one who lost marks on the road section stood any chance in the rally this year and this makes it all the more unfortunate that one or two British competitors, experienced enough to know better, jeopardised the chances of several compatriots by obstruction on the snowbound passes.

No photographer ever gets up near the tops of the passes where the conditions are really bad, and there is therefore no pictorial record of what went on, but for many miles the snowploughs had only been able to smooth out a track of single car width. On this ribbon of packed snow, reasonable if not spectacular progress was possible, even without chains, but any effort to pass another car meant plunging into deep loose snow which immediately swallowed up the power and defeated the manoeuvre. Passing in safety, therefore, required co-operation from the car in front in pulling over at the first suitable point were there was a level or downhill stretch which would assure an easy recovery after entering the heavy snow. Unfortunately, there were several processions of four or five British competitors were held up, all frantically sounding their horns, behind slow drivers who could not keep up the pace and would not give way.

If a car suddenly appears behind you, when previously the road was empty, it is a fair assumption that it is travelling faster than you are. There is no harm in taking the hint and trying to speed up, but if you cannot lose him there is a clear duty to pull over and give him the chance to get ahead.

Some people went to the other extreme and stopped to help fellow-competitors in positions where they could not possibly restart themselves without fitting chains and losing time, which could never be made up. We counted ourselves lucky to get through non-stop, for if we had no chains on our wheels, we had at least no snow on our boots.

Any attempt to build up a reasonable time margin in these conditions means proceeding in a series of controlled slides uphill and down, the drivers with a trials background seem happiest at the job, as they are fully accustomed to keeping the throttle wide open when the car is at about 45 degrees to the direction of travel.

On the earlier part of the road section a few impressions stand out vividly from the rest. First of all, the astonishing enthusiasm in Britain. In Scotland coalminers and schoolchildren lined the roads to watch the cars pass, and in Ruabon and Wrexham it seemed as if the whole populations were pressing onto the road, three or four deep, waving the drivers on as though it was a long-distance road race instead of a rally at closely controlled speeds. The present public enthusiasm for motoring sport in Britain is something never known before, and if the matter is handled properly, we could have Continental-style long-distance rallies and road racing on closed circuits with overwhelming public support in quite a short time.

The class-winning Jupiter of Robinson/Ellison at the end of the 1951 Monte Carlo Rally. The six around the car are the drivers of the three works-entered Jupiters. *From left to right:* Robert Ellison, Tommy Wise, Horace Grimley, Gordon Wilkins, Bill Robinson and Raymond Baxter. (JCC)

The same enthusiasm is to be found in France but not so much in Belgium. In Holland, however, the peak was reached. Customs formalities took less than 30 seconds and on entering the country each British crew was presented with complete route directions for the passage through Holland printed in English. Every important turning was marked by signs, which glowed in the light of the headlamps, and every major junction was guarded by smart police in black uniforms. Through the main cities we were guided by motorcycle police, who looked like TT riders in their white crash helmets and black leathers, and certainly rode to fit the part. Most of the roads were covered in black ice, but if ever we showed a desire to travel faster than the convoy, one of the escorts would immediately detach himself and beckon us on. He would then lead us in a fantastic chase through the deserted streets at over 50mph. Their ability to travel on two wheels on ice, while we were using all our efforts to keep going in the right direction on four wheels, excited our unreserved admiration.

In Belgium, on both the inward and outward loops, the situation was quite the reverse, and no guidance at all was received. A reader's letter in last week's issue seems to suggest that this was because nobody remembered to tell the Belgian police that the Monte Carlo Rally was happening. However, the situation was restored on re-entering France, and the usual admirable traffic control by the French gendarmerie gave competitors an easy trouble-free run through Rheims to Paris, where further mobile police provided high-speed escorts into and out of the city, the dense and rapid traffic of the French capital providing quite as much excitement as the ice-bound roads of Holland.

Another thing that astonishes the British rally competitor is the lavish hospitality offered to crews en route. For the Glasgow contingent it started with open house at the Royal Scottish Automobile Club before the start, and at Lille there were quantities of champagne, far greater than a prudent crew would absorb. At Liege the Royal Motor Union, organisers of the famous Liege-Rome-Liege trial, presented each crew with a hamper, much too large to go into a car the size of ours. Besides sandwiches and fruit, it contained such welcome items as bottles of wine, packets of cigarettes and veal steaks wrapped in cellophane. At Amsterdam a delightful restaurant was turned over to competitors, who enjoyed meals from a menu on the generous Dutch scale and, as parting gifts, were presented with small bottles of gin and slabs of chocolate by pretty girls in National costume.

In Rheims, the great champagne producers co-operated most effectively with the local automobile club in its efforts to fortify the fatigued crews.

In Paris the *Action Automobile* excelled themselves as usual. Each British crew was taken care of by a beautiful girl, gowned in the manner one normally associates with Paris, and, after champagne and refreshments, they were sent on their way with quantities of ham, fruit, aperitifs and liqueurs. Perhaps the Paris control was the hardest of all to leave on schedule, but then that is usually the trouble in Paris, rally or no rally.

At Bourges there was a well-stocked buffet in the former bishop's palace, opposite the lovely cathedral, and the Clermont Ferrand, the control was in a local sports stadium. From then on there was little time to enjoy hospitality, but things continued to tumble in through the windows of the car. At Grasse there were bottles of the local perfume, but it has not so far been possible to verify the claims that these were immediately opened and drunk by the tired crews, who were now thoroughly accustomed to receiving alcoholic refreshment as a parting gift.

Inevitably the Llandrindod Wells control did not compare favourably with the others, but the mayor did present us each with a guidebook, including a view of Station Crescent and the Post Office. A happier impression was left by the magnificent buffet offered by one of the local garages at Lee, which has now become a recognised stopping place for competitors on the route down to Folkestone.

Monte Carlo itself provided a curious incident in the cocktail party at the Exotic Gardens. After a long trek up the steep hill behind Monte Carlo, about half of the guests were unable to obtain any refreshment stronger than a glass of soda water, and in case the revelry should get out of hand on this unaccustomed intake, they were shepherded off the premises by uniformed officials blowing whistles. Fortunately the ball at the Café de Paris and the gala dinner at the Sporting Club were more in accordance with the Monte Carlo tradition.

The comic and farcical incidents during the rally and after would, of course, fill a book. There was the British Ford Anglia crew who failed to notice that, from Valence onwards, early time margins were cancelled at each control to make things more difficult, and happily occupied themselves practising brake tests outside the final control, when they should have been checking in. Then there was Prince Lanza di Trabbia, henceforth known as Rip Van Lanza, who slept his way into a heavy time penalty after stopping outside the Clermont Ferrand control with an hour in hand. Prince Lanza gave me a run along the Corniche in his Alfa Romeo 1900 afterwards, and it seems there is some proposal that Alfa Romeo should give him and his crew a dinner at which they are presented with an alarm clock.

Then there was the man who fell asleep and got himself locked up for the night in one of the more exotic night clubs. After waking up at about nine in the morning, he broke his way

Raymond Baxter and Gordon Wilkins driving through Monte Carlo to a class second in the 1951 Monte Carlo Rally. (JCC)

out, only to fall into the hands of two gendarmes, who proposed to arrest him for breaking and entering. He protested that he was breaking and exiting.

The 4½-litre Delahaye used by Thevoux and Chiron is a post-war model not hitherto seen much in competitions. The front suspension is Dubonnet and there is a De Dion axle at the rear. The chassis is usually fitted with special bodywork by the French *carrossiers,* and none of the literature I have seen makes any specific claim to the weight of the whole car. The two cars that finished in the first ten had very light special bodywork with every surplus ounce pared off the panelling and fittings, and the one used by Chiron had the popular lightweight seats made of rubber stretched over a tubular framework. It must be emphasised, however, that they were thoroughly practical in style, with large space within for four or five people.

Chiron's car was well streamlined with a fully swept back, but the winning car used by Trevoux had a more conservative notched back with big rear windows. This results from Trevoux's experience in being hustled in last year's Mexican road race by transatlantic thrusters, who did not hesitate to close up and give him a nudge from the rear. It is a considerable shock to a driver bred in the well-ordered European road racing tradition when, to quote Trevoux's own words, 'I suddenly find there are horses, which I do not have under my foot.' Hence the large rear window on his latest car.

With three carburettors, as used for the rally, the 4½-litre six-cylinder engine, which has pushrod operated overhead valves, normally gives 137bhp, but the inspection after the event showed that proper advantage had been taken of the modifications permitted by the regulations, and it seems reasonable to suppose these engines were giving about 180bhp.

Well, it is all over, and now a lot more of us are entitled to wear the little round badge with the bar, which indicates the year, we finished on time. More than ever, we envy the veterans with the long strings of bars that seem to dangle almost to their knees. Trevoux for example, has ten of them; one of the best consecutive sets is that of Col Barnes, of the RAC, who has seven in a row.

1951 Le Mans
Gordon Wilkins

Gordon wrote a two-page article for The Autocar *dated 6 July 1951 entitled 'Drivers impressions of some of the 24-hour-race cars.' He was allowed to drive the C-type Jaguar, which he waxed-lyrical about, but also wrote this about his Jupiter:*

During the race I had plenty of opportunity of seeing how the other cars handled, while sharing with Marcel Becquart the wheel of the Jupiter number 66, which won the 1½ litre class. Whatever the acceleration away from the corners, there were not many cars which could get away from the Jupiter in the winding stretches. Several times it went drifting fast into swerves before Arnage, with a much faster car behind it, and by the time it emerged the Jupiter had gained several lengths. It was particularly happy at White House, too, and gave us a very comfortable ride.

Of the three Jupiters entered, the one run by T.H. Wisdom and Tommy Wise was a prototype known as the R1 incorporating a number of modifications. The main chassis components are similar to those of a normal Jupiter, but simplification of the frame design had permitted a considerable weight saving, and further weight was saved by a slim body with cycle-type wings. The normal type Jupiters driven by Hadley and Goodacre, and Becquart and myself were below 15cwt, but the R1 was nearly a hundredweight lighter, and was able to pull the high 4.1 axle, which was originally proposed for the standard Jupiters. Thus equipped, it was cruising down the straights at 5200rpm on top, equivalent 105mph. The compression ratio had been raised to about 8.5 to 1, giving a power output in the region of 65bhp, but unfortunately gasket trouble eliminated the car from the race. Meanwhile, Bert Hadley, driving the other standard Jupiter, retired when the centre of one of the collars retaining the valve springs pulled out, another example of the lessons which racing provides.

Although there were still several Simcas in the race, our pit control took the wise step of slowing the third car down. The Simcas were still going very fast, but one by one they dropped out and soon after 4 a.m. I had the signal that the Jupiter was alone in the 1500cc class. Our only trouble was some misfiring caused by rain and spray reaching the distributor at the height of the storm, because the car had been prepared for a motor race rather than a regatta!

On the Sunday morning, when the field had greatly thinned out by retirements and crashes, the race seemed to be full of Aston Martins, for they were circulating fast and safely in undiminished numbers. To bring home five cars out of five starters, with four of them in the top ten places, is a tremendous feat.

Gordon then detailed other cars, which I am not going to reproduce here, but he finished with an interesting point about Bert Hadley's Jupiter, which I am sure most people will not have known. – NS

If a driver runs into trouble he has to get himself out of it single-handed and if anyone departs from the pits, even to give him verbal advice, disqualification is the result. This is why Hadley's Jupiter was posted as a disqualification and not a retirement. When the car failed to appear, a worried driver left the pit area to find out what had happened, and although he had no contact with Hadley other than to ask him what was the trouble, disqualification was the result. This regulation may need review in the light of scientific progress. The pilots of the three Cunningham cars were in touch with their pit all the time on two-way radio sets which were carried in the cars. The pit could call up the drivers for reports and the drivers were free to ask the pit for advice. If this can be done by radio, but not by personal contact, the regulation might become a farce.

Economy Plus – Victories in Fuel Economy test for Jowett Javelin (67.868 mpg) and Morgan Plus Four (57.8mpg)
Gordon Wilkins
(As reported in The Motor, 30 July 1952)

Immense improvements in mileage per gallon since a very similar event was tried out a year ago were the feature of the 'News Chronicle' National Road Fuel Economy Contest, which was run off by the Cheltenham Motor Club last Friday and Saturday. Few can have anticipated that, with entries limited to essentially standard cars, and an 828-mile route around England, Wales and Scotland to be negotiated at a speed of not less than 29mph average, entrants would be able to show mpg figures around double those which many owners of similar cars regard as creditable.

The results suggest that the event was something of a 'benefit' for members of the Technical Press, the two classes into which the cars were divided being won by members of staffs of The Motor and The Autocar respectively! The winning car in the two-seater class was a Morgan 'Plus Four' two-seater driven by Joseph Lowrey, running on very thin (SAE5) oil, and with small carburettor jets which did not prevent the car making best times of the day in the standing-start acceleration tests. The winning car in the 4-6 seater class was a Jowett Javelin saloon which Becquart handled so successfully in the RAC Rally, driven on this occasion by Gordon Wilkins, who also using thin oil (SAE10) and with the radiator almost completely blanked off, had an engine vigorous enough to give him second best saloon car time (behind a Ford Zephyr Six) in the acceleration tests.

Fuel consumptions were measured as cars completed the 828-mile set route, fuel fillers and bonnets being sealed between refuelling checks set at 130-190-mile intervals, and the total amount of fuel needed to restore the original level in the tank being checked at the finish. Although the high order of concentration required to maintain utmost economy on such a long journey, with only a single refreshment break in a period of thirty hours, provided something short of excitement for the competitors, a truly representative variety of motoring had to be tackled. First there was the Friday morning rush of go-to-work cyclists around Gloucester, and a little later, the traffic of Newport and Cardiff had to be negotiated. Byways leading over the Mynnyd Eppynt hills to Llandrindod and onwards towards Lake Vwyrny were quiet on a weekday but no less rough, winding and steeper than usual. Industrial traffic around Warrington, Wigan and Preston caused many a delay, so that it was a relief to cross Shap Fell as the sun set and to enter Scotland at Gretna Green through the seemingly everlasting northern twilight.

Edinburgh, at around midnight, provided a very warm welcome for the competitors at the S.M.T. garage, but soon the road back to England had to be taken, with low cloud and sleeping sheep combining to obstruct the way across the hills to Carter Bar.

As Saturday morning advanced, the aggressive traffic of the A1 had to be tackled, then a crossing of the midlands via Leicester, Coventry and Stratford-on-Avon before the return to the final acceleration test at Cheltenham early on Saturday afternoon.

On the road it was only too evident that drivers had very widely divergent views about the most economical methods of handling a car. Too many had failed to appreciate that the most economical ratio in any gearbox is neutral, and that the most economical engine is one not running – brakes alone should be fully adequate to restrain the speed of a modern car down the longest Welsh hill.

The results produced many surprises, and eliminated an anticipated challenge from foreign cars. Amongst the smaller models, the much fancied Fiat 500 could not better 57½mpg and lost heavily to Morgans and an HRG on the acceleration tests. In the class for cars with four or more seats, the extreme economy of Wilkins's 67¾mpg in the Javelin surprised the Renault and Morris Minor crews, the two most 'fancied' Renaults going out of the running when Jack Newton blew a gasket and Jack Lucy had trouble with a non-standard carburettor.

In sum, whatever this event lacked in entertainment value it fully made up in the technical interest. Next year, when the 100mpg may well be reached by a 'baby' car, it is hoped that the event will have been approved for support by car and component manufacturers, who should be able to learn a great deal from it.

Fuel Economy Contest
Gordon Wilkins
(As reported in *The Autocar*, 1 August 1952)

Jowett Javelin wins with 67.8mpg

The first National Fuel Economy Contest, held on Friday and Saturday of last week, was sponsored by *The News Chronicle* and was organised by the Cheltenham Motor Club. Two well-known motoring journalists put precept into practice by taking the premier awards. Gordon Wilkins of *The Autocar*, driving a Jowett Javelin saloon with Alan Lamburn as co-driver, won the class for cars with four to six seats and made the best performance in the whole event by recording the lowest fuel consumption, regardless of engine size. His figure for the whole route of 828 miles, starting from Cheltenham, going through Wales over some of the most difficult mountain roads and then on through Lancashire to Edinburgh, and returning via the Great North Road and the Midlands was 67.8mpg. J. Lowrey of *The Motor*, with C.H. Bulmer as co-driver, driving a Morgan Plus Four with the 3.7 to 1 Le Mans axle made best performance in the class for cars with two to three seats, with a figure of 57.8mpg.

Both the winning crews adopted a similar driving technique, keeping the engine working at its most efficient condition and coasting wherever possible, but on the Jowett Javelin special care had been taken to reduce rolling resistance to the minimum and at one point it was able to roll for 9 miles without having to use the engine at all.

The team award was won by three Morgans and other outstanding individual performances were made by M.A. Reid and G.H. Lucas, who recorded 63.69mpg in a Morris Minor, and J.V.S. Brown and G.B. Ashton who achieved 54.6mpg in an HRG. Colonel Lucy, last year's winner, had hoped to achieve nearly 80mpg with his Renault, but a last-minute carburettor change destroyed his chances and he could not equal last year's result of 62.4mpg. The 1951 runners-up, Mr and Mrs Jim Readings, took third place in the class for cars with four to six seats, having improved the consumption on their Morris Minor to 62.96mpg.

The results were based on a formula which took into account the result per gallon recorded on the road section, the seating area measured according to the methods used in *The Autocar* Road Tests, and performance in two quarter-mile acceleration tests, one at the beginning of the event and another at the end.

Among the cars up to three seats, the best aggregate performance on acceleration was made by Lowrey, who scored 20.4 and 20.0 seconds in the two runs in his Morgan. In the opposite class the best performance on the first run was by A.F. Roberts who recorded 23.2 seconds in a Ford Zephyr, but the second run was a little slower and was beaten by Wilkins, who recorded 23.2 seconds with the Javelin saloon.

There were forty-nine starters and three of these retired in the course of the road section, one with a broken oil pipe and one with a blown gasket. Particularly unfortunate was A.E. Tumim with a Standard Eight who had to retire from the contest with gearbox trouble after recording over 50mpg. The average speed on the road section was only 29mph but the difficulties of the course were such that several competitors failed to achieve the required speed and after a difficult run over the Welsh mountains, nine crews lost marks at Llandrindod Wells. The Friday mid-day traffic in Wigan, Warrington and Preston also exacted a heavy toll in lost time and seven competitors lost marks at the time control at Cabus, near Garstang, in Lancashire. The turning point at Edinburgh was reached about midnight on Friday and all the competitors were on time. They then had an hour in which to refuel and take a meal before starting on the return run. There was a time control at Boroughbridge, after which further difficulties were encountered in the form of the usual traffic jams in Coventry, Warwick, Leamington, Stratford-on-Avon and Evesham, so once again the modest average speed of even 29mph proved impossible for seven competitors.

The organisation of the event presented several novel problems and the difficult part of sealing and unsealing fuel tanks and bonnets quickly and efficiently at each time control was ably handled by the Cheltenham Motor Club, who showed themselves capable of organisation on a national scale, admirably backed up by the resources of *The News Chronicle*.

A detailed study of the results reveals many technical points of interest. It is clear that variations in driving method can cancel out all the gain owed to careful preparation and it was shown, for example, where an overdrive is fitted the theoretical advantage is not sufficient to compensate for inadequate preparation or driving technique.

Cars had to be standard models on normal tyres, but modifications were permitted to carburettors and ignition systems. Special care was taken by several competitors to maintain a really steady throttle opening, and one driver completed the event driving in socks, without shoes.

One of the outstanding performances was made by Miss Jennifer Whitehall, who won the novices award at the age of nineteen, by achieving 59.3mpg in a Renault 750 saloon. She was driving on L-plates, not yet having taken her driving test.

Bite of the underdog.....
Gordon Wilkins writes from first-hand experience of the competition Jowetts and Yorkshire's moment of success trouncing the best France could produce on their home ground.
(Taken from *Collector's Car* magazine, October 1979)

I went back to Le Mans this year, after a ten year absence, to see how the old place had changed, and to celebrate the 40th anniversary of my first drive there in one of the works Singers. I stayed at the Modeme, where a faded plaque over a garage commemorates glorious days still earlier, in the 1920s, when it was taken over by the Bentley team during Le Mans week.

In 1939 Bill Jones and I shared the cost of preparing the car, insurance, petrol, oil and tyres, hotel bills and transport to and from the circuit, driving the car out and using my MG 1½-litre tourer to carry the stores. We did it all for about £100 each. The cars were fully equipped for use on the road and the circuit was composed of French rural roads, bricks at Indianapolis, gravel elsewhere.

By the 1950s, when I was back at Le Mans racing Jowett Jupiters, it was still a road course though now smoothly surfaced in tarmac and the cars were still close to those you could buy, none more so than the Jupiters which won the 1500cc class three years in succession. Today, Le Mans cars are monstrosities designed solely for thrashing around on a gymnastic circuit between lines of Armco. To use them on the public highway would invite instant prosecution, and the only way you can tell an open car from a closed one is because you can see the top of the driver's helmet among all the other advertisements on an 'open' car.

But why were Jowetts racing at Le Mans at all? Nobody had any such ideas when the post-war Javelin was designed. It all started in 1910 when the two brothers Ben and Bill Jowett began building light cars with flat-twin engines, which gained a great name for reliability and economy, as they went chugging up and down the Yorkshire Dales at the cost of about one penny a mile. But the brothers seem to have been just about as horizontally opposed as their engines, and from time to time each shut himself in his own office, refusing to speak to the other one, so by the Second World War management had passed into other hands. Gerald Palmer, formerly a draughtsman at MG, was invited to design a new car for world markets, which could be launched when the war ended.

The Javelin, like the Mini that came later, was the creation of one man; more so in fact as Gerald Palmer designed the whole car, including the engine, whereas Alec Issigonis had to adapt an existing engine to save time and money. Today, looking at the side elevation of the Javelin, it is astonishing to see what a large proportion of the length is devoted to the passengers and luggage. Today's transverse engines and front-wheel drive do no better.

The flat-four engine with the radiator above and behind it was close under the toe board and there was a flat floor with no propeller shaft tunnel as in those days a high ground clearance was considered essential to cope with 'colonial' roads in export markets. The car was originally designed with the existing facilities at the small plant in Idle, near Bradford. Without the benefit of expensive press tools, the first prototype had all four doors that were interchangeable, but by the end of the war management policies had changed and Briggs Bodies were engaged to build conventional steel unit bodywork at a new plant near Doncaster. This pushed the Javelin into a price class that had not originally been intended and created a demand for more power for which the engine had been designed.

Nevertheless, the design stood up remarkably well when the management decided on a competition programme. Class wins in the 1949 Monte Carlo Rally and the Belgian 24-hour race at Spa were among the first successes and a Javelin won the saloon car class in the RAC Rally.

Soon afterwards I borrowed this car to compete in the Cheltenham Motor Club's National Road Fuel Economy Contest, sponsored by the *News Chronicle*. The cars had to be strictly standard, but there was no restriction on driving methods. With tyres inflated to 60psi, SAE10 oil in engine and transmission and the radiator fully blanked off to conserve heat, I managed to win the cup for the best performance, covering the 828-mile route through England, Wales and Scotland at a minimum average speed of 29mph, with overall consumption at 67.86mpg. Rolling resistance had been reduced so much that I could push the car on the level with one finger. Using the full throttle, switch off and coast method, which was then little-known outside the USA, where the Shell engineers had invented it in competitions run for their own amusement, I managed to coast with a dead engine for 14 miles on the Welsh section of the route. Unfortunately, Jowett were so pleased with the result that they could not resist advertising it and were promptly fined £200 by the SMMT because it was not an approved event.

The thing I most wanted to do with a Javelin was to score in the Alpine Trial, but in those days *Autocar* staff men really had to earn their modest pittance. I was expected to take part in the event, winning if at all possible, but also to report and take photographs. All went well on the night run from Marseilles to Cortina d'Amprezzo and the next day there was a fast circuit round the mountains. Having worked the Javelin into a leading place in its class, I handed over the wheel to Horace Grimley, Jowett's experimental engineer, who had a long experience in competition driving, going back to record breaking at Brooklands in 1926.

For some time we followed Nancy Mitchell who was driving her HRG beautifully, taking each corner in a controlled drift. Suddenly Horace said, 'If she goes on like this, she could get in trouble!' and glanced in my direction. That was it. The tail of the Javelin came round; we spun twice and ended the event wedged between a tree and a stone wall.

Gerald Palmer had returned to MG and with the arrival of Roy Lunn as chief engineer, work began on a two-seater sports car with the American market in mind. ERA, then under the control of Leslie Johnson, were engaged as consultants and Professor Dr Eberan von Eberhorst, who designed the 1938–39 Auto Union Grand Prix single seaters, was put in charge. His light tubular chassis with the improved front suspension devised for the Javelin by Roy Lunn had outstanding road holding. At Le Mans in 1950 Tommy Wisdom and Tommy Wise won the 1500cc class at record speed.

My next engagement was the 1951 Monte Carlo Rally, where three Jupiters were entered and three finished, winning the manufacturers' team prize. My main memories of this event are of the fantastic enthusiasm of people who could not buy new cars but lined the route from Scotland through Wales to Dover up to four deep in places, just to see the cars go by. Then the lavish hospitality as we left the austerity of Britain behind and drove through Holland, Belgium and France.

To be sure, the Mayor of Llandrindod Wells presented us with a guidebook, including a view of Station Crescent and the Post Office, but on the Continent our only regret was that we had not brought a bigger car, as pretty girls loaded us up with hampers of food, bottles of wine, packets of cigarettes, bottles of gin and slabs of chocolate. In Paris each one of us was looked after by his own hostess, in a Paris gown, who plied him with champagne and refreshments and parting gifts of ham, fruit, aperitifs and liqueurs. So generously refuelled, we were well equipped to face the rigours of snow and ice in the Massif Central.

The final test in Monte Carlo marked the turning point between gymnastic special tests of the pre-war era and the road race on ice, which is what the present rally has become. We had to do six laps of the Grand Prix circuit, in which four were marked for speed and consistency, but there was also an acceleration test where we had to brake in the middle, putting the front wheels over a line, reverse back over the line then rush toward the finish. We did alright, but it cost Louis Chiron the rally as he was unbeatable on the circuit but fumbled the gymkhana bit.

However, the Jowett was ill received by the Simca team, who could not understand how their light modern cars whose engines had been breathed upon by the great Amedee Gordini and handled by such racing stars as Trintingant and Scaon, could be so crushingly defeated by those rather ponderous convertibles from the wilds of Yorkshire, handled by a load of garage proprietors, journalists and radio reporters. They lodged a formal protest and our cars were impounded to discover what work the devil had found for Idle hands. It was probably the first time most of the present had seen a Jowett stripped. Not a pretty sight. However, they were obliged to confirm we had no more than declared quantity of cubic centimetres and after some searching questions about the valve diameters and the shape of the inlet tract, our victory was confirmed.

In fact, the limitations of the Jupiter had been laid bare for all who had eyes to see. Starting with 50bhp at 4000rpm with a compression ratio of 7.2 to 1 which was the highest that could be used with the dreadful British Pool petrol of the post-war years, the engine was persuaded to give 68bhp on a 9.25 to 1 compression for the 1952 Le Mans cars, but with much anguish along the way as we were to discover in the 1951 event.

With a split light alloy crankcase and long bolts to hold the cylinder heads down, the engine had began to blow gaskets as the power was increased. This was cured by using Wills gas-filled steel rings in place of the conventional gaskets, but once the compression ratio reached 8 to 1, prolonged high speed running produced failures of the crankshaft, which in its original form had sharp angles between crank pins and crank webs. One crankshaft broke in the 1950 RAC Tourist Trophy. The crankcase was stiffened, the crankshaft was modified and lubrication improved, but at Le Mans in 1951 the first of the new R1 Jupiters suffered a failure of the boss holding a cylinder head stud, leaving Becquart and I to win the class in an ordinary Jupiter.

For the 1952 Le Mans race we had three R1 Jupiters and the latest engine modifications. They weighed about 180lb less than the cars with standard bodies and the frontal area was lower, but improved scuttle construction increased the torsional rigidity and improved the road holding.

The race coincided with an official drive to counteract the bad impression that overcharging and poor service were making on tourists visiting France. The slogan was 'Priorite au Sourire' and any visitor who felt aggrieved by overcharging or poor service was invited to lodge a formal complaint. The Jowett team, staying at the Hotel du Saumon, felt they had plenty to complain about, when they were charged for dinner they could not eat while away on night practice sessions and were refused packed meals to take to the course with them. As I spoke French I was elected to lodge a protest with the Syndicat d'Initative. The result was staggering. We came down to breakfast next morning to find the hotel officially closed, with a Gendarme guarding the door and Madame the proprietress weeping copiously and complaining that she was ruined. New arrangements were swiftly agreed but the hotel was not permitted to reopen until I signed a statement of satisfaction, and thereafter our tables in the dining room were screened off from the rest, so that other visitors should not be irritated by the sight of the princely fare we were receiving.

Marcel Becquart and I had to miss a practice session, as our engine had mysteriously blown up and we had to start the event with a new engine which had been hastily installed and was barely run in. We did not realise how fortunate we were. During the race, both Bert Hadley and Maurice Gatsonides suffered broken crankshafts, with catastrophic effects on the engine, although the cars and drivers survived.

While I was sitting in the pits during an off duty spell, after the second engine had blown up. I noticed Charles Grandfield, the chief engineer, was doing some sums and looking rather thoughtful. He had been checking records of the two failed engines and it dawned on him that our crankshafts had a life of precisely twenty-four hours at racing speeds. Two cars were out and Becquart and I were due to break our crankshaft as we approached the finishing line!

Fortunately, the opposition was once more fading away and we were able to reduce speed on Sunday morning so that the crankshaft held together until we scored the third consecutive class victory for the Jupiter. As far as I remember, the crankshaft broke on the way home. *

And so Jowetts' brief period of glory drew to a close. They were no longer masters of their own destiny, because the price of the Javelin was really dictated by the amount that Briggs charged for the trimmed and painted bodies, to which Jowett merely added the mechanical parts. Ford bought Briggs and the Jowett company changed hands once more. The new owners sold the plant to International Harvester, but rather like the Labour Government who cancelled the RAF's brilliant TSR2 and then sent the prototype away to be used as a target for artillery practice, the Jowett management sawed the R1's in half, so that they could never again run publicly to embarrass them. Fortunately, some apprentices, who had more regard for a valiant attempt by a little company to enter the big league, and a better sense of history than have been displayed by so many management's in the British motor industry, managed to join two halves together again, so that one R1 Jupiter remains in running order.

The bite of the underdog article was reproduced in the Jupiter Owners Auto Club magazine By Jupiter, issue number 1 of 1994. This produced a reply from Phill Green in issue number 2. I am reproducing Phill's excellent letter as it gives more information about the 1952 Le Mans and corrects Gordon's account. Phill was employed in the Experimental Department and was heavily involved with the stillborn CD project and competition work. – NS

The letter, dated 5 April 1994, reads:

How super to be reminded of Gordon Wilkins again and to read his 1979 'Collector's Car' article in last quarter's edition of *By Jupiter*. It certainly does bring the memories flooding back as sharp and clear as ever.

Until the time that the Motor Show moved from its traditional home of Earls Court in London to the NEC I used to meet up with Gordon every year on Press Day – in fact I also used to meet up with Donald Bastow each year and we used to take a walk round the show together. I was with Vauxhall Motors at this time.

Gordon and I would often talk over the 'Good old Jowett days', and, in fact, I still do have a photograph of him and Mrs Wilkins joining one of the Experimental Department's celebrations. It was taken at the Bankfield Hotel, between Saltair and Bingley, and the occasion was a dinner for the department, their wives and girlfriends. Chris was the girlfriend in those days, and we have been married for forty years this year – we actually had our wedding reception at the Bankfield! Ain't life full of coincidences? *(Here's another one – The Jowett Car Club held its 100th Anniversary of the first Jowett National Rally in May 2006, and the hotel we used was the Bankfield. – NS)* Anyway, the crowd of us were obviously celebrating one of our successful rally seasons – it could have been 1952 – because Marcel Becquart was there as also was Madame Serande. Roy Lunn, Charles Grandfield, Donald Barstow, Reg Korner and Horace Grimley were also in the picture. Happy days!

Gordon made mention of the 1952 Le Mans R1 Jupiter which he and Becquart brought successfully to the finish line for Jowett's third class win in a row in the *Collector's Car* article. As he said, two cars went out with broken crankshafts. Very permanent! However, he is not quite right in his final remembrance. The crankshaft did not break on the way home, because I nursed it back to Bradford in one piece.

Under strict instructions from Arthur Illingworth and 'Digger Metcalfe,' I gently nursed the car up the A1 from London, trying desperately not to open it up. I remember it was a beautiful sunny day and I even stopped at the Ram Jam Inn north of Stamford, just to give the car a rest.

Before reaching Newark, the A1 in those days had a number of very inviting swinging curves which, under normal circumstances, could be taken almost flat out. Don't forget, the A1 wasn't a dual carriageway in those days, and if you were appreciably off line, could play some rather breath-taking tricks on you. As I approached these bends ever so sedately a Riley 2.5 came ploughing up behind me, just itching for a dice. What a quandary! Did I contain my baser feelings and continue gently on my way, or did I join battle! I took a deep breath, took my courage in both hands – and floored the pedal! After a glorious 2 miles, during which the Riley nearly lost it through one of the fast bends decided to disappear backwards at a fair rate of knots, I was able to return to my sedate perambulations up the road to Bradford.

You can imagine the relief I felt when I drove in through the gates at Idle. We immediately took the R1 into the Experimental Shop and lifted the engine out. Obviously, as I stripped it down, I was very anxious to see if any lasting damage had been inflicted on the crankshaft. We cleaned it off and treated it with the required liquid before putting it on the department Crack Detector. It just looked as if it were covered in rather large spider's webs. They were all over. It was absolutely covered in hairline – not so hairline – cracks. You can imagine, I heaved a very heavy sigh of relief. Gordon could very nearly have been right!

Gordon Wilkins
Extract from his obituary
(Published in *The Times*, Tuesday 15 June 2007)

Gordon Wilkins began his professional life in the 1930s, when he was just in his twenties, and was still attending motor shows and filing stories into his nineties.

He combined writing with participitation in motor sport that included disciplines as diverse as muddy trials and the 24-hour Le Mans race. Fluent in French and German, he worked extensively throughout Europe.

Born and educated in Liverpool, Wilkins began in the advertising department of the weekly *The Motor*, and moved to the editorial side in 1933. He took up photography and demonstrated artistic skill, contributing hundreds of sketches, cartoons and illustrations to the magazine. He also took a course in engineering to make himself competent to write technical articles.

A frequent visitor to Germany, he could claim to be the last survivor of those journalists who had attended the 1939 launch of the Volkswagen. It was on the way back from that year's Berlin motor show that he and a colleague attempted to achieve 100 miles in the hour in a Lagonda V12. 'Sadly we couldn't quite make it, because Hitler hadn't made enough road,' he once recounted. 'It was almost in the bag until right at the end we ran out of autobahn. I tried my best, sliding around on horse droppings and passing farm carts. We achieved something over 98 miles in the hour.'

Wilkins became involved in motor sport, joining a trials and rally team run by a Savile Row tailor. Their drivers were distinguished by their potent, modified Ford V8's and by being the best dressed of all the competitors. Wilkins really wanted to go racing, and was asked by a neighbour to share a Singer at Le Mans in 1939; they finished a respectable eighteenth overall.

The early war years were spent were spent in the research department of the Bristol Aeroplane Company, before Wilkins moved in 1944 to work with the former Bristol aero-engineer Sir Roy Fedden on the Fedden car, an unconventional design powered by a rear-mounted sleeve-valve radial engine. Wilkins was responsible for the styling of this visionary but misguided project, and recalled the car as being notably lethal to drive.

By 1947 the Fedden project had folded, and Wilkins joined *The Autocar*, where he ultimately became a technical editor and was known for filing detailed and highly readable accounts of the motor industry outside Britain.

He continued to enjoy motor sport and in 1949 he drove one of Jowett's Javelin saloons in the Monte Carlo Rally finishing 161st. In 1951 his factory-entered Jowett Jupiter was tenth overall and second in class.

That year and in 1952 he also won his class at Le Mans in a lightweight Jupiter *(together with Marcel Becquart – NS)*, and in his final sortie to Le Mans in 1953 he co-drove an Austin Healey to fourteenth overall. In 1957 he helped to secure various twenty-four-hour and seven day records in Italy, driving a special streamlined Fiat Abath.

In 1953 Wilkins left *The Autocar* to go freelance. He became one of the most prolific writers in his field, at one stage contributing to twenty-seven magazines throughout the world. In the 1960s and 1970s, he combined this work with compiling the *Daily Express* Motor Show Guide.

Wilkins was the anchorman for the *Wheelbase* TV programme, and he continued to be involved sporadically with television in later years. He also translated various motoring books from French and Italian.

From 1980 to 1992, when they moved to their final home in rural southern France, Wilkins and his wife, Joyce, who was very much his professional partner, were able to live in a palazzo in northern Italy, thanks to the then friendship of an Italian count.

Affable, urbane and with an engaging modesty, Wilkins was aware that he had led a fortunate life; however, those who spent time with him soon came to appreciate that he had earned this through talent and hard work.

His wife predeceased him, and there were no children.

Gordon Wilkins, journalist and broadcaster, was born on 6 October 1912, and he died on 11 April 2007 aged ninety-four.

1951 Monte Carlo Rally
Taken from Tales of My Time *by Raymond Baxter, in collaboration with Tony Dron*
(Published by Grub Street of London 2005)

Raymond Baxter had been a broadcaster and journalist for well over fifty years; he drove a Jupiter in the 1951 Monte Carlo Rally with Gordon Wilkins. This new book is the only time I have seen in print any of his reminiscences of these events, apart from a couple of forewords he wrote for other people's books. I will quote from all three of these, as there is only limited material available. In his own book this is what he said: – NS

After the war, the historic but minor manufacturer Jowett hired Professor Robert Eberan Eberhorst, a brilliant German engineer of pre-war reputation with Auto Union. He designed the unconventional Jowett Javelin four-seater and later the two-seat sports version soft-top, the Jupiter. ★

Jowett invited me to Brands Hatch to have a go in the Jupiter with Gordon Wilkins. As a result we were offered a works drive in the Jupiter in the 1951 Monte Carlo, with me as co-driver.

We finished eleventh and second in class and the three Jupiters won the manufacturers' team prize. I met all my broadcasting commitments, which built up an audience, and I reckoned we were in business.

Sadly for me, the Monte went pear-shaped next year. Gordon and I had a works Jaguar Mark 7. His wife turned up at midnight, at the control at Saint-Claude in the Massif Central, on the last night. It was a snow-bound year and critical that we should make time immediately after that control on some fairly fast roads before the mountains. We left two minutes late! I was furious and Gordon stuffed us into a snow-filled ditch.

At the start of my first Monte in 1951, outside the Royal Scottish Automobile Club in Blyhswood Square, Glasgow, I took my live microphone for a walk down the line of competitors, and that was how I first met Jackie Reece. He and his cousin, Peter, had already won a reputation with their bog-standard Ford Anglia. As I approached, Jackie was tinkering at the carburettor with a broken nail file.

'Final adjustments, Mr Reece?' I said.

'I am j-just c-coaxing the last ounce of p-power from the m-mighty m-motor.' I did not know until then that Jackie had a pronounced stammer, but it would clearly have been rude to break off the conversation.

'As your car is standard, you have no rev counter. Won't that be a problem in the mountains?' I asked.

'Not at all,' said Jackie. 'When the knob on the end of the g-g-gear lever glows cherry red, I change up.'

Jackie Reece became one of my dearest friends. When his uncle died he inherited Blake's of Liverpool – 'We sell Fords for a living and Aston Martins for fun,' he would say, and partly because of that we shared an Aston Martin DB3 on the Monte Carlo in 1958.

★NB. I have typed this quote as it appears in the book, but clearly this is incorrect, as it is well documented that Gerald Palmer designed the Javelin in all respects. As regards the Jupiter, Eberhorst designed the tubular chassis only, the mechanicals were basically from the Javelin and the body was designed in-house by Jowett's designer Reg Korner.

Sadly Raymond died on 15 September 2006 at the age of eighty-four, he was the face of the BBC programme Tomorrow's World *for twelve years from 1965, and had a knack of making science simple. He was an excellent commentator and was sought out for important sporting and state occasions such as the annual Festival of Remembrance, the funerals of Lord Mountbatten of Burma and Sir Winston Churchill, also the Coronation in 1953. During the war he flew Spitfires and became a squadron leader. He also commentated on Concord's first flight and covered air shows such as Biggin Hill. He had been the Vice President of the Jowett Car Club for at least forty years, and will be sadly missed by us all. – NS*

Raymond had also written about the Monte Carlo Rally in general terms as forewords to other people's books on the Monte. I am including extracts from each of these. – NS

Rallying to Monte Carlo
By Mike Couper
(Published by Ian Allan Ltd, 1956)

The Monte Carlo Rally is by no means the only rally of its kind in the International Calendar. It is not the toughest test available to man and machine. It has neither the largest entry nor the most brilliant organisation. It is not exclusively reserved to the privileged few, neither on the grounds of skill or financial resources. I doubt if it is fair to say that it is more publicised than all its rival marathon drives!

Once it was all of those things, but those days are separated from the contemporary world of motoring by those six years, during which so many sporting drivers found themselves in the cockpits of aircraft, the turrets of tanks or on the bridges of fighting ships.

But yet the Monte Carlo Rally still manages to retain a unique appeal to those who consider that there is more to motoring than the daily trip to the office, and the weekend with the family in the country.

Precisely why this should be is difficult to state in a succinct analysis. That it is so is indisputable, and should you doubt this claim, ask anyone who essayed this improbable journey across Europe, during the vagaries of this mid-winter climate.

'Doing the Monte' is like being a dog owner. Once you start it is difficult to stop, consider the case of the author of this book.

Raymond goes on to talk about Mike Couper in detail, but finishes the foreword off like this:

To me as a comparative newcomer, with only five cracks at the Monte to my name, Mike is as much a permanent feature of the event as the Col de Braus, or the annual visit to the Casino.

Perhaps this is because when I first started in motoring, he went out of his way to be kind and helpful, in the most unobtrusive way possible. He in fact is a sporting motorist of great experience and a gentleman. Who better to write a book on the 'Monte'?

Raymond Baxter

Destination Monte
By Peter Harper
(Published by Stanley Paul, London, 1964)

It is often said that husbands and wives going rallying together provide the greatest factor but one in the divorce rate. Certainly if you get in a car with someone, close the doors on the outside world, and emerge eighty-odd hours and over 2,000 miles later, you will have got to know a lot about your companion; and he about you.

I have been lucky enough to share a car with Peter Harper under these circumstances – and, what's more, I have even been asked again! I have been in the same team, competed against it, and I have watched him and the team in action many times from the privileged position of the professional reporter. What I have seen I like – very much.

Raymond then goes on to talk about Peter at length, but then refers to a very unfortunate problem he had with Peter – travel sickness!

On that awful occasion when, as his co-driver, I was horribly sick during the final test of the Monte Carlo Rally. Every time I attempted the vital calculations concerning our arrival time at the control, I nearly died, and hoped I might. Beyond doing these sums I was worse than useless to him for at least four hours. He just went on driving as fast as he possibly could all the time.

Later, when we were refuelling, still during the test, he called for buckets of water, and did his best to wash the marks of my shame from the car, while sternly ordering me to stay and rest in the left-hand seat. But this he does not mention himself.

Peter does in fact cover this event in some detail in the book:

Travel sickness is a rally hazard manfully endured by many a skilful Navigator or co-driver. I am reminded of this when I think of the time I teamed up with the BBC's Raymond Baxter and started out of Frankfurt.

The final test was again behind Monte Carlo in the mountains and again I had carried out a recce. It wasn't as thorough as the recces we do now, but nevertheless I knew the road fairly well. This proved to be fortunate as it was shortly after this that Raymond was violently car-sick. This was nothing new among navigators. It was something to do with being thrown around while looking down and reading, and it seems much more prevalent at night.

I thought his sickness would quickly pass, but he got steadily worse until one time I was sure he was practically unconscious. I began to wonder if I could forge his signature at the time control. The object of the test was to make your given times on the road sections while going round first time in the dark. The circuit then had to be done in daylight, but it was also a regularity test, so daylight timings on each section had to correspond with the timings made in the dark.

Here was also a secret check for exceeding the maximum average allowed. I thought this secret check could be imposed only on one stretch of road, and checked my speed there to avoid any possibility of being disqualified. As soon as daylight broke, Raymond started to take an interest in life again, but the strange thing was that on one section I was a few seconds slower in daylight, when I did not have the inconvenience of driving in the dark and was without the worry of knowing whether Raymond was alive or not.

We won our class, finished fourth, and were the best British car. Some consolation for Raymond, who hadn't enjoyed the most comfortable of rallies!

RAYMOND BAXTER

After I had typed the above extracts, I realised that Raymond had in fact also written an account of his 1951 'Monte' recollections for the Jowett Car Club. In June 1982 the club held its National Rally at Holker Hall in Cumbria. The organisers had invited Raymond to the event, but sadly, he was not able to attend. He did, however send a letter together with a 'scribble' which was published in the rally programme. I am reproducing both the letter and the 'scribble', though it is hardly that! – NS

16 February 1982.
Dear Mr Nicholson,
Thank you for your letter of the 6th.

It was kind of you to invite me to your celebrations but, unfortunately, as you surmised, I have already committed myself to be elsewhere on 5/6th. I can only ask you to accept my apologies together with good wishes for the success of your event.

However, I enclose a 'scribble' in the hope, as you suggest, that it may provide a programme note.

Again my apologies but please convey my warmest greetings to your members.

Yours sincerely, Raymond Baxter

Now for the 'scribble':

A woman, it is said, never forgets her first lover. A man, I am sure, never forgets the car on which he did his first Monte Carlo Rally.

That alone would ensure for the name of Jowett a very special place in my memory and affections for, much to the surprise of many, we managed to do rather well, Gordon Wilkins and I brought our Jupiter into ninth place in general classification, as I recall. Certainly we were second in the class to our team-mate Bill Robinson, and with Tommy Wise in his Jupiter, we cleaned up the famous Team Prize – the 'Challenge Charles Faroux', for a nominated entry of three cars of the same marque. That was in 1951, the year my son was born – which was another good reason to remember the date. Indeed, as my wife never fails to remind me, immediately after that happy event I went off motoring, leaving her holding (literally) the baby. On our return the 'works' gave us a celebration dinner in Bradford. The menu was dedicated to the theme 'Bringing home the bacon' and the handsome silver mug presented to each driver still decorates my study.

Actually 1951 was a comparatively easy year as far as the weather was concerned, so the very lively performance of the Jupiter stood us in good stead. Even though it was pretty hard work. What 'Monte' has not been, if one was out to win as opposed to merely finishing?

It was also the first Monte Carlo Rally the BBC broadcast from a competitors' point of view. We did 'live' reports every night at 1015 on the Light Programme and built up, I think it fair to say, a considerable audience amongst people not particularly interested in motor sport. And we were still doing that fourteen years later.

But those were the 'good old days' when, although the competition was as keen as it ever has been, motoring even at that level of major International events was still fun rather than big business. I, for one, was very proud to be a works driver in a British manufacturer's team which was prepared to 'take on' and 'see off' the rest of the world.

Raymond Baxter

ROY LUNN

Roy Lunn took over as chief designer at Jowetts in 1949, replacing Gerald Palmer who had moved back to Morris. He wrote a most interesting letter to Steve Waldenberg, which he published in the December 1986 issue of The Jowetteer. *At the time Steve was the editor of* The Jowetteer, *and, in fact, he still prints it for the club. I have edited Roy's letter slightly, as the first part related to some photographs he donated to the Club at that time. – NS*

After all these years I still look back on the Jowett period of my life with special fondness for all its happy memories. These are awakened once a month with the delivery of *The Jowetteer* to my home in Florida, which I very much appreciate.

Charles Grandfield employed me as Chief Designer in 1949 to replace Gerald Palmer who had returned to Morris. I was twenty-three years old and although I had worked at AC Cars and Aston Martin, the assignment at Jowetts was totally unexpected. Charles became my teacher for the following four years, which turned out to be very eventful, challenging and a great learning experience for a young engineer. Picking up the continuing engineering on the Javelin, working with Eberan von Eberhorst on the original Jupiter, evolving the CD line of vehicles, generating the R1 and R4 Jupiter sports cars, the involvement in racing and driving in rallies for three years with Marcel Becquart was beyond any young man's dreams for four years. In that period there was always something happening and the work on the regular models was punctuated by interesting test trips around Europe and going to racing events and rallies.

The CD series of vehicles and the R4 sports car derivatives was the major problem at the time. The two-cylinder versions of the CD were underpowered but could have the four-cylinder unit as per the R4 model. Through all these projects, Charles Grandfield and later Donald Barstow gave me a tremendous foundation for my future career. They tolerated me as a pedantic young engineer and gave me great encouragement to create.

At the end of 1953 I left Jowetts and unhappily learned later of the sale of the company and cessation of car production. Although it was a great disappointment it was still a hell of an education. After leaving Jowetts I started the Ford Research Establishment in Birmingham and gathered some of the old team from Idle. On moving to Dagenham and after several interesting programmes, I emigrated to the States in 1958 and headed Ford US Advanced Engineering. This gave the opportunity for designing not only advanced road cars, but anything from a single-seater flying car, a 170,000lbs GVW super highway truck, the Mustang 1 and a variety of other vehicles leading to the GT40 and the MkII and MkIV vehicles that won Le Mans in 1966, '67, '68 & '69. This was particularly gratifying for me, as my first effort to win Le Mans was in 1949 with the DBII Astons. It was, however, much of what I learned in working on the winning Jupiters in the 1.5 litre class at Le Mans between 1950 and 1952 that gave the background to the Ford's success.

In 1971 I became Director of Jeep Engineering and later, Vice President of Engineering for all American Motors and Jeep products. This was also a gratifying experience culminating in the Eagles, the Renault's introduction and the Jeeps through to the present models. I retired from this position in 1983 and started and became President of a subsidiary of American Motors, called Renault Jeep Sport Inc. This turned out to be my fourth involvement in racing after Aston Martin, Jowett and Ford. It provided challenges for creating Jeeps racing in the US and Mexican off-road events such as the Baja as well as track racing with other specially prepared models. One memorable experience was to drive in the 1984 Paris – Dakar event to reconnoitre what would be required to compete on a future occasion. In 1984 we also won the Front Wheel Drive Racing Championship with two specially prepared Renaults.

Another interesting programme was the designing and building of an affordable racing vehicle for SCCA (Sports Car Club of America). This machine was designed and prototyped in three months and put into production ten months later. It is a $10,000 machine and comes partially assembled and is raced in a class by itself. Modifications are not allowed and the winning is by skill of tailoring and driving rather than dollars.

Renault Jeep Sport inadvertently became the largest producer of track racing cars in the world and has produced 465 of these little machines to date. They are raced all over America with often as many as sixty as cars in an event. While generating this little machine, I was reminded of the R4 which was created in a similar time span.

I retired again at the end of 1985 and after three months was persuaded to start a new career last April. I am now the Vice President of Engineering for the AM General Corporation that manufacturers trucks and Jeep-type products for the US Army. This is keeping me busy and it seems I never have time to get old.

Once again I can only say thank you to my associates at Jowetts, particularly Charles Grandfield and Donald Barstow, who gave me the background that made my career so rewarding and successful.

I still have the original R4 emblem mounted at the back of my home bar which, together with the monthly *Jowetteer*, constantly reminds me of those happy Jowett years.

Roy Lunn was the co-driver with Marcel Becquart in the RAC Rallies of 1951 and 1952. Unfortunately, I have no personal accounts of his for either of these events, but he was in correspondence with Keith Wear, the club's film librarian, in 1992, where he talked about a Continental test drive in a prototype CD registered HKW272, and is detailed below:

I remember the test run very well, it was in late 1951. The CD was designed to be built as either RH or LH drive, so it was converted to LHD for the trip, which took place in the early spring of 1952. I was accompanied by Ted Fannon who worked in the Experimental Department.

We headed for the south coast, crossed on the ferry and drove across France via Rheims, Dijon and down to Annecy where we visited Marcel Becquart, with whom I had driven in the RAC Rally. From here we went to Lugano in Switzerland, where we picked up our third traveller. He was the son of the Lugano Jowett dealer and had trained at the factory and was consequently very knowledgeable about Jowetts and naturally spoke Italian.

The three of us set off into Italy, hitting the Mediterranean coast at Genoa and headed south to Pisa. I still recall driving down the coast road with the blue Mediterranean on the right, and on the left one could look inland over the newly budding olive trees to the snow capped mountains. I remarked on the beauty to Ted, who was a very loyal Yorkshireman. After a moments silence he commented 'Yorkshire could look like this if it was cleaned up a bit.'

The rest of the trip took us south to Rome, Naples and Pompeii, then across to the Adriatic. We went north through Pescara, Ancona, Rimini and across to Bologna and back to Lugano. That is how I remember the route, but as I did the journey again later in the R4, I may have the sequence out of order.

The trip was most successful not only from durability testing aspects, but also for general vehicle capabilities and characteristics. As I recall we did nothing but normal service the whole trip.

I have vague recollections of the filming you mentioned and the trip over to St Moritz but I cannot remember if it was before or after the swing round into Italy. ★ I do remember driving down the multi hair-pinned road with Ted shouting he wanted danger pay. As I recall we went back across France via Lyon, Nevers, Le Mans and Rouen and then back to England.

★*The filming Roy mentions is in respect of a 3¾-minute cine film Keith asked him about, a copy of which is in the club film archive, which was taken on this trip. – NS*

MARCEL BECQUART

Marcel Becquart played a very important part in Jowett's racing programme, and was probably the most successful Jowett driver of all. Naturally, most people tend to think of the two Le Mans class wins in 1951 and 1952, but there were other notable successes. In the 1952 Monte Carlo Rally he finished first in the 1500cc class and fifth in the general classification, which was the highest placing Jowett ever achieved in this event. In 1953 he was on track for an outright win, but disaster struck with the ventilation fan breaking away and going through the radiator on the final speed test in the Col de Braus, so was not able to finish the stage, but he was still an official finisher.

He teamed up with Roy Lunn in a works Jupiter in the RAC Rally in 1951. The following year he was to enter the Farina Jupiter, but it was rejected as it was a non-standard car. Roy Lunn came to his aid by making his Javelin registered HAK743 available to him, so partnered him a second time. Marcel produced a stunning speed test up Oliver's Mount in Scarborough and clinched first place in the saloon class.

He had originally been placed first in class in the 1953 Tulip Rally in the Javelin HAK743, but was later disqualified when the car was found to have a minor non-standard alteration to the exhaust system. Needless to say, Marcel was furious with Jowett's and never drove for them again. – NS

Rallying
By Marcel Becquart
(As published in the *Jowetteer Yearbook* of 1970)

I drove in my personal 20 CV Hotchkiss in rallies in 1947, '48, '49 and '50. I had been first in the Monte Carlo Rally in that year.

At that moment, the General Manager of Hotchkiss since many years before the war was Mr Ainsworth (still living in Paris). But in 1950 the shares in the company went to Peugeot and they changed the management. Mr Ainsworth became the European sales manager for Europe for the Jowett Company, which was just coming onto the market with the Jupiter.

I bought through Mr Ainsworth a Jupiter chassis and sent it to Torino to Farina for the body (only two cars have been made so far...) *(there were in fact four made in total – NS)* I drove that car in the 1952 Monte and finished fifth in general classification. I drove it again in 1953, but the ventilation fan went through the radiator in the Col de Braus on the final test, so could not finish.

I drove a works Jupiter in the 1951 RAC Rally with a young engineer from the factory, Roy Lunn (well known, actually, in the Ford Company, he is the designer of the Ford Mustang), and we made in many tests the best time, but we were far down in the general classification, as we got lost several times on the road section. In 1952 in a Javelin, still with Roy Lunn, we won the general classification (closed cars) of the RAC. (Geoff Imhof in an Allard won the open class.)

I also drove in the 1951 and 1952 Le Mans with Gordon Wilkins and won the 1500cc class in 1951, being second (Porsche was arriving!) in 1952. *

It was very sad news for me when I learnt that the factory was going to close, as the new R4 Jupiter (designed by Roy Lunn) was coming, and was very promising. I drove it during an experimental journey with Roy Lunn, and I am very sure it would have been a very good and successful type.

*Clearly this gives the impression Porsche beat Jowett into second place in the 1500cc class in 1952, which was not the case. It should be noted, however, that Jowett had some good luck, as the Porsche was in fact leading by twenty laps with four hours to go, when it was disqualified for failing to switch the engine off when refuelling in the pits. The R1 went on to win the 1500cc class as the sole survivor in the class, but at a slower average speed of 72.94mph, covering 210 laps, a total distance of 1,751.58 miles, taking thirteenth place in the overall placings.

Another interesting but little publicised fact, in Jowett circles anyway, was that a Porsche did in fact beat the R1 in this race; it was entered in the 1.1 litre class. The car in question was a 1,086cc Porsche driven by Auguste Veuillet and Edmond Mouche, they covered a total distance of 1,836.4 miles at an average speed of 76.51mph, covering 220 laps, taking tenth place in the overall placing. This makes Marcel's comment as being second to the Porsche in 1952 more understandable. It was obvious to Jowett that the car was now totally outclassed, but picked up this win due to the unreliability of the other much faster cars in the 1.5 litre class and the good fortune of the smaller Porsche being entered in the 1.1 litre class.

It was therefore the last year that Jowett's entered; this was clearly the right decision as a Porsche won the 1500cc class in the 1953 event at a record average speed of 86.28mph, an average speed of well over 13mph faster than the R1. – NS

The Jowett Car Club archive holds copies of our club magazine The Jowetteer *back to 1961; they were produced, however, for many years before this date also. A club member sent me a photocopy of a Jowetteer magazine dated November 1952, which is now in the club archive. This was a good issue for me, as there was a potted-history on Marcel Becquart and his racing achievements up to that date, which I reproduce below:*

Our President
Marcel Becquart

For the interest of all members we have gleaned some facts and figures concerning our President, which we here compile into a short history, starting with his private life and interests,

Line up of the team of three R1 Jupiters prior to the start of the 1952 Le Mans. *From left to right:* Marcel Becquart seated in 45; Tommy Wise and Charles Granfield are standing between 45 and 46; Roy Lunn is seated in 46; Horace Grimley is stood to the right of 46 and Maurice Gastonides is seated in the third car. At this stage it was on the reserve list, but was later accepted for the race, carrying race number 64. (JCC)

then enumerating the thirteen Rallies and Events which have contributed towards his rise to fame in a relatively short space of time.

Marcel Becquart was born in Brussels of French parents – celebrated his fortieth birthday this year at sea, en route for the Rally Morocque. He is married to a Welsh girl, and they have a son of seventeen years and a daughter of thirteen. He is in business as a leather watch strap manufacturer and employs forty workers. His hobby in the main is stamp-collecting, and he is reputed to have one of the best collections in Haute Savoie. He also has an excellent library which includes many of the best British Classics, of which he and his wife are particularly fond.

In the motor racing world, Marcel remains an amateur, since he pays his own entry fees – the Le Mans entries being his own and not the factory's; prize monies he splits into thirds, one to his co-driver, one to his mechanics tending his cars, and a third for his own use. He claims the British Amateur has the most wonderful spirit, sticks to the regs. & gives a good clean fight – this is not always the case with the professional, who has to win at any price; in consequence of his voiced experiences in this direction, he has provided a Trophy for the best performance by a British Amateur driving in International Rallies; this has now been passed to the British Trials Drivers' Association, and will be run for next year.

He is also President of 'Commission Sportive' of the Mount-Blanc Automobile Club, and for six years has run the Evian-Megeve Rally, very popular with the British drivers, fourteen entering in 1951 and sixteen this year.

Here is some detail of the thirteen rallies Marcel has entered since 1949:

1) 1949 brought Marcel to his first rally, The Monte Carlo Rally, in which he drove a Hotchkiss, and was placed fortieth. No road marks were lost, however it is interesting to note that he has never lost road marks on a Monte Carlo.
2) The Lyons-Charbonnieres – all went well until reaching Le Puy where he went into a skid, and after five somersaults retired. Reason; speed too high for the wet road.

3) Rally De L'Iseran – took second place in his class driving an 1100cc Simca.
4) Outright winner in the 1950 Monte Carlo Rally, driving a Hotchkiss.
5) The Lyons-Charbonnieres again, driving a Hotchkiss, finished third in general classification and first in his class – having the best performance of all classes in the hill-climb test.
6) Roy Clarkson persuaded Marcel to enter for the first *Daily Express* Rally, forgetting Marcel held a French Competition Licence and was therefore not eligible. Endeavours were made to get the French Licence cancelled in favour of a British one, but the French National Club declined to do this, and the result was that Marcel was allowed to start and follow the rally without being eligible for an award. As fate would have it, he went out with a broken piston in Wales and retired anyway – as also did Roy Clarkson, in order to take Marcel and Henri Secret to Torquay. This was indeed a sad introduction to British Motor Racing for Marcel, and was little better for Roy, who was, after all, responsible for introducing him to it.
7) The 1951 Monte Carlo Rally in which he drove a Hotchkiss with Octal Box (Electric gearshift) – it selected the wrong gear in the acceleration test. In the regularity test at Monte Carlo he came through the chicane too fast, striking the kerb, which flung the car round and the spare wheel flew off into the sea. Everyone thought that this was Henri Secret (his co-driver until the 1952 Monte). Marcel was placed fiftieth, but was credited with his fastest lap of two minutes fifteen seconds.
8) 1951 Le Mans, Marcel had by this time secured a Jupiter to which he had fitted a Farina body (this car appeared at the 1950 Paris Show). Whilst awaiting a chassis modification from Jowetts, Marcel had to use a Works car for both Le Mans and the RAC Rally; he was winner of his class in the Le Mans.
9) 1951 RAC Rally, again best in class in the Rest & Be Thankful, also best performance in class at Bournemouth, but in the Blackpool test he had to use reverse gear on two occasions owing to the short lock on the Works Car, and being slowed by this, was placed fifth in class in the rally.
10) The 1952 Monte Carlo Rally – fifth in general classification, and second in his class. It appears that in the early stages of the rally, he hit a dog and badly crumpled the front of the Jowett, shattering one of the headlamps, but drove so fast that at Paris there was time to repair the full damage before checking in at the control, after which he returned to the repair shop and had the front end painted before driving on to Clermont Ferrand, and at the finish, there was little sign of any damage at all.
11) The 1952 RAC Rally, Closed Cars – best in his class at the Rest & Be Thankful Hill Climb, and also at Mount Oliver Final Test in Scarborough.
12) 1952 Le Mans – First in class driving Jupiter R1.
13) Rally Morocque, driving a Peugeot, Marcel was leading in the Anfa Six-Hours (Le Mans Formula) but after four and a half racing, the wires came off the control box, leaving him with only first and second gears. After repairs, however, he finished fifth in general classification.

We are all looking forward to meeting Marcel at the AGM on 1 December.

John Bolster Tests 'That Tulip Rally Javelin'
(*Autosport*, 25 September 1953)

It is always interesting to try a car that has 'been in the news'. In recent months, there has surely been no more sensational story than Marcel Becquart's disqualification in the Tulip Rally, which vitally affected the results. He drove what was outwardly a standard 1953 Javelin, except for the usual elaborate rally equipment, and he certainly put up an electrifying performance with it. Unfortunately, the sleuths discovered that the exhaust system had some trifling modification, and that is, apparently, against the rules.

The RAC Rally of 1952, where Roy Lunn allowed the French driving ace Marcel Becquart to drive his Javelin after his Farina-bodied Jupiter had not been accepted as an entrant, as it had a non-standard body. This is at the start of the Oliver's Mount stage, where Marcel had a storming run to take the class win. (Charles Dunn/JCC)

Thus, the organisers had no alternative but to exclude poor Becquart, though he was probably unaware of the slightly non-standard pipe. Anyway, the Javelin in Tulip tune, and with its extra equipment, is now on the market. My friend, Robin Richards, recently offered to lend it to me for a few days, and so I repaired to the showrooms of Messrs Richards and Carr, at 35 Kinnerton Street, London SW1, where the vehicle was on view.

There I found a bronze coloured four-door saloon, which had none of the 'porcupine' look so common among rally cars. The powerful Marchal headlamps fitted into the normal mountings, and a fog lamp of the same make was clipped unobtrusively to the bumper. There was built-in defrosting of the rear window, and the windscreen also had this provision. There were innumerable extra pockets and lockers, too, some of them labelled rather amusingly in French as well as English.

The most noticeable alteration was in the seating for a bench-type front seat had replaced the separate arrangement. It had a permanent central arm rest so that the driver and passenger were held in their proper places, however violent the manoeuvres in progress. The principal object of all this was to allow the passenger to sleep. He was provided with a comfortable head rest, an aircraft-type safety belt, a footrest, and padding at strategic points. In fact the machine had all the equipment which an experienced competitor could desire.

As far as the car was concerned, it would appear that the engine was of virtually standard series 3 specification, but most carefully balanced and assembled. It did not pink on ordinary pump fuel, but it certainly revved with exceptional freedom. One might say, in fact, that this vehicle gave the best of both worlds, for it had most of the performance of the Jupiter, while offering the much greater passenger accommodation of a Javelin.

Marcel Becquart slides the Javelin round a corner on the Oliver's Mount section in the International RAC Rally of 1952. (JCC)

The finish control, Scarborough, in the 1952 International RAC Rally. (Charles Dunn/JCC)

Marcel Becquart with the Farina-bodied Jupiter, one of only four made; he was to have successes with the car even though it was not eligible for the 1952 International RAC Rally. (Le Blanc/JCC)

On the road, the Javelin got going in fine style. I think that the suspension may have been somewhat stiffened, for certainly one could fling the car around in a most violent manner without appreciable rolling. Having checked the speedometer, which showed only a small degree of optimism, I took some acceleration figures. As a mean of runs in both directions, I was able to record a 0-50mph time of 13 3/5 seconds, and 0-60mph 19 1/5 seconds were occupied.

The Javelin has a steering column gear change, which is as good an example as any I have handled. Nevertheless, I shall always prefer a floor-mounted lever, on the right (*a la* Rolls-Royce) for choice, but a good central control (Bristol fashion) can be very pleasant. However, if one must follow the modern style, the rigidity of construction and low frictional losses of the Jowett design ensure that precise control which is essential for rally tests.

To drive, this is a small narrow car, and it can be taken through quite heavy traffic at apparently impossible speeds. Naturally, there is a temptation to compare it with the Jupiter, though the two models are not really competitive. Of course, the room in the body is the Javelin's greatest virtue for rally work, but in other respects, the sports two-seater by the same maker comes into its own. Although both cars handle equally well on dry roads, the Jupiter has an incredible mastery of wet and greasy surfaces that neither the Javelin nor almost any other car can equal. Then there is the question of engine accessibility, which is quite excellent for the speed model, but frankly mediocre in the machine under review. For the majority of users, however, a four-door saloon is the correct wear, and that is that.

This particular engine seemed to revel in high-speed work, as a properly prepared competition unit should. 40mph was easily exceeded on second speed, and a full 60mph could be reached in third. The maximum velocity was just on the sunny side of eighty, which is certainly good going for a roomy saloon with only 1½ litres to pull it. The small size of the power unit paid dividends in fuel economy, for 30mpg could be attained at reasonable cruising speeds, and even the most brutal driving failed to bring the consumption below the mid-twenties.

The 'flat four' Jowett engine is not so unobtrusive as a good 'in line' unit, partly because it is largely of light-alloy construction. The exhaust has a typical and unusual sound, but curiously enough this particular example seemed quieter than standard. In spite of that the future owner would be well advised to replace it with the normal manifolding if he intends entering international rallies, for one disqualification is surely sufficient!

There remains the question of using a rally-equipped car for everyday motoring, and I would say that the attention paid to the lighting, demisting and windscreen washing equipment would pay dividends compared to the less lavish arrangements of a standard car. I had no occasion to use the snow shovel or, for that matter to strap my passenger down, but the extra lockers and pockets were of great convenience which any driver would appreciate.

BERT HADLEY

Bert Hadley had several drives for Jowett including the 1951 BRDC Silverstone One-Hour Production Race, Le Mans and the RAC TT at Dundrod. Then the 1952 RAC Rally and Le Mans. Charles Grandfield knew Hadley, as they had worked together at Austin in pre-war days. I do not have any direct quotes from Bert Hadley, but I have been lucky enough to obtain some correspondence between Hadley and Grandfield from March 1952 regarding preparations for the RAC Rally of that year, which makes interesting reading. I am most grateful to Geoff Roe of the pre-war Austin 7 club for giving me these copies. – NS

Dear Bert, Thank you for your letter of the 3rd instant and the copy of the BARC Regulations, these will be very useful. I am sorry I cannot send you any regulations for the RAC Rally, since I have only one copy, so you will have to bother the RAC for them.

I am enclosing some correspondence which has arrived from the RAC, concerning the matter of insurance; we shall look after that for both you and the car personally so there will be no need for you to take any action with Muir Baddal.

Tom Wise's address is: 'Whitestacks', Scotton, Nr Knaresborough, Yorks and you certainly better give some close attention to the methods of manipulating the motor car, since we shall be relying very much on the Hadley effort to keep the good name flying, especially as there seems to be every possibility that Marcel Becquart will cancel his entry in view of the RAC refusing to accept his Farina Bodied vehicle. Marcel's reaction is, 'My vehicle is built on a chassis on which more than 250 have been made, it is heavier than the normal vehicle, it was accepted for the Monte Carlo Rally', so he is definitely of the impression that the RAC are victimising him. Anyway at the moment there is a brisk interchange of cables between here and Annecy and I hope to get his entry finalised one way or the other within the next day or two.

Kind regards, Charles, 5 March 1952

Dear Bert, Thank you for your letter of the 8th instant, I am very glad to know that Bill Butler has decided to drive with you, I am sure it will be a very strong crew.

Regarding the date when you pick up the car, we are not going to let you have it too early otherwise you may wear it out and probably break it, and I suggest that you and Bill might come up to the Works here on Saturday 29th, when you could leave your private cars here, picking up the Jupiter and proceeding to Scarborough sometime on Sunday 30th where accommodation has been booked for you at the Grand Hotel for the Sunday night, when you then start the rally on Monday.

Regarding the question of Bench versus Bucket Seats, I wonder if you really appreciate the comfortable nature of the Bucket Seats fitted to 107, these were the ones fitted to the car when it won the Monte Carlo Rally and were said to be extremely comfortable by Messrs. Wilkins and Baxter. They are certainly very well padded and the passenger's seat gives side support so that he is not violently thrown about when asleep. If, however, you still think that the Bench Seat would be more suitable let me know and we will change it. But since there is a little difference in leg length and overall height between you and Butler, I think it would probably be best if you each had a Bucket Seat with an individual adjustment.

Regarding the big pedals, we will have these fitted to your car, and I am quite sure you will find room for two small suitcases without under-lining the word small too much.

I am enclosing a letter which has been received from the Esso Petroleum Co., please would you disregard this, since we have a definite agreement with Shell and they will be supplying special fuel at certain points which I will acquaint you with after having attended a Meeting with Shell tomorrow.

Regarding the Bonuses we will see that you are not out of pocket in this respect, if a good performance occurs.

Kind regards, Charles, 11 March 1952
78 Red Lane, Kenilworth, 14 March 1952

Dear Charles, Many thanks for your letter of the 11th instant.

It will be necessary for us to arrive at Bradford during the afternoon of the 29th – I have to attend a meeting in the morning. I trust this will be in order.

I am quite agreeable to bucket seats as you suggest, thanks for the pedal alterations. According to 'Motor' report on 106 the luggage accommodation equals two suitcases 24' x 14' x 8' dimension, so I think we will manage. Perhaps you will let me know if this is not so – don't bother to write if my assumptions are correct.

I note the Esso letter and your remarks.

Tell Tommy Wise that I will try and find out about the Singer Le Mans job. I have better contacts for this purpose than Bill these days. Incidentally, the Singer could be a very potent entry – the 1½-litre power unit as fitted to the SM1500 has plenty of scope for boosting. The Company have plenty of problems however at the moment with 850 export cars idle for whom no overseas buyers can be found. They have discharged 300 people, so under such circumstances they may not run.

Frankly, I welcome plenty of opposition. It is much better I think from our point of view. Walk-overs are a dead loss anyway from a publicity point of view.

I trust that my Goodwood aspirations are receiving the Grandfield touch.

Kind regards, Bert

Dear Bert, Thank you for your letters of 12th and 14th instant, I do not think we can do anything for the Easter Monday Meeting at Goodwood, although we shall try and do something for later events.

I am enclosing herewith a letter from C.C. Wakefield's again offering you hundreds of pounds of bonus, and I am also enclosing an Agreement from Shell which I would like you to sign and send it back to me, this then puts us in the clear with Shell.

There is also enclosed a letter from the *Yorkshire Observer* and they apparently need your photo for some low-down publicity purpose.

Regarding the Luggage Compartment in 107, it is smaller than the Motor suggests, since the car has been fitted with an extra petrol tank, giving you 18 gallons tank capacity, we do not want to take the tank out because it is such an awkward job to get it out, but the size of the luggage compartment is 2ft 7in x 9in x 12in. Can you make this do for your small kit during the rally, regarding the other stuff which you might need at the weekend, you can leave this with me and I will get it over to Scarborough in time for your return.

Thanks for the possibility of getting information about Singer; we should be very interested to know more about it.

Kind regards, Charles, 17 March 1952

BOB FOSTER

Bob Foster was a garage proprietor and drove Jowetts on several occasions, including the 1951 Daily Express *Rally, 1952 Monte Carlo Rally & RAC Rally, 1953 Monte Carlo Rally & RAC Rally. This letter was from his son, Ian, where he detailed the cars used and the events undertaken. – NS*

FAK 798 was a privately owned Mk1 Javelin, owned by my father. The photo shows him at the wheel and his brother-in-law, George Holdsworth as they were in the 1951 *Daily Express* Rally. In 1952 a semi works Mk2 EPR 999, was acquired for George and my father to enter the Monte Carlo and RAC Rallies. Some press cuttings are also enclosed for your interest. For 1953 EPR 999 was retained for a further season, including another Monte Carlo. The 1953 photo from the Monte Carlo Rally taken from the rear end of the Javelin, shows that my father and George were joined by Bobs' younger brother Noel.

The Monte Carlo results were not headline making but the 1952 RAC Rally did produce high drama. I have some press cuttings of the story in the daily papers but they are stuck in an album and I cannot send them to you. At the end of the rally the results were published showing my father and George Holdsworth as the outright winners in the Javelin. The result was changed the next day after the celebrations; following a protest from the eventual winner. Apparently, after allowing only three cars through, one of the special stages became blocked by a crashed car and the whole of the rest of the field were delayed and therefore lost time unfairly. Bob and George were one of the three cars safely through but the organisers cancelled the special stage altogether after the protest and this gave victory to another entry.

In the years concerned the Javelin was up against Jaguars, Citroens, Lancias and Sunbeam Talbots. The car therefore was at a considerable power disadvantage throughout. I believe that a gearbox had to be changed on one of the British Rallies and EPR 999 hit a lorry on the road between stages in the 1952 Monte. Apart from that I believe that the car was reliable during three years of hard competition and I know that the Fosters were all Jowett enthusiasts at the time.

I have no particulars but as a small boy I remember that talks between my father and Jowetts took place in 1953 regarding an entry of a Jupiter in that years Le Mans 24-hour race. I regret that nothing ever came of the talks.

Ian Foster,
Wimborne, Dorset

I received these excellent letters from Alan Broderick, who was one of Bob 'Fearless' Foster's employees. I greatly enjoyed reading these and could not resist publishing them here. – NS

1) I worked for Bob Foster in Poole in the early '50s; Bob won the Lightweight TT in 1936, on his honeymoon, and the Junior TT in 1947. He was World Champion in 1950, rode some fast and fearsome machines and was known as 'Fearless Foste', he had a prosperous motorcycle business in Poole.

He drove a Jowett Javelin in the Monte Carlo rally and kept his Javelin for several years. One morning he intended to drive up to Birmingham and Coventry to the huge and prosperous BSA and Triumph factories. In his usual tearing hurry he called: 'Alan, check my oil!' I was unfamiliar with car engines and gazed at the Flat Four without identifying the oil filler. The air intake was prominent and I poured a pint of XXL down it before realising my mistake. 'Either it will "hydraulic" and bend all the con rods or it will clear; I've got to be off!' cried Bob, and rushed off. It was quite dark in Ashley Road for several minutes after he had gone, and, 'It smoked all the way to Birmingham,' said Bob later. He was not amused when George Savage, a BSA executive, said innocently as he saw him from the factory, 'I didn't know that these were a two-stroke.' I was never allowed to live this down and was known as 'oily brod' ever after. Yet Bob lent me the car on many occasions and I did my courting in it. Foster was a lovely man and 'a real Englishman'.

2) Bob Foster drove his Javelin in a couple of Monte Carlo Rallies. He died in 1985. He was a martyr to asthma all his life but earned the nickname 'Fearless Foster' because he rode some fearsome things which did not steer very well; before the War he rode a supercharged AJS four-cylinder racer and was electrifying. He won the Lightweight and Junior T.T. and was comfortably in the lead on the big works Guzzi in the 1949 Senior T.T. when it packed up on the last lap.

The 1953 Monte Carlo Rally had repercussions for him. On a deserted road one Sunday a Traffic Police Officer booked me because my International Norton left a trail of sparks when I was cranked over enthusiastically. My colleague Barry Cortvriend was forced off the road one night by an oncoming car; he pursued it, stopped it, and cursed the driver, who reported him to the police. We both appeared before Wareham Magistrates Court whose Chairman was Admiral Sir Reginald Plunkett Ernle-Earle Drax, who was Beatty's Flag Captain at the Battle of Jutland in 1916. Sadly he regarded motorcyclists as fiercely as he had glared at Von Hipper's battlecruisers and fined us £10 each, which was a week's wages then.

In the same week one of our mechanics, Derek Powell, a leading Road Racer whom Foster supported and who lived in the New Forrest, peppered a New Forrest pony with his shot gun, as it had trampled his garden and bashed his baby's pram. His neighbour reported him and Derek ended up at Winchester Assizes and was fined £300 or three months in jail. The pony was unhurt.

All these cases were reported on the same evening in the *Bournemouth Echo*, which also did not like motorcyclists, under separate headings. Foster had paid Derek's fine and provided us with a solicitor, although we had asked him not to, but he was furious as we were all described as 'working for Bob Foster'. He had us on the mat. Fearless was not happy, and said, 'People will think I run a Fagin's Den here, with you three reprobates!' His secretary, Jean, said quietly; 'The post has come, and I think you ought to read this Mr Foster'. It was a letter from the French Police informing him that he had been quite heavily fined because he had knocked off a French Cyclist, without injury, with his Jowett Javelin in the previous year's Monte. 'Oh Dear,' said Derek, 'Now people will think that we run a Fagin's Den here, won't they?' Foster glared, and then, to his eternal credit, began to laugh. So did we, helplessly, until Foster, gasping and laughing, threw us out.

A collection of some newspaper clippings of Bob Foster's rally exploits make very interesting reading, as there was some considerable controversy regarding the outcome of the RAC Rally of 1952, Bob being less than happy with the outcome. These should really be in the 'What the Papers Had to Say' section, but had several quotes from Bob, so I felt it was more appropriate to continue with these here:

1952 Monte Carlo Rally
Bob Foster for Monte Carlo

The president of Bournemouth Motor Club, motorcycle and car trials driver and Parkstone motorcycle dealer, forty-year-old Bob Foster, enters his first Monte Carlo Rally. He leaves in his Jowett Javelin registered ERR999 next Friday for Munich (writes Dickie Boot, BT motoring correspondent).

'We'll look like a Christmas tree when we leave,' said Bob. 'I'm getting too old for open cars, so we've chosen a saloon model. We are expecting trouble and I expect we will find it.'

With Bob go his thirty-eight-year-old Birmingham brother-in-law, George Holdsworth, and Les Tanner from Stroud.

Motorcycle champion's first Monte Carlo Rally

Bob Foster, the Parkstone motorcycle enthusiast, this year enters his first Monte Carlo Rally. He will drive from Munich through Holland, Belgium and Paris down to Monte Carlo in his Jowett Javelin, which is entered in the 1500cc class. The car is at Ashley-road, Parkstone now, being prepared for the rally, later this month.

Extra lamps are being fitted and snow chains carried to help with the treacherous weather expected south of Paris. Experiments are being made with instruments to help with the exacting eliminating trials at Monte Carlo.

In the team will be Bob's brother-in-law, George Holdsworth of Birmingham and Les Tanner of Stroud, who drove just in front of the Foster-Holdsworth car in the *Daily Express* rally last November.

The team will do spells of four hours driving and then six to eight hours of navigating – or trying to get some sleep on the back seat of the car. 'We shall take some food over with us, but we shall pick up supplies on the Continent as well,' Bob told me.

The car crosses the Channel on the 18th, and will then be driven from Calais to Munich. This will give the team a day or so in which to rest before the rally begins. This year's record British entry of ninety-one cars means that some British drivers are having to start from the Continent, only sixty-nine starters being permitted from Glasgow. The Munich starters will leave at 8 p.m. on 22 January.

Bob is familiar with a lot of the route, as in the summer he drove a lorry down it, in the French Grand Prix. 'It was hard work driving a truck on the mountain passes,' he confessed. The rally route lies through Clermont Ferrand to St Flour, Le Puy, Valence, Gap, Digne and Grasse to Monaco. The whole of this mountainous road – nearly 500 miles long – is subject to heavy snow and ice.

Bob, who is just getting over a heavy cold, commented; 'They say the snow is only waiting for the rally to start. At the moment I don't feel much like going; but opportunities like this don't come along every day.'

November 1952 *Daily Express* International Rally
(Written by Basil Cardew in Hastings on Friday)

Motorcyclist wins car rally and drives off without knowing

Bob Foster, a crack motorcyclist for twenty years, last year's 350cc racing champion, but unknown as a car driver, today won the *Daily Express* National Motor Rally. It is only the second rally he has ever entered, and he just could not believe he had won. He had told Joy, his wife, as she drove him back home to Parkstone in Dorset; 'We can forget it – I had a bad cold and I muffed the final test'.

Right enough, he was sneezing like a grampus and in the fast-to-the-kerb test he was thirteen inches out. That was one inch too much and ten points were lost.

He had come through the 1,200 miles road section without losing a mark, only two other cars were unpenalised by the time they finished the tests on Honister and Newlands passes, and he was 'clean' in two of the other three tests too.

When I telephoned him that he had won Bob said blankly, 'Incredible, just incredible'. He went on to say, 'Still, the fact that I have won shows you that even the raw newcomer had a chance. We drove in old man's comfort – heater, flasks, rugs, everything – but my cold came on at Cardiff and got worse all the time.'

Foster's car was a Jowett Javelin saloon, and for co-driver he had his brother-in-law George Holdsworth from Birmingham. When we 'old men' – Foster is forty and Holdsworth thirty-eight – reached Hastings, with so much better chance than they knew, some good men were in the running, including Geoffrey Imhof, Norman Garrad, Ken Rawlings in the Vanguard 'special' and last year's winner Geoffrey Holt.

But two other cars skittled these challengers, an open MG handled by Mr and Mrs Alan Hopkinson of Chesterfield and an HRG, also open, with J.V.S. Brown and R.W. Kettel aboard.

Of the 428 cars that started from eight different centres on Wednesday 360 of them completed the 1,200 miles of rain, fog and mud in more than forty-seven hours of driving. For more than seven hours today (Friday) they streamed into Hastings and took their final tests on Castle Hill and on the seafront. Tonight after the mayor's reception, most of them will be cleaning their cars ready for tomorrow's concourse d'elegance – beauty competition if you like – on the sea front. Then comes the rally ball at the end of a great four-day motoring festival.

Here are the final results, and the marks shown against the competitors are marks lost. The winner is the one who loses fewest:

1. A.R. Foster & L.G. Holdsworth (Jowett Javelin) 15.031 marks – Silver cup and £50.
2. Mr & Mrs R.A. Hopkinson (MG) 15.316 marks – £25.
3. J.V.S. Brown & R.W. Kettel (HRG) 15.564 marks – £15.
4. K. Rawlings & L.J. Tracey (Vanguard special) 15.586 marks.
5. D.G. Griffin & A.G. Robbins (MG) 15.677 marks.

The winners from each of the eight starts were as follows:
Plymouth, J.G. Reece & P.B. Reece (Cooper)
Manchester, Mr & Mrs R.A. Hopkinson (MG)
Leamington, J.V.S. Brown & R.W. Kettel (HRG)
Norwich, A. Anderson-Wright & R. Baxendale (Singer)
Cardiff, A.R. Foster & L.G. Holdsworth (Jowett Javelin)
Glasgow, G.S. Rollings & W.F. McCormick (Healey)
London, A.D.C. Gordon & B. Spencer (HRG)
Harrogate, D. Howard & B.S. Jepson (Morgan)

Basil Cardew wrote from Hastings again on the Sunday:

Drink to the next time says winner-who-loses...

Bob Foster out of Rally prize list – on a recount.

Over a drink at the prize-giving last night Bob Foster, who for twelve hours thought he had won the *Daily Express* National Motor Rally, and Alan Hopkinson, who did win, shook hands and made a pledge.

The pledge – to 'fight it out' in next year's rally. Bob Foster said, 'I have lodged a protest – purely as a point of principle. There's nothing personal in this you know.'

Bob Foster and George Holdsworth in their Javelin EPR 999 at the Paris control in the 1952 Monte Carlo Rally. (Photo Plage/JCC)

Another view of the Paris control. (Photo Plage/JCC)

The Foster/Holdsworth Javelin in the 1952 'Monte'. (JCC)

Alan Hopkinson said, 'Thanks old man, we'll have another tussle next year, but I don't think your protest will succeed.' It didn't, the stewards had a meeting this morning and ruled it out. Now what was this protest about? Well during the forty-seven hours' driving part of the rally, there was a driving test on a Lakeland mountain pass. Only three cars – and Bob Foster's was one – got there 'clean.' But it was to be recorded that something had gone wrong with the timing equipment. So after an all-day meeting on Saturday, the stewards decided the only way to be fair to all the 360 competitors who finished the course – out of 428 starters – was to wash-out the Lakeland mountain test altogether.

So the markings had to be revised, and because Bob Foster lost ten marks at one go – in the fast-reversing tests – he dropped from first place to 'nowhere.' *(NB. Bob was in fact placed sixth after the recount. – NS)* The cars which had been 2-3-4 moved up to 1-2-3. None of them in the whole rally had lost as many marks as Bob Foster did by 'muffing' that test on the sea front. Only one other provisional winner was ruled out by the revised markings, that was Major RS Smith, who would have won the 3000cc class in his Sunbeam Talbot. At the prize-giving which preceded the great rally ball, it was announced that the *Daily Express* was giving consolation prizes to this unlucky pair, £50 to Bob Foster and £10 to Major Smith. The crowd gave a cheer for that news.

Mrs Marguerite Hopkinson, who was with her husband in the rally-winning MG TD which started in Manchester, said: 'I drove more than 400 miles so I was no passenger. Alan taught me to drive; in fact we broke off our engagement umpteen times while he was trying to teach me. But after I passed my test all was peace.' Said Alan, who is thirty-five, 'She's a sound driver and particularly a good navigator. We pulled off the Circuit of Ireland earlier this year and thought your rally was tops.'

Foster/Holdsworth at the Reims control in the 1952 'Monte'. (Photo Plage/JCC)

The 1951 Alpine Rally - 'Private Entry'
By Dr Thomas Smallhorn
(As published in The Motor, *3 August 1951)*

It might be of interest to the ordinary Javelin owner to hear the experiences of another ordinary Javelin owner who has used his car both for his profession and for family conveyance, and also for competition. In the course of my profession this car has completed 50,000 miles. When I decided to enter the 'Alpine' of 1951 it was only because of reasonable wear and tear that a reconditioned engine was installed in this car and the extra precaution taken of fitting an oil filter. Alfin brake drums, by Wellworthy, were added. The degree of the tune obtained was by close attention to the standard tuning notes issued by Jowett Cars Ltd, maintaining the standard compression of 7.2 to 1.

Foster/Holdsworth at the Grasse control in the 1952 'Monte'. (Photo Plage/JCC)

Bob Foster and George Holdswoth driving in snowy conditions in the 1952 Monte Carlo Rally. They would finish thirty-seventh in the overall classification. (Erpe, Nice/JCC)

Bob Foster and George Holdsworth driving through the snow of the Col de Braus in the 1953 Monte Carlo Rally. (Photo Junior, Nice/JCC)

Bob Foster and George Holdsworth at the end of the 1953 Monte Carlo Rally. (Photo Junior, Nice)

Beyond these modifications the car was standard, maintained by an ordinary Jowett agent; but in the course of its life scrupulous care had been taken to ensure that the lubrication was as advised by the manufacturers. The tyres were standard Michelin 5.25 x 16, and the oil used was the grade of Mobiloil advised by the manufacturers. The brakes were standard fully hydraulic Girling.

It was clear from the beginning that the Javelin could maintain time only if it kept its full reliability, for, as the enlightened know, the Alpine this year was run to a thirty-minute time limit which precluded any possibility of mechanical adjustment whatsoever, unless of a minor character, or unless the car was fast enough to maintain schedule time completely. Many readers will have no doubt been over the passes – Galiber, Iseran, Izoard, St Bernard, Stelvio, Falzarego, Pordoi and many others, but to contemplate an average of nearly 35mph over the passes, which reach to a height of nearly 9,000ft is beyond the ordinary realms of the family motorist; let me state quite clearly that the Alpine is the great test, *la grande epreuve,* of the touring car. No other test has yet been devised which gives such assurance to the ordinary motorist of the reliability of his car.

Not unnaturally, in the extremely severe tests, I lost considerable time, but the maximum loss at any one stage was sixteen minutes, and that was on the Stelvio after an eighteen-minute stop at a railway crossing at the bottom of the pass. I was fortunate enough to make up two minutes in the Javelin over this climb; the speed of the climb only surpassed in the class by two Jowett Jupiters and two HRGs. But, unfortunately, I could not make up the heavy loss caused by that long wait. It was possible for other competitors in low-built sportscars to pass under the horizontal bars of this railway crossing, whereas the Javelin was too high.

The car on its *autostrade* speed test easily maintained its average for 120 miles, although the outside temperature was 105 degrees in the shade and a certain amount of time was lost between Bolzano and Cortina d'Ampezzo, again owing to road delays and traffic lights.

In the fifth day of the trial, a word now, incidentally, much more suitable than 'Rally' for this event, the sections were extremely 'tight' and in the final section only 100 miles, which included the climbs of Forclaz and the Great St Bernard, only four minutes were lost. It may not be realised that the principal of driving in the Alpine is to make up time on the downhill grades on the cars with low horsepower. On the uphill grades with average slopes of about 1:8 of 17 to 20 miles, time is bound to be lost, especially as, in the consecutive hairpins, which on climbs like the Selvio contain as many as ten complete changes of direction in 2km, it is impossible for any car in existence to maintain 35mph average, and the hairpins bring one down to speeds of 20mph or less. It is, therefore, to the great advantage of a car to have enormous reserves of horsepower.

The maximum speed of the Javelin is about 35mph in second and 55mph in third, whereas some of the biggest cars will exceed 75mph in second. Therefore, the only method of making up time on the low horse-power *voitures* is downhill, by means of superlative brakes which are absolutely fade-proof; at any rate, by means of adequate performance by completely fade-proof brakes my average never dropped below the 34mph minimum required by the organisers.

On the sixth day the organisers devised a test which I think must stand as the most severe of all time. They timed short sections of 100 miles or less over two passes and to the top of a third, this allowing no possibility of recovery on the downhill section of the third pass; and as a *piece de resistance* that included the climbs of Glandon, an appalling descent of the Croix de Feu and then the climb to the top of the Galiber, about 2 miles of which was unmade road. The Croix de Feu was further complicated by avalanches, which had, in many cases made the road extremely treacherous; yet the Javelin over this section only lost twelve minutes.

The oil was changed once during the trial; the water temperature never exceeded 85 degrees, even at the top of the full-throttle climb of the Galibier. Third gear was used for a total of 300 miles and second for 50 miles in a 2,000-mile test. On the ordinary road sections the time was maintained with ease and at the end of the trial five people were brought back from Cannes to Dunkirk in two days, without even bothering to service the car.

The only troubles encountered were a blocked fuel line, which was blown out at a filling station using an ordinary airline and gave no further trouble, and some vapour blocks on top of the Gross Glonkner. The front tyres were changed as a precaution at Innsbruck.

I feel that as a seal on the performance of this car one ought to add that it was second in class on the final test at Cannes. After all of which I'm afraid that DCT993 will find it rather tame to be back on its rounds in Lincolnshire.

Post – Alpine Road Impressions
After the successful run in the Alpine Trial, DCT993 was handed over to a member of *The Autocar* staff to see how an ordinary production car stood up to the very strenuous operating conditions.

Inside the car the cockpit had been 'doctored' in a strictly operational way. To prevent dazzle, the top of the facia, the steering wheel, and, in fact, all parts that could cause reflection in the windscreen had been painted a dull black, while lighting on extra instruments (ammeter and oil pressure) were cleverly shielded, again to prevent screen reflections.

From cold the engine was a little difficult to start, firing almost at once, but requiring several applications of the button before it would continue to run. Once warm, the engine ran evenly, with tick-over speed perhaps a little faster than usual. All controls were functioning well, although the free movement on the clutch and brake pedals suggested that slight adjustment was required, but no more than would have been needed after an equivalent distance of normal motoring. The engine felt very lively and had none of the 'tiredness' that often follows competition work. It was flexible, would pull well, and there was only a slight tendency to pink at low speed on a gradient.

The steering column gear change mechanism (the Javelin is fitted with one of the best of its kind) was still light and very responsive, with absolutely no lost motion. Rather more noise than usual came from the indirect gears, especially on the overrun, although the axle was very quiet. In top gear the car purred along in a very smooth manner it is the sort of car that wants to go places, and gets there quickly too. The Javelin held the road well, the steering was light and responsive, had that extra sense of control provided by a slight, yet definite understeer, which allowed the car to be positioned in a way that inspires confidence. A certain amount of squeal came from the right-hand front wheel, even at quite modest speeds on sharp corners. The ride in both front and rear seats was good and the shock absorbers were still up to their job.

Apart from a few minor adjustments mentioned, the car was in very good condition and will no doubt continue to give its owner many thousands of miles of economical high-speed motoring. The Javelin is a first-rate car judged by any standards.

An interesting footnote to this story is also added, it was a letter published in the December 1997 issue of Classic Cars *magazine written by Dr Smallhorn's son, Anthony, and it would appear that the doctor's car had been deliberately delayed. The letter reads:*

Jowett Journeys
I was very interested in the article on Jowett Javelins (The car Issigonis wasn't allowed to build, October 1997 issue) and thought that readers might like to know a little more about their rallying history.

A team of three Jowetts were prepared by my father and his friends as privateers for the 1951 Alpine Rally. The drivers and navigators were:
Tom Smallhorn and Charles Lillicrap.
Ralph Kennedy and Pam Smallhorn
Tom Wisdom and Pat Hall

My recollection is that only my father's car, DCT933, finished, and that they were fifth in their class and in the top twenty overall, but possibly members of the Jowett Car Club can verify this.

DCT933 would have fared better and possibly won its class had my father and Charles Lillicrap not been held up at the bar of a railway crossing which had been deliberately closed against them by the French crossing keeper. This sporting gesture allowed the four following cars of the HRG team to fold their windscreens flat and pass beneath the bar. We believe that this cost DCT933 its class lead, and possible class win.

My father, Marcel Becquart, and many others, continued to rally Javelins for several years with factory support.

The Autocar road-tested DCT933 after the 1951 Alpine, recording a maximum speed of 96mph, which is not bad for a 1.5 litre family saloon.

My understanding from Jowett owners is that DCT933 is still in existence in Denmark. If anyone has further information about its whereabouts, I would be extremely interested.

The 1952 Monte Carlo Rally
By Bo Boeson & Goran Norlander

In the autumn of 1951 Bo and I decided that we would enter the 1952 Monte Carlo Rally with my new Jowett Javelin. We knew from our experiences that a number of minor changes had to be made to the car, in order to face all difficulties that might occur when driving over 3,300km (2,050 miles) from Stockholm to Monte Carlo in winter conditions. North of Stockholm is an area with a number of small curvy hills with sand pavements, where we used to drive around to test various equipment.

We learnt the hard way that the weak part on the Jowett were the bearings in the engine, one of the reasons for this might have been difficulties in maintaining an acceptable oil temperature at hard driving. The short boxer motor gave proportionally a smaller cooling surface for the oil, compared to a straight engine. Anyway that was my theory! To prevent this I installed in tandem with the oil filter, a Volkswagen oil cooler. This cooler was mounted on top of the motor just behind the radiator. This also increased the oil volume which was good for this type of motor. Thanks to this cooler we saved the motor at an incident during the race.

The carburettors have a ring to balance the petrol injection with the air velocity controlled by the throttle, a sort of ventury. In mounting one size larger rings we made the motor more 'lively' which is important in Alpine driving with quick toe and heel shifting in the hair needle bends, also acceleration was improved. These larger rings did not add any motor power, and the idling revs had to be increased, I believe petrol consumption suffered, but that was of less importance. We had four spare sparking plugs with the corresponding key mounted on a bracket under the hood for quick changes.

Already at the start in Stockholm the temperature was far below zero, and we had a radiator screen We spent a lot of time on the headlights, as in snow, fog or heavy rain the visibility was reduced by the headlights reflecting some light vertically, thus lighting up the snow or fog near your eyes. We made in aluminium some shades like the peak on a hat that were fixed to each headlight, they were about eight inches long. The undersides were painted in a mat black so light was not thrown back up. We also fitted three fog lamps to the car, also a spotlight on the roof that could be operated from the inside. It was not only used for reading road signs, but also for guiding the man at the wheel. The co-driver pointed the beam into the curves before arriving there, then following the bend until the car was on the straight again.

Snow tires were of the utmost importance, and from other courses we had experienced a Finish tyre called *Wittmer* which had a thick layer of rubber with squared or rectangular points one inch by two. They gave an excellent grip in the snow, but of course less in ice. We wanted something better so we started to experiment, which led to an original snow chain mounted on the front wheels. We cut a groove in the centre line of the tyre about ¾in wide and ½in deep. We then let the air out of the tyre and forced in a motorcycle chain, which was the exact circumference of the groove. After that the tyre was pumped up about 50 per cent higher than normal and the chain was then securely fixed in the tyre centre line and sticking up a little above the tyre surface.

The result was that when breaking hard all four wheels locked, but the chains on the front wheels functioned as skates and so we could still steer the car. Thanks to this we could, during the snowy part of the rally, go faster and more safely than our competitors. We took two spare tyres with chains mounted and also two jacks and suitable wrenches. We trained on fast front wheel changes, and finally we were able to do this operation in 1½ minutes from stopping the car and starting again.

Finally we installed an extra petrol tank of about 60 litres (13 gallons) in the trunk towards its front wall. This tank was connected by a valve to the normal petrol pipe. The back seat served as a bunk for a nap now and then, but it was not very comfortable, especially as it had to be shared with some luggage. Among other things, we had to bring our tuxedos for the final banquet. So on 22 January 1952 at 4.40 p.m. we started on our big adventure, thirty-nine cars started from the Swedish capital, twenty-one Swedes, eleven Finns, four Danes, one Norwegian, one Dutch and one French. We were numbered 148 to 189, two did not come to the start and we were at the end of the line with number 186.

In winter it is already dark at this hour and it was bitterly cold, as I remember it was 15 or 20 degrees below freezing, and of course there was snow. The Swedish roads were well cleared from snow, so it was fairly easy driving south at the stipulated minimum speed of 50kph (31mph), which included service stops, between control points. Every minute delay gave a 10-point penalty; over two hours accumulated delays meant automatic disqualification.

After only about 200km (125 miles) the motor started to run unevenly and gave less and less power, and finally it stopped altogether. It started again on the first attempt and ran well for a while, but the procedure was repeated. We searched for a cause, but found nothing wrong with the sparks or fuel supply etc. We managed to reach the first checkpoint in Huskvarna after about 330km from the start. Somebody there said that the carburettors were freezing up. We were not allowed to do any repairs at the checkpoint, or even open the bonnet, but as soon as we were back on the road again we stopped and wrapped each carburettor in newspaper, and after that we had no further problems of that kind.

We continued over to Helsingborg by ferry, about a twenty minute crossing to Denmark. At this time there were speed restrictions all over that country, the maximum speed being 60kph (37mph). It seemed to us that the entire Danish police force was out that night, and everybody was driving very correctly.

The next engine trouble showed up a little later, a stuck valve, what to do? Then we remembered a bottle of Redex that somebody had given us before the start. A wonder elixir to mix with the petrol to get smooth running and to clean the motor. Why not try it! In the middle of the night we stopped in a little square in Copenhagen, no traffic and people all sleeping in their beds. We took the air filters off and poured the liquid directly into the carburettors with the motor running at fairly high revs. There was no wind, and a fantastic amount of smoke was produced and the entire square disappeared in a heavy dark cloud. The valve loosened and we quickly put the air filters back on and disappeared before the fire brigade showed up. We concluded that Redex after all must be a good product.

The next stop was Kosor 110km (68 miles) from Copenhagen, where we had to take another ferry across the Great Belt to Nyborg on the Danish island Fyn. The crossing takes about one and a half hours, with a boat leaving every hour. Nobody wanted to miss the scheduled one, and there was also the risk of there being no space left on the ferry. This meant everybody was increasing their speed to arrive first at the ship, near the harbour we were all racing! As far as I know, the police only caught one Swedish driver speeding, as it was everybody got on board in time.

As soon as we were onboard I went to the lounge and found an armchair where I immediately fell asleep. Disturbed by some noise from the ships moorings I woke up and thought we were in Nyborg, and rushed down to the car deck – but we were still in Korsor! After that I could not sleep any more on that crossing.

Bosse and I share everything (except the long-legged two-cylinder models). The costs, including the entry fee, and also the time at the wheel were equally split up. Every two or three hours we shifted, as there were also several co-drivers duties. A part of the navigation in difficult conditions, he should lead the driver by indicating verbally what the road looked like. For instance, 'Sharp curve ahead, then straight 100 metres, snow in bend etc.' When it was dark he had to follow the road with the roof-mounted spotlight, as we had the steering wheel on the right-hand side, he also had to tell if the road was clear for overtaking another car. Only during easy driving conditions was he allowed to take a nap.

After Nyborg we crossed Odense, where H.C. Anderson used to live and wrote his wonderful tales. Another slow 200km (125 miles) brought us to the German border, and it was a relief not having to watch the speedometer anymore. Outside Hamburg we were met by a police motorcyclist who escorted us through the city at full speed, we could hardly keep up with him at 75mph. At every street crossing there were other police officers stopping the traffic, here and there people were crowding to see the big show!

There were no motorways in Europe at this time, except for a few in Italy and Germany. The very first was built by Fiat from Turin to Milan to test their cars, and Hitler copied the principals from this autostrada and built the first autobahn from Hamburg to Bremen, 120km (75 miles).

Goran Norlander and Bo Boesen at the Stockholm start of the 1952 Monte Carlo Rally. This was in fact Goran's car on which extensive testing in snow had been carried out in their native Sweden before the rally. (Junior/JCC)

The Norlander/Boesen Javelin had chains fitted to the front wheels in the 1952 'Monte' which were very effective, as it was one of the fastest cars in the snowy conditions that were experienced that year. (JCC)

We followed this road which was not completely repaired from war damage; many bridges were temporary one-line military constructions.

After Hamburg the front wheel bearing started to make a noise, how could we solve this problem? We did not have a spare with us or the special tools needed, so we had to get external help. In Germany we could not expect to find a repair shop with English inch-tools, nor a suitable bearing. Arriving at the checkpoint in Hengelo, at the German-Dutch border, we called at 11 o'clock in the evening at the Jowett representative in Amsterdam, who was keeping night watch.

It was snowing and we were in a hurry to make up spare time, he met us at 3.30 a.m., just before the checkpoint at Amsterdam, by then we were 45 minutes ahead of schedule. He guided us to his workshop and the doors were opened, we hardly had time to stop the motor before the car was being lifted up. All tools and parts for the wheel-bearing repair were placed on a white cloth, and four men attacked the car. Some overlooked various things while the bearing was changed. When the wheel was back we discovered that the inner rubber gasket that prevents grease to come into the brake drum was still on the table! A number of words 'impossible to translate' in Dutch and Swedish were loudly expressed.

We rushed out to have our road book stamped in the control, which was fortunately close to the Jowett garage, and we arrived three minutes before the time limit. Then back to the workshop, wheel off, bearing off, gasket and final assembly. We were delayed 45 minutes, but were back on the road again towards Brussels. The owner declared generously, with big gestures, that the whole operation was on the house

We succeeded in making up the lost time, partially thanks to a dedicated police motorcycle in La Haye, like his colleague in Brussels; he guided us through the town on full throttle. His motorcycle was fitted with a sidecar, and I can still see the sidecar now lifting off the road on high-speed right turns. After Brussels we continued across the Ardennes to Reims in France. We passed through a wonderful old town called Dinant in a steep valley near the border. This is where we saw a very tall chimney, which became famous in the last war, as the RAF pilots on missions into Eastern France or Southern Germany used it as a landmark.

The Norlander/Boesen Javelin at the Grasse control in the 1952 'Monte'; note the smoke coming off the front brakes. (Photo Plage/JCC)

At every checkpoint the local car club offered tea, coffee, or soft drinks and sandwiches, sometimes they gave us a local souvenir. In Reims, the capital of the Champagne district, offered champagne, as much as you can drink while waiting to start again, no food! As we were tired, one glass was enough; our Finnish friends however, accepted gladly the kind offer from the Reims Automobile Club. Shortly after, on our way to Paris we saw their car, an Austin if I remember correctly, as a wreck in a field. Bosse and I thought that we had seen them for the last time. In Paris the checkpoint organised by the French Automobile Club, which were magnificent, to get there we strolled along the Champs Elyssees like any other tourist. From there we continued on to Bourges.

One of the Monte Carlo principals was to assemble competitors from all corners of Europe. When leaving Stockholm we met drivers from Oslo in Halsingborg, and in Hamburg the Germans from Munich showed up. In Amsterdam the people coming from Monte Carlo and also Glasgow joined us, and from Reims the cars starting in Lisbon used the same road. Finally in Bourges the Italians showed up coming from Palermo in Sicily. Then all of us had made more or less the same distance from the start, and the most difficult part of the rally-road ahead became common, across the Massive Central Alpes Maritimes. To avoid crowding on the roads and in the checkpoints, starting points were spread out. We had the Oslo drivers behind us, and before the Swedish group were the English.

The next control point was Clermont Ferrand, and on this section it started to snow heavily, we switched our front wheels with the steering chains and arrived on time in Clermont. On the way to the next stop at Le Puy, it started to become very difficult. After Le Puy we headed on the shortest route to Valence, but after a while, as there were no other cars on this way we understood that something was wrong. A man along the roadside explained that the road was blocked further up. It seemed that other drivers had been informed about this in the Le Puy checkpoint, except for us and a couple of Swedish drivers. We turned back and took a longer road to Valence. It was snowing very heavily and the road was very curvy, and as we caught up with others, we were also delayed by difficulties in over-taking slower cars. How many we saw off the road or stuck in snow walls that night, we did not have time to count. We could not make up all the time we had lost by choosing the blocked road, so we arrived in Valence eight minutes delayed, which gave us an 80-point penalty, but there was nothing we could do about that.

Now all our preparations we had done before the start for good snow driving came into use. It was dark, heavy snowfall and much snow covering the pavements and a very curvy road, ideal winter racing conditions! We had a special 180-degree curve-technic, especially useful when going downhill. I will try and explain: Approaching a left hairpin driving on the right side of the road, I turned the wheel sharply to the left, blocked the brakes and then turned the steering wheel completely to the right with blocked wheels. This made the car skid more or less sideways into the curve with its back still swinging round. Once in the bend with the front more or less pointing in the right direction breaks off and full throttle in first or second gear. Still skidding we then accelerated out of the curve in the opposite direction. The procedure could be done with good control thanks to the steering-chains on the front wheels. It was only possible to make this manoeuvre when we were alone on the hairpin bend, very often however, that night, there was one or several cars stuck in the snow in the bend.

From Valence we climbed up to Gap where we joined the Route Napoleon. At my turn at the wheel, daylight came and it was snowing less, but there was still plenty of it on the road. Somewhere after Digne an English driver refused to let us pass, which was unusual, after several kilometres of horn-blowing and blinking of lights, I took my chance. The road was cleared, but not to its full width, and the snow wall was on the road and not on its side. I forced the car over it with the two left wheels, and managed to pass the car. We were throwing up snow high above us with the bumper. What we did not notice was that the little valve under the radiator was opened by the snow pressure and our radiator was slowly being emptied. The thermometer climbed to boiling, but as we were short of time, and the next stop was at Grass, which was not far away, we agreed upon to take a chance that the motor would take it.

A few kilometres before the centre of Grass the snow had gone and a Mediterranean sun gave us hope. Our snow chains could not take the bare asphalt and one after the other broke and disappeared.

Then! – The most scaring few seconds in my life came in the last downhill to Grass. We were speeding and braking intensely this last distance. In the final long narrow downhill, that ends with a tight bend just before the square, where the checkpoint was situated, our brakes failed due to overheating. The curve was full of spectators, children, balloons, grandmothers, etc. and there was no chance to get round that sharp curve at 80 km/h. I remember that I cried to Bosse 'NO BRAKES'! Pulling on the handbrake did not help much, but gearing down to second brought our speed down a little. We took the last curve on two screaming wheels, and all we saw of the public were the soles of their shoes. Trembling and sweating we got out of our smoking car and had our road book stamped in time. Some people applauded as they thought that this was skilful controlled driving! I can still see that bend and the people when I close my eyes.

When the brake drum gets overheated it changes its form due to dilatation and becomes conical instead of cylindrical. The brake linings do not then touch the drum inner surface with more than an edge, with little or no braking efficiency. Once the drum has cooled off, it takes its original shape, and the system works normally again.

After the car had cooled down a little, we continued to the first service station, there we changed the water and oil, or rather what was left of it. The oil-filler was completely silted up and looked like it had been dipped in tar. Soot flakes were floating on the oil, and it seemed as if the heat in one way or other had carbonised the oil. Without doubt the VW oil cooler had saved our engine from collapse.

Driving along the Promenade Des Anglais in Nice in a very high mood, we were stopped by a polite policeman informing us that there was a speed limit of 40 km/h (25mph) to be respected.

And finally after some seventy hours of non-stop driving we arrived at the finishing line in Monte Carlo. As we came in among the first of the English cars, it was obvious that we had done a good race, and people were applauding. According to the participation numbers, we had passed about 100 cars since Le Puy.

A proud moment!

Our three Finnish friends that crashed outside Reims were waiting for us, still affected by Bacchus' favourite products. 'Are you still alive?' 'Yes St Peter has given us permission today' they answered happily.

The car had to be parked in a special area, and not to be touched until the final test, but all we needed was a shower and twenty hours sleep. The rally committee had reserved a room for us and most drivers in the magnificent old-fashioned Hotel Beau Rivage. The next day, Saturday 26 January, the inspection of the cars was done, and we passed without any comments.

The final test was run on Sunday on a 74.4km (46.2 miles) circuit starting just above Monte Carlo and climbed up a pass called Col de Braus at an altitude of 3,280ft. It had snowed again, and the palm trees were leaning under the unusual weight of snow on their leaves that morning, but rapidly the sun melted it. Also the road was free from snow except a little at high altitudes. All other traffic was stopped at this circuit. The best fifty cars participated in this final test.

Once again the average speed was set at 50km/h (31mph), but the three checkpoints were secret. This increased considerably the difficulties, as practically a constant speed must be held. More than half the distance, however, was on Alpine roads, where 50km/h was almost impossible to respect. I drove, but I must admit that I was very nervous before the start, but once on the way and concentrating on the road, it was gone.

Bosse had his own time/velocity landmarks that we had worked on before the start, but on some parts of the road it was impossible to keep to the schedule. The whole circuit was done without any incident, but at one spot we almost crashed. Going downhill after the 'Col' the road was cut in a niche in the mountainside, and we were supposed to turn off to the right into a tunnel, which I did not observe in time. Anyway I made a sharp turn and the car skidded on the wet asphalt, but, maybe thanks to St Peter again, there was a dry spot just in the tunnel entrance. We did dust off the car against the tunnel wall, but no scratches.

Later the same day the results of the Col de Braus test were announced, and we were second! What joy and happiness, our 129 seconds penalty points were only beaten by another Swedish driver, Gunnar Olsson who had 96 points. He had an odd vehicle, a Henry J Kaiser car. Now the total results could be determined.

Drivers without any penalties only totalled 15, and the final test classified them 1 to 15. The overall winner was Sydney Allard in his own make of automobile with 130 points at the Col de Braus circuit and second was Sterling Moss with 134 points in a Sunbeam Talbot, a very good English score! The best Jowett Jupiter with No 1 on its rally plate was driven by a Frenchman, Becquart, who started in Lisbon and finished fifth with 162 points.

We were nineth in our class for standard 1.5 litre cars and overall sixteenth. If it had not been for the late eight minutes in Valence, and as we were one point better than Sidney Allard in the final test, we would have won the whole thing; such is life! The final test winner, Gunner Olsson had twenty-one minutes delay on his way to Monte Carlo and was placed nineteenth.

About 350 cars started this twenty-second Monte Carlo Rally in 1952 and 163 crossed the finishing line, but out of those thirty-nine were disqualified due to exceeding the two-hour delay, or for other reasons. Most of the penalties were collected between Le Puy and Valence, due to

Journeys end! Goran Norlander and Bo Boesen congratulate each other at the end of the 1952 Monte Carlo Rally. (JCC)

the fact that several roads in that area were impassable. An interesting observation is that fourteen out of the first fifteen drivers, without penalty, started in Lisbon or Monte Carlo. They were the first in the rally order and had the chance to pass this part of the course before the heavy snowfall that caused the road blockades. The only penalty free driver from the north was Sidney Allard, who had a fantastic rally. From newspaper reports I learnt that six people had been killed, but I do not know if that is true.

A number of more or less professionals participated, but Mercedes Benz showed for the first time what a professional rally team is. They started in Lisbon with three cars, all in white. The drivers were all pre-war Auto Union F1 aces, Caracciola, Kling and Lang. At each checkpoint, there was a white van or rather a lorry, with servicemen in white overalls decorated on the back with the three-pointed star, waiting for them. I believe that Mercedes must have had at least two of these lorries following the rally. They finished eighteenth, twenty-sixth and thirty-fourth. The most famous French driver was Louis Gironde, but he went off the road in his Alfa Romeo. It was fantastic, that once in a lifetime we were able to beat all those famous racing drivers, including Sterling Moss in the final test.

On Monday there was the Comfort Competition, nothing for us. The day ended with a big ball for all rally competitors. The last day, Tuesday 29th, a parade was organised that ended up at the castle court, where the Prince of Monaco distributed the prizes. Our placings of nineth in class and sixteenth overall and second in the final test did not qualify us for any prizes, but we were very satisfied, as these results were far better than we had ever expected.

One important thing we learnt from this rally was that the seats must be comfortable, as after many hours, pains in the back occur due to reduced blood circulation. Also it is of the utmost importance that the co-driver gets a rest as often as possible. To solve these problems before the next Midnight Sun Rally in Sweden, we bought, when passing Paris on our way home, a couple of Citroen 2CV front seats. These chairs were made of steel tubes, and the seat back was just rubber bands about an inch wide. The back could be folded down and thus it became a short bed. They were very light and served us from there on all our other rallies. For the next rally we installed safety belts, anchored in the floor behind each seat, nobody had ever seen that before in an automobile in 1952.

1952 Monte Carlo Rally, amongst other events
By Fred Bassett

My wife and I were the proud owners of a Jowett Javelin from 1951 to 1954, I wish now that I had kept her longer. Being keen rallyists she had a tough life but served us well. I did one RAC Rally in her, which was a disaster, as one of the tests was ten racing laps round Silverstone her big end bearings went, as did those on two other Javelins.

Together with my wife and I did a number of Club Rallies in her, which included the London Rally in which we won the team prize. The other two members of the Jowett team, all in Javelins, were Skelton Ginn and the other chap was called Odell. The conditions were very bad that year and only Skelton Ginn and us finished, but as no other team finished complete, we were the best that did, so qualified for the team prize!

She had her odd little habits, she regularly broke the throttle cable, so we got used to carrying some piano wire with us, and we could change it in about five minutes. She also used to jam the starter; this meant carrying a special spanner and getting under the car to clear it. This did embarrass my wife on one occasion when it happened in Sloan Street just outside her bank. Spectators were slightly surprised to see my wife get out of the car and, with a spanner in her hand, disappear under the car to carry out the repairs required, before we beat a hasty retreat!

The car was extremely good in floods despite the position of her engine. If you took a right-angled rubber tube and fitted it over the exhaust pipe, so the exhaust came out upwards for about nine inches above its normal level, the car did not seem to mind having its engine partly under water.

I took part in three Monte Carlo Rallies, but I have to say, never in the Javelin, in 1951 I competed in a Ford Pilot and finished 29th out of 365 entrants. In 1952 I was co-driver with Mackenzie, the *Daily Telegraph* motoring correspondent, in a works Sunbeam Talbot 90. This car was works-prepared, but was not factory-supported. It was an identical car to that driven by Stirling Moss, who finished second behind Sydney Allard in his Allard. The conditions were particularly severe this year, and when we arrived in Monte Carlo, we were more than an hour late, so were not classed as finishers. Our start number was 366 out of 368 starters, so we were always right at the tail end, which was rather depressing.

It was when I was competing in the 1952 event that my wife decided she would set off in the Javelin with her mother and a friend to meet us in Monte Carlo! She drove on 'Wyresoles' which were extremely good on ice. She ran into trouble about 200 miles south of Paris, when another car threw up a stone and broke the windscreen. As the only Jowett agent in France was in Paris, she had to head back there for a new one, but when she got there they had none in stock! A new one arrived three days later, but it was the wrong size, I was told that the export

The 1953 Monte Carlo Rally saw the return of Goran Norlander and Bo Boesen, this time in Bo's Javelin. (JCC)

Goran Norlander and Bo Boesen at the end of the 1953 Monte Carlo Rally; they were the only Jowett entrants to start from Stockholm. (Photo Junior, Nice)

cars had a different sized screen, which is why it was wrong, but I am not convinced that this was the case at all. *(Neither am I. – NS)* However the French are very good at improvising and they made up a special surround that looked very odd, but it worked! Eventually she arrived down in Monte Carlo the same day that we got there, so all was well. Four of us plus the luggage came back from Monte Carlo in the Javelin.

I think it was 1951 when Jupiters finished first and second in class, Ellison drove the first and Raymond Baxter the second. Raymond Baxter was a good friend of mine and I worked with him whilst broadcasting the Monte over a period of years, and twice for the ITV. He invited me to join the Jupiter team on a celebration run around the 'circuit' in Monte Carlo after the presentations had finished. There were ten of us in or on one Jupiter, four inside the car operating various controls. There were three people draped over the bonnet and three across the back. Raymond was the centre anchorman at the back, he was in the middle and I was to his right. I was nearly lost overboard with every left-hand corner, but we survived!

My last Monte was in 1956, driving a Borgward, but this came to a rapid end when my Italian co-driver put us up against a tree in thick fog in the Alps. After that I commentated on every Monte upto 1963, normally with the BBC, but as mentioned above, twice for ITV.

1952 *Daily Express* National Motor Rally
By G.H. Rushton
(As published by me in the April 1997 issue of *The Jowetteer*. – NS)

Following my request for Jowett information published in the Daily Telegraph *in 1997, I received an interesting letter and photo from Mr Rushton telling me about this event. He wrote:*

Seeing your letter in the *Telegraph* motoring section, I enclose this photo. I don't know if it is of any use for what you want. *(Yes it was! – NS)*

The car was purchased from Wilf Parrish Ltd of Preston in 1951, it was not my car, but I am on the picture next to the car wearing glasses. (The car carried the registration number NTF263 and had rally plate number 427.) The photo was taken at the start of the *Daily Express* Rally in 1952. We managed to finish third in the saloon class after having to replace a broken throttle cable in the Black Mountains at about 2.30 in the morning.

The car had several more trophy wins in local club rallies and events; it proved to be a very good car, but a bit dodgy to maintain and service. In all; well advanced in looks and style. It was exchanged for a Jupiter later on, to do sprints etc. This I had no part in, and have no 'gen' on it. I hope the photo is some good to you and will fit in with what you require.

Bradford with 'Go anywhere' characteristics
By E.H. Dennis (The 1953 London to Exeter Trial and others)
(As published in the Jowett Car Club Yearbook for 1972)

Back in the late forties and early fifties when I had to combine family motoring, business motoring together with what competition I could find at the time and money for, I was offered a new Bradford. I liked the first one so much that I had three or four more, changing them at the rate of one per year. In thirty-five years of road motoring at home and abroad including twenty-five years of competitive motoring – mainly production trials, some sporting, some speed hill climbing, driving tests, rallies and a little racing, I never enjoyed a period more than that with my Bradfords. Unfortunately, I've kept no records of performances etc, but recall that in driving tests I could hold my own with almost any saloon. For normal family use we often undertook long journeys, for example, on a Sunday in June 1953 I took my very elderly Great Aunt, my mother and father-in-law to Sussex from Cornwall and back in the same day. This was a distance of 500 miles, and though being notorious for having a 'heavy right foot'; I cannot ever recall one of the Bradfords letting me down.

I had such faith in their toughness that the very first run I gave one new one was to climb over the moor – around the bracken and rocks to the summit of our local mountain. This was Roughor, which is 1,350ft high, a mountain which few others, if any, outside a Land Rover variety would tackle. Traction was wonderful too, and in trials I found that I could wipe up any opposition provided the gradient was not too steep. If it was I would have to resort to 'pumping' the clutch whilst hollering to my passenger to keep forward to promote wheel spin to build up the revs, and so when done, to charge down to the tail-end to transfer the power into grip and forward motion again.

I entered one of my Bradfords registered OAF81 (appropriate for a Cornish 'spud basher') in the 1953 London to Exeter Trial, one of the three M.C.C. classic long-distance trials. *The Motor* reported on its climb of the very long and rough Finagle Bridge as 'An outstanding effort, the Bradford chugged its way without a falter.' Of Pin Hill *The Motor* said, 'Others had a lot of wheel spin, whereas Dennis in a twin-cylinder Jowett Bradford merely went steadily up, just a little faster than expected.' *Autosport* reported, ' Dennis's ordinary Jowett Bradford never looked like failing, though the writer has seldom seen such bouncing by a passenger, who appeared to leave his seat by at least 3ft and come down again with a sickening thud.'

In one of the Exeter Trials, the M.C.C. introduced a hill known as Applington, which was very rough and rutted; but being not too steep, so I knew the Bradford would be able to cope with it and it did. *The Motor* saying, 'Indicative – although only a few standard production sports cars are claimed to have achieved a premier award, the M.C.C. still provide in the Exeter and Lands End at Easter, a fair chance for a well-driven normal vehicle with a reasonable allocation of weight on the rear wheels. Confirmation of this fact comes from the fine performance on many hills of E.H. Dennis's Jowett Bradford, pictured here on the last hill of the trial, Applington.'

I entered a Lands End or two, arriving home on one occasion at 3 a.m. after twenty-four hours of continuous motoring, only to find that my wife had accidentally slipped the Yale lock catch and I nearly bashed the door down! I cannot recall, however, ever failing to collect an award in any of these long distance, or any other trials driving test which I entered the Bradfords in.

As I finished with each one, which I bought new, I passed them on to our construction business for use there. In time we built up quite a fleet, all to be seen round North Cornwall, complete with loaded ladder racks, 'up to the gunwales' and grossly overloaded with workmen and their equipment. One Bradford was taken over by my second son, Paul, who learnt to 'trial' on the hilly and wooded ten acres in front of the house. I wonder if my love, and subsequently, his love for them led him to Bradford City, where he now keeps company with yet another Jowett (Miss) – though his contact between Bradford and Cornwall is now kept by his Malvern Morgan.

My experiences with the Javelin were rather short-lived. Being always a speculator, I was offered two new Javelins when I hardly had the price of a spare tyre for one of them. I took delivery on a Friday night and worked like mad over the weekend trying to flog them before my cheque was presented the following morning. I managed it – but only just – by selling one to a gullible, but kindly uncle, who gave me a £25 tip for my bother, and the other to an architect in Truro. Although by then I let him have it at cost as at this stage panic was setting in.

It was a pity I had to dispose of them like this as I had been looking forward to owning one properly, and keeping it; but when the moment came I hadn't the cash to hold on. As a boy I had always loved the Lancia Aprilia from afar and I felt that with the Javelin I would have got what earlier I would have expected from the Aprilia. Now I drive a Jaguar V12 amongst others, but

E.H. Dennis climbing Afflington Bank in his 1948 Bradford Utility, with the Cornish registration number OAF81, in the 1953 Exeter Trial. *The Motor* had been impressed with his performance, saying, 'Others had a lot of wheel-spin whereas Dennis in his twin-cylinder Jowett Bradford merely went steadily up, just a little faster than had been expected.' (*Autocar*)

none of them give me the thrill of taking on something twice my size and supposed potential and beating them to it – as did the Bradford. Owners of big cars such as Humber Super Snipes etc. could always be relied on to do something desperate in retaliation after seeing the Bradford flash past them, when they thought they were 'motoring'. Little did they know that I'd been building up my momentum from about half a mile behind.

How can one praise a vehicle without appearing to shoot the line about oneself – I don't know! All I do know is that I am passing on to other Jowett enthusiasts the message that there is another who is more than glad that at sometime he, and the Jowetts, kept company together.

The Tulip Rally 1953
By Count van Zuylen van Nijevelt
(Taken from The Jowett Car Club website)

In 1952 I drove a Jowett Javelin in the Tulip Rally and had come close to winning it, which unfortunately finished on the Circuit of Zandvoort, when the radiator screen did not want to come down and the car started to boil. In 1953 I was determined to do a good job in this fabulous little car, so this is why I did not mount a radiator screen, but little flaps which I could pull away on with a rope. I know that we prepared the car very well indeed.

Another thing we did was to try a downhill section which was a rolling test, no engine! First of all I tested it in France to see if adding weight would help. I did the same circuit over and over again, with very exact timing with the car full of sandbags and empty. I discovered that it made no difference, a heavy car took more time to start rolling, with more skidding in the corners and more brake pressure required. A light car starts a little quicker, but then did not gain momentum that quickly, but much faster in the corners, and less braking required; I chose to keep the car as light as possible for the test.

Also, of course, the tyre pressure was very important, the harder the tyres, the faster it would go. Then during the rally before the special test, everybody was pumping up their tyres, and I did the opposite. I made them almost empty and then drove a few kilometres waggling the steering wheel from left to right over and over again to try and wear off the side of the tyres. Then just before the start of the test I had them pumped up as hard as I could possibly think it would be safe. As the sides of the rubber had gone, I was literally driving on a very, very narrow little piece of rubber. That was why I was the fastest on that down hill race. Needless to say I had arranged for new tyres immediately after that down hill section!

In an original Auto Revue of 15 May 1953, I see that my time in that test was 1.39.4, and the runner up was, believe it or not, was Banks in his Bristol in 1.40.1, he would go on to be second overall. Becquart in his Jowett Javelin had a time of 1.45.8 in that test.

In the hill climbs he beat me twice, but later he was disqualified because he had used Jupiter parts. In the final test at Zandvoort he was only 1.2 seconds faster than me, and I am still proud of that achievement.

Number 1 in the classification was my Jowett Javelin, followed by:
2) Banks in the Bristol.
3) The Frenchman Grosgogeat with a Dyna-Panhard – very fast!
4) My good friend Jetten in a Vauxhall.
5) The Appleyard couple in a Jaguar.
Then we also won the team prize for Jowett's with myself and the Dutch teams of Scheffer/Willing and Homan/de Boer.

I will never forget the prize giving in Hotel Huis ter Duin, every time I go there I cannot help thinking of that ceremony when the big boss of the Rallye Piet Nortier handed me the first prize. He waster Duin, every time I go there I cannot help thinking of that ceremony when the big boss of the Rallye Piet Nortier handed me the first prize. He was crying, because he was so proud that his Rally was won by 'the boys', as we were called. We were the youngest team, the first Dutchmen to win the Tulip Rally on the 5th anniversary of the rally and also the team prize, it could not have been better!

I still relish those memories.

Hugo

The Tulip Rally 1954
John Gilley

I had a request for Jowett information published in The Banbury Guardian, *which produced this unexpected, but most welcome, interesting reply. – NS*

A long time ago I rallied a Jowett Javelin in the Tulip Rally, 1954 to be precise. The Javelin was owned at the time by Henry Burke, who then lived in Ilkley, but now lives in Jersey. He was the registered entrant and I was his co-driver. The car was registered HKY 777, and our rally plate number was 157.

We unofficially teamed up with two other Dutch-owned Javelins, who were numbered 156 and 158. The mere fact that we stayed together in consecutive numbered identical cars meant we were given a enthusiastic welcome wherever we went.

We remained together to the end of the rally and crossed over the finish line together to a rousing reception.

The previous year's rally was won outright by a Javelin. *(This was Count van Zuylen van Nijevelt as detailed in the entry above. – NS)*

The start of the 1953 Tulip Rally shows Marcel Becquart in HAK743 ahead of Nijevelt in the Dutch Javelin registered NT-43-85. This year's event ended in chaos with numerous disqualifications due to non-standard alterations to cars. Provisionally Becquart won the class, but to his horror he was disqualified due to alterations the factory had made unbeknown to him; it would be the last time he drove for Jowetts. This paved the way for Nijevelt to move from second in class to first, and even better for him, the rally as a whole, due to how the points were allocated! (JCC)

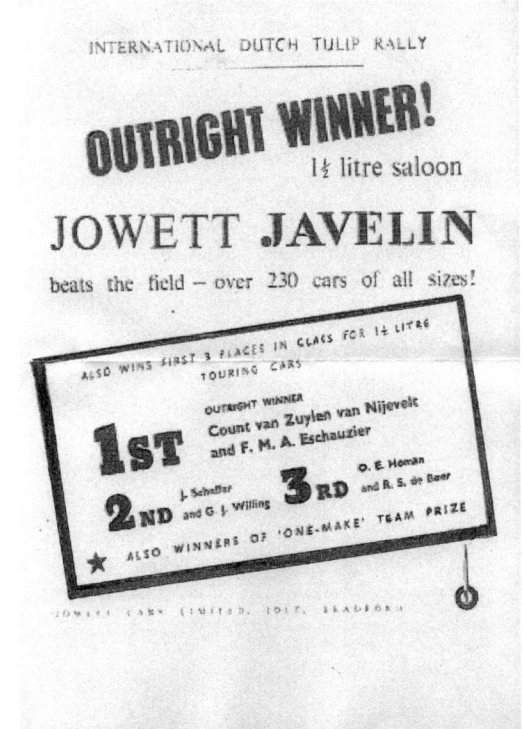

Nijevelt showing off his novel way of opening and closing the radiator muff at the start of the 1953 Tulip Rally. (JCC)

Ken L.W. Cooke, Goodwood Sprint October 1954

This is a bit of self-indulgence on my behalf, as Ken raced my Jupiter registered JBE4 at this event in October 1954. I found this out as a club member in 1998 told me that he had bought some photos of his Jupiter racing at a 1950s event from a photographer, *Ferret Fotographics*, who specialised in vintage motor sport pictures. He told me there were also a couple of pictures of JBE4 racing as well, needless to say I bought them both, as prior to this I had no idea my car had been used in competition. Both pictures were taken at the Goodwood event, and stated on the backs that the driver was K.L.W. Cook.

I have since found out that he also drove the car in 1953 at a hill climb at Tarrant Rushton Airfield near Bournemouth, and a sprint at Brunton near the villages of Ludgershall, Collingbourne Dulcis and Collingbourne Kingston, a short distance north of Andover. This was a third of a mile course used in the 1940s and 1950s; the start banner was slung between two barns, one of which housed the timekeepers.

Since I bought the photos of JBE4 racing at Goodwood, I had tried to trace K.L.W. Cook, as this sounded a particularly interesting part of the car's history. I tried contacting the secretary at Goodwood, with no luck, but she suggested that I write to The British Automobile Racing Club to see if they could help. I wrote to them but their records did not go back as far as 1954. I also contacted the West Hants and Dorset Car Club, but had no reply from them. By chance, I typed in K.L.W. Cook into the Google search engine on my computer and it came up with K.L.W. Cook Electricals of 1 The Broadway, Andover. This looked too good to be true, as all three known races that he entered JBE4 in were in this area.

I spoke to a gentleman called Cliff at K.L.W. Cook Electricals in April 2005, he confirmed that the business had been set up by Ken Cook in approx. 1953, when Ken retired in 1994 the business retained the original name. I told him it was Ken I really wanted to talk to, as I wanted to know if he had owned a Jowett Jupiter. Cliff said that he knew he had done, and that he had used it in competition events! Sadly he told me that Ken had died in 2004 aged ninety. He did however give me the phone number of his widow, Eva, they had lived together for over fifty years, but he must have decided to make an honest woman of her, as they married a year before he died!

I rang Eva up and she told me that Ken had set up the electrical business in 1953 and at the time he had traded in a pre-war Riley for JBE4, and this was the only car he owned at the time. She said that come rain or shine he delivered new Television sets to people with the hood down, placing the TV on the seat next to him. He had to have the hood down, as he could not slide the TV's in through the open door with the hood up, he had to place it on the seat from above. He kept the car for a couple of years, but needed a more suitable vehicle for his business. She confirmed that they both had a very soft spot for the car, which was their favourite of all the cars that they owned.

I attended the Classic Car Show in Birmingham in November 2006 with my wife, Jane, and had another stroke of luck. The same photographer *Ferret Fotographics* had a stand there and to my amazement he had a photo of JBE4 racing at the 1953 Tarrant Rushton event for sale, needless to say I bought it! I am most grateful to them for giving me to reproduce these in this book.

Some reminiscences of a life in Jowetts

Reg Korner

Reg Korner was chief designer at Jowetts and was responsible for the body design of the pre-war 8 and 10hp models. He also designed the body for the post-war Jupiter, in record time. I have included this letter in the book as it also gives a good insight into the workings of Jowetts in these exciting times for them. – NS

I arrived at Jowetts in 1936; Willie Jowett was Managing Director, Ben having retired a short while before.

Ken Cooke drove my 1952 Jupiter registered JBE4 in a hill climb at Tarrant Rushton Airfield near Bournemouth in 1953. (Ferret Fotograpics)

Ken also raced my Jupiter registered JBE4 at Goodwood in October 1954. (Ferret Fotographics)

A Bradford-registered Javelin HKY777 with its proud owner, John Gilley, ready to start the 1954 Tulip Rally. (JCC)

The firm was rather cut off from the rest of the car trade, which was either in the Midlands or further south, and not many men would risk moving up there.

I had to train mechanical draughtsmen to draw bodywork details. Most of the machinery was rather old, some from the First World War, when the Government helped them to re-equip, as they did during the Second World War. It is surprising how many firms were saved by the wars. Most of the machines were belt-driven, power being supplied by a single-cylinder gas engine, which hopefully, was started up each morning by Horace Grimley hauling on the belt!

The first models I designed were the Eight and Ten; these models were identical, the eight with the flat-twin engine, and the ten with the flat-four engine and were the last models produced prior to the war.

On the outbreak of war, Mr C.C. Reilly was made Managing Director, and due to his drive and connections in London, the firm was soon working on large and exceptionally varied production of armaments.

Near the end of the war Mr Reilly asked me to start thinking about body designs for a new car. Styling was a problem as other firms were turning out pre-war models. The other problem was how to make a design of about 200 per week at a reasonable price.

Plastics were in their infancy at that time and we carried out some interesting experiments with thermo plastic sheets which could be easily formed and were self-coloured. These were discarded because of the effect of contraction and expansion at varying temperatures, and they were also too costly. We had a sample door made of moulded plywood, as used on Mosquito aircraft. This was strong and light but too expensive for large production.

After many experiments, I designed the first prototype Javelin, having a steel framed construction with aluminium panels clinched on round the edges. One of these prototypes had a clear plastic panel in the roof, forward of the central pillar. These prototypes created considerable interest when on test, with numerous requests to have a look under the bonnet! Mr Reilly had one exciting moment when, during a fairly fast run, the bonnet catch failed and the bonnet flew up. Fortunately we had put some louvers in the bonnet for cooling purposes, through which we could see and he brought the car up safely to a stop! *(The same thing happened to Horace Grimley, as detailed by his son Victor. – NS)* Another experience happened when he had just finished demonstrating the car to some financiers with a view to raising some more capital for the firm – he drew up outside the Savoy Hotel, and on opening the door the handle came off in his hand!

In the end Briggs Bodies offered to make an all steel body at their war-time factory in Doncaster, the design and tooling being done in Dagenham. This necessitated a number of fairly high speed journeys down the Great North Road via Doncaster – I think the record for the journey to London was four hours – no M1 in those days.

In 1950 Mr Woodhead told me that the firm had definitely decided to put a sports car on the market using the chassis designed by Prof Eberhorst. He left the design of the body to me, but insisted that the first prototype should be ready in time for the New York Show in four months time. This meant working long hours, but I had a good Body Experimental Shop then under Bill Poulter.

An aluminium panelled body seemed essential to keep the weight down. Several bodies had been made by outside coachbuilders but most of them were rather heavy. I had heard that a body panelled in aluminium which had been on view at an earlier show had been covered in dents, caused by people leaning on them with their elbows, so I decided to make this one out of 16swg. The tubular chassis was not particularly strong torsionally, so it was necessary to insulate the body from it by mounting the body on silent blocks. Inboard headlamps allowed for a good line on the wings and also protected them.

I always considered that the normal folded hood ruined the appearance of a sports car and that good weather protection was only possible with wind-down glass windows. This was a problem, but was accomplished by an unusual method of folding the hood which still could be quickly erected, which was equally important. I still think this is the best type for an open sports car.

We managed to complete the first Jupiter a few days before the American show. Charles Grandfield and Horace Grimley and I ran it around the hills for a couple of hours in very foggy weather, none of us daring to take any risks.

The next day it was on show at the works before being shipped to America for the show, where it was well received and, I understand, it was the most photographed car in the show. *(As published in the March 1987 issue of* The Jowetteer. *– NS)*

Mike Wilson

Was the official timekeeper for the Jowett team at Le Mans for the three years that they entered, 1950 to 1952, and was a great friend of Tommy Wise, the 1950 winner who ran a garage business in Guiseley near Leeds.

He was co-driver and navigator for Tommy in the 1950 Monte Carlo Rally in Tommy's Javelin which carried the entry number 120 and was registered FAK920, they, like most Brits at the time, started from Glasgow. They made such good time they had time to stop off for a meal at Tommy's house in Leeds on the way down! They ran into heavy snow south of Nevers, and eventually finished fifteenth in class.

Nikki Wise (Tommy's daughter) mentioned a nice little story about this event, Mike's Auntie Olive decided to knit them some bobble hats to keep them warm on their long journey. This she lovingly did in green and white stripes. They duly arrived in Glasgow just before an 'Old Firm' derby between Celtic and Rangers, and had parked up amongst a large number of Rangers supporters. They were jostled and given a hard time by the supporters, as their lovely hats were in Celtic colours. As soon as they realised what was happening, they removed their hats and beat a hasty retreat!

The Ron Ayres Javelin leaving the Paris control point during the 1954 Monte Carlo Rally. (JCC)

The Ron Ayres Javelin registered MOK326 in action at Col de Leques in the 1954 Monte Carlo Rally. (Charles Dunn/JCC)

Another view of the Ron Ayres Javelin in action in the 1954 Monte Carlo Rally. (Plage of Cannes/JCC)

He also co-drove and navigated for Tommy in the ex-Le Mans winning Jupiter from 1950, registered GKW111, which Tommy had bought from Jowetts in two Alpine rallies as a private entry. On the first occasion in 1951 they retired after hitting some cyclists, who were injured and needed hospital attention. The car was too badly damaged to continue. The following year they were back with extra horns fitted, but sadly, the engine was to fail 20 miles from the finish.

Dudley Noble - Motoring Correspondent

Another famous motoring and travel journalist I wanted to mention in this book was Dudley Noble, during the 1920s and '30s he drove Rover cars for the factory to gain as much publicity for the marque as he could. One of his most memorable exploits was in January 1930, when he raced the 'Blue Train'. At the time this was the fastest and most glamorous way to reach the French and Italian Riviera, and was used mainly by the rich and famous. He had noticed that the train took almost twenty-four hours to travel from Calais to its terminus at Vintimille, just over the Italian border from Menton. He, like most people, assumed that it travelled all the way at 60+ mph, but careful examination of the timetable showed that it averaged at something like 40mph for the full journey. This was due to long delays crossing Paris, it also stopped at Dijon for a change of locomotive, and more delays crossing Marseilles, where the engine was changed again. This idea found approval from the Rover board, as it was a glamorous idea, which Dudley thought would make an excellent news story.

A full account of this adventure is in Dudley's excellent book, *Milestones in a Motoring Life*, published by Queen Anne Press Ltd in 1969, but to cut a long story short, they had planned to beat the train from Calais to the Riviera. This attempt failed as they encountered thick fog for a considerable time. After falling behind the train they decided to continue down to the Riviera at a more leisurely pace and have a go on the return journey. This they did, and they beat it back,

The Ron Ayres Javelin leaving the car ferry *Lord Walden* during the 1954 Monte Carlo Rally. Ron said that they had had a trouble-free run down to the south of France, as the weather had been very mild that year, with no snow to contend with. (JCC)

Nice shot of a Jupiter registered KTM555 closely followed by a Jaguar XK120; it was owned and driven by Mr K. Crutch of Markgate. This picture was taken at Silverstone, but sadly the event is unknown, although must have been during the mid-1950s. (Charles Dunn/JCC)

I could not resist using this photo, as it was on the front cover of my first book *Jowett 1901–1954*, but at the time I did not know the event or the driver and had asked for any information about it. I have just heard from George Mitchell, who told me he was the driver and it was his car, the navigator being his good friend George Hugh Baird. The event was the Grouse Rally which took place in Scotland in August 1957. George is well known in Jowett circles and has held various posts for the club from the early 1960s. (JCC)

At the start of the 1952 *Daily Express* Rally are Wilf Parish (left) and navigator G.H. Rushton (centre with glasses). Mr Rushton said that they finished third in their class, but lost time having to replace a broken throttle cable. (JCC)

A very early Javelin registered FAK798 at a night control in the *Daily Express* Rally of possibly 1952. (JCC)

A Javelin registered PPF886 in action in the *Daily Express* Rally of possibly 1952. (JCC)

The same car in action again, but sadly the event is unknown to me. (JCC)

which created great excitement in the *Daily Express*, as one of Dudley's passengers was a reporter from that paper. It was a clever piece of marketing which I am sure that the Jowett brothers would have been proud of.

Dudley and his wife, Marianne, travelled to France, and elsewhere, on a regular basis and published details of their exploits in their travel magazine called *Milestones*. On at least one occasion they travelled to the south of France in the Jupiter SC prototype which was registered HKW 197. I am not sure how this came about, but a picture of the car appeared in their book, *With your Car in the South of France*, published by Frederick Muller Ltd, London in 1959. This is a very atmospheric book and gives a lot of information on how to get there and the best routes to use, some of which take in part of the 'Monte' route. A section at the end of the book would have been of interest to prospective entrants, entitled 'The car for the journey'. As they had done this route in the Jupiter, I am sure that some of their suggestions could have been influenced by the Jupiter.

I said it was a tenuous link with Jowett's, but I feel justified in this piece of self-indulgence on my part, as it is relevant to the basic principles of this book, together with the fact that their book has this nice picture of the Jupiter HKW 197 travelling at speed towards a chateau called Louis de France, a hotel on the banks of the River Loire at Muides.

The section 'The car for the journey' reads:

It is natural that a motorist should give his car some special care and attention before he takes it abroad, but I would stress the desirability of not giving it major operations without allowing time for it to settle down again before departure. Sometimes, if the cylinder head has been removed and replaced, or the cylinders rebored, little troubles develop which can readily be put right at home, but might be a problem to rectify once on the road in a foreign country. Leaky gaskets between cylinder head and block, or joints in the water circulation system, can give rise to serious delays if they have to be renewed with parts sent out from home.

The manufacturers of most British cars are well alive to the needs of owners who go motoring abroad, and if you have the space, it is wise to take one of the packs of spares which are available on a sale-or-return basis. It is even wiser to have made friends with the manager of your local service station so that, in the event of something being required which is not in the kit, he can get a proper replacement part for your particular model sent out. Both the motor manufacturers and the motoring organisations know how to forward such parts, so they stand the best chance of getting through customs red-tape without delay. If you are a member of either the AA or RAC you should carry their foreign touring guide in the car as it contains a great deal of useful information, including details of their respective 'Get your car home' schemes in the event of a total breakdown.

The only troubles I can myself remember having centre mainly on the tyres, and once I found the jack was not right for the car, while on another occasion the wheel nuts had been screwed up so tight at the factory that the wheel brace provided in the toolkit was insufficiently strong to undo them. This certainly was a problem, with the tyre flat! Beware, too, of rusted-up bolts to the wheels. It is commonsense to carry the car's instruction book around, even if it is in English and therefore not understandable to a French mechanic. Also in an emergency is one of those large charts which the Wakefield Castrol Oil company issue for the most popular model cars, intended to help with lubrication but conveying a clear indication of the layout of the chassis without words.

Apart from the spares referred to, I always take with me a can or two of spare oil, as one's recommended brand is not to be had everywhere abroad, and in any case it costs more there. It is also useful to have a small can of brake fluid, as this way likewise may not be easy to come by in an emergency. Some distilled water for topping up the battery is another of the items for which I always find room – I have got myself a gadget known as 'Purawata', which holds about a pint of ordinary tap water. When the container is squeezed the water is forced through a very efficient filtering cap screwed into position, and the fluid that emanates from the nozzle is chemically pure and thoroughly suitable for batteries. It is surprising how the electrolyte in the cells boils away during a long trip in hot weather, especially if the battery is located under the bonnet.

If night driving is on the programme, it is best to have yellow bulbs fitted into the headlamps, and adjust the dipping mechanism to suit driving on the right. Unless, however, one is going to drive either a long distance after dark, or frequently, one can get by with yellow transparent discs stuck over the headlamp glasses. French motorists and lorry drivers are not too happy if faced with a beam from clear white headlamps; they, of course, are obliged by law to fit yellow bulbs.

There is one further 'must', so far as I am concerned, that is a copy of the current Michelin Guide, without which I would not think of touring France. Once one learns to use it properly there is simply no end of invaluable information it can impart where hotels and restaurants are concerned, and I do advise all who want to get the best out of their trip to carry a copy in the car. But first – and do this one quiet evening at home – go carefully through the explanatory pages in front of the book and master the meaning of the numerous signs and symbols. The effort on your part might be well repaid.

To finish on a stronger Jowett note, Dudley was the motoring correspondent with the Investors Chronicle, *so I am also reproducing a road-test he did for them on the Javelin, which he clearly rated very highly. – NS*

The Jowett Javelin
Dudley Noble
(*The Investors' Chronicle*, 3 February 1951)

During recent weeks I have had the opportunity of trying out one of the real post-war designs of car, the Jowett Javelin. When this was introduced to the British public some four years ago, in May 1947, it caused no small stir because of its original design and unusual appearance. In the intervening period it has proved itself to possess a road performance and degree of reliability truly justifying the faith of its sponsors, Jowett Cars Ltd. The new Javelin won its class (1½ litre) in the Monte Carlo Rally in 1949, while in last week's edition of this famous event, its young brother the Jupiter put up a fine performance by being in the first six placings and winning the 1½ litre team prize.

Taking stock of the Javelin today, what appeared four years ago to be advanced styling is no more than representative of the modern trend of design. But, while in outward appearance the Javelin may now be less individual than it was, it remains unique among British cars for its engine. No other manufacturer has adapted the 'flat four' or horizontally-opposed type of four-cylinder power unit, which is a basic feature of the Javelin.

That such an engine has special merits is undoubted One of them is smooth running, for the cylinders are in pairs, in a straight line on either side of the crankshaft, so their piston movements, being opposed, may be said to cancel themselves out. In the important matters of power and economy this type of engine also seems to have advantages, for the Javelin, although of only 1,486cc (say 13hp nominal), actually develops more than 50bhp and will pull the car along at 75mph, cruising comfortably at a mile a minute when the conditions allow. Its petrol consumption, on the other hand, is notably low, and 28-30 miles in the gallon are obtained under normal conditions of driving.

But perhaps the most useful aspect of the flat-four engine is that it occupies so little room. It is about as compact a type as could possibly be designed, and allows the very maximum of space to be put at the passengers' disposal. The result is that the interior of the Javelin's body is surprisingly roomy, giving plenty of space for leg-stretching even though the rear seats are placed well forward, and so get fullest benefit of the efficient springing system.

When one drives a Javelin for the first time there is a 'different' feel which is a little difficult to explain – let me hasten to say that this is a pleasant sensation. It is, I think, a combination of the unusual smoothness of the engine with the individualistic movement of the springing, which is by means of torsion bars at both front and rear. Naturally, the feeling wears off, but one continues to marvel at the extraordinary efficiency of the suspension, which smoothes out the bumps and potholes in a quite uncanny fashion and lets the car ride over bad roads with an absence of shock and pitching. The car corners with great stability and holds the road very well indeed.

The car I tried was a saloon de luxe which costs £695 plus purchase tax; there is a standard model at £595 plus purchase tax. The difference between them is in detail, the de luxe model having full hide upholstery as compared with plastic and cloth, while the facia board of the more pricy model is in walnut grain; there are also various extra fitments which make for comfort and convenience for the additional money. Common to both models are the essential Jowett Javelin features of excellent passenger and luggage accommodation. There is adequate ground clearance for rough roads and tracks, and the accessibility of the engine and its ancillary parts is outstandingly good. The grille at the front pivots and can be swung up in a few seconds (or can be removed entirely) to reveal the whole power unit and provide access to the twin carburettors, valves and so forth. The gearbox is a four-speed, with synchromesh to second, third and top, and with a lever control on the left-hand side below the steering wheel.

The Jowett Javelin was one of the first British cars to be fitted with a curved windscreen, which definitely increases the driver's range of vision to each side; in fact, visibility is good throughout – a feature that has a considerable bearing of the comfort of the rear-seat passengers. Great care has been taken to dust-proof the body, which is of all-steel construction and has six lights and pull-out handles to the four doors. This is, altogether, an extremely well-thought-out and practical car, and one which has deservedly a high degree of popularity in export markets as well as the home market.

John Bullock

Once again, this following item is a bit of self-indulgence on my behalf, as the story is not strictly speaking a racing or sporting event, but it does involve John Bullock, the well-known motoring correspondent, and is connected with the Jupiter racing team. It is also such a good story it would have been a shame not to include it! – NS

High Risk in a Jupiter
John Bullock
(*Classic Car Weekly*, 7 December 1994)

The shoppers in St John's Wood, London, who heard a crash, saw me leap from my damaged car and make off the road as fast as I could, would have every reason to think I was a hit and run driver and give chase, writes John Bullock.

They weren't to know that the Jowett Jupiter I was driving was full of cans of high-octane fuel that could have exploded at any moment!

The Jupiter was one of the Le Mans team cars and I was on the way to Silverstone to put it through its paces. Its racing engine needed high octane fuel, which meant that I had to carry enough with me to get to and from the Jowett headquarters in Albermarle Street and do several circuits of the track.

As a result the car resembled a small bowser with its highly inflammable contents – all rather illegal and neither Jowett nor I wanted anybody to know. Looking back we seemed willing to take a lot of foolish chances in those days.

After a Jowett Jupiter, driven by Tommy Wise and Tommy Wisdom, had won the 1½ litre class at Le Mans in 1950, three cars were entered the 1951 race.

That year it was the Jupiter driven by Marcel Becquart and Gordon Wilkins which was successful, but Wisdom still managed to put up the fastest lap of 80.60mph.

It was after this success that the jovial John Baldwin, Jowett's popular publicity manager, invited me to test one of the team cars and I naturally jumped at the chance.

The only way to get to Silverstone, however, was for me to drive it there myself and John's last words as I set off from Albermarle Street that morning had been, 'For goodness sake keep out of trouble, and don't get caught with all that high-octane on board.'

I thought my best plan would be to cut across country and keep to the minor roads, but I hadn't accounted for the absent-minded driver of a rather battered Standard.
He shot the lights at St John's Wood and hit the Jupiter with a resounding crash behind the driver's seat, only inches away from the cans of extra fuel I was carrying.

As soon as I realised that luck was on my side and fuel didn't seem to be leaking from any of the cans, I made my way back to the car.

Perhaps the police were having their lunch or didn't wish to become involved, but none appeared on the scene. With the help of a rather crest-fallen driver of the Standard, the battered Jupiter was pushed into the relative safety of a side street.

The driver agreed to stand guard while I arranged for a local garage to tow away the damaged car and carefully remove the cans of high-octane.

Then I rang Mr Baldwin to tell him the bad news.

After I explained what had happened there was a moment's pause, then he said. 'I bet you could do with a drink. Jump into a cab and I will meet you at the Ritz. A stiff drink and a spot of lunch will soon have you feeling better. Look on the bright side; if those cans of fuel had exploded we'd probably both have been for the high jump.'

The publicity manager was a true professional who knew how to make the best of a situation.

We became close friends and I was delighted when Becquart and Wilkins won again in 1952, despite water getting into the fuel – making it the third successive year that the Jowett Company from Bradford had carried off the 1½ litre class at Le Mans.

It gave me an opportunity of giving Jowett some well-deserved publicity, but I decided against test driving any of that year's team cars. I felt I might have used up all my luck.

What the Papers Had to Say

1949 Monte Carlo Rally
(Taken from an unknown paper dated 9 February 1949)

Members of the five English teams which drove Javelin cars in the recent Monte Carlo Rally had some entertaining reminiscences to tell at the dinner which Jowett Cars Ltd., makers of the Javelin, gave to them in Bradford last night.

They drove 2,000 miles in two days and three nights from Glasgow to France, Belgium, Holland, back to France, and through to Monte Carlo. They had little sleep, but all did well, and for one spell of bad luck, would have done better.

The team in charge of Mr T. Wise, of Guiseley, took first prize in the 1½ litre class, and a St Annes team under Mr R. Smith took third – a great tribute to their skill and endurance and the quality of the Javelin.

The team prize would also have probably been gained had not one of the cars not been involved in an accident. It had put up an excellent performance, but late at night on a tricky stretch of road, the driver, Mr A.H. Grimley, one of the members of Jowett's staff, saw a French lorry almost upon him. He instinctively pulled to the left instead of the right, as he should have done in France, pressed on his brakes and came to a stop, but was struck by the lorry.

The French driver was co-operative, but he insisted that the accident was reported. The nearest policeman was 5 miles away. He had to be got out of bed, but as there was no injury, he was not interested. He referred the team to another public representative, who also had to be got out of bed to draw a plan of the scene. The result was nearly four hours' delay, and in spite of the excellent performance which the team and car did afterwards make, the prize was lost.

Mr H. Woodhead, managing director of the firm, paid tribute to all who had taken part. He has great confidence in the Javelin, a confidence that is shared by Mr A.H.G. Hume of English Racing Automobiles Ltd., who was a member of one of the teams, and who said if he were to enter a car in the next rally; the Javelin would be his choice. *(NB. this is just what did happen, see the article 'And thus it came to pass' in which he drove the winning Javelin in the 1949 Spa 24-hour race. – NS)*

1949 Tulip Rally
(From an undated newspaper clipping)

Both owners of Jowett Javelin cars, W.H. Robinson of Dalton-in-Furness and J. Towers Leck of Ullverston are joint entrants of the International Tulip Rally motor race of Holland.

They start from Glasgow shortly after 4 p.m. today, with 1,700 miles of British, French, Belgian and Dutch roads ahead. Mr Robinson's car is being used.

Mr Tommy Wise, recently very successful in the Monte Carlo Rally, is also driving a Javelin and is starting from London.

1950 Monte Carlo Rally ... – Guiseley driver beats snow in rally dash, told, 'It's a daughter'
Tommy Wise
(Taken from the *Yorkshire Observer*, 26 January 1950)

A Bradford-made Jowett Javelin, driven by T.C. (Tommy) Wise, of Green Croft, The Green, Guiseley, put up a good performance among the British cars competing in the Monte Carlo Rally.

Mr Wise, who set off from Glasgow on Sunday, arrived at Monte Carlo yesterday, but will not know his exact placing until Saturday, after the acceleration, braking and other tests.

Awaiting him in Monte Carlo was a cable informing him that yesterday his wife had presented him with a daughter. Mrs Wise is in a nursing home at Rookeridge, and both mother and daughter are doing well. Mr & Mrs Wise also have a six-year-old son, Timothy.

Mr Wise is a member of the Yorkshire Sports Car Club, was a private entrant in the rally. Last year he won the 1½ litre class. The British Allard took first, forth and sixth places in the first results known in the rally yesterday – in breaking and acceleration. The Allards were those teamed by S.H. Allard, G. Warburton, L. Potter and A.G. Imhof. In the acceleration test S.H. Allard's time of nineteen seconds was two seconds better than that of his nearest rival, last year's winner, J. Trevoux (France) driving a Delahaye. Allard has little chance, however, of winning the rally for he arrived at Monte Carlo with a smashed wing and headlamp, caused by crashing into a skidding car in the mountains. Allard was the second of the Glasgow starters to reach Monte Carlo.

First was P.C. Harper and C. Evan Cook in a Hillman, who had a puncture 2 miles from the finish, losing nine minutes, and probably, their chance of finishing without penalty. The rally in which 282 cars started on Sunday night ended last night with only 135 vehicles left in the running. There were 181 cars that reached Monte Carlo, but forty-six arrived too late. The whole Rhone Valley and all the Alps roads over the last lap were in a howling snow storm. Many cars had damaged mudguards, bumpers and radiators, telling a tale of skids and crashes on snow and ice-bound roads.

Checks will be held today on cars' engines, and another test for a combination of speed and steadiness will be held tomorrow. The winners are expected to be announced on Saturday night.

Monte Carlo Rally 1950
Tommy Wise
(*Yorkshire Evening Post*, 23 January 1950)

The heading reads, 'Tommy Wise checks in near Doncaster', the photo shows Tommy checking in at Punch's Hotel Doncaster with Messrs Wilson and Noble. – NS

Snow, ice, fog and tortuous mountain roads are some of the hazards to be overcome by the Monte Carlo Rally drivers of the 278 cars which left six centres yesterday on the first stages of their 2,000-mile journey.

Hundreds of motoring fans greeted the cars just outside Doncaster, by 12.30 a.m. only Tommy Wise of Leeds had failed to clock in. He later arrived, 'Just popped in at home for a meal,' he explained.

Soon after 1 a.m. the last rear light vanished south into the night bound for Folkestone.

People who knew Tommy would tell you he was a real Yorkshire character, and this was just the sort of thing you would have expected him to do! NB. The article also quoted numbers of starters from the six centres, I have omitted these to avoid confusion, as clearly they were wrong and did not add up by a considerable amount.

Monte Carlo Rally 1950 - 'They went off to Monte Carlo early this morning - with a pick and shovel'. Four men take part in 2,000-mile drive
(The Southend Pictorial, 21 January 1950)

Early on Tuesday morning four prominent Southenders, muffed-up in flying suits, fur-lined boots and gauntlets, set off in a Jowett Javelin on the first stage of a 2,000-mile journey to take part in the famous Monte Carlo Rally.

The crew of this car is Mr Arthur Porter, chief driver and owner, of Highlands Boulevard, Leigh; Mr Ralph Bernard, co-driver, of London Road, Westcliff, and Messrs David Clough of Hadleigh Road, Leigh, and R.C. Golding of Boston Avenue, Southend, who will be navigators for the whole journey.

This Southend crew will begin their arduous journey officially on Sunday, when they start from Glasgow, making for Folkestone, where the Channel crossing will be made.

Then follows a difficult route through Europe through France, Belgium, Luxemburg and Holland, reaching Monte Carlo after a night and day drive of 2,000 miles, checking in at control points set up approximately 250 miles apart.

The crew will snatch their sleep in the rear seat of the car. There will be precious little time for washing and shaving and probably as they are winding their way through the passes of the Alpes Maritimes southwards towards Monte Carlo, their best friends will be a pick and a shovel, the most necessary equipment on every car, to deal with the deep snow and ice on the roads ahead of them.

The route has to be completed at an average speed of 31.7mph, and special allowances have been made for the sea journey by British competitors.

The Southenders conceived the idea of this trip after a golfing weekend. The four wives were approached, and, after some hesitation, the necessary consent was given. Now the 'rally widows' sit back and await news of their husbands' progress.

The 1950 Monte Carlo Rally
R.P. Ellison
(The Blackpool Gazette & Herald, 21 January 1950)

Two Fylde men set off tomorrow for the Monte Carlo Rally, the premier sporting event of the motoring world.

They are Mr Walter Mason, a thirty-eight-year-old Blackpool solicitor, and former adjutant of the Blackpool Regiment, and the St Annes motor agent R.F. Ellison, who will be hoping to improve on his last year's performance when he was placed third in the class for cars up to 1½ litres.

Both will be travelling in Mr Ellison's Jowett Javelin, a 14hp saloon, which has to cover 1,990 miles at an average speed of 32mph, with no allowance given for meals or sleep.

The Fylde men are in a British contingent of sixty, the cream of over 300 applications, who will line up at Glasgow for a journey all hope will end in Monte Carlo.

Later, in The West Lancashire Evening Gazette, *25 January 1950:*

'Car wrecked – no injuries – further details later'

These were the words on telegrams received today at the homes of the two St Annes competitors in the Monte Carlo Rally.

They were sent from Painhermitage Drome, a hamlet between Paris and Lyons in the early hours of the morning by Mr R.F. Ellison, a motor agent and Mr Walter Mason, a Blackpool solicitor, who were driving Mr Ellison's 14hp saloon car in the rally.

This afternoon Mr Mason telephoned his wife from Painhermitage Drome to tell her that the car had run off the road and was wrecked. Neither he nor Mr Ellison had been injured but they were wondering how they were going to get home.

Last night telegrams told their families that they had arrived at Rheims after a good run and were continuing to Lyons. It was reported today that competitors met with thick snow during the night on the last 500 miles of their 2,000-mile trip.

Up to that time the six contingents from Glasgow, Lisbon, Monte Carlo, Florence, Oslo and Stockholm had reached Paris. Yesterday they had been driving in weather, which was in general comparatively mild. After leaving Paris for Nevers and Lyons the drivers ran into blinding snowstorms, which severely tested their powers.

A later Reuter message from Paris says that, driving through a blinding snowstorm from Paris to Lyons, only six starters from Glasgow arrived without penalty marks.

The comparatively good weather of the rally's opening days gave way yesterday to snow, and many competitors who had said at Paris that the rally was a 'joyride' arrived in Lyons today more than an hour late, with completely different opinions. After Lyons the drivers had another 300 miles to cover on the last stages of their 2,000-mile trip.

1950 Le Mans – Javelin Jupiter on its way to make debut in 24-hour road race
(*The Telegraph & Argus*, Friday 16 June 1950)

With a team of six, the Javelin Jupiter, made by Jowett Cars Ltd, Idle, entered the 24-hour Le Mans road race on 24-25 June. They left Bradford today on the first stage of their journey to France.

After an overnight stay in Folkestone, the Jowett party will sail from Dover tomorrow for the Continent, where practice will start almost immediately. The Jupiter, a stripped-down version of the two-seater luxury sports car which made a sensational debut at the Society of Motor Manufacturers and Traders show in New York, has been entered in the race to test it under arduous conditions.

There will be tough opposition from America, Argentina, Belgium, Great Britain, France, Italy and Czecho-Slovakia in one of the premier sporting motoring events in Europe. Painted in English Racing Green, the Jupiter will be driven by T.H. Wisdom and T.C. Wise, who is well known in the north as a trials competition driver. The rest of the team is made up of two mechanics, timekeeper and a team manager, Mr C.B. Grandfield, who is engineering manager at Jowett's. Mr Grandfield told *The Telegraph & Argus,* 'We think we have a very good chance in the 1½-litre category.'

A descendent of the famous Javelin, the Jupiter has a modified version of the Javelin 'flat-four' engine, with 1½-litre capacity and overhead valves. Petrol consumption is from 28 to 30 miles per gallon. The car is constructed on a tubular alloy steel chassis for strength and lightness. The standard version can reach 90mph, while the racing version can reach 98mph.

1950 Le Mans – Jupiter made a record in Le Mans race, but Bradford car 16th
(Unknown newspaper clipping dated 26 June 1950)

Although Louis Rosier of France, with his son Claude as co-driver, won the fastest ever 24-hour Le Mans road race yesterday in a 4½-litre Talbot, a Jowett Jupiter, made by a Bradford firm, is believed to have set up a new lap record.

The Jupiter driven by Tommy Wisdom and Tommy Wise was placed sixteenth, and the record was broken in its category – 1500cc. The former record was set up in 1935 by an Austin at 75.5mph. The Javelin Jupiter team manager, Mr C.B. Grandfield, said that he believed they had put the record up to 75.6mph.

In the index of performance, won by an Aston Martin, the Jupiter was classified eleventh. It went the whole twenty-four hours without a change of tyres. The Jowett team plan to motor back to Britain today via Boulogne.

Pierre Meyrat and his co-driver, G Mairesse, also driving a Talbot were second, third was a British Allard driven by Tom Cole and Sydney Allard. Louis and Claude Rosier covered a record 256 laps in 23 hours 54 minutes 2.2 seconds. Meyrat and Mairesse completed 255 laps in 23 hours 55 minutes and 4.7 seconds. The British Allard covered 251 laps. British cars took six out of the ten top places, only two of the sixteen British entries failing to finish.

Rosier broke the lap record at 103.8mph; he also set a new Le Mans record by covering 3,464.85km (2,152.94 miles) in twenty-four hours and by driving twenty-three hours and fifty minutes non-stop himself, his son drove only ten minutes. Lord Selsdon's Ferrari, driven by the one-armed French driver, Jean Lucas, overturned at the wicked Terte Rouge bend and fell into a ditch, Lucas is in hospital. Mme. Germaine Rouault's French Simca also overturned after completing 142 laps. Regine Gordine, who was driving, was unhurt, but the car was badly damaged.

1950 *Daily Express* MCC Thousand-Mile Rally
John Batten
(*Eastbourne Gazette*, 15 November 1950)

Forced to retire from Motor Rally ... bad luck for local team

The only local competitor in last week's national motor rally to Torquay, organised by the Motor Cycling Club, was forced to retire owing to ignition trouble, after covering almost 1,000 of the 1,200-mile course. The car was a Jowett Javelin saloon entered by Mr John Batten, Eastbourne's former Director of Publicity, with his brother-in-law, Mr Stewart Bendall, as co-driver, and Mr R. Ticehurst, the Mayor's secretary, as navigator.

Mr Batten told the *Gazette* reporter that he and his crew, though naturally tired after some thirty-two hours' continuous motoring, thoroughly enjoyed their first experience of a motor rally. It was a great disappointment to them to have to give up after running so well to time at most of the controls, and they hope to enjoy better luck on the next occasion.

The Jowett Javelin saloon was started from Leamington Spa on Wednesday afternoon and its course to Torquay was via control points at Weymouth, Folkestone, Worcester, Doncaster,

Southport and Chester. The route from Chester, which all competitors had to follow, was not made known to them until the start and was via Brighton, Ross-on-Wye and Lynton. It included the well-known Welsh peak, Bwlych-y-Groes, and took competitors over a roundabout route though narrow lanes in Wales.

The rally was promoted by the *Daily Express*.

Daily Express Rally 1950
Douglas West
(*The Whitstable Times*, 1997)

The popular classic Jowett Javelin was a favourite of one of Whitstable's best-known doctors – Dr T. Callender.

Back in the 1950s the staff at the George Fitt Motor Company (The Jowett agent's for Whitstable) entered a number of rallies in their own Jowett Javelin saloon.

The Jowett Javelin in the Douglas West photograph was entry number 337 in the *Daily Express* Motor Rally held between 7-10 November 1950.

The people in the photograph, left to right are: Phil Barber, Joe Turner, Harold panther, Mrs H. Callender, Cyril Jackson and Dr T. Callender.

Douglas West described the event for *The Times*; the route for the rally was from London to Penrith in Cumberland and back to Hastings. The rally ended with five tests for acceleration, braking and reversing. The total distance was 1,000 miles; it was enjoyable, but nonetheless very hard work. I cannot remember the results but it did show commendable pluck and skill.'

Monte Carlo Rally 1951
R. Nelson-Harris
(*The Bulletin & Sports Pictorial*, 24 January 1951)

The Monte Carlo rallyists set off yesterday with a 2,000-mile trip ahead of them. There were sixty-six official entrants who left Glasgow, six of them were Scots. Mr R. Nelson-Harris was one of the starters seen yesterday loading his car for the trip ahead. *The picture shows Mr Nelson-Harris loading his open Javelin boot with bags, ropes and shovels etc. – NS*

Monte Carlo Rally 1951
T. Wise & H. Grimley
(*Yorkshire Post*, 27 January 1951)

Target – Monte Carlo. Ready for the off for Glasgow, their starting point in the Monte Carlo Rally, after last-minute tests on Harrogate roads on Sunday, are well-known competition motorists, Mr 'Tommy' Wise and his co-driver Mr A.H. Grimley. Mr Wise lives at Scotton, Knaresborough, and his car is a Jowett Jupiter. *The picture shows Tommy stood by the driver's door and Horace at the passenger side. The Jupiter, registered GKY106, was one of a works team of three. – NS*

Monte Carlo Rally 1951
R.P. Ellison & R. Robinson
(*Lytham & St Annes Express*, 3 February 1951)

Local garage proprietor, Robert F. Ellison, aged forty-five, who with co-driver Bill Robinson of Dalton-in-Furness, won four cups in the Monte Carlo Rally, was given a civic welcome on reaching Lytham St Annes, his home town, yesterday.

Driving from London, Mr Ellison's car – not the prize-winning Jowett Jupiter – broke down 2 miles from Lytham. He finished the journey in a borrowed car, and was met at the town's boundary by the mayor and was escorted to the Town Hall by thirty cars whose owners are members of the Lytham St Annes Motor Club.

He said that French competitors were astonished by the performance of their Jowett, which came in first in the 1½ litre class.

'In the elimination tests at Monte Carlo the best French car lapped the course in 2 minutes 36 seconds. Their team were amazed when our time was five seconds better on a course unfamiliar to us.' He added, 'They thought our Jupiter was fitted with a racing engine and requested that our car needed careful checking. The referee spent a day and a half stripping our engine before being satisfied that it was a standard production one. Ours was the only British car to be vetted so thoroughly.'

1951 Sestriere Rally ... 'They finished 22nd in Sestriere Car Rally'
(The *Derby Evening Telegraph*, 5 March 1951)

Three young Derbyshire motorists returned to Derby last night, after finishing twenty-second in the arduous Sestriere motor car rally. More than 350 teams were entered in the rally, but fewer than 100 finished the course.

The Derbyshire competitors, all officials of the Derbyshire County Car Club, and all driving in their first Continental Rally were, James Walker (twenty-seven) the club chairman, of Old Hall Littleover, Alan Bemrose (twenty-one), trials secretary, of Hazelbrow, Hazelwood Road, Duffield and John Dalton (twenty), of Windmill Lane, Belper, the club secretary.

Driving their Jowett Javelin in turn, they travelled from London, through Dunkirk, Rheims, Lyons, Marseilles and Turin to Sestriere. They left Derby market-place on Thursday 22 February and arrived at Sestriere, after a 1,300-mile journey on the Saturday afternoon.

Mrs M. Bemrose, Alan's mother, told the *Telegraph* reporter that telegrams from the Derbyshire team reported that they were leading at every check point until slowed up by snow after leaving Monte Carlo.

Apart from some difficulties in the mountains, they had a comparatively smooth journey. They returned through Turin, Milan, Como, Lucerne and Paris, arriving in London on Saturday evening after travelling over 2,500 miles.

They brought back with them a Sestriere Rally plaque, awarded to all competitors who finished the course.

1951 International Tulip Rally
Syd & Eric Abrams
(*Salford Evening News*, 21 April 1951)

Raisins Will Be Three-Day Race Diet

Manchester garage owner Mr Syd Abrams, and his son Eric of Waterloo Street, Cheetham Hill, travel to Harrogate tomorrow for the start of the 2,000-mile Tulip Car Rally.

They make their bid for a Tulip Trophy in a 1949 second-hand Jowett Javelin, in which they will eat and sleep for the next three days and nights to complete the course.

'Fruit and raisins give plenty of energy, they are the food we will carry,' says Mr Abrams.

As the car crosses the Dutch border, officials will put a garland of tulips on it.

1951 Sheffield Ace Club's Midnight Trial
Mrs J. Wood
(*Sheffield Star*, 27 July 1951 … Car Trial a Family Triumph)

With her two small daughters – Anne, aged four, and Stephanie, aged six – on the rear seat, and husband Jack as navigator, Mrs J. Wood, of the Sheffield and Hallamshire Motor Club, driving a Jowett Javelin, beat over sixty other competitors to win the chief trophy in the Sheffield Ace Club's Midnight Trial.

In addition she earned the cup for the best performance by a Sheffield and Hallamshire Motor Club member, and free servicing of the car for the next twelve months.

Her success is the more meritorious because she had been busy selling programmes at the Gamston race meeting, before dashing back to Sheffield for the start of the trial, and driving throughout the night.

Anne and Stephanie are quite experienced 'rallyists', having frequently accompanied their parents, or grand parents, Mr and Mrs John Wood, on treasure hunts etc.

1951 Ulster Tourist Trophy Race, Dundrod
W.J. (Billy) Skelly

13 September 1951 … Ulster Drivers Face Their 'Medical', and Cars Undergo Scrutineering

While Royal Automobile Club Officials probed under the bonnets of forty of the world's fastest sports cars in a Belfast garage today, the drivers were undergoing a strict medical test to ensure they are fit to take part in Saturday's Ulster Tourist Trophy race.

Ulster is one of the few places in the world where such an examination [is still held] and yesterday some anxiety had been felt that some of the driver's would fail to pass. But all those examined this morning by Dr W.N. Jones, of Ballymena, met the required standard.

It was a busy scene in the Adelaide Street garage of Harry Ferguson Ltd, as the business of Scrutineering went on. As soon as each car drove into line, officials got busy checking engine and chassis to make sure that it was a completely standard production model.

The first hitch to occur concerned the youngest driver in the race, nineteen-year-old Billy Skelly from Scotland, who was competing in his first TT. There was nothing wrong with Billy's sleek Jowett Jupiter, however, except its colour – a bright red.

And when it had been examined the officials told him – 'You must have that painted green before this evening's practice.' The reason is that the International race green is the colour for British entries, Italian cars are red and French are blue.

Said Billy, whose father owns a garage in Motherwell: 'that's easy, I have some green paint here.' Then he and his mechanic got to work on the car.

Daily Graphic, 14 September 1951

Forty TT Men Pass the Test

Forty men, who will drive some of the world's fastest sports cars in the Ulster TT race on Saturday successfully, passed the compulsory medical fitness test in Belfast yesterday.

All the cars passed the scrutiny of the RAC officials except that of one competitor, who had to do a last-minute job with a paint brush to get the car through.

He was nineteen-year-old Billy Skelly (Scotland), competing in his first TT in a Jowett Jupiter, who was told his bright red car would have to be green, as under International rules, only Italian cars may be red.

1952 Monte Carlo Rally
RV (Robbie) Russell
(*Middlesbrough Evening Gazette*, January 1952)

'Civic send-off to Monte Carlo'

Three Tees-side motorists, entered for the Monte Carlo Rally for the first time, have almost completed their preparations for the start at Glasgow on Tuesday.

Heading the team will be Robert Russell, co-partnered by Mr Stan Eddy and Mr Bob Waller. All are members of Stockton and Middlesbrough motor clubs. They will be driving a Jowett Javelin.

Special preparations to the car include a new type pencil beam spotlight – hitherto only available for export – hand searchlight for reading signposts, roof rack for carrying spare wheels, interior rack for holding thermos flasks and sandwich tins, and even a plug for operating an electric razor. Special supplies of petrol have been laid on along the route.

The three men aim to have three hours' driving, three hours navigating and three hours rest throughout the three days and nights of travelling. They are due at Monte Carlo 3.30 p.m. on Friday after covering 2,100 miles at a minimum average speed of 32mph.

Weather reports at the moment are not promising; the road over the Alps has already been blocked this week.

There were over 140 English entries, seventy were accepted as having taken part last year and another twenty-two entrants were allowed, Mr Russell's entry was one of them.

The car is a private entry but will be one of a team of three Javelins; the others have been entered by Major P.K. Braid of London and Mr Nelson-Harris of Surbiton, Surrey.

NB. Robbie Russell owned Harewood Garage in Thornaby, which was the Jowett agency for the town. He took part in the Monte Carlo Rally and also the Tulip Rally in 1952. When the team set off for Glasgow on the Monte, they were flagged away by the Mayor of Thornaby, Councillor H. Drinkel, from outside Harewood Garage. The car was registered GPY373 and carried an entry plate numbered 129.

Robbie was a prominent man in the town and was a founder committee member of the Teesside & District Union of Golf Clubs in 1956. He became captain of the club in 1957 and its president from 1959–91. – NS

1952 Monte Carlo Rally
David Jones
(*Sevenoaks News*, 7 February 1952. Reached Monte Carlo without time limit)

A man doing half a dozen jobs more or less simultaneously on Friday afternoon was Mr David Jones, director at Sevenoaks Brickworks. Reason was that he had just got home after motoring about 3,000 miles as a Monte Carlo Rally competitor, and was busy catching up with business matters.

It was the first time that he had entered a motoring event of this sort, and while discussing business with his father and secretary, having a telephone conversation and passing the time of day through the window with an employee, he found the time to tell the *Sevenoaks News* that he had enjoyed the run and would like to go again next year if he could manage it.

Tommy Wise and Horace Grimley pose to have their picture taken with their works Jupiter prior to leaving Harrogate to travel to Glasgow for the start of the 1951 Monte Carlo Rally. (JCC)

R. Nelson-Harris loading his Javelin with ropes and other essentials at the Glasgow start of the 1951 Monte Carlo Rally. (*The Bulletin & Sports Pictorial*/JCC)

Mr Jones, who lives at Redbank, 22 The Drive, Sevenoaks, was the third driver in a private team led by Major P.K. Braid of Surrey. The other member of the team was an old friend of Mr Jones, Major Gordon Eastwick-Field of Bournemouth, and their car was a Jowett Javelin.

Starting from Glasgow, the journey had to be made at an average speed of between 31mph and 41mph. On the way to Folkestone, Mr Jones had time to chat to his wife on the Maidstone by-pass. At Folkestone the team managed to talk themselves in to the stewards' quarters of the SS *Dinard* and had a good sleep as they were taken across to Boulogne.

The team were doing well until near Le Hague, where their car blew a cylinder head gasket. They had a spare, but this job on a Javelin is a tricky one, and took them one and a half hours. Despite covering the distance to Brussels, 'quicker then ever before!' they were just over half an hour late.

The police – 'at enormous speed, despite considerable traffic' – escorted them out of Paris! Although there was bad weather, including a blizzard, they managed to reach Monte Carlo within their two-hour time limit, which qualified them for a place and a 'gong'. It was then Friday afternoon and they went to bed until the following morning. The rally might be over, but their troubles were not! When they went out to see the first fifty competitors go through the Coldbraus test, they blew another gasket!

After this they motored 25 miles downhill without using any petrol. 'It was some of the best cornering I have done in my life,' commented Mr Jones with a smile.

At Monte Carlo they 'fed will, lived well, and slept little'. Mr Jones travelled back with another driver and had a 'good look' at the Alps on the way. During the journey they encountered another blizzard – 'and had a private rally of our own!'

Mr Jones had enjoyed the journey very much, but next year's rally seemed a long way off on Friday afternoon, and the *Sevenoaks News* left him to more immediate Brick Works matters.

RAC International Rally of Great Britain
L.C. Procter
(*The Evening Sentinel*, 28 March 1952)

Two members of the North Staffordshire Motor Club, Mr Cecil Heath in his Jaguar and Mr L.C. Procter in his Jupiter *(NB. the text said Javelin, but it was wrong – NS)*, are taking part in next week's five-day International Rally of Great Britain, in which 250 cars will compete in an arduous 2,000-mile trial from Scarborough to Silverstone (where ten laps are covered round the famous circuit) and on to the south coast, up through Wales and on to Blackpool and Edinburgh, where the appropriately named hill 'Rest and be Thankful' will be negotiated. They then travel back through Carlisle to Scarborough, again with tests en route in the Lake District. Their co-drivers are Mr B.J. Brittle and Mr J. Randles, all of whom feature in the photograph.

The Jaguar XK120 carried the rally plate number 148 and was registered OVT700, the Jupiter carried the rally plate number 174, but its registration number is only partially visible PE****. – NS

1952 RAC International Rally
D.C. Hodgson
(*The Evening Argus*, 8 April 1952)

3 Back from Tough Rally

Three East Sussex men, who competed in last week's RAC International Rally of Great Britain, successfully finished the gruelling 1,800-mile course. They returned home after running up a normal motorist's mileage for two months in only five days.

R.V. Russell, the proprietor of the Jowett agents Harewood Garage of Thornaby-on-Tees, together with his co-driver, Mr S. Eddy, at the Glasgow start of the 1952 Monte Carlo Rally. (JCC)

From left to right: R.D. Barrack of Aberdeen, J.B. Campbell of Aberdeen and John Lawrence of Cullen are seen adjusting the rally plate prior to the start of the 1952 International Tulip Rally. (*Evening Express*/JCC)

Prior to the start of the 1952 Tulip Rally, a Scottish team comprising of (from left to right) John B. Campbell, John Lawrence Cullen and R.D. Barrack. (*The Press & Journal*/JCC)

They were Mr D.C. Hodgson of Aster Cottage, Water Mill Lane, Bexhill, Mr John Batten of Grange Road, Eastbourne and Mr R. Mackenzie Low of Dorset House, Hastings Road, Bexhill.

Neither Mr Hodgson, owner of the 1950 Jowett Javelin saloon, nor Mr Low had taken part in a rally before. Although they were not in the prize list, the crew managed to get through the road section without losing marks, and Mr Hodgson will receive a finisher's plaque from the RAC.

The rally ranks with the Monte Carlo and Alpine Rallies as one of the toughest motoring events in the world, and attracted some famous continental drivers as well as many well-known British competitors.

1952 RAC International Rally
Marcel Becquart & Roy Lunn
(By John Bullock, motoring correspondent for the *Yorkshire Observer*, 7 April 1952)

Frenchman's Rally Win in a Borrowed Bradford Car

Driving a Bradford-built Jowett Javelin, which he borrowed at short notice, French 'ace' Marcel Becquart, at Scarborough on Saturday, won the closed car class in the second International Rally of Great Britain.

Becquart's own Italian-bodied Jowett Jupiter which he brought over from France was banned by the rally officials because it was not fitted with a standard body.

Roy Lunn, chief designer of the Jowett Company, heard of Becquart's difficulty and offered to lend him his own production model, and accompany him as co-driver on the 1,800-mile rally.

Becquart's superb handling in the final reliability speed test at Oliver's Mount, Scarborough's road-racing circuit, won him the award.

Handled Easily

'I did not have the opportunity to practice any of the tests, but the Javelin handled very easily, and we had a very pleasant trip,' he said. Much of the credit must go to Mr Lunn, who not only helped design the car, but also shared the wheel over much of the toughest road sections of the rally.

Mr and Mrs R.H. Wilkins pictured prior to the start of the 1952 6th International Eviant-Mont Blanc-Megeve Rally. The rally was over a 940-mile course over roads mainly in Switzerland. They started the rally by flying to France with the car. (*Sidcup Times*/JCC)

L.C. Proctor in his Jowett Jupiter with his friend Cecil Heath in his Jaguar XK120 prior to the start of the 1952 RAC International Rally. These two gentlemen were both members of the North Staffordshire Motor Club. (*The Evening Sentinel*/ JCC)

Results
Open cars: 1 A.G. Imhof (Allard) 183.8 marks, 2 J.C. Broadhead (Jaguar) 185.0 marks, 3 E.I. Appleyard (Jaguar) 186.6 marks.
Closed car class, up to 2500cc 1 M. Becquart (Jowett) 222.6 marks, 2 R.P. Lane (Riley) 227.0 marks, and 3 A.P. Warren (Riley) 230.4 marks.
Closed car class over 2500cc 1 P.W.S. White (Ford) 240.4 marks, 2 J. Greenock (Allard) 243.0 marks, 3 J.C. Smith (Jaguar) 243.6 marks.

1952 RAC International Rally
Marcel Becquart
(From an unidentified clipping by Thomas H. Wisdom)

The second RAC International Rally, which ended in Scarborough on Saturday, was one of the sternest tests of a car ever held in this country. While it is impossible to stage in Great Britain a test as severe as the Monte Carlo Rally or the Alpine Trial, the event this year, aided by the bad weather and some extremely well-designed tests, combined to make it a fine event.

Of the 251 entrants, nine of whom did not start, there were 199 finishers, and because of the tests everyone had been penalised. The best performance in the event and winner of the open car class was Geoff Imhof with his big 5¼-litre Cadillac-engined Allard, second was the Jaguar XK120 of J.G. Broadhead, followed by the well-known competition car of the same make driven by Ian Appleyard.

Marcel Becquart, with a Jowett Javelin, took the honours in the small closed car class and a Ford Pilot in the unlimited car class.

The fact that so many different makes appeared on the leader board suggests that this was a really fair test. No fewer than 1,400 officials were engaged in running the event, and although a large number of protests were lodged, few were allowed by the stewards.

1952 Tulip Rally
Robert (Bob) D. Barrack
(*Bon-Accord*, 17 April 1952)

On Sunday morning a sleek, stylish Jowett Javelin car, with a bright red and yellow plate on the front and rear bumpers, will burble its way smoothly out of Aberdeen on the main road south – bound for London and the starting point of thirty-eight British cars competing in the famous Tulpen Rallye of Holland.

At the wheel will be R.D. Barrack, the well-known Aberdeen garage proprietor. Acting as co-drivers and navigators will be Mr J.B.G. Campbell, Aberdeen, and Mr J.N. Lawrence, Cullen. These three motor sport enthusiasts will represent the Aberdeen and District Motor Club in the rally.

For Messrs Barrack and Lawrence it will be their first 'Tulpen', and there is little doubt that they will be depending on the experience of Mr Campbell, who will be making his third rally visit to the land of the tulips. In 1949 he was placed eighteenth and in 1950 he was second in the elimination test.

'No, I have never driven on the wrong side of the road before,' driver entrant 'Bob' Barrack told your 'Personal and Otherwise' reporter. Mr Campbell, who is managing director of Messrs P.N. Shinnie Ltd, remarked: 'We will be taking part as a team in the rally but when we return we will be competing against each other on Crimond Aerodrome Race Circuit on 24 May.

As for the car it is a standard 1951 model and, apart from super tuning the engine, she will be as she left the factory. Mr Barrack has fitted a special map-reading shelf on the back of the rear seat so that the navigator of the day will have the least possible trouble in the maximum of comfort.

The car has to be in London on Sunday for scrutineering and 'sealing' ready for the Monday morning start at 4.18 a.m. In all there will be 300 cars in the rally from all over the Continent.

The only other known Scottish entrant is Gordon McKerracher of Glasgow who will be driving his XK120 Jaguar.

1952 International Tulip Rally
John B.G. Campbell
(*The Press & Journal*, 21 April 1952 … North-East Trio set off on Tulip Rally)

Three determined Scotsmen worked late in London tuning up the car in which they set off at 4 a.m. today on the first stage of the 1,700-mile International Tulip Rally.

Mr John B.G. Campbell, forty-three-year-old 'veteran' of the team, who lives in College Street, Aberdeen, declared; 'We won't win, but it will be a good man that beats us!'

And his two co-drivers, forty-two-year-old Mr Robert Davidson Barrack, of Richmondhill Road, Aberdeen and Mr John Lawrence, the thirty-year-old 'baby' of the team, from The Wakes, Cullen, agreed.

Their work completed, they turned in for the last night they will spend in bed until Thursday. Driving in turn, for stretches of about 200 miles each, they will spend every hour of the next three days and nights in their Jowett Javelin, super-tuned saloon, with the lion flag of Scotland proudly streaming in the wind from the off-side front wing.

The rally route will take the trio over the toughest country in France, Belgium and Holland until they reach journey's end at Noorwick-an-Zee (near The Hague) on Thursday. None of them speaks any language but good Scots – but they are not worrying. The two younger men have complete confidence in Mr Campbell's navigating – and he has ample confidence in himself!

On the journey down to London from Aberdeen, the car 'went like a bomb', in Mr Lawrence's words. They are quite certain that they will put up a creditable performance against the 300 other competitors.

When they get back to Scotland they will meet up again in four weeks time at Crimond – in a race against one another, as they have so often done before.

1952 Le Mans
Tommy Wise
(*Telegraph & Argus*, 12 June 1952 … 'Hat-trick Bid')

Three Jowett Jupiters are now in France, ready to take part in the 24-hour race at Le Mans on Saturday, and with them have gone strong hopes of winning in the 1½ litre class for the Bradford firm for the third year in succession.

If they do succeed in doing this – and the cars are some of the fastest in their class anywhere in the world – the Jowett Company will be the only firm to register three wins in three attempts.

The cars, which are capable of between 115 and 120mph, are the latest R1 version of the Jupiter, and have been specially built for the race in France. In many respects these models (all works entries) are similar to the successful Jupiter touring car which won the 1½ litre class at Le Mans in 1950 and 1951. They are, however, lighter and there are a number of new features.

Two of the crews have already been named, Tommy Wise, of Harrogate, who was successful in 1950 will again drive with Midlander H.L. Hadley as his co-driver; the second will be driven by Marcel Becquart, the famous French rally driver, and Gordon Wilkins of Cheltenham (who won the 1½ litre class last year). At the wheel of the third Jupiter is M. Gatsonides, the Continental racing driver; he will travel with a Dutch driver, who as yet has not been named.

Excellent driving, excellent cars – a combination which should ensure that the Bradford firm of car makers, which has taken part in competitive events only since the war, should add to its laurels on Saturday.

Northern Echo, 12 June 1952 – Bid for Le Mans hat-trick, Harrogate driver in British team

A team of three Jowett cars, capable of 120mph, has been flown to France in an attempt to win the 1½ litre class in the 24-hour race at Le Mans on Saturday for the third consecutive year. The cars, the latest R1 versions of the Jupiter, have been specially built for the race. A prototype model raced last year, but retired with cylinder head trouble.

The new car is lighter and has a high compression engine with exposed cylinder heads, and a forward curving exhaust pipe. The headlamps have been built into the wings and the car has been fitted with quick-action fuel and water filler caps.

Tommy Wise of Harrogate, who was successful in 1950 will again be at the wheel of one of the cars. The main opposition is expected to come from the new German Porsche, which has been redesigned.

1952 Le Mans – Jupiter wins class award at Le Mans for the third time
(Unknown newspaper clipping)

A Bradford-built Jowett Jupiter, driven by Marcel Becquart and Gordon Wilkins won the 1½ litre class in the gruelling race at Le Mans yesterday.

As with last year, the Jupiter was the only 1½ litre entry to finish, and was the third Le Mans success for the Jowett Company in their first three attempts – a world record for any one firm.

The Jupiter's victory was all the more credible because the Jowett team were dogged by extreme bad luck from the start.

The reserve car driven by Maurice Gatsonides ran into trouble earlier in the race and was forced to retire. Then the leading Jupiter driven by Bert Hadley hit a sandbank in the early hours of yesterday morning and was too badly damaged to continue in the race.

Meanwhile Marcel Becquart, the French rally driver, who was sharing the wheel of the remaining Jupiter with Gordon Wilkins – the last year's winning team – was far from happy at the way their car was performing.

When Becquart brought the car into the pits it was found that the official petrol issued to the Jowett team had a considerable amount of water in it. All the petrol for the race was supplied by the Le Mans officials to ensure that all the cars ran on the same quality of octane.

After a pit stop of one hour and twenty minutes for additional petrol to be obtained and the tanks to be drained and replenished, the Jupiter was back in the race but many laps behind. Leading the class was a very fast Italian Osca and a German 1½-litre Porsche. The Osca suddenly developed mechanical trouble and had to be pushed more than 2 miles to the pits. After working feverishly the mechanics managed to get the car going again, but a lap later it was forced to retire.

Soon after the officials flagged off the remaining Porsche and the French drivers, Martin and Picard were disqualified for failing to stop the engine of the Porsche when refuelling at the pits.

With all opposition out of the race Becquart and Wilkins drove steadily throughout the remainder of the twenty-four hours.

The Jupiter they were drove was the latest R1 version capable of 120mph and with a lighter redesigned two-seater body.

1952 Le Mans
Marcel Becquart & Gordon Wilkins
(*Southern Daily Echo*, 17 June 1952)

'Le Mans Racers Home'

Marcel Becquart and Gordon Wilkins, winners of the 1½ litre class in the 24-hour Le Mans race, landed at Southampton Airport today with the winning Jowett Jupiter aboard a Silver City freighter aircraft from Cherbourg.

They won the race for the second year and brought off a 'hat-trick' for Jowett's in the class.

1952: The 6th International Eviant-Mont Blanc-Megeve Rally
R.H. Wilkins
(*Sidcup Times*, 19 July 1952)

'They fly to car rally'

Flying to France on Sunday to take part in the sixth International Eviant-Mont Blanc-Megeve Rally is Mr R.H. Wilkins of 1 Valley Road, St Paul's Gray, who is the proprietor of hairdressing saloons in Sidcup and Petts Wood. He will be accompanied by his wife Mrs J Wilkins, and their friend, Mr W. Edwards, who will act as navigator.

The rally, which will take place on 24, 25, 26 and 27 July, is a course about 940 miles, over roads in Savoy, the Jura, and the Ain to Vercors, Dauphine and Volals, in Switzerland.

The rally is mainly a test of road reliability; there are twenty-five time controls for the whole course, which includes thirty mountain passes. Those, which are likely to prove most difficult, are the Val D' Ieere, the Col du Golver and the Col du Lauteret in France, and the Col de la Forcolz in Switzerland. There are also two hill tests of different aspects, and the average speed for the whole of the rally is 32mph.

Principle prizes are 400,000 francs and 150,000 francs for the first and second in the general classification and 100,000 francs for the ladies cup winner.

There are eleven British entries this year and Mr Wilkins will be driving his Jowett Javelin, which he keeps especially for competition work. Features of the car include special competition headlamps, an extra petrol pump to stop vaporisation at altitudes and most of the controls have been duplicated in case of faults.

This is the first time that Mr Wilkins has taken part in an international rally, but he has recently won a first-class award in the British Automobile Racing Club's Eastbourne Rally, and the Sussex Cup in the Kinetic Border Deal Rally. He also gained a finishing award in the Arc's International Rally.

The Sidcup Times *later reported that Mr and Mrs Wilkins had to pull out of the rally on the second day with back axle trouble. It was said that at that point they had only lost ten minutes. They entered the race the following year in an XK120 Jaguar. The* Sidcup Times *carried the article about the 1953 rally which was published on 17 July 1953. – NS*

1952 Daily Express International Rally
Gerald Hoyle
(Southport Guardian, 15 November 1952)

Last 60 miles beat rally drivers

After two days and two nights of fault-free driving, Southport's entrants in the 1,250-mile National motor rally were defeated by engine trouble.

The MG sports model entered by Mr Ralph Darby of 14 Rookery Road, and co-driver Mr Frank Mawddsely of 30 Rawlinson Road, was only 60 miles from the Brighton finishing line, when a piston breakdown dashed their hopes.

The Javelin saloon driven by Mr Gerald Hoyle of 93 Preston New Road was halted 100 miles from Brighton when a throttle cable broke.

Up to then Mr Hoyle and his crew – Mr Don Wood of 4 Allerton Road, and Mr George Rushton of 25 Longford Road, reached every checkpoint on time. They were in the first six in the Lake District test. *(NB. the Javelin owned by Gerald Hoyle was registered NTF263 and carried the rally plate number 427. – NS)*

1953 Monte Carlo Rally
W.G. (Bill) Pitcher & Les Brooke
(Coventry Evening Telegraph, 16 January 1953 … Off to Monte Carlo)

During the Monte Carlo Rally, which starts on Tuesday, day-to-day reports on the progress of the competitors will be given in the *Coventry Evening Telegraph*.

Our motoring correspondent, accompanied by Mr David Francis, the Midland manager of Mintex Ltd, will be following the competitors through Holland, Belgium and France to Monte Carlo. The first report from Glasgow will appear on Tuesday.

The car which will take them on their 2,000-mile journey is the Sunbeam Talbot, registered LHP823, which Stirling Moss drove to second place in last year's Monte Carlo Rally.

The only privately entered Coventry competitors are Les Brooks and Bill Pitcher, who were wished bon voyage by Councillor Harry Weston before leaving for Glasgow. They are driving in their Jowett Javelin, which is registered LWD818.

1953 Monte Carlo Rally
F.M. Baker, Jack London & Jimmy Brown
(Sussex Daily News, 19 January 1953)

One each for the road – the road to Monte Carlo, Mr Jack London of Chichester Terrace, Brighton with Mr F.M. Baker of Ovingdean Grange, Brighton and Mr Jimmy Brown of Hove drink a glass of champagne as a toast prior to setting off to the Glasgow start of the Monte Carlo Rally. Rally fashion note, the woollen caps are in Coronation colours.

NB. The picture shows the three men standing round their Javelin-registered MCD124 toasting each other with a glass of champagne. They are all wearing woolly pom-pom hats, which must have been coloured red white and blue! – NS

THE only privately entered Coventry competitors, Les Brooks (right) and Bill Pitcher, are wished bon voyage by Councillor Harry Weston before leaving for the Glasgow starting point of the Monte Carlo Rally in their Jowett Javelin.

Syd Henson, of Coventry, who is a familiar figure at most rallies, will be at the wheel of this Ferodo-entered Sunbeam-Talbot (right). He will be accompanied by Alan Collinson, the competitions manager, and Bert Balkam, test house manager. The car, which Syd Henson took on the 1952 Alpine Rally, will be fitted with a special counter to record the number of brake applications during the 2,000-mile journey. Syd Henson is seen on the left of the picture.

Bill Pitcher and Les Brook prior to the start of the 1953 Monte Carlo Rally, being flagged away from their home town of Coventry by Councillor Harry Weston to start their long journey to the Glasgow start. (*Coventry Evening Telegraph*/JCC)

Jack London and his crew pose for their picture to be taken for their local paper prior to setting off on the long drive from Brighton to Glasgow ready for the start of the 1953 Monte Carlo Rally. (*Sussex Daily News*/JCC)

One each for the road—the road to Monte Carlo. Mr. Jack London (Chichester-terrace, Brighton), Mr. F. M. Baker (Ovingdean) and Mr. J. Brown (Hove) drink a champagne toast on Saturday before setting off to Glasgow, their starting point in the Monte Carlo motor rally. RALLY FASHION NOTE: The woollen caps are in Coronation colours.

TELEGRAPH & ARGUS. 31.12.52

Bradford F.A. Cup pairings

Bradford and District F.A. cup draws are as follows:

1953 Monte Carlo Rally
Marcel Becquart
(*Belfast Telegraph*, 28 January 1953)

French Car is 'first home' at Monte Carlo

A French nobleman, the Marquis Francois de Noailles, at the wheel of a Simca Aronde, had the distinction of being the first rally competitor to reach the finish line at Monte Carlo today.

Spectators saw the clean-shaven Frenchman, who had started at Lisbon, reach the end of his 2,000-mile run without losing a single point.

The second in was a Porsche manned by a Swiss team, and the third was a Jowett Jupiter driven by French drivers.

Officials said they thought an unprecedented number of competitors would get through this year, and that a special elimination test was almost a certainty.

The first all-British team to reach Monte Carlo was that of Tommy Wisdom and K. Simpson in a Ford Zephyr. They had driven from Lisbon.

Later the Glasgow starters – most of them British – began to arrive in a steady stream.

1953 Tulip Rally
W.G. (Bill) Pitcher and H.L. (Les) Brooke
(*Coventry Evening Telegraph*)

The only local competitors in this year's International Tulip Rally, which finished last week, Bill Pitcher of Rugby and Les Brooke of Coventry, arrived home slightly bruised, and with a battered Jowett Javelin.

Yet both were happy; they had finished sixth in their class and were grateful still to be alive.

The Tulip Rally differs from others in that it features special tests and special stages. In the former it is possible to gain bonus marks, while in the latter it is possible only to lose marks. And once marks are lost it is impossible to make them up in other sections.

While taking a long, shallow corner quickly during the first special stage in the Ardennes, a rear tyre burst, and in their own words, 'a tree came out of the hedge and hit them!'

The tree probably saved their lives as it prevented them from falling down a steep bank. After clambering out of the car in a slightly dazed condition, they were horrified to see one of the rear tyres was hanging over the edge of the bank.

Once the Jowett had got all four wheels back on to the road, and they had changed the burst tyre, it was found that the car would still go. The tree had hit a cross member which had prevented more serious damage.

Pitcher and Brooke arrived at the finish without loosing a mark, but as they had lost a great deal of speed they were unable to gain any bonus marks. Their record however was good sufficient to give them sixth place in their class.

When I spoke to Les Brooke about the rally generally, he told me that it had been scrupulously fair, and magnificently organised. The organisers had kept strictly to the rules and believed that no one who had lost marks or who had been disqualified had any justifiable complaint.

Many of the other Jowett Javelins in the race had been modified slightly, which at first seemed rather unfair to the local drivers. But they later learnt that certain modifications were allowed providing that the organisers were notified before the event.

Some people maintain that the most important part of a rally takes place before you get in to a motor car – in reading the regulations.

NB. this was a really good effort by Pitcher and Brooke, who still managed a very respectable forty-eighth in the general classification, despite the considerable damage to the car. – NS

1953 Tulip Rally
Count van Zuylen van Nijevelt
(From an undated clipping)

Never in the history of motor sport has there been such confusion in the official results as there was after the conclusion of the Fifth International Tulip Rally, which finished at the weekend at the Zandvoort racing circuit for speed tests, the reverse way of the track being used, so those with knowledge of it should not benefit.

Originally it was announced that J.W.B. Banks and M. Porter were the outright winners in their Bristol saloon, and they were duly acclaimed as such. Next in order in placings were L.G. Elliott (Sunbeam Talbot), M. Grosgoeat (Panhard) and Ian Appleyard (Jaguar). Then the protests rolled in. There were more than forty of them, and after deliberations lasting for more than twenty-four hours there were many alterations.

First Elliott was disqualified for an alleged non-standard engine modification. Next was Marcel Becquart, announced originally as winner of his class, was out, as it was alleged that his Jowett Javelin was fitted with a Jupiter engine. This had the effect of increasing the points of Count van Zuylen van Nijevelt, whose Jowett Javelin came up in Becquart's place as the class winner and ultimately, as the outright winner of the rally.

The unfortunate Banks, however, did not benefit from the disqualifications as he was in a different class, and his bonus marks remained the same.

Before all this confusion there was a mild sensation at the disqualification of the Ford Zephyr team; in this case the scrutineers preventing the cars taking place in the final tests as they alleged that the cars contravened the regulations by having external oil filters, a fitment incidentally, which did not result in any power gain.

Mrs Nancy Mitchell, also driving a Zephyr, went out on the same score when she looked an almost certain winner; thus letting in Mrs Greta Molander to win the ladies' prize in her Saab.

Other disqualifications of British drivers were those of Mr Jack Kemsley and P.C.E. Harper, whose Sunbeam-Talbot was alleged by the scrutineers to have non-standard brake drums. In each instance none of these competitors had incurred any penalties en route.

In the end the outright winner was Count van Zuylen van Nijevelt in his Javelin with the previous outright winners Banks & Porter were second with the Bristol saloon – a car in use every day and one that has covered a considerable mileage. Marcel Grosgoeat retained his third place in the Panhard, P.J. Jetten came into forth place with a Vauxhall Velox at the expense of Ian Appleyard in his Jaguar, who was now fifth in front of M. Damote in a Fiat.

To say the competitors – especially the British – were disgruntled, was to put it mildly. Many had vowed it was the last time they would compete in this event, as the same cars would have been ruled as complying with the regulations in similar events.

It appears that in certain circumstances, if the slightest of modifications had been mentioned on the entry forms, some of the disqualifications would not have taken place. Particularly this seems to be the case of the Ford Zephyrs. The reason it was not mentioned on the entry form was because it did not give any more additional engine power.

Another case in point was that of a Volkswagen driver who was disqualified for the sole reason that he had fitted a sports coil.

In the case of the Ford drivers it meant loosing any chance they may have had in the drivers' touring car championship, for it affected Gatsonides, British trials champion Cuth Harrison, and Jack Reece. To a lesser degree, although of great importance, was the downgrading of Ian

Appleyard to fifth place, for although not depriving him of the lead in the championship, it lost him valuable marks.

The framing of the regulations do, however, give the driver of a small-engined car an equal chance to the one handling the fastest car in the rally, on account of the awarding of bonus marks for performances set up in the five tests, the first four of which were assents of passes in the Ardennes, Vosges and Jura mountains.

There were also some errors in the time-keeping in the Zandvort test. For example, Elliot's time was found to be a minute in error, and on rectification this reduced him from second to fourth place. But at the last moment, his Sunbeam-Talbot – the same car which Stirling Moss drove in the Monte Carlo Rally – did not comply with the rigorous standard specification. As a result Jetten's Vauxhall Velox took fourth place, but not without surviving more than one protest.

The winning Javelin had several modifications, all of which had been listed by the entrant. The owner had lightened the car slightly by divesting it of comfort and even by the fitting of window straps in the place of the normal window winders.

The Dutch team of Jowett Javelin drivers also won the team prize, the other drivers being J. Scheffer and O.E. Homain.

Although a Dutch driver won the event for the first time since the rally was promoted five years ago it made the fifth consecutive win for a British car. Ken Wharton with a Ford won in 1949, 1950 and 1952 and Ian Appleyard in a Jaguar in 1951.

1953 North Wales Motor Rally
Councillor A. Hugh Rutt
(*Flint County Herald*, 1 May 1953)

Councillor A. Hugh Rutt of Greenfield, an enthusiastic motorist won a First Class award for closed cars up to 1500cc in the North Wales Motor Rally during the weekend.

Councillor Rutt, who was driving his Jowett Javelin car, is a member of the Rhyl and District Motor Club, the South Caernarvonshire Motor Club and the Denbigh Motor Club. His navigators in the rally were Mr Cedryn Jones of Rhyl and Mr Bob MacLellan of Denbigh.

There were fifty-seven competitors from North Wales, Cheshire, Lancashire and Staffordshire, with two groups starting simultaneously from Chester and Rhyl on Saturday night and finished at Rhyl on Sunday morning. The 309-mile course over the mountains took approximately eleven hours.

There was a test on the Horseshoe Pass and elimination tests were held at the Rhyl promenade car park.

Councillor Rutt was also a member of the Rhyl and District team, which won the team award. The other members of the team were G.S. Budge and Stan Kennedy.

Cllr H. Waterhouse referred to Cllr Rutt's success in the rally at Monday's meeting of the Urban Council, and members expressed congratulations to him.

1954 Monte Carlo Rally
Arthur Lewis & Dr Dick Osborn
(*Birmingham Mail*, 14 January 1954)

Doctor and Partner in Monte Carlo Bid
A Water Orton farmer and Stetchford doctor, who team up for next week's Monte Carlo Rally, take it in turn to provide a car for this classic test in motor sport.

Bill Pitcher and Les Brook pictured at the end of the 1953 Tulip Rally, the car was badly damaged after a tyre burst and they hit a tree. They managed to get the car home sixth in class, forty-eighth overall, which was a very brave effort. (*Coventry Evening Telegraph*/JCC)

Councillor Hugh Rutt (pictured in the car) with his navigator, Cedryn Jones, at the end of the 1953 North Wales Motor Club Rally, where they won a first class award for closed cars up to 1,500cc. (*Flint County Herald*/JCC)

Francis Dundas and his co-driver James Payne were two Dumfries entrants in the 1954 Monte Carlo Rally. The picture was taken while they were loading the car in Dumfries prior to setting off to Glasgow for the start. (JCC)

Arthur Lewis, a farmer from near Birmingham, pictured with his Javelin prior to the start of the 1954 Monte Carlo Rally. His co-driver was Dick Osborn, a local solicitor; they used the solicitor's Austin A70 to enter the previous year's rally. (*Birmingham Mail*/JCC)

This time, the farmer, Arthur Lewis, who runs the 160-acre Attleboro Farm, is providing the car – a Jowett Javelin – for Dr Dick Osborn, of 615, Church Road, Stetchford, and himself.

Last year they went together in an Austin A70 on the doctor's entry form, but near Valence the gearbox failed, leaving them to struggle with bottom and top gears and nothing between. They got to Monte Carlo, but too late to qualify for the final tests.

They have planned and schemed again to try and avoid all foreseeable trouble, and in optimistic mood they will leave Birmingham on Saturday for Glasgow, the starting point on Monday for the gruelling 2,000-mile drive to Monte Carlo.

Farmer Lewis, who is a member of seven Midland motor clubs, has taken a prominent part in car sport for several years. Last year he won a class award in *The Birmingham Post* rally with Ron Ayres of Whiteacre, Coleshill, who will be navigator to Mr Lewis and the doctor in the Monte Carlo.

Another Jowett entrant is J.M. Tew of Kelmscott Road, Harborne, with is co-driver E.C. Marsland.

1955 Monte Carlo Rally
Commander J.B. Laing
(Bath Chronicle & Herald, 15 January 1955)

'Bath man in Monte Carlo Rally'

Among the hundreds of starters for the 1955 Monte Carlo Rally, which starts on Monday, is a Bath man. He is Commander J.B. Laing, a bachelor of 4 Devonshire Buildings, Wellsway, Bath, who is with the Admiralty at Fox Hill.

Together with a London doctor, Dr L.R.S. Taylor, and a Surrey accountant, Mr Tony Hartnell, he will start for the south of France from Glasgow.

The three men will take it in turns to drive Dr Taylor's 1953 1500cc Jowett Javelin – one of two taking part in the rally. Dr Taylor, with other drivers, competed in the same car last year and completed the course.

Commander Laing, who has been in Bath since February last year, has held a driving licence since 1931, but he is quite a newcomer to the motor car rally world.

He was initiated when he took part with his brother and Dr Taylor in the London Motor Club rally last September, when he drove another Jowett Javelin and finished bogged down in a field.

The commander, who is a native of Limpsfield, Surry, is very modest about their prospects this year. He thinks they have no chance of winning. 'But we hope to enjoy ourselves, and I think we will be doing well to finish the course in the time allowed,' he said.

The car in which he will compete in is being driven to Scotland by Dr Taylor, and Commander Laing left Bath by train today.

The rally should prove to be an exciting adventure against some of the world's most skilled drivers.

Bath Chronicle & Herald, 21 January 1955 – It is believed that Commander J.B. Laing of 4 Devonshire Buildings, Bath, who is stationed at the Admiralty, Fox Hill, Bath, was disqualified from the Monte Carlo Rally near Paris on Wednesday. Commander Laing was one of a team driving a 1500cc Jowett Javelin.

1955 Monte Carlo Rally
Mrs Jo Ashfield
(*Wimbledon Borough News*, 21 January 1955)

Wimbledon woman does well in the Monte Carlo Rally

Competing in the Monte Carlo Rally for the fourth time is Mrs 'Jo' Ashfield of Wimbledon Park Road. Starting from Glasgow on Monday she was reported on Tuesday to have got down to Dover and crossed the Channel without losing any marks. She was expected in Monte Carlo yesterday (Thursday).

Her co-drivers of the Ford Zephyr are Mrs R. Wilton-Clarke and Mrs V. Farlow-Jones.

In other Monte Carlo Rallies and minor ones such as the Alpine Trial and Rally Gastronomique, Mrs Ashfield has driven Sunbeam Talbots and Jowett Javelins.

The last woman driver to win the Monte Carlo Rally was Mrs M. Vaughan, in 1935, with whom Mrs Ashfield has been associated.

Mrs Ashfield is married to a stockbroker, has two sons, fifteen-year-old Philip and sixteen-year-old Michael. But only Philip shares her unbounded enthusiasm for motor racing.

MCC National Motor Rally
Dowsett & MacDonnell
(*Hastings & St Leonard's Observer*, November 1956)

National Car Rally Finishes Here Today

The first competitor in the MCC National Motor Rally, which finishes at Hastings today, is expected to enter the borough at 10 a.m. for the final tests at Castle Hill, Robertson's Hill and on the sea front at Caroline-place. The Mayor (Alderman F.T. Hussey) will be there to greet him.

Messrs Dowsett and MacDonnell with their Jupiter before the start of the 1956 MCC National Motor Rally, they started the rally at the London start, and finished at their home town of Hastings.

Local entrants Mr. Dowsett and Mr. Macdonnell with their Jowett sports car.

About 150 cars set out from seven different rally starting points on Thursday morning and later that day converged on Harrogate. The night was spent motoring about the Yorkshire Moors on the first of the navigational exercises. At dawn the leading competitors arrived at Honister Pass for the first test.

Competitors then saw a good deal more of the Lake District and took another test at Hardknott Pass before moving south to Chester.

Last night they took the fourth test on Bwich-y-Gioes, a famous hill, and motored on through winding Welsh roads, this section comprising the second navigational exercise.

Daylight this morning found them on their way to Hastings, and by the time they arrive over 1,200 miles will have been covered in forty-eight hours of motoring.

The three local entries will be watched with interest – Mr W.G. Edgerston's Sunbeam numbered 104, the Milton brothers in their Austin numbered 78 and Mr Alan Dowsett in his Jowett Jupiter numbered 76. All three started from London.

This evening there will be a civic reception for competitors and officials at the White Rock Pavilion, and the prize-giving takes place at the Queen's Hotel, the rally headquarters, tomorrow morning.

Entrants include last year's winner, Mr S.P.A. Freeman, who is once again driving his 1938 MG TA sports car, and Miss Angela Palfrey, winner of the 1955 ladies award, driving a Morgan, also J.C. Wallwork, winner of the 1954 RAC Rally, is driving a Triumph TR2.

Members of the Hastings and East Sussex Car Club will be staffing the final control point at Beauport Park and assisting at the tests in the Borough.

NB. The Jupiter was registered MCD28 and carried rally plate number 76. – NS

The Ferranti Motor Club Rally
M.I. MacDonald
(*The Scotsman*, 10 October 1956)

The weekend rally of the Ferranti Motor Club, covering a 300-mile route from Kincardine to the Devil's Elbow to Tomitoul, attracted twenty-two entries. The winners were M.I. MacDonald with K.J. Lyon as navigator in a Jowett Javelin. Runners-up were J.D. Ross and R.R. Bryce in a Hillman. L.F. Benzies and J.S. Duncan in an Austin '8' took third place.

Bibliography

Books

Frank Gray, *My Two African Journeys* (Methuen & Co. Ltd, 1928)
T.C. Bridges & H. Hessell Tiltman, *The Romance of Motoring* (George G. Harrap & Co. Ltd, 1933)
Mike Couper, *Rallying to Monte Carlo* (Ian Allan Ltd, 1956)
William Boddy, *Brooklands: The Complete Motor Racing History* (1957 & 2001)
Dudley & Marianne Noble, *With Your Car in the South of France* (Frederick Muller Ltd, 1959)
Lord Montagu of Beaulieu, *Lost Causes of Motoring* (Cassell & Co. Ltd, 1960)
Tom Wisdom, *Touring Abroad* (Odhams Press Ltd, 1960)
William Boddy, *Montlhery, the Story of the Paris Autodrome 1924 – 1960* (Cassell & Co. Ltd, 1961; reprinted by Veloce Publishing, 2006)
Peter Harper, *Destination Monte* (Stanley Paul, 1964)
Tom Wisdom, *High Performance Driving for You* (Odhams Press Ltd, 1966)
Dudley Noble, *Milestones in a Motoring Life* (The Queen Anne Press Ltd, 1969)
T.R. Nicholson, *The Age of Motoring Adventure* (Cassell & Co. Ltd, 1972)
Stanley Sedgwick, *Motoring My Way* (B.T. Batsford Ltd, 1976)
The Hon. Mrs Victor Bruce, *Nine Lives Plus* (Pelham Books Ltd, 1977)
Rupert Prior, *Motoring – The Golden Years, A Pictorial Anthology* (HC Blossom Ltd, London, 1991)
Paul Clark & Ed Nankivell, *The Complete Jowett History* (Haynes, 1991)
Michael Allen, *Gatso – The Never Ending Race* (Gatsometer BV, 1993)
William Leonard, *Rallies and Races – Gatsonides' Adventures* (The Greyhound Press, 1995)
Gerald Palmer & Christopher Balfour, *Auto-Architect: the Autobiography of Gerald Palmer* (Magna Press, 1998)
John Bullock, *Fast Women* (Robson Books, 2002)
Geoff McAuley and Edmund Nankivell, *Jowett Javelin and Jupiter – The Complete Story* (The Crowood Press, 2003)
Raymond Baxter with Tony Dron, *Tales of My Time* (Grub Street, 2005)

Other Sources

The Autocar
The Motor
Motor Sport
Classic & Sportscar magazine
Classic Car Weekly
The Times
The Independent
The Sun
The Investors Chronicle
Collectors Car Magazine
The Klemantaski Collection

Jupiter Owners Auto Club
Jowett Car Club
The Pre-War Austin Seven Cub
Vintage Motor Cycle Club

Local Newspapers

Yorkshire Observer
Scotland Pictorial
Blackpool Gazette & Herald
Telegraph & Argus
Eastbourne Gazette
Whitstable Times
Bulletin & Sports Pictorial
Yorkshire Post
Lytham & St Anne's Express
Derby Daily Telegraph
Salford Evening News
Sheffield Star
Daily Graphic
Middlesbrough Evening Gazette
Sevenoaks News
Evening Sentinel

Bexhill Evening Argus
Bon-Accord
Aberdeen Evening News
Aberdeen Press & Journal
Northern Echo
Southern Daily Echo
Sidcup Times
Southport Guardian
Belfast Telegraph
Flint County Herald
Birmingham Mail
Bath Chronicle & Herald
Wimbledon Borough News
Hastings & St. Leonard's Observer
The Scotsman
North West Evening Mail

Other Titles Available from The History Press

Jowett 1901–1954

NOEL STOKOE

When the Jowett brothers set about designing their first car, little did they know that they would end up building thousands of Jowetts. A few cars were built prior to and during the First World War, but it was the construction at Idle, Bradford of a new factory that saw Jowett expanded to become Yorkshire's major car manufacturer. Always quirky, always fun, Jowett's were the best engineered and designed of all the light cars. The post-war Javelin and Jupiter models were successful too.

978 0 7524 1723 3

Jowett: Advertising the Marque

NOEL STOKOE

With their large, purpose-built factory constructed at Idle, Bradford, the Jowett brothers' car manufacture recommenced in 1920. Two important appointments in respect of advertising and publicity then took place; the first was Harry Mitchell, who produced Jowett advert and sales brochures. The second was Gladney Haigh, who took over writing sales booklets and adverts in 1927. The advertising was quirky and fun and, above all, was different to anything that had gone before or since.

978 0 7524 3535 0

Minimal Motoring:
From Cyclecar to Microcar

DAVID THIRLBY

From the dawn of motoring, light cars have played a major part in the growth of the car. Many famous makers started with cycle cars including Lagonda, Morgan and Fraser Nash. The cycle car boom period was from 1910-1930 and the start of the Second World War killed any car-ownership aspirations overnight. During the 1950s, however, a series of manufacturers from BMW to Bond, from Messerschmitt to Mochet and from Peel to Powerdrive manufactured economy cars and the 'microcar' was born.

978 0 7524 2367 8

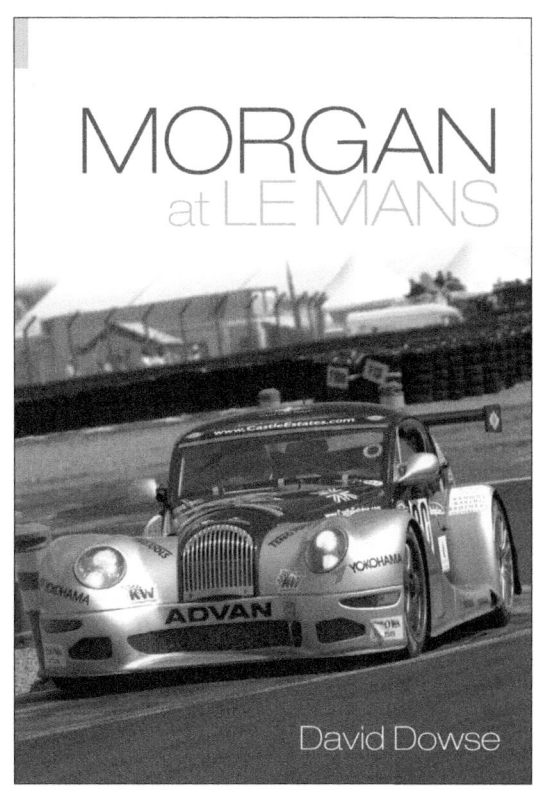

Morgan at le Mans

DAVID DOWSE

A minnow in a rather large pond – that was Morgan at Le Mans. There they were, one of Britain's smallest car manufacturers, competing with the big boys of Ferrari, Porsche and Mercedes. The story of their Le Mans is one of triumph and tragedy, of David against Goliath, yet they managed to gain entry to the exclusive race and, despite their car retiring at the eighteenth hour in 2002, they had made a huge impact on the crowds. In 2004, Morgan returned to Le Mans, finishing the race to the cheers of thousands of Brits who had crossed the Channel to see the team triumph.

978 0 7524 3488 9

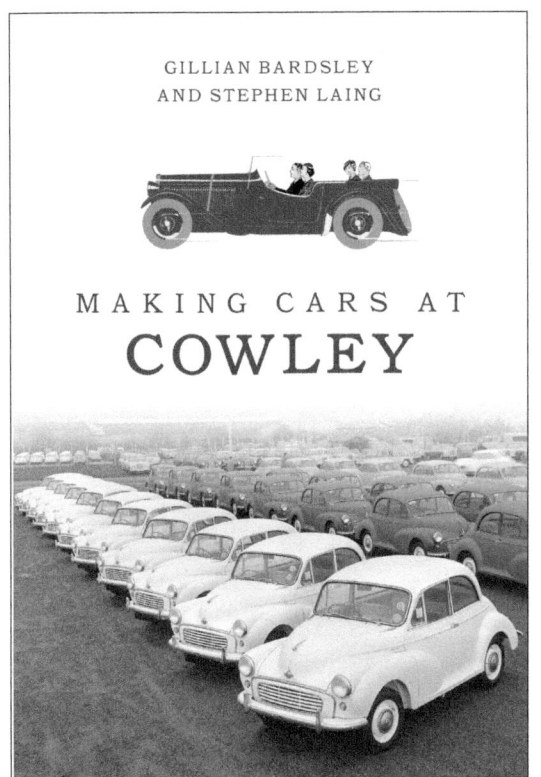

Making Cars at Cowley

GILLIAN BARDSLEY AND STEPHEN LAING

In 1913 an ambitious young businessman named William Morris converted a derelict military college on the outskirts of Oxford into an assembly hall for motor vehicles. He thus opened the first chapter in one of the most extraordinary success stories of the British motor industry, becoming Lord Nuffield and a multi-millionaire in the process. From Morris Motors and Pressed Steel, via the British Motor Corporation and British Leyland to its role as part of BMW and their successful manufacture of the new Mini, car manufacture at Cowley has been a significant player. Though the old factory chimneys have given way to more modern developments, Oxford today would be a very different place without its influence.

978 0 7524 3902 0

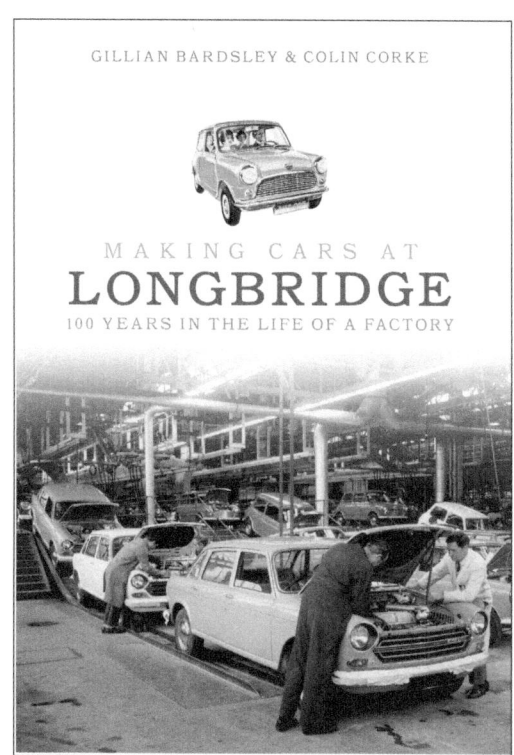

Making Cars at Longbridge:
100 Years in the Life of a Factory

GILLIAN BARDSLEY AND COLIN CORKE

For ninety-nine years cars were made at Longbridge. Less than a year off its century, the factory closed and 6,000 lost their jobs. The story of Longbridge is full of tragedy and the loss of car making there has dealt a huge blow to the Midlands' manufacturing base. But it is easy to forget that the factory produced millions of motorcars, including some of the most famous designs ever made and that it was once an employer for tens of thousands in Birmingham.

The first cars to roll off the production plant were Austins and some of the most recognised marques and models have been made there; from the original Austin 7 of the 1920s to the Mini of 1959, as well as the Austin 1100. In later years the factory also made Rovers and MGs.

978 0 7524 3741 5

Rolls-Royce From the Inside:
The Humour, the Myths, the Truths

REG ABBISS

For generations, people have been fascinated by the magic of 'The Best Cars in the World', the majestic carriages of Rolls-Royce, and the rich and powerful who own them. A Rolls-Royce is much more than a car that dreams are made of. It is a British icon which symbolizes a privileged way of life and generates passion and admiration even among the many millions who have no hope of acquiring one.

Packed with fascinating stories and anecdotes, *Rolls-Royce from the Inside* is a humorous celebration of a century of excellence and achievement by skilled artisans and craftsmen whose coachbuilt motorcars have long been described as the Pride of Britain, Envy of the World.

978 0 7524 4324 9

Visit our website and discover thousands of other History Press books.
www.thehistorypress.co.uk